THE PRINCIPLES OF **FIGHTING**

ROBERT SWEET

ISBN: 1-4392-2515-X
ISBN-13: 9781439225158
Library of Congress Control Number: 2009900275

Visit www.booksurge.com to order additional copies.

But friendship, as between our heroes,
can't really be: for we've outgrown
old prejudice; all men are zeros,
the units are ourselves alone.
Napoleon's our sole inspiration;
the millions of two-legged creation
for us are instruments and tools;
feeling is quaint, and fit for fools.

Eugene Onegin, Alexander Pushkin

INTRODUCTION

In the second century AD, the Roman emperor and philosopher Marcus Aurelius wrote his celebrated *Meditations*. In that work, he lays out his precepts for living with others:

o   Reverence heaven and succor man.

o   Love in sincerity the fellow creatures with whom destiny has ordained thou shalt live.

o   Should [a man] interpose with main force, take refuge in equanimity and tranquility, and turn this obstacle into an occasion for the exercise of another virtue.

o   We are all created to work together, as the members of one body... Whence, to work against each other is contrary to nature.

o   My present work [should] be that of a rational and social being who acts under the same laws as God Himself.

o   If thou canst, show the sinner the error of his ways. If thou canst not, remember that for these occasions the virtue of kindliness was given thee, and that heaven itself shows mercy to evil-doers.

o   When thy neighbor sins against thee, consider first what is thy relationship to mankind, reflecting that we all exist to serve each other, and that, in especial, thy life-work is to champion thy fellow-creatures as the bull defends his herd and the ram his flock.

o   Meekness and gentleness are not only more human but also more manly.

o   What a wonderful power is man's, to do naught save what will receive the approval of God.

Much of Aurelius's reign was taken up with warfare. On crossing the Danube into Dacia, Pannonia, and other Roman territories in 166 or 167, the Quadi and Marcomanni massacred Roman citizens, razed towns, and took vast numbers of prisoners; they then invaded north Italy. Taking advantage of Roman disorganization, the Costoboci crossed the Carpathians and sacked cities and towns as far south as Greece. In 170, Aurelius retook the lost territories. Three years later, the Sarmatian Jazyges attacked from the west; Aurelius inflicted a defeat on the Jazyges in a battle on the frozen

Danube. In 175, Avidius Cassius, virtual prefect of the eastern provinces, proclaimed himself emperor; after Cassius was murdered by his own soldiers, Aurelius had many of his accomplices executed and punished Antioch and Alexandria for aiding him. In 177, the Quadi and Marcomanni, joined by the Hermunduri, again crossed the Danube and were again defeated by Aurelius. In 179, Pannonia was attacked once more...

Why could Aurelius not live by his precepts? Why was he forced to fight, against his wishes, against his ideals?

The Human Mode

Ancient Greek literature is modal. Modes are the generic states and phases of existence, each defined by contrast with other modes. The chief modal distinction is between human beings and the gods; human beings are mortal, the gods immortal. But there are also modal distinctions among human beings, a hierarchy of value and being, distinctions of status, wealth, sex, age, and *arete*, or virtuousness. In Greek plays, the mask shows a character's mode, shows whether the wearer is a youth or a man, a girl or a matron, a slave or free, rich or poor. (The characters in Greek plays are not individualized, as in modern plays, but rather archetypal and universal.) The posture of each character also suggests his mode; he stands erect or bent (as in supplication), taut or at ease. In the *Bacchae* by Euripides, writes the great Greek scholar William Arrowsmith, "we observe...that...Pentheus is a *boy*; but he is also a *king*; these two salient facts then combine to produce a third, his spiritual intransigence and pathetic susceptibility to Dionysus, and these 'traits' are then given depth by contrast with old Teiresias and Cadmus."

A being's mode is the degree to which it is "yoked" to necessity. "Necessity is the criterion which divides each 'species' of existence from the other... Implicit, often explicit, everywhere in Greek literature is a great hierarchy of being which runs from absolute, untrammeled Olympian possibility at the top, to sheer, wretched subjection to total necessity at the bottom..." (Arrowsmith) The human mode is to suffer necessity — death, life, collisions of power, suffering, joy, sexuality, the "rhythm that holds mankind in its bonds." Greek literature is filled with images of constraint and binding, of coercion and obligation, with metaphors of yoking and wrestling. To the Greeks, the gods, and the necessities they represent, are not *moral*; they are "pitiless, awful, inscrutable, careless power." They are by turn kind or cruel, without cause or sense. The gods lack compassion because they do not suffer necessity (or only seldom so); they do not understand what it is to suffer and be mortal. In the *Alcestis* by Euripides, a chorus of old men kneel as they sing of the "goddess" Necessity:

O Man,
against her hard, relentless coming on,
all your craft and intellect are weak.
There is no power in your spells and Orphic songs;
no virtue in your herbs, your healing lore. Nothing,
nothing can resist her coming on. Only patience.
Suffer and submit.

Necessity is stone,
Implacable. She has no face
but rock; no human shape or likeness owns,
no cult, nor shrine. She heeds no sacrifice.
She is force, and flint; no feeling has, no
pity. None.

To know oneself, in the Greek sense, is to know one's mode, one's place in the scheme of things. To the Greeks, human beings fall on a scale from high *sophia* — those who are wise, who understand themselves and their mode — to *amathia*, unteachable, ungovernable, ignorant of themselves and their necessities. Between high *sophia* and *amathia* is low *sophia*, opportunistic cunning and shrewdness, calculation and expedience, the wisdom of "trimmers and compromisers." It is chiefly through suffering that we come to recognize our mode, to think human, or mortal, thoughts. Suffering teaches us that we are not exempt, that we, too, are subject to necessity; we *suffer* into moral dignity and compassion, into "an anguished acceptance" of our mode. In the *Heracles*, the hero, broken by suffering, says, "And now, I see, I must serve necessity," and follows the king Theseus like "a little boat in tow."

To be hubristic is to think one's mode higher than it is, to be "the garden that thinks it is a jungle." The person of hubris fancies that the ordinary rules and conditions of human existence do not apply to him, that he is exempt — from necessity, limits, suffering, failure, anything untoward, humiliating, or hurtful. He may be contemptuous of his mode, ignorant of it (as with the young), or innocent of it (because of good fortune). An instance of the first is Odysseus from Euripides's *Hecuba*: possessed of great power, he does just as he pleases with others, all the while speaking the language of morality and insisting that his cruelty is forced upon him by necessity. An instance of the second is the title character of Euripides's *Hippolytus*: he is proud of his chastity, fancies himself something he is not; but he is a man like all other men and feels passion. An instance of the third is Admetos in the *Alcestis*: "Youth, good fortune, and exemption from all human necessity and need have left him humanly undeveloped... All his traits of character, quite without exception, derive from his modal innocence and inexperience." (Arrowsmith) He is *a-dametos*, the "untamed," the "unbroken." The person of hubris threatens to destroy himself and (if he is sufficiently powerful) his society; he increases his and the group's suffering.

Selfishness and the ESS

In *The Selfish Gene*, the Oxford zoologist Richard Dawkins writes, "The basic unit of natural selection is best regarded not as the species, nor as the population, nor even as the individual, but as" the gene. A gene is a molecule, DNA; it is a replicator: it makes copies of itself. Each gene vies with a rival gene, or allele, for survival in the gene pool; natural selection determines which genes survive and which do not. All successful, which is to say long-lived and numerous, genes are selfish. "Any gene that behaves in such a way as to increase its own survival chances in the gene pool at the expense of its alleles will...tend to survive. The gene is the basic unit of selfishness." (Dawkins) Were a gene *not* selfish, it would simply not be here.

The successful gene will be that which makes the body in which it lives (and which it contributed to making) more likely to live and reproduce than the body would have been had it had the rival gene. This body, or "survival machine," is quite as selfish as its genes; if the body is to survive and reproduce, it must find and catch food, elude predators, mate, feed and protect its offspring, and so on. "Natural selection favours genes that control their survival machines in such a way that they make the best use of their environment. This includes making the best use of other survival machines, both of the same and of different species." (Dawkins) To increase their chances of survival, mammalian survival machines live in groups. "For mammals," writes Edward Wilson in *Consilience*, "social life is a contrivance to enhance personal survival and reproductive success." Within the group, the individual must tailor what he does to the context, chiefly to what others in the group do; in doing so, the individual is following an evolutionarily stable strategy, or ESS. A universal ESS is that an individual should see to his interests at the expense of those weaker than himself. (Or, as Balzac said, "Wolves do not attack wolves; they attack sheep.")

The unit of cooperation is that of conjoined self-interest; the more the conjoining of self-interest, the more the cooperation. The conjoining of self-interest within each wolf, for instance, is far greater than that within a pack of wolves. "The genes in a pack of wolves don't all stand to gain from the same set of events in the future. A gene can foster its own future welfare by favouring its own individual wolf, at the expense of other individual wolves." (Dawkins) This is why an ESS *is not optimal for the group as a whole.* Two of the strategies Dawkins considers are "hawk" and "dove." A hawk fights all out and retreats only when badly injured; a dove pretends it will stand its ground, but always runs away if a hawk attacks. (An individual tends naturally to be a hawk or a dove, but may be more or less so depending on the context.) "Any group in which all individuals mutually agree to be doves would be far more successful than a rival group sitting at the ESS ratio [of 7/12 hawks and 5/12 doves]... Even though a 'conspiracy of doves' would be better for *every single individual* than the evolutionarily stable strategy, natural selection is bound to favour the ESS... [I]n conspiracies of doves, a single hawk does so extremely well that nothing could stop the evolution of hawks." (Dawkins) (The reason the social insects such as ants cooperate so is that only the queen can reproduce; all the other ants "reproduce" through her.) Natural selection instills in each mammal both the instinct to do what is best for itself and the instinct to do what is best for the group; these instincts are not, however, of equal strength: the first is far stronger than the second. In groups of mammals, altruism — increasing the survival chances of another *at the expense of one's own* — is illusory: the individual who *seems* to be performing an altruistic act is in truth increasing his own chances of survival.

Any species that comes into being through natural selection is selfish; since our species came into being through natural selection, it is selfish. *The human species is not exempt;* it is not one whit less biological than the others. A human being is a member of the Order Primates, Infraorder Catarrhini, and Family Hominidae. Our modes are life, species, and individual. What is true of the other species is true of ours; the same processes are at work. "...[B]y and large," writes Wilson, "people behave in their daily lives as though somehow guided, whether consciously or unconsciously," by the principles of evolution by natural selection. "The same arts and tricks that boys will now try upon you for balls, bats, and half-pence," wrote Lord Chesterfield to his son, "men will make use of with you when you are a man, for other purposes." We take a highly instrumental view of other creatures, whether of our own species or of others; our chief consideration is how they might contribute to our comfort and convenience. "Let us not be angry with men when we see them cruel, ungrateful, unjust, proud, egotistical, and forgetful of others," said Jean de La Bruyere; "they are made so; it is their nature; we might just as well quarrel with a stone for falling to the ground, or with a fire when the flames ascend." The mode of life is to be selfish; what the Greeks called the gods, is biology.[1]

---

1 Of all La Rochefoucauld's maxims, the longest by far is that on "self-love," or selfishness. La Rochefoucauld is describing perfectly the workings of our genes. A portion:

> Nothing is more violent than the desires of self-love, nothing more deep-laid than its designs, nothing more skilful than its maneuvers; its subtleties are beyond description... Its depths cannot be plumbed, the mists which lurk in its chasms cannot be pierced. In those abysses, hidden from the sharpest eye, it carries out unseen a thousand marches and counter-marches; unseen even by itself it there engenders, feeds, and raises a host of loves and hatreds of which it is itself unaware; among its brood are some so monstrous that, when at last they are revealed by the light of day, their parent fails to recognize them or at least refuses to accept them as its progeny. In the obscurity that envelopes self-love are born those ridiculous convictions which it cherishes about itself: from that murk derive the errors, the ignorance, the crude and foolish ideas which it conceives concerning its own nature. Thence springs its belief that its passions are dead when they do but slumber, that it has withdrawn from the race the moment it is no longer in motion, that it has abandoned lusts which are merely satiated...

Since we are mammals, we, too, must follow ESSs, we, too, must do what is fitted to the group. However *we* might prefer to live, we must adapt ourselves to the context; we cannot do just as we please. In the perfect expression of an ESS, Montaigne writes:

> I once tried to employ in the service of public dealings ideas and rules for living as crude, green, unpolished — or unpolluted — as they were born in me or derived from my education...a scholastic and novice virtue. I found them inept and dangerous for such matters. He who walks in the crowd must step aside, keep his elbows in, step back or advance, even leave the straight way, according to what he encounters. He must live not so much according to himself as according to others...according to the time, according to the men, according to the business.

This is one of the necessities: that we live "according to others." "Instead of decency, self-discipline, and competence," said Sallust, "there was [in Rome] insolence, corruption, and rapacity. Although I despised these things, being quite untainted by baseness, my insecure youth was nevertheless corrupted, in the presence of such great vices, by the desire for honors and gain and became their prisoner." Rarely is a predetermined, fixed mode of behavior adaptive. Being kind and compassionate does not reflect a "higher state of consciousness" if within a vile group; it simply reflects maladaptation. A virtue is not an ESS if the population in which

It is capricious, and at times can be observed to labor with the utmost diligence and incredible perseverance to obtain that which can be of no advantage and may indeed be actively harmful to it, but for which it continues to strive because that is what it wants. It is bizarre, and will often exert all its energy for some totally frivolous end, will relish the most insipid pleasures, and will preserve its pride in the most contemptible undertakings.

It is to be met with in all stages of life and among all conditions of men; it lives everywhere... It can adjust itself to all circumstances and, equally, to a change of circumstance. It will even be found among the ranks of those who are its declared foes, and it can be seen seated at their council table. And what is most remarkable is that, in their company, it will hate itself, it will plot its own overthrow, it will strive for its own ruination; for it cares only that it should exist, and so long as it continues to be it is quite willing to do so as its own enemy... At the moment when it is driven back and defeated in one corner of the field, it will be advancing victoriously in another. And when we think to have routed it at last, we will discover it still glorying in its own defeat.

it is displayed is not virtuous. To have a higher state of consciousness is to recognize which behavior is best fitted to the particular group. (The more powerful the individual, the more he influences the ESS. The provocations of Richelieu and Napoleon made the other European states do things they would very much have preferred not to do; the ESS becomes more hawkish with a Richelieu or Napoleon in the group.)

Quite as much as other creatures, we follow the great ESS: please the strong and satisfy our needs at the expense of the weak. No less than other species, our coming into being through natural selection makes us *exquisitely* sensitive to gradations in, and highly respectful of, power. (Which attribute do we give our gods? That of great power.) Among human beings is an infinity of asymmetries, of modes; miniscule before agriculture, these asymmetries became elephantine with it. Much as we might prefer that it not, each mode, each order of being, "suffers the cumulative [necessity] of the orders above it in an ascending curve of freedom and power." (Arrowsmith)

We are rather careless toward those with little power; once the consideration, can this person help or hurt me, has been satisfied, we do as our interests and whims direct us. When the French King Henry IV protested against an alliance the Grand Duke Ferdinand of Tuscany had formed with Spain, the Duke replied, "If the King had had forty galleys in Marseille, I would not have done what I did." Richelieu once complained to his King that, since France had only the slightest of navies, "the King's subjects have not only been constantly deprived of their property but of their liberty [by pirates]; our neighbors have considered themselves justified in selling us their goods on their own terms and in taking ours at whatever price they choose to pay." Richelieu himself "nearly always destroyed his opponents provided he could do so with impunity. If his adversaries were persons whose rank precluded such action, he tried to win them over by appointing them to high position." (Auchincloss) While a member of the Institute of Sciences and Arts, Talleyrand composed a document recommending that France not try to conquer other European states (which were strong), but rather territories in North Africa and elsewhere (which were weak). Morality, honor, moral law, decency, the gods, principles, civilized custom, the rule of law — to all these the weak appeal; the strong do as they please.

The celebrated negotiator William Ury concedes that adversaries will negotiate only when their power is somewhat equal. At one point during the Roman civil war, Caesar wrote Pompey that "this was the one time to negotiate peace, while they were each confident and appeared to be equally matched; but if fortune tilted even slightly towards one of them, the one who thought he had the advantage would have no interest in a negotiated peace, and the one who believed that he was about to take the whole would not be content with a fair share."

We would dearly like to live in concord with our fellows, to live by our ideals; but we have *needs*, and we satisfy those needs within a group some of whose members are strong and some weak. Often we cannot see to our interests without wounding those of others. "Only God can make something out of nothing," sighed Richelieu on having to tax the poor white to finance the war against the Habsburgs. "Whoever escapes with clean breeches from handling the affairs of the world," said Plato, "escapes by a miracle." Rarely is an ideal a match for self-interest; rarely is honor a match for need:

o Though Cicero hated Caesar for vitiating the Roman republic, prudence dictated that he write a work praising the dictator. Of it he said, "In these matters we have already become callous and cast off all *humanitas*," or dignity.

o Richelieu detested the *paulette*, the selling of offices, and wished to abolish it; the *paulette*, he wrote Louis XIII, was "prejudicial…to the purity of justice." But once the war against the Habsburgs began, Richelieu could do without neither the *paulette*'s annual payments nor the dependency it created in the office-holders.

o Edward Gibbon, the first volume of whose *History of the Decline and Fall of the Roman Empire* was published in 1776, was "the enemy of empire as a political form, and a friend to the freedom of nations." In the *History*, Gibbon writes, "There is nothing perhaps more adverse to nature and reason than to hold in obedience remote countries and foreign nations, in opposition to their inclination and interest." He was strongly opposed to his country's war against the American colonists. Since his estate produced too little income, Gibbon needed a government sinecure. Not once did he, while a member of the House of Commons, speak out against the war; indeed, he wrote a state paper, the *Memoire justificatif*, criticizing the French for their support of the colonists. In July 1779,

Gibbon was appointed to the Board of Trade and Plantations at a salary of £750.

o   In 1787, the young Wellington wished to be promoted within his regiment, the 76th. An officer was required to recruit men into the army; since to do so properly would take time and be costly, Wellington hired a crimp, a man who would dragoon the unemployed and destitute into service — something for which Wellington was later very much ashamed.

o   In his novel *Sybil*, Benjamin Disraeli depicts the horrific lives of the working poor in the northern mill and coal-mining towns of England. He speaks of his country's being "two nations," the rich and the poor, and he attributes the squalor and hopelessness of the poor to the accumulation of capital, to the very existence of the rich: "A spirit of rapacious covetousness, desecrating all the humanities of life, has been the besetting sin of England for the last century and a half." Some years later, while Disraeli was a member of the House of Commons, a bill arose proposing that the government be permitted to *inspect* the country's mines; one of the greater coal-owners in the country, Lord Londonderry, pronounced it "infernal." So greatly did Disraeli need Londonderry's support that he both spoke and voted against the bill.

Certainly we do not speak of what we do. It is not in our interests to do so; others must think well of us, that we care more for the interests of the group, *their* interests, than we do our own. And we wish others to do, not what we do, but what is good for the group. "We present ourselves in two aspects," said Montaigne, "the actions in one fashion and the speeches in another." In his *Memoirs*, Talleyrand glosses over many things; that which he prefers us not to know, he simply does not mention. Some years ago, a group of Microsoft programmers recommended via e-mail that the company create codes to disable rivals' software, but that it do so secretly, since the world at large was certain to disapprove. In *Only the Paranoid Survive*, Andrew Grove, then CEO of Intel, writes, "I believe that the prime responsibility of a manager is to guard constantly against other people's attacks..." But what of his directing Intel's General Counsel to file as many lawsuits as possible against other chip makers? Or of the European Commission's charging that Intel denied crucial design data and access to new Intel chips to customers that buy computer chips from competitors? Not a word is said of these things...

In truth, our ideals are more for others than for ourselves. We wish to do as biology prompts us, what is pleasing and pleasurable; we wish others to live in a way that furthers our interests. We hate limits on ourselves; we wish others to be hemmed in, to be hedged about. "Solon represents himself now as himself, now in the shape of a lawgiver," said Montaigne; "now he speaks for the crowd, now for himself; and for himself he takes the free and natural rules." He quotes the courtesan Lais: "I do not know about their books, or their wisdom, or their philosophy, but those men knock at my door as often as any others." Sallust wrote works on Roman virtue and morality; to Caesar he insisted that the cause of Rome's dissolution was the pursuit of luxury and wealth. So corrupt was Sallust as governor of the Roman province of Africa Nova that he was put on trial in Rome and acquitted only after paying colossal bribes. "And Xenophon, in the bosom of Clinias, wrote against Aristippic sensuality." (Montaigne) While natural selection governs *our* behavior, we dearly wish it not to govern others'.

The pursuit of interests is also why alliances fluctuate so. What Lord Chesterfield said of life at court is true of society in general: "Nothing in courts is exactly as it appears to be; often very different, sometimes directly contrary. Interest, which is the real spring of every thing there, equally creates and dissolves friendships, produces and reconciles enmities; for as Dryden very justly observes, 'politicians neither love nor hate.'" The more power Caesar attained, the weaker his alliance with Pompey grew, as Pompey was forced to seek other allies as a counterpoise to Caesar. The wife of Louis XIII, Anne of Austria, for years conspired with his brother, Gaston d'Orleans, against his policies; but once she had a son, so determined was she that her child rather than Gaston would be the future king of France that she turned against her co-conspirator. Talleyrand and Tsar Alexander conspired for years against Napoleon; following Napoleon's abdication, Talleyrand turned against the Tsar on his becoming quite as acquisitive as Napoleon. "There are certain families," said Jean de La Bruyere, "who...ought never to be reconciled to one another; however, now they are good friends, for those whom religion could not induce to lay aside their feuds, interest, without much trouble, has linked together."

As we pursue our objects and others theirs, collisions of interests naturally occur. Society is a cockpit, an arena of conflict. Getting to our object is like crossing a field or bog: we must sometimes lay down stones as a bridge, sometimes go round obstacles, and sometimes simply hack our way through. Fighting is one of the ways to lessen the asymmetry between oneself and the strong, to lift one's mode, to lessen the likelihood of one's being imposed upon by others. All relationships *should* be symbiotic; in general, the more the asymmetry between the parties, the less the symbiosis. Fighting is one of the means by which one *forces* a relationship to be symbiotic. The great law of natural selection is this: a creature must have power of some sort to survive. *Fighting is a form of power.* "Covenants without the sword are but words," said Hobbes, "and of no strength to secure a man at all."

The Maladaptation of Our Species

The human brain is "a patchwork of makeshifts," jury-rigged from 400 million years of evolution by natural selection, adapting now to this environment, now to that one. Within our brain lie those of fish, amphibians, reptiles, primitive mammals, and hominids. "The human brain preserves the three primitive divisions found throughout the vertebrates from fishes to mammals: hindbrain, midbrain, and forebrain." (Wilson) The neocortex, where consciousness lies, sits atop bestial and fractious lower brains; this is why we so often do not know why we think and feel as we do, why so often feel such an admixture of emotions, why so often find it difficult to control ourselves. "Mankind is made up of inconsistencies," said Chesterfield. "Our jarring passions, our variable humours...produce such contradictions in our conduct, that I believe those are the oftenest mistaken, who ascribe our actions to the most seemingly obvious motives..." "I fear that we are such gods or demigods only as fauns and satyrs," said Thoreau, "the divine allied to beasts." Our species is Sophocles's Philoktetes: bow raised to heaven, dragging his putrefying foot along the corrupt ground.

Compounding the dysfunctionality of the human brain is our being wildly maladapted to the world we have created. One of the great misconceptions about evolution is that it fits a species perfectly to its environment.

For a whole host of reasons, species are *not* perfectly designed, not perfectly fitted to their environments. One of those reasons is that the environment to which a species has adapted changes: "Natural selection," notes Wilson, "...does not anticipate future needs." For millions upon millions of years, we lived and evolved in small kin groups. This world was our Garden of Eden; that in which we now live is quite foreign to us. Natural selection crafted us for a world with which we have done away; we are both Dr. Frankenstein and his monster. It is quite queer, this laying down of modern society upon our species. Our species is now asked to do all sorts of things quite new to us; all of a sudden (in evolutionary terms), we are asked to tabulate figures, file briefs, administer large organizations, engage in diplomacy among nation states, design machines — none of which we were required to do during the millions of years of our evolution. It is little wonder we so often make a hash of things.

There is great variation in our species. All the members of our species, being life, are selfish, but the variation in certain traits — intelligence, morality, talent — is almost certainly greater than in any other species. Each human gene has on average 14 haplotypes, or variants, and no one variant is in the majority. Furthermore, each environment to which a group of genes adapts is unique. The variation in our species is quite simply infinite. It is the variation in intelligence that concerns us here. Think of all of life as being on a bell curve for intelligence; the ability to think abstractly does not begin to the left of our species, but rather somewhere in the middle of where our species falls on the curve. Just as a squirrel cannot understand what a book is, so, too, can many human beings not understand what others can. (Nothing, perhaps, makes governing a society so difficult as does this great variation in human intelligence.) *Most human beings are quite poor at abstract thinking.* As Cicero observed, philosophy is not for the multitude. Richelieu hated deliberative assemblies because he recognized that the intelligent would always constitute only a small minority.

The most intelligent members of our species create the societies in which their far less intelligent peers live. (Science, for instance, is a child of the intelligent.) The *general* human intelligence is insufficient in the world the intelligent have created; the genes for intelligence evolved in a far simpler world. The median human intelligence was more than sufficient through most of our evolution and continues to be so in simple groups or societies; but in wildly complex, industrialized societies, it is not. The degree to which a creature follows instinct is roughly a function of intelligence; the less the intelligence, the more instinct governs. *Most human beings follow the promptings of the lower realms of the brain, realms fitted to a very different context.* But even the intelligent are quite at sea in most realms of modern society. The more humanity learns, the more each individual must specialize and, in specializing, remains ignorant in all else. Since all intelligence is of a kind, the most intelligent in a particular field craft that field, and so even those quite intelligent in other fields cannot understand it.

Natural selection also crafted human beings to think in the short term rather than the long. "Selfish genes...have no foresight. They are unconscious, blind replicators. A simple replicator...cannot be expected to forgo short-term selfish advantage even if it would really pay it, in the long term, to do so." (Dawkins) Most human beings are quite as short term as their "simple replicators;" most cannot see that what benefits them in the short term may very well doom them in the long. (This is why, for instance, we pollute now, though our doing so may well make the earth unlivable in the future.) Because most members of our species think abstractly only poorly, they live in the present, a bit in the past (which requires only memory, after all), and only slightly in the future. This is why most human beings learn best by catastrophe: it is both *now* and *concrete.*

Because of the dysfunctionality of the human brain and human maladaptation, most human beings simply do not know which acts are in their long-term interests and which not. In the modern world, most people simply do not know what they are doing. This is why human beings so often "miss the mark," or, in Latin, sin; ours is the peccant species. This is the human perversity commented on throughout history, that human beings often do not do what is in their interest. Cicero observed that the assassination of Caesar was planned "with the courage of men but the understanding of boys." Much that humanity does, it does with the understanding of boys. Dostoevsky felt that human beings must be free, but in being free will destroy ourselves.

Much of humanity commends what it should condemn, and condemns what it should commend. "As long as mankind shall continue to bestow more liberal applause on their destroyers than on their benefactors," said Gibbon, one of the better students of humanity, "the thirst of military glory will ever be the vice of the most exalted characters." At the beginning of the Roman civil war, Cicero said of Caesar, "This insane, miserable fellow has never had the least inkling of the good!" That the Roman Empire might soon collapse because of the ineptitude and corruption of its government, and that Caesar would make that government far better, Cicero could not see. Many people will gladly permit those who please them to harm their interests and refuse aid from those who displease them. Gaston d'Orleans, the brother of Louis XIII, induced the duc de Montmorency to rebel against the King; Richelieu tried to dissuade the duc. The duc rebelled and was executed. Of Richelieu Montmorency's widow said, "It has taken me years of strict penance to forgive him," of Gaston, "He has shown me such kindness that I always include him in my prayers." On seeing humanity's folly, some think, "I will save humanity from itself," others, "I will take advantage of that folly." The latter have always met with more success than the former.

When asked why he has mastered fencing and shooting, though quite opposed to dueling, the Count of Monte Cristo replies, "When one lives among madmen, one should train as a maniac." On occasion you must fight simply because others do not know what they are doing.

The Feeling of Insignificance

One of the ways in which modern society is not suited to our species is that it rarely satisfies the needs of self-love, particularly male self-love. Our feeling of significance was created and satisfied in small kin groups. Modern society is neither small nor kin; the infinite, atomistic society of today is quite unable to meet needs formed by life within small kin groups. We increase our chances of survival by living among and cooperating with other human beings; to ensure that we *do* live among and cooperate with them, natural selection crafted us to care very much what they think of us. We thus take much of our feeling of significance from others. Natural selection also crafted us to care that the other members of the group care about us (for the simple reason that they protect us to the degree they care about us). To increase our chances of survival still further, natural selection had us feel significant to the degree others acknowledge our superiority, since with this acknowledgement comes control (over food, mates, and the affairs of the group). But few of the members of modern society either think or care about us; the great male instinct to be celebrated and without peer, to be acknowledged as superior and thus direct affairs, cannot possibly be satisfied in a "group" of six billion human beings.

To feel significant, human beings commit every species of cruelty and folly. Of Pompey the ancient playwright said, "Through our misery you are great." "The pride of one man," said Gibbon, "requires the submission of the multitude." The multitude themselves are quite willing to sacrifice their interests to feel significant; Caesar felt that they "often purposely cast many idle slurs upon their superiors, in the effort to draw them into strife, so that they might seem to be their equals and of like importance with them, in case they should get anything similar said of themselves." (Cassius Dio) Richelieu's opponents felt that *they*, rather than he, should formulate and carry out the policies of France. They were far too conceited to see that they were incompetent and he a genius, that they would only make a hash of things. But even had they been able to see, they would not have cared a fig. They did not care whether they could do a good or bad job; they cared only that *they* do the job. They would gladly usurp that which they could not do. (Nothing, perhaps, has been so ruinous to society as has the general human unwillingness to stand down.) While natural selection prompts all human beings to seek power — so that they might control their world and thus survive — it bestows on only a small minority the wherewithal to use power judiciously in modern society.

Morality

Morality is little else but a concern for the group. For millions upon millions of years, the social group was the kin group; cooperation among the members was natural, because biological. Furthermore, the members of these groups followed a simple policy of tit for tat: if a member of the group cooperated with others, they cooperated with him; if he did not, they did not — and he soon came to cooperate. Tit for tat *forced* us to be moral, however selfish we might have wished to be. In the social groupings of today, we are not conjoined biologically, and the constraint of reciprocity is far looser. We feel far less compulsion to be moral toward those to whom we are not related.

So complex is civilization that we find it difficult to make moral judgments. In small kin groups, it was quite clear how cooperating with the other members of the group increased one's own chances of survival, quite clear what was beneficial for the group and what hurtful to it, quite clear who was cooperating and who not. It is not so today; morality is now *highly* abstract. Since human beings are generally poor at abstract thinking, we are also generally poor at moral thinking. Was it moral or immoral for Caesar to conquer Gaul, for Richelieu to subjugate the Huguenots and so wound the German states that they took centuries to recover, for Microsoft to put countless firms out of business? We cannot say. Gibbon felt it would perhaps have been better had the Roman Empire itself never existed. As he gazed at Rousseau's tomb, Napoleon remarked, "The future will tell us whether it would not have been better if neither I nor Rousseau had ever lived." But the future has not: we still do not know. A hero, said Aristotle, is "either a beast or a god" — we have never been certain which.

On losing the natural constraints of kinship and strict reciprocity, human groups created the restraint, not only of law, but also of religion. A religion comes from a moral genius, from the higher realms of the human brain; it says: "Do not follow the dictates of the lower brain. Do not go only with power; treat those without power well and fairly, too." Few of the followers of a religion, however, are moral geniuses. Most go with the lower rather than the upper realms of the brain; most understand the religion as little as they do the world. *The quality of a religion depends on the quality of the follower.* Most understand religion less as a *constraint* — be selfless and share; do not hurt others; be compassionate; succor the weak — than as a flattering of their self-love, a confirmation of their specialness and goodness and a guarantee of God's favor and protection. When most human beings speak of their religion, we hear, not the voice of the moral genius, but that of the lower realms of the human brain: "God loves me; I am of the Elect; my wishes (prayers) influence God" (I am significant; I control my world; I am less vulnerable).

"Give your ideas to the mob," said Dostoevsky so truly, "and when your ideas come back to you, you won't recognize them." The ancient Romans associated the goddess of love (Venus) with military victory; the Bavarians sculpted Apostles onto their cannon; the French hung the regimental colors taken at Austerlitz on the walls of the cathedral of Notre-Dame. Nothing so distorts moral judgment, said Confucius, as does self-interest. Most of humanity has a primitive, child-like moral system: that which I think good for me, is *morally* good, that which I think bad, *morally* bad. As Arrowsmith said of the Cyclops, their religion is their belly. Humanity has had quite as much difficulty transitioning from a partisan to an egalitarian God, as it has from the occult to science.

In our species, there is quite as much variation in morality as in intelligence. Just as there is a bell curve for intelligence, so, too, is there for morality; some human beings are far less moral than others, care far less about the interests of the group. Some of this variation is due to genetics. "Now suppose that human propensities to cooperate or defect are heritable: Some members are innately more cooperative, others less so. In this respect moral aptitude would simply be like almost all other mental traits studied to date." (Wilson) Some of the variation is due to experience. Only a minority of human beings have suffered so deeply, and for so long, that they have developed understanding and compassion. Like the Greek gods, they do not feel compassion because they have experienced little necessity; they do not think "human thoughts." The best wine comes not from the richest grapes, but from those that have "suffered" an insufficiency of water and nutrients. Furthermore, the Greeks felt that suffering gives *sophia* only to the strong; the weak it simply deforms. In our species, strength is no less rare than wisdom. Most human beings either have learned or suffered too little, or simply do not have the genetic wherewithal, to attain high *sophia*. In the *Electra*, Orestes observes that only those of high *sophia* feel compassion; those of *amatheis* do not.

While morality will *sometimes* stay the hand of the moral, it will only rarely that of the immoral. The moral will refrain from doing immoral things more than will the immoral; at the very least, the moral will feel compunction at hurting others. (A good person, said the Russian philosopher, is one who does bad things with disgust.) The moral person is torn by conflicting claims, the immoral not. "A man's general character may be that of the honestest man in the world," said Chesterfield. "Do not take this probity upon trust, to such a degree as to put your life, fortune, or reputation, in his power. This honest man may happen to be your rival in power, or interest, or in love; three passions that often put honesty to most severe trials..." Immorality is put to no such trials. Morality is an obstacle the moral will usually respect and the immoral not; what Germaine de Stael said of Napoleon is quite as true of the immoral: "He owes his success as much to the traits he lacks as to those he possesses."

To hope compassion will keep others ever from hurting you, is to hope in vain. Compassion is quite as rare as all the other moral virtues. The limit to our feelings of pleasure and pain is our body; the feelings that come from beyond our body, through empathy, are but a faint echo of what we feel within ourselves. We could all say, with Monsieur de Villefort in *The Count of Monte Cristo*, "Look at me, Madame...: have men treated me as a brother? Have they loved me? Have they considered me? Have they spared me? Has anyone ever begged pardon for Monsieur de Villefort, and has anyone ever granted a pardon to Monsieur de Villefort? No, no, no! Struck, struck, and struck again!" The *general* human morality is quite as low as the general human intelligence. "Without government is anarchy," said Gibbon. "The good of the community" — that is, morality — rarely by itself constrains us.

Other Casus Belli

o   Generally speaking, the more that is to be gained, the more one must fight. Fighting is one of the ways in which to obtain what economists call "excess rents," to bring about distortions in the economic system, to tilt things one's way. Rarely can such rents be obtained or, once obtained, maintained, without fighting. Had Microsoft not fought, Windows would not be on 95% of all PCs. (Investors would do better to invest in firms that fight well than in firms that do not, or to short the stocks of firms into whose industry a Microsoft has entered.) "Let there be wealth without tears," said Aeschylus; that he would wish for such a thing shows its rarity. "The art of making yourself rich, in the ordinary mercantile economic sense," said John Ruskin, "is equally and necessarily the art of keeping your neighbour poor." Some at least of your neighbors are apt to resist.

o   On occasion great need compels us to fight. "Marriage," said Jean de La Bruyere, "which ought to be a source of all felicity, is often to a man a heavy burden which crushes him through want of fortune. For his wife's and children's sake he is sorely tempted to commit fraud, to tell falsehoods, and to obtain illicit gains." We take Talleyrand's dictum for our own, and it supersedes all other laws and precepts: "One must never be counted among the wretched poor." And the further from the wretched poor, the better.

o   As with Aurelius, on occasion we must fight because another is resolved on fighting us. Most often the motive is resources, power, or a mate; but it may be far less rational. Fury, for instance, requires an object; but most of the fundamental causes of fury — the selfishness of life, the maladaptation of our species, overpopulation, environmental degradation, a civilization's decline — are too abstract to act as the object. Individuals or groups thus become the object.

o   On occasion we must take revenge. Few things cause us quite so much remorse as not inflicting retribution on those who have consciously hurt us or our family deeply; and few things are quite so satisfying. To strike the person who has wounded your interests and treated you with deliberate cruelty, is to make him feel a remorse he should feel, but does not. Be certain he will hurt others as blithely as he did you. Take your revenge on him, and he will be far less apt to do so; take your revenge, and you will aid the group. Furthermore, only rarely is restitution freely given; it must almost always be obtained by force.

❦

In a world in which selfish genes create survival machines with needs and vulnerabilities; in which the strong see to their interests at the expense of the weak; in which human beings have "jury-rigged" brains over which we are only imperfectly in control, and are wildly maladapted to the environment in which we live; in which the moral constraints of kinship and strict reciprocity are largely absent — in such a world, we must sometimes

fight. Fighting is one of the necessities, one of the many disagreeable con-
comitants of evolution by natural selection. "Whoever defends not his
water-tank with his goodly weapons will see it broken," said the pre-Islamic
poet Zuhayr ibn Abi Sulma. "Whoever suffers people always to be riding
upon him, and never spares himself humiliation, shall come to rue it." The
Romans would open the doors of Janus Geminus, the shrine of Janus, when
Rome was at war and close them when the city was at peace; between the
7th and 1st centuries BC, the Romans closed the doors only twice. Knowing
how to fight well is as indispensable in life as any of the other social skills.

Aurelius could not live by his precepts because it would not have been
an ESS for him to do so. Only if all others had followed his rules of conduct could he himself have followed them. As an ancient historian said,
Aurelius was "by nature a saint and a sage: by profession a ruler and a warrior." His *mode* was that of Emperor; like Admetos, Aurelius was a man of
innocent hubris who "suffered into" an understanding of his mode (as is
quite clearly shown by his later meditations, which are far less hopeful than
the earlier). "The world is too vile," murmurs Lily Bart to a friend in *The
House of Mirth*. "It's not a pretty place," the friend replies. "And the only
way to keep a footing in it is to fight it on its own terms." Lily rejects her
friend's advice and dies young and poor. Dawkins informs us that "hawks"
and "bullies" (which are rather like hawks) do best in computer simulations of groups, Wilson that "the abundant evidence of history [is] that
cooperative individuals generally survive longer and leave more offspring."
Which is it? It is not quite so simple as either. The hawk must cooperate,
the cooperative individual be hawkish, *at certain times toward certain others*. The
most successful individual is *both* cooperative and hawkish: cooperative now
with this group, now with that one, hawkish now toward this group, now
toward that one.

As unpleasant as fighting is, its alternatives may be far more so. When in
a Council meeting a fellow minister protested that war with the Habsburgs
would bring great hardship, Richelieu retorted, "That applies not only to
this war but to all wars, but it can be no reason why we should deliberately
choose a peace on the most feeble, wretched, and scandalous conditions!"
Whoever is always peaceful, lives by a dictated peace; the slave almost always leads a peaceful life. During her Regency over her son Louis XIII, the
Queen Mother gave in to everyone and resisted no one; the result was loss

of territory, anarchy, and impoverishment. Only by fighting did France achieve security and peace. "Death is nothing," said Napoleon, "but to live defeated is to die every day." By not fighting, by letting others impose their *putative* necessity upon you — not a true necessity, but necessity as a cloak or mask for other motives, a corrupt and false necessity — you may suffer intolerably, a suffering that may annihilate your humanity. At the end of the *Hecuba*, she and Polymestor scramble about on all fours, bestialized by their suffering.

Fighting takes a certain degree of self-esteem. While on a voyage to Rhodes as a young man, Caesar was captured by pirates. The "prisoner" insisted on quiet when he wished to sleep, forced the pirates to listen to the poems and speeches he composed, and smilingly said he would pursue and kill them once free — which he indeed did. Indignation is a fitting response to deliberate, conscious mistreatment.

In the tit for tat between the strong and the weak, it is government that is to strike the tit. But governments do so only imperfectly, and much of life is simply not subject to governmental control. Law is protective to the degree it corresponds with morality, is justly applied, and is enforced; on each of the three law is lacking. Much that is legal is immoral, and law will gladly serve any master. Richelieu would have historians and jurists study international laws and treaties; never once could he not use what they found to justify what he did. And Intel files lawsuits against its rivals simply to impede them.

∽

Fighting has gotten a bad name; it should not be so. Fighting itself is neither moral nor immoral; only its *object* can be said to be so. Was Caesar immoral to end oligarchic rule in the Roman Empire, Richelieu feudalism in France? Only if you think the oligarchy of the late Roman republic, and late French feudalism, good. We may count the ability to fight well, when applied to a just cause, among the virtues. To be moral is *not* to fight no one; to be moral is to fight those who vitiate life and civilization. As Richelieu observed, sparing certain lives "causes the death of a great many others." Hawks and bullies prefer that most of the population be doves, because then they do so very well. In computer simulations of groups, notes Dawkins, "nasty" behavioral strategies flourish only while "softy" strategies exist; once the softy strategies die out, so, too, do the nasty ones. That the moral are far less willing to fight than the immoral has always hurt societies; the moral would do far better to follow revanchism, a policy of retaliation. Fighting is one of the means by which to restore the constraint of reciprocity to modern life. Our chief concern should be for, first life, then civilization; fighting may foster life and civilization, and not fighting harm them. If you truly wish to make the world a better place, you should sometimes fight.

Human beings lie along two general continua. One continuum runs from concern for the group to concern for oneself, the other from concern for the long-term to concern for the short. Those who are concerned about the long-term well-being of the group, must ever and anon fight those who are concerned only about their short-term interests. The latter are partisans, not of the group, but only of themselves. (One of the great failings of our species is that we have not learned how to ensure that high political position go only to those who are concerned about the group and the long term.) We should not feel remorse at hurting blackguards; we are doing society, and perhaps them, a favor. For many, a thrashing is as condign as it is salutary.

It is in the interests of the individual to further the interests of the group. Not to do so is to hurt oneself over the long term. The lower understanding sees that one is a biological creature and must do certain things to survive, the higher that one is a member of a group and benefits from aiding that group. Many human beings simply do not understand that they are "a piece of the continent, a part of the main," that they are part of the group, that *its* interests are *theirs* as well. Our lower understanding prompts us to care about the kin group (why we all do so); but only the neocortex prompts us to care about the non-kin group (why only a minority do so). "Civil society," said Mommsen, "but slowly and gradually attains to a perception of the interdependence of interests." Only a minority of human beings attain "to a perception of the interdependence of interests," come to care deeply about the group. (The more civilized the society, the more the concern for the group among its members.)

In a species that arose through natural selection and is thus selfish, that simply does not know what it is doing, that which is most to be feared is impunity. All human beings hate limits; all wish to do just as we please. But doing so would not be in our interest, because not in the interests of the group. None of us should be without limits; all must oppose and be opposed. Just as it is best that a balance of power exist among states, so, too, is it best that a balance of power exist among individuals. Socrates felt that a magic ring that could make its wearer invisible, and thus able to do just as he pleases, would corrupt even the best and wisest of men. While under investigation by the Justice Department for possible antitrust violations, Microsoft refrained from engaging in some of the practices that had led to the investigation. Where the gods do not impose limits, human beings must.

In Alduous Huxley's *Crome Yellow*, a Mr. Scogan says:

> The Caesars...are characters functioning, so to speak, in the void. They are human beings developed to their logical conclusions... When I meet someone for the first time, I ask myself this question: Given the Caesarean environment, which of the Caesars would this person resemble — Julius, Augustus, Tiberius, Caligula, Claudius, Nero? I take each trait of character, each mental and emotional bias, each little oddity, and magnify them a thousand times...
>
> Perhaps...it's as well that Denis hasn't been permitted to flower into a little Nero, and that Ivor remains only potentially a Caligula. Yes, it's better so, no doubt. But it would have been more amusing, as a spectacle, if they had had the chance to develop, untrammelled, the full horror of their potentialities. It would have been pleasant and interesting to watch their tics and foibles and little vices swelling and burgeoning and blossoming into enormous and fantastic flowers of cruelty and pride and lewdness and avarice.

Impunity is quite as harmful to its possessor as to its victims. The possessor, whether an individual, organization, or state, almost always overreaches, and in overreaching falls. Too few human beings have the wisdom to see that the impunity they now possess is transient. During the Peloponnesian War, at the height of its power, Athens sent a delegation to the island of Melos. "We will not trouble you," said the delegates, "with specious pretences, either of how we have a right to our empire because we overthrew the Persians, or are now attacking you because of a wrong you have done us…since you know as well as we do that right, as the world goes, is only in question between equals in power, while the strong do what they can and the weak suffer what they must." *But Melos was wholly without strategic significance*; there was no *necessity* in Athens's taking the island. As Arrowsmith observes, true necessity is difficult to see, especially for those with great power. Athens soon lost the war and, with it, its empire.

Only through force can certain objects be attained. Caesar did not *ask* the Roman rich if they would rather share their colossal wealth or retain it, the poor if they would rather emigrate to new colonies to farm or continue living in Rome, receiving free corn and attending games and festivals. Richelieu did not *ask* the feudal lords if they would rather relinquish their castles, serfs, and political independence or retain them. *Asking* would have achieved nothing, would have taken Caesar and Richelieu no closer to their objects. Rarely can one create without first destroying; it is natural for that which is to seek to continue itself, for that which is to be reactionary. And most human beings venerate the inherited order (if it is at all just). Only by suffering a civil war, Caesar's dictatorship, and civil war again could Roman society create a new, more functional government. (Whether destroying betters or worsens civilization depends on the morality and wisdom of the destroyers and their successors. It is well to remember that, as immoral as the government of the Tsars was, that which supplanted it was far more so.)

∽

Fighting is to attain a certain object — a resource, market share, the betterment of the group, emotional satisfaction — or to prevent another from doing so. To fight is to attain the object by force; fighting is thus distinct from competing. To compete is to let merit determine the outcome; to fight is to lessen or nullify the merit of the other. If, in a foot-race, two runners run as fast as they can and the fastest wins, they have competed; if the runners trip and catch at each other as they run, they have fought. The distinction between fighting and competing is determined not by the field, but by what is done; a diplomat may find himself fighting quite as much as any general. And two rivals may simultaneously fight and compete. Fighting is sometimes light and sometimes thick, sometimes of long duration and sometimes of short, sometimes legal and sometimes illegal, sometimes bloody and sometimes bloodless. The ultimate goal in fighting is to attain your object as swiftly as possible while having your interests hurt as little as possible.

It is not really true that might is right; rather, it is the *victor* who is right. It is simply because the victor is so often mightier that this is thought to be so. But it need not be. "The art of war is an art with principles," said Napoleon, "and these principles must never be violated." It is not by chance that Caesar, Richelieu, Napoleon, and Gates won victory after victory; they followed certain principles well. Did *Fortuna*, the Roman goddess of chance, favor Caesar over others? No: Caesar applied certain principles better than did others. Chance plays a role; but the better the principles are applied, the less of a role does chance play. To think *Fortuna* will be with us whether we do certain things or not is to be hubristic. Victory does not come as a matter of course, by itself, simply because *I* am *I*; it comes in a rather scientific fashion, by following certain principles well. In the *Iliad*, great men are divine *because* they are exceptional: "A hero is a hero, not because he enjoys the favor of a god but because his [greatness] requires a god's presence to account for it." (Arrowsmith)

The principles are immutable. "In the art of war," said Napoleon, "nothing is lost, nothing created." They are the same whatever the context; of Napoleon's Egyptian campaign a military historian said, "It is indeed less suited to serve as a distinct military lesson than his other campaigns, for the climate as well as the enemy were too much unlike those to be met with in Europe. Still, the great principles of warfare, true under all circumstances, were here, too, acted on, and may here also be studied." The principles are the same whether applied by Caesar or the common workman — the difference lies simply in scale. They apply equally to competition, as they do to war, social reform, epidemiology, business, and sports. The principles are usually applied simultaneously, or at least in rapid succession; they reinforce one another, each done well fortifying the others.

While the principles themselves are overarching and unchanging, the way in which you apply them is not. Each situation is unique; each calls for a unique application of the principles. How you strike, when you strike, where you strike — all these may change. Napoleon would work out the best possible method of attack and then modify it according to circumstances. "One engages," he said, "then one sees." Here you will win by first demoralizing the opponent, there by first stoking his self-confidence; here by continually attacking, there by withdrawing for a time; here by showing clemency, there by giving no quarter; here by adapting yourself to his dispositions, there by forcing him to adapt to yours; here by striking a single point, there by striking multiple points. Simply knowing the principles did not make Napoleon a great fighter; after all, a child could learn them. (Indeed, this is why he decried "maxims" of fighting, though his own writings are filled with such maxims.) It is because Napoleon applied the principles creatively and with great intelligence that we remember him.

Size and strength matter little, where the principles are applied well. With 50,000 small Italians, Caesar conquered Gaul; he then defeated Romans who controlled the whole of the Roman Empire save Gaul. Richelieu, a frail man directing a frail state, vitiated the much stronger Habsburg states of Spain and the Holy Roman Empire. In his first campaign in Italy, Napoleon won a series of brilliant victories with a ragged army of raw French recruits; indeed, in most of his battles Napoleon had fewer troops than did his opponent. Talleyrand, an infirm man with no position to speak of, hastened Napoleon's fall. In its early years, Microsoft bested far stronger rivals such as IBM, WordPerfect, and Borland International. While soldiery matters, it does so far less than does the intelligent application of the principles. Had Caesar, Richelieu, Napoleon, Talleyrand, and Gates *not* applied these principles, they would most certainly have been destroyed by their far-stronger opponents.

You should apply these principles even when as strong as, or stronger than, your opponent; otherwise, you may see your interests wounded or find yourself bogged down in a protracted fight. (While you fight one rival, another may attack you.) The military historian David Chandler writes that Napoleon "disliked having to force a full-scale, fully arrayed frontal battle — that is to say, marching directly against the enemy to fight him on ground of his (the adversary's) choosing — for such battles were inevitably expensive and rarely conclusive." Whatever your strength, you should only rarely ever oppose force to force.

The best study of these principles is the lives of those who applied them best. Just as we read great writers to learn how to write well, so, too, should we study great fighters to learn how to fight well. Doing so, said Napoleon, "is the only way to become a great general and to grasp the secrets of the art." "Truly Caesar ought to be the breviary of every fighting-man," said Montaigne: "he was the true and sovereign model for the art of war." Clausewitz's *On War* should properly be titled *On Napoleon*, since it is little else but a study of Napoleon's campaigns. Indeed, so superior were Caesar and Napoleon as generals that their chief difficulty was not in winning, but in inducing their opponents to fight. In fighting, these men knew what they were doing. For the purposes of learning these principles, it does not matter whether those applying them were in politics (Richelieu and Talleyrand), politics and the military (Caesar and Napoleon), or business (Gates): the principles are the same.

Unlike Aurelius, these men did not seek to live by ideals. Not for these men was the "obstinate legal formalism" of the Roman constitutionalist Cato, who preferred "to let the republic go to ruin in due course of law than to save it in an irregular way." (Mommsen) These men cared only for two things, their supremacy and their object; all else mattered little. It was not, for these men, a question of the ends justifying the means; they did not care one whit about justifying their means (at least to themselves). To them, it was all quite simple: to achieve certain ends, they must use certain means, means that fit the world as it is. Caesar remarked that he would reward even murderers and thieves if they had once aided him. (The historian Strasburger detects a certain "immoralism" in Caesar's writings, in that he sometimes records acts that others would regard as unscrupulous. Caesar is coaxing the reader into seeing the world as he does.) Richelieu's sole object on coming to power was to unify France; but as it was necessary to divide France in order to come to power, he did so.

In considering Richelieu's *Le Testament politique*, the Oxford historian Anthony Levy writes, "It is a characteristic of [neostoicism] that there are no objective ethical norms. Virtue consists essentially in the vigour with which the will strives to achieve the perceived good [or object], but in a context in which moral grandeur is divorced from strictly ethical values. Corneille... creates morally heroic...characters like Cleopatre in *Rodogune*, who are ethically evil." (Here Levy uses "moral" to mean confidence in the rightness of one's actions.) Neostoicism would seem to have been the ethic of all these men. (It is well to remember that their opponents were not innocents and fought quite as much — just not quite so well.) These men were, however, rarely cruel, and then only when it served their interests; being cruel takes time and rarely contributes to attaining an object. "Unlike his master," writes Auchincloss, "Richelieu was never cruel. He was merciless because he thought that mercy incited disorder." What Auchincloss said of Richelieu could be said of them all, that he was "merciless out of policy alone;" for Richelieu, "the [execution] block was a place of business, no more."

It must be remembered that, except in rare and fatal instances, *all these men applied all these principles.* You mustn't go away from this work thinking, "Oh, yes, Caesar was the fellow who would win at all costs, and Richelieu the one who was dead-set on his object." One could just as easily speak of Caesar's fixation on his object and Richelieu's mettle. Caesar saw his object no less clearly than did Richelieu; Richelieu's determination was quite as great as Caesar's. Neither could have attained his object without applying all the principles; to have been successful at applying any one of these principles, they had to be successful at applying them all.

It is more efficacious — and thus more moral where the object is good — to fight all out. "A decisive battle is far less costly in human life and misery," notes the Oxford historian Felix Markham, "than the attrition of a protracted campaign." "The sharpest methods are the mildest," said Richelieu, "because the quickest." "After exhausting all the means of adjustment," writes Burckhardt, "Richelieu acted in hopeless cases quickly and sternly if the good of the State demanded it, because any half-measures would have been disastrous." In defending the Tuileries against a mob in October 1795, Napoleon ordered his troops to fire ball rather than blanks. "For the populace," he later explained, "hearing a great noise, are a little frightened after the first discharge but, looking around them and seeing no one killed or wounded, they pluck up their spirits, begin immediately to despise you, become twice as insolent, and rush on fearlessly, and it becomes necessary to kill ten times the number that would have been killed if ball had been used in the first place." Of kindness in fighting Clausewitz said, "Kind-hearted people might of course think there was some ingenious way to disarm or defeat an enemy without too much bloodshed, and might imagine this is the true goal of the art of war. Pleasant as it sounds, it is a fallacy that must be exposed: war is such a dangerous business that the mistakes which come from kindness are the very worst."

❦

Only a small minority of human beings *like* to fight; most would far prefer never to have to do so. Richelieu did not *wish* to fight the French aristocracy and the Habsburgs; he would much rather have been born into a world in which France was a functional, unified state quite the equal of the Habsburgs. But he was not. No one *likes* natural selection; no one would have chosen to create us through such a process. But that we evolved by natural selection is certain, and we would do well to understand its consequences, since we must live with them.

Fighting is only one of the many ways to attain our object. "War is nothing," said Clausewitz famously, "but the continuation of policy by other means." Just so: war is a *continuation* of policy, not its beginning; the other means should be tried first. Of Richelieu's Auchincloss observes: "They might be bloody or not. The most effective would be chosen — that was all." To Richelieu, continues Auchincloss, "there was no room in politics for little men. Only a great man could be trusted to reconcile a life of personal rectitude with one where murder for the state was on occasion required..." Just so with fighting: it is not for the little.

DO OR DIE

Of Pompey Mommsen said, "He lacked no condition for grasping at the crown except the first of all — true kingly courage." In fighting, too, "true kingly courage" is the first of all conditions. "The art of war," said Clausewitz, "deals with living. . .forces. Consequently, it cannot attain the absolute, or certainty; it must always leave a margin for uncertainty, in the greatest things as much as in the smallest. With uncertainty in one scale, courage and self-confidence must be thrown into the other to correct the balance." "The moral is to the physical," said Napoleon, "as three is to one." Indeed, Wellington felt that "Napoleon's mere presence with his army was worth 40,000 men."

Once you have begun to fight, nothing matters but prevailing — nothing. "The essential quality of a general-in-chief," said Napoleon, ". . .is the determination to win at all costs." To Metternich he once remarked, "You haven't learned to despise your own life and the lives of others when that is necessary." It is so in fighting. To the Persian king Darius the Macedonian deserter Amyntas said, "Alexander is sure to come wherever he hears Darius to be." Such resolve communicates itself and weakens that of your opponent. You should fight as the mythical Lancelot jousted: while his opponent would instinctively pull back a bit just before contact, Lancelot would not.

To fight without resolve, to be fainthearted and engage in half-measures, is to increase the likelihood of defeat. The more determined you are to prevail, and the more determinedly you proceed, the less risk you run. In his commentaries, Caesar often remarks that "our only hope of safety lay in courage." Without the feeling of do or die, you will not be able to do that which your intellect shows you you must. Time and again, the opponents of Caesar, Napoleon, Richelieu, and Gates could have been victorious had they simply not been too afraid to attack. "On those who lack courage," said Mommsen, "the gods lavish every favor and every gift in vain." You must remain resolute even while down, must be resilient and stout-hearted. Caesar observes that the Gauls are "eager to start wars, but their minds are soft and lacking in determination when it comes to enduring defeats."

To succeed in fighting, you must — only during the fight, and only toward your opponent — be utterly selfish. It is your interests that must prevail; you must wholly disregard your opponent's. You must not feel compassion for your opponent; compassion weakens resolve. You must strike without compunction. In the French Revolution, the Directory, or council of dictators, would preface an execution by declaring the victim hors de la loi, "outside the law." He was shorn of all rights; anything could now be done to him. In the same way, you *must deem your opponent* hors de la loi, *not entitled to the customary kindnesses.* "Kind, trustful, and forgiving as I was," *remarks the Count of Monte Cristo,* "I made myself vengeful, secretive, and cruel — or, rather, impassive like fate itself, which is deaf and blind." *So you must make yourself in fighting.*

In the early second century BC, the Roman poet and dramatist Ennius wrote, "The Roman commonwealth rests upon ancient customs and the men [who practice them]." By the first century BC, the late Roman republic, the ancient customs no longer fit the context, and the men who practiced them were of far lower quality.

Though the population of Rome had grown from 200,000 to perhaps one million; though Rome was now a Helleno-Oriental, rather than chiefly Italian, city, consisting of Syrians, Berbers, Celts, Germans, Libyans, Iberians, Phrygians, and others; and though Rome now controlled much of the Mediterranean world, the Romans continued to govern themselves and their dominions through political structures developed for a city-state. An oligarchy of rich or aristocratic (or both) families administered the state through the Senate and law courts. It was rule by individuals rather than by institutions (the state had, for instance, no civil service); these individuals represented both their own interests and those of (fluctuating) clients, cities, towns, and less powerful individuals.

The structure of Roman government permitted the mass of peoples of Italy little say, the peoples of the provinces none at all. The whole system was tilted toward the rich; it was a plutocracy, rule by Cicero's "army of the rich." By law, a candidate had to possess at least 100,000 *denarii*; and since political office was unpaid, only the rich could give themselves fully to politics. That which contributed most to electability — an illustrious family, military prowess, eloquence in the courts, patronage and a substantial *clientela*, the giving of shows and feasts — was the province of the rich. The *comitia centuriata*, which elected the Roman magistrates, the consuls and praetors, was structured so that the rich would predominate. And since all elections took place in Rome, even the *comitia tributa*, which elected the junior magistrates and tribunes of the people and voted on legislation, tended to represent the interests of the rich, since only well-to-do rural citizens could come to Rome to vote.

Riches and slaves flowed into Rome from the cruel exploitation of the provinces, chiefly of Asia and North Africa. The ruin of Roman morality followed upon the ruin of the provinces; by the late republic, most of the Roman rich cared nothing about the group. A comment by Plutarch on Caesar's first consulship typifies the view of the priviledged class: "He at once began to work in favor of the poor and distressed classes by proposing measures for the founding of new cities and the distribution of land. This was a lowering of his great office." To the rich, the Roman masses were simply "the bilge of the city," the small middle class "artisans, shopkeepers, and all that scum." (Cicero) The senators, *equites* (the equestrian class), *publicani* (which included the tax-farmers), and others of the upper class cared only to introduce new delicacies from Africa and Asia Minor or to vie with one another in the provisioning of luxuries to mistresses. And the more luxuries were valued, the more riches were sought to obtain them. Military command was viewed simply as a chance to acquire riches through conquest. The rich would use the law courts to destroy whoever stood in their way of making money. Whichever Senatorial families fell behind would incur great debts, or resort to peculation or extortion or both, to buy office or luxuries or to construct palaces or country villas, the price of which continually rose. Indebted senators would vote as their creditors — or a foreign ambassador who had paid a bribe — asked. Once bankrupt, they would agitate for civil war in hopes of cancelling their debts. (That this was the object of their insurrections is shown by their motto, "a clear sheet.") The infusion of Greek culture further contributed to the decline in the old Roman morality, as the Romans took, not the best of Greek culture, but "its frivolity and luxury, its pleasures and vices." (Gelzer)

The disproportion between the rich and the poor, high in the early republic, became higher still in the late; Rome was now a city of "millionaires and beggars." 2,000 or so Roman families had inconceivable riches, all others very little. (Not since 167 BC had the rich paid direct taxes.) Cicero observed that a Roman aristocrat required an annual income of at least 25,000 *denarii* — this when a legionary received 120 or so *denarii* a year. Only to themselves did the rich show solicitude; the mass of Romans lived in squalor. Between one-third and two-fifths of the population of Italy, and at least half that of Rome, were slaves. The poor could not hope to compete against slaves and freedmen, first, because the propertied class preferred slave to hired labor (since slaves were generally less costly), and, second, because the slaves and freedmen were trained and financed by their masters or former masters for a share of the profits. Either with the riches they had amassed from the provinces and public contracts, or through the violence of their slaves, the upper class acquired the small farms of Italy, and large landholdings took the place of small. (The Senatorial families alone came to possess half the land of Italy.) The rich would also have their slaves enclose the public domain lands (thus preventing the peasantry from using those lands). Small farmers, displaced from their own land, and unable to find work on another's, would move to the towns and cities (chiefly Rome), where they earned a living as best they could. Simply to eat, a free man would sell himself as a gladiatorial slave, "to let himself be chained, scourged, burnt, or killed without opposition." The legionaries were drawn almost entirely from the rustic poor; conscription made them poorer still, as they were paid very little, and their farms (and families) fell to ruin without their labor. Since the oligarchs refused to give them lands on which to settle once released, the veterans would "roam the land with their wives and children, homeless and hounded."

Caring only about its short-term advantage, the oligarchy grossly maladministered the Empire. It is difficult to say which was worse, what the Senate did, or what it left undone. The criminal, the dissolute, and the indolent flocked to Rome from throughout the Empire. The oligarchs did little to police the city, in which banditti killed at will, and street-riots were frequent; to lessen the wild fluctuations in, for instance, the supply and prices of goods and the money supply; to widen or clean the streets; to lower the price and improve the construction of houses (on which speculators made vast fortunes, and many of which collapsed); to prevent the frequent conflagrations; to regulate the flow of the Tiber. While the mass of Romans sat idle, much of Italy lay uncultivated; scarcities of food were common in Rome. Traveling in the countryside was unsafe, and kidnappings common. The rich so mistreated their slaves that rebellions were frequent (that of Spartacus being but one of many). (To make up for the loss of slaves following the uprisings of the 60s, some of the rich forced indebted peasants into servitude — as the law permitted them to do.) No less than the provinces, Italy was a patchwork of laws and administrative forms the Senate did little to make uniform.

The Senate carried out Rome's wars incompetently. "The object of its highest care was, not that the frontiers might be defended, but that they should not need to be defended quite immediately by itself." (Mommsen) Roman dominions formed an archipelago round the Mediterranean that the oligarchy did nothing to unite. It was piratical rather than Roman fleets that sailed the Mediterranean, plundering at will; trading companies, ship-owners, and even Roman ports were forced to pay the pirates tribute. The provinces seethed under Roman maladministration and exploitation. The oligarchy granted Roman citizenship, or even the lesser Latins rights, to very few communities, and then only under duress. (Indeed, it was only during Caesar's childhood that Rome granted citizenship to the *Italians*; once organized into self-governing communities, the Italians now had no say in either their own governance or that of Italy.) Without Roman citizenship or Latin rights, provincials were at the mercy of rapacious Roman governors, who could confiscate their property with impunity. The governors viewed the provinces as they did their country estates; they could do just as they pleased, and it pleased most to plunder, rape, enslave, and murder (but not to govern: the provinces suffered from brigandage and lawlessness). A town suffered as much in quartering Roman troops as it did in being taken by storm. The economies of the provinces declined greatly under Roman rule; no word was so hated in the Mediterranean world, observes Mommsen, as was "Rome."

The Roman state was wildly disorganized; in Rome quite as much as in the provinces, the people were "neither governed nor governors." The Senate was nothing but a "talking shop;" there was simply no mechanism for addressing the true problems of the Empire. So dysfunctional was the government of the late republic that "it was virtually impossible to do anything for Rome." (Meier) The oligarchy had repeatedly to resort to temporary military commands, to regents or quasi-monarchs, to sort out its affairs; the government of the late republic thus oscillated between anarchy and dictatorship. (The oligarchs were also not in the least fitted by education to administer an empire, since they valued learning quite as little as they did good governance.) Quite simply, the Roman Empire was on the verge of dissolution.

No one, however, was permitted to alter the structure of government. The Senate consisted of *optimates* and *populares*; the *optimates* sought the continuance of the inherited order and the primacy of the Senate, the *populares* to increase the power of the popular assembly as a counterpoise to the aristocracy. Most of the senators were *optimates*, and most were aristocrats from Rome. A small minority of the senators were, however, of the equestrian class, most of whom were municipal gentry; the *equites* almost always sided with the *optimates*. (Senators held their seats for life; though membership in the Senate was not strictly hereditary, most of the senators in the late republic were descended from senators.) The *optimates* cared, *uber alles*, about the continuation of the inherited order (or at least those elements of the order that favored their interests). When Marcus Calpurnius Bibulus declared at the beginning of his consulship that no innovations would take place during his tenure, he was expressing the great value of the *optimates*. The more a senator defended the status quo, Sallust tells us, the more he was considered "good." One of the reasons the *optimates* resisted making conquered territories provinces and opposed enfranchising the Latins was that doing so would compel them to reform the political system; and once the *optimates* did make a territory a province, it was governed, not by Rome, but by a military dictator.

Why were the *optimates* so keen on preserving the inherited order? For half a millennium the Romans had ruled their city and its possessions through that order; the order was not "an entity to be shaped," but rather "a shared ambience in which life could go on as before...not a means to an end — such as the guaranteeing of work and prosperity — but the very element in which [they] lived." (Meier) Cicero observed that *res publica* was the same as *res populi*, "the property or concern of the people," the commonwealth itself. And the less the inherited order could deal with the great problems of empire, the more the *optimates* clung to it; the solution to the dysfunctionality of the order they felt to lie, not in its alteration, but in a still keener emulation of their ancestors. (In truth, the *optimates* did *not* do as their ancestors did; those ancestors showed a far greater, and far shrewder, liberality to the Roman people and their Italian allies.)

The priviledged classes, the oligarchs and financiers, resisted reforms also because reforms might lessen their power and thus their wealth. (It was the Senate, for instance, that awarded the public contracts.) The oligarchs favored the existing system because its weakness let them do as they pleased. (They could, for instance, commit crimes with impunity.) Furthermore, the Roman aristocracy viewed dominion over others as an element of its *libertas*. Rome was freer than all other states by virtue of its imperial strength; and of the Romans, the aristocrats were freest. The aristocrats felt that "a man was most free when he had the fullest right to enforce his own will" (Brunt), that others *should* be poor, others *should* be slaves; to accede to the wishes of the lower orders would be to demean themselves. To the Roman aristocracy, "the liberty conceded to the people at Rome was tolerable only in so far as it was specious." (Brunt) "The good is what pleases the good," said Cicero, "the good" (*boni*) being the oligarchs.

The oligarchy resisted all but the slightest reforms also because whoever instituted a reform might become too popular and thus too powerful. Within the Senate, a premium was placed on equality and conformity; the senators distrusted and opposed *any* individual who sought more power than others, even those, such as Gnaeus Pompey, who did so to strengthen the Senate. The senators preferred to place nullities (such as Bibulus) in high position, since nullities could neither govern well nor come to dominate. Whenever forced by a crisis to appoint a competent individual dictator, the senators would fully expect him to stand down once the crisis had passed. The unfortunate consequence of the *optimates'* suppression of the *populares* and their reforms was that reform must needs come from elsewhere.

Individuals such as Pompey and Julius Caesar would chaff at the bit, obtain a military command, add to Roman dominions, and become far more powerful than their fellow oligarchs. The more such individuals freed themselves from the restraints of the oligarchy, the more power they could attain, and the more able to free themselves further. The powerful men would ally themselves with whichever party could most further their interests, now with the *optimates*, now with the *populares* and the populace they represented. The men generally preferred, however, to ally themselves with the *populares*, as the masses were far more willing to follow than were the *optimates*, who insisted on equality, whatever the true state of things. (As the Oxford historian W. Warde Fowler observes, all democratic movements in the late republic soon turned into the ignorant masses following a demogogue; the Romans were prepared by neither education nor culture for democracy.) The contest was not, however, simply between the powerful men and the *optimates*; it was also between the powerful men themselves. That individuals such as Caesar and Pompey could acquire such power, that governors rather than the Senate determined Roman policy in the provinces, that Roman soldiers would obey their commanders rather than the government in Rome, shows how very dysfunctional the system had become.

Pompey wished to be liked and respected by the senators and Roman society in general, to be allied to the Senate while being recognized as *princeps*, the first man of Rome; he wished to serve the Senate as it recognized his supremacy. Pompey did not understand that few of the senators respected achievement, and that anyhow they were quite unwilling to grant anyone a position of primacy. Understanding the senators far better than did Pompey, and thus neither liking nor respecting them, Caesar did not care a fig whether they liked or respected him. He was far less concerned with preserving the inherited order than with addressing the practical problems of governing the Empire. Caesar's "standards required [others] to be measured not by the yardstick of the possible, but by that of the necessary." (Meier) The *optimates* wished to do the possible, Caesar the necessary; he wished to take up that which the Senate neglected, Rome's vital interests. Roman government must be reorganized upon wholly new lines. The *optimates* drew a distinction between Rome and its provinces (indeed, even between Rome and much of Italy); to Caesar, the Roman Empire was of a piece. The *optimate* world was that of a city-state and its provinces, Caesar's an empire. (That the *optimates* insisted all voting be done in Rome, though Roman citizens lived throughout Italy and the provinces, clearly shows their worldview.) Whereas most of the *optimates* lived only in Italy, and chiefly in Rome, Caesar would spend much of his adult life in the provinces.

To better the Roman Empire was to displease the Senate; only in the teeth of its opposition could one save the Empire. To Caesar, the republic was "nothing — a mere name without form or substance," the *optimates* simply immoral individuals ruling in their own interests. And if the Roman Empire was in truth ruled by individuals, should the best individual not rule? Would that not be the most sensible and functional government? Was the rule of a superior individual not preferable to that of inferior individuals composing a factious oligarchy? Was it not all quite simple? Pompey had clearly shown in the East that a judicious individual governed far better than did an injudicious group. And if *Pompey* could rule so well, what could Caesar, greatly his superior, not do?

❦

In 60 BC, Caesar formed an alliance with Pompey and Marcus Licinius Crassus, the richest man in Rome, to attain certain objects for each. In league with the *populares* and *equites*, the triumvirate soon obtained for Caesar one of the two consulships for 59. As consul, the highest magistrate in the Senate, Caesar did all he could to vitiate the inherited order, fully exploiting the maladaption of the late republic and the ineptitude and irresolution of the senators. He was quite high-handed — so much so that Rome's two consuls were sardonically said to be Julius and Caesar; most of the senators simply boycotted the meetings of the Senate. Not only through his legislation (which strengthened Pompey), but also by so violating custom and precedent Caesar greatly weakened the inherited order.

One of Caesar's chief reasons for seeking the consulship was to obtain the governorship of a province or provinces. Through one of his supporters, the tribune Publius Vatinius, and with the support of Pompey, Caesar acquired the governorship of the Roman provinces of Gallia Cisalpina (to the south of the Alps) and Illyricum (the littoral to the east of the Adriatic). Soon afterwards Pompey also induced the Senate to confer on Caesar the governorship of Gallia Transalpina (to the west of the Alps). The conquest of Gaul would provide Caesar not only with riches with which to buy influence and fund public buildings and games, but also a large *clientela* of legionaries. The expansion of the Roman Empire would further strain the Roman political order, the addition of new Roman citizens further enfeeble the senatorial regime. (By thus simultaneously strengthening himself and weakening the Senate, Caesar also hoped to make it quite impossible for the *optimates* to prosecute him for his acts as consul.) And the addition of Gaul to Roman dominions would be the beginning of Caesar's first step toward creating a great empire.

In Gaul, Caesar would be able to show his great superiority, to show *why* he should be considered the first man of Rome. In the little, constrained world of Roman politics, Caesar could show his superiority only slightly. Life in Rome hemmed him about; to live in Rome was to be trussed-up. Caesar was filled with the ancient Roman passion for achievement, a passion quite lost on most of his contemporaries. (That which was a spur to

Caesar, only flummoxed his compatriots.) Through his conquest of Gaul, Caesar would achieve true *dignitas*, a term connoting both rank *and* worth. Caesar felt the senators had corrupted the concept of *dignitas*, that while worth should lead to rank, they had acquired the latter without ever possessing the former.

The linchpin of Caesar's Roman policy while in Gaul would be the continuation of his alliance with Pompey and Crassus, the keeping of the two at variance with the *optimates*. Caesar must isolate the stronger elements in Roman politics; combined, they would be a strong counterpoise to Caesar. The interests of the three now corresponded (a correspondence furthered, in Pompey's case, by his marriage to Caesar's daughter, Julia); Caesar must ensure that they continue to do so at least until he himself had attained great power. Then, should Pompey and the *optimates* ally themselves against him, he would have some chance of opposing them. Furthermore, Caesar had had certain laws passed while consul that greatly weakened the inherited order; the *optimates* must not be permitted to rescind those laws, to undo his work as he had undone theirs. While conquering Gaul, he would winter in Gallia Cisalpina whenever possible so that he might influence Roman affairs. Much of what Caesar would do in Gaul would be to influence Roman politics; and much of what he would achieve in Rome, his victories in Gaul would make possible.

∽

Gaul corresponded to present-day France, Belgium, southern Holland, Germany west of the Rhine, and most of Switzerland. Though it was not quite so simple, in *The Gallic War* Caesar divides the Gauls into three main groups, the Celts in the south, the Belgae in the north, and the Aquitani in the southwest. Southern Gaul, filled with Roman (and, earlier, Greek and Etruscan) merchants and farmers, was far more Hellenized and Romanized than northern. The Gauls were organized into states; those to the north were ruled by kings, those to the south by proto-Roman councils and magistrates. Within the latter, as in Rome, the councils consisted of aristocratic families who cared little about the interests of the group. The Gallic states contested territory and formed ever-shifting alliances; stronger states exercised a hated and exploitative hegemony over weaker states. Gaul north of Gallia Transalpina was independent (though Rome maintained alliances with many of its states). A sense of national unity, fostered by a common language and religion and wars with Rome and the Germanic states, pervaded the country.

Neither the Roman Senate nor the Gauls themselves wished Gaul to fall under Roman sway. The Senate did not wish to add to Roman dominions and thus further strain the government, and it certainly did not wish Caesar to acquire the power the conquest of Gaul would give him. The Gauls were far too well acquainted with Roman maladministration and exploitation in Spain and Asia ever to wish to be a Roman tributary. In his commentary on the Gallic war, Caesar gives two reasons for intervening in Gallic affairs. First, the chieftain of the Germanic Suebi, Ariovistus, was making conquests in eastern Gaul and Germans continuously crossing to the left bank of the Rhine; only fifty years before, the Germanic states had almost taken Rome itself. Second, these incursions were forcing the Gallic Helvetii to migrate west; not only would the Germanic states occupy their territory, but, since the Helvetii were old enemies of Rome, they would doubtless seek to turn the neighboring Gallic states against the Romans. (So alarmed was the Senate by the Germanic incursions and Helvetic migration that it sent legions into the country during Caesar's consulship.) Caesar argued that Rome must possess a buffer territory between Italy and the Germanic states, and that only by occupying Gaul could Rome prevent future Germanic incursions. (Some Gallic states, or factions within them, had shown themselves quite willing to call on Ariovistus to aid them against their enemies, and Ariovistus would soon tell Caesar that he viewed Gaul as his.) Whether he truly considered the Germanic states a danger, or whether that was simply a pretext, Caesar's object required that he conquer Gaul; any resistance by the Gauls he would view as rebellion.[2]

At the proconsul's command were three legions in Gallia Cisalpina and one in Gallia Transalpina. On his own initiative, Caesar would soon raise an

---

2 Suetonius states that Caesar "lost no opportunity of picking quarrels — however unfair and dangerous — with allies as well as hostile and barbarous states, and marching against them." This is as frequently quoted as it is untrue. Caesar would not have attacked his allies, so badly did he need them; to non-allies, he showed clemency whenever possible. While it is true that Caesar required "reparations" (that is, tribute) of subject states, he asked far less than did Rome's governors elsewhere — to have asked too much would have increased resistance — or exempted loyal states altogether.

additional two legions in Gallia Cisalpina. Most of these legionaries would not be Roman citizens (though Caesar would treat them as if they were), the beginning of the Gallicization of his forces. His staff consisted chiefly of the elite of the *populares*, the most gifted of whom was Titus Labienus.

In the spring and summer of 58 BC, Caesar inflicted defeats on first the Helvetii and then Ariovistus, forcing the first to return to their territory in eastern Gaul, the second to flee across the Rhine. Caesar thus stabilized, at least for the present, the territory along the Rhine. He permitted the Germanic states that had long ago settled on the left bank of the Rhine to retain their domains; these states, as politically isolated from the Gallic states as from their Germanic kinsfolk, would have little choice but to be allies of Rome — a nice check against the hostile Gallic and Germanic states. That Caesar was determined to control Gallic affairs far from Gallia Transalpina shows that he viewed the whole of Gaul as a Roman possession, and the Rhine as a boundary of the Roman Empire.

The successes that brought the submission of most of the states of central Gaul, and the wintering of the Romans there, served only to unite most of those of northern Gaul. In the winter of 58/57, a force of 300,000 Belgae and their allies marched to their southern frontier. Caesar raised a further two legions in Cisalpine Gaul and with eight marched north to meet them. The Remi and other Belgic states, wishing to throw off the yoke of the stronger Belgic states, submitted to Caesar without a fight. As was his policy in Gaul, Caesar insisted that their aristocratic families provide him with hostages; with their fathers, brothers, and sons in Caesar's possession, these families were far less likely to agitate for war against the Romans.

On learning that the Belgic force was drawing near, Caesar constructed a fortified camp upon a hill with a river on one side and a marsh on another. Though the two fought minor cavalry skirmishes, neither was willing to cross the marsh in force. The Belgae tried to storm a Roman outpost on the river and destroy the bridge by which the Romans received supplies, but Caesar repelled them with cavalry and light infantry. Recognizing that they could not take the Roman positions, and running short of corn, the Belgae decided to return to their towns and villages and come to the aid of whichever state Caesar might attack next. So eager were the Belgae to return to their homes, however, that their departure was more flight than march. On seeing this, Caesar had his cavalry and three legions pursue them; before returning to camp that night, they were able to kill a great many of the Belgae. Caesar then marched from town to town in the western Belgic territory, where states that only a few weeks before had sworn to destroy the Romans now capitulated.

In the eastern Belgic territories, however, the Nervii and their allies, the Viromandui and Atrebates, as valiant as they were unwilling to submit, created a new force to resist the Romans. On marching into their territory, Caesar learned that the main force of the Nervii was awaiting the Romans on the other side of the Sambre river. The Nervii had been told by Gauls within Caesar's camp that, in the Roman order of march, each legion would be followed by its baggage train. They resolved on attacking the Romans on seeing the first baggage train; they would thus be able to destroy each legion as it came up. Whenever near an enemy, however, Caesar would mass his legions; as they marched toward the Sambre, the Romans observed the following order: Caesar, the cavalry, and light infantry in front, followed by six legions; then, the baggage train followed by two.

The Roman scouts had found a hill by the river well-suited to fortification works. On arriving, the cavalry and light infantry crossed the river and drove off some Nervii horsemen. As they did so, one by one the legions arrived; the soldiers at once set to work gathering supplies and constructing their camp. (Caesar had the officers remain with their legions should they be attacked by surprise.) The Roman baggage train now arrived; as it did so, the Nervii erupted from the woods on the opposite bank, driving the cavalry and light infantry across the river and falling upon the scattered Romans.

Wild confusion reigned among the Romans; their forces were widely dispersed over difficult terrain criss-crossed with hedges. Pitched conflicts took the place of a line of battle; most of the soldiers fought without helmets, and with shields still in their leather coverings. Each soldier fought wherever he stood, whether with his own cohort or another. As Caesar could not communicate with his officers, they did whatever their situation demanded. Labienus, commanding the seasoned ninth and tenth legions on the Roman left wing, drove the Atrebates down the slope and across the river. The two legions in the center were equally successful, driving the Viromandui down the hill. Their doing so, however, isolated the Roman right wing (where Caesar was), upon which the main force of the Nervii now fell. The Nervii also poured into the Roman camp and round its baggage train; thinking the Romans lost, the Gallic cavalry and Numidian slingers and archers fled.

The Nervii outflanked the twelfth legion and attacked it from both sides. So crowded were the soldiers round their standard that they had difficulty fighting; most of their officers had fallen, and no reserves were to be had. The legion began to fall back under the relentless onslaught. Caesar seized a shield from a soldier and threw himself into the front line, calling on some centurions by name, encouraging others, and instructing them to draw the units apart so that the soldiers might have space in which to fight. The soldiers took heart and began to fight resolutely once again.

Caesar now raced to the nearby seventh legion, which was also being attacked from both sides, and also falling back. Bit by bit, he brought the two legions together and ordered them to wheel round so that they might fight back to back. Aid now arrived: the two legions protecting the baggage train, and the victorious tenth legion of the Roman left, fell upon the Nervii from all sides. The Gallic cavalry and Numidian archers and slingers rejoined the fight; even the Roman wounded fought while leaning on their shields. Their situation hopeless, the Nervii fought no less fiercely; as the Romans hewed down line after line of them, the survivors, fighting from atop the bodies of their fallen, hurled the Romans' pikes back at them. Their valor earned Caesar's highest respect.

Of 60,000 Nervii warriors, only 500 survived, of their 600 senators, only three. Caesar showed clemency to the survivors, requiring only that the Nervii surrender their weapons and give hostages, and commanding the neighboring states to respect their territory.

Caesar now lay siege to a town of the Atuatuci, one of the few states still unwilling to recognize Roman suzerainty. Frightened by the Roman siegeworks, the Atuatuci feigned submission so that they might take the Romans by surprise in the middle of the night. Their attack failed, and the Romans stormed the town. Caesar had all the Atuatuci survivors, 53,000 or so, sold into slavery. While generally hewing to a policy of clemency, Caesar would punish treachery with great severity.

Caesar now received word from Publius Crassus, the son of his ally and his legate to Brittany and northern Normandy, that those states had submitted. The legions went into winter quarters in Gaul, their commander first in Illyricum and then Gallia Cisalpina. It seemed to Caesar that his work in Gaul was very nearly finished, that the country was now all but a Roman province. But the Romans had achieved victories only over certain states in certain parts of Gaul; much of the country had yet to see a Roman legionary. Certainly the Gauls in these territories — and indeed even those in the states that had submitted to Rome — did not view themselves as Roman subjects.

The Romans, too, seemed to think that Gaul was now theirs; and even if it was not, they were thrilled at the victories of Roman arms over the fierce Gallic states. The Senate granted Caesar a *supplicatio*, or festival in honor of a victor, of fifteen days, the longest ever bestowed on a Roman commander. Pompey wished it to be understood, however, that he was still the first man of Rome, whatever Caesar's successes. The more power Caesar gained through those successes, the more Pompey must seek to augment his own. By engineering a grain shortage in Rome, he was able to induce the Senate to vote him a *curatio annonae*, a five-year commission to organize the grain supply throughout the empire, thus linking his power in the provinces to that in Rome and giving him a strong hold over the city.

Since both Pompey and the Senate wished to weaken Caesar, preferably by relieving him of his command in Gaul, might they not now become allies? Pompey indeed tried to draw closer to the Senate — without, however, severing his ties with Caesar. What Pompey could not see was that he could be the ally of the Senate or of Caesar, but not of both. He also could not see that the Senate disliked and distrusted him for aiding Caesar in weakening the republic and that — what he could never see — the *optimates* would grant him what he most wished, recognition of his primacy, only temporarily if at all, and certainly never in earnest. The Senate indeed wished to draw Pompey away from Caesar — *not* so that it might be allied with Pompey, but simply to weaken them both (and thus regain its supremacy). Now seemed propitious: the triumvirate had achieved its objects; what further objects could it possibly have?

Doubtless Caesar was delighted at the Senate's aloofness to Pompey, at his having nowhere to turn. But he must also have recognized that, as his power grew, the Senate would be forced to accept Pompey as its ally, however much it would prefer not to do so. And the *optimates* were once more insisting that Caesar's governorship was illegal and should be rescinded. To save themselves, Caesar must once more bind Pompey to himself.

In April 56, Caesar invited Pompey to visit him at Luca, the town in Gallia Cisalpina nearest Rome. Here he laid out for Pompey the context: that the Roman ruling class would never give Pompey what he wished, recognition of his supremacy. Why continue to seek that which would never be granted? Speaking so, Caesar was able to induce Pompey to reconstitute their alliance. Pompey would become consul for the following year, receive command of the two Spanish provinces for five years (to match Caesar's own), and be acknowledged as the supreme member of the triumvirate. Caesar would gladly give Pompey anything he wished — until Caesar could be certain of Gaul and thus his power. (That Caesar would grant Pompey a position to his rear and acknowledge his primacy shows how little he feared him.) The Senate could not again discuss Caesar's *imperium* in Gaul or his successor until March 1, 50, and he would become consul for 48. This law, and another governing the allotment of provinces to proconsuls, ensured that no one would be able to become governor of Gaul before 48. It was critical to Caesar that this be so: if there were to be an interval between the end of his governship and the beginning of his consulship, if he were to become a private citizen, his enemies would be able to arraign him for crimes committed while consul in 59 and while governor of Gaul. Crassus, with whom Caesar had met the month before and also induced to rejoin the alliance, would become Pompey's fellow consul in 55 and receive command of the province of Syria (where Pompey had many clients, thus intertwining their interests). By giving the triumvirs provinces, large armies, and the highest political position in Rome, by dealing a further blow to the egalitarianism of the Roman ruling class, Caesar greatly vitiated the inherited order, and this without harming his own interests in the slightest.

Notwithstanding the (weak) opposition of the *optimates* and other antimonarchical groups — who did little else but absent themselves from meetings of the Senate and dress in mourning — by filling the voting booths with their supporters, and by forcing all the other candidates to stand down, Pompey and Crassus were soon elected consuls. As consuls, the two would have little difficulty obtaining what the triumvirs sought. The anti-monarchists would continue to oppose the triumvirs by electing *optimates* whenever they could and by persecuting the triumvirs' supporters through the jury-courts (which they still controlled). A natural correspondence would arise: the more Caesar, Pompey, and Crassus acted like monarchs, the more anti-monarchical Roman society would become.

In the winter of 57/56, the Veneti, a seafaring state in southern Brittany, induced the other states of Brittany and northern Normandy to join in rebelling against Rome. Soon the whole of the coast from the Rhine to the Loire had risen up. Patriotic Gauls from throughout the country flocked to join the rebellion, the first act of which was the taking hostage of Roman officers sent to collect corn.

By early May, Caesar was in Brittany. He divided the legions into five groups; while four held down the rebellious states elsewhere, he with one conducted the land attack on the Veneti. Only at sea, however, could the Veneti be decisively defeated: on spits of land or high upon cliffs, the Venetic towns were as difficult to take by storm as they were easy to resupply by sea; and whenever the Romans succeeded in taking a Venetic town, its inhabitants simply sailed off to another. In the late summer, the fleet Caesar had ordered built on the Loire arrived; it was, however, far smaller than the Venetic, and its ships of far lower quality. The Romans could neither board nor attack the high decks of the Venetic ships, from which the Veneti could hurl missiles down upon the Romans; and the iron beaks of the Roman ships would simply recoil from the oak planks of the Venetic.

As Caesar and much of the Roman army watched from cliffs, the two fleets met. Caesar had had his men attach sickles to long poles; the Romans would position the sickles by the halyards that attached the yards to the masts and then row hard away from the Venetic ships. The yards and sails would collapse, and the Roman soldiers board the maimed ships. The Veneti tried to put out to sea (where the Roman vessels could not follow), but the wind died, and ship by ship the Romans destroyed the Venetic fleet. Since the Veneti had taken Roman envoys hostage, put at risk the vital corn supply, and fomented rebellion, Caesar showed little mercy: he had all their councillors executed, and all other members of the state sold into slavery.

Elsewhere in Brittany and northern Normandy, the Roman legions were quite as successful in bringing the Venetic allies to heel. The legions wintered among the newly pacified states, Caesar once again in Cisalpine Gaul.

During the winter of 56/55, two Germanic states, the Usipetes and Tencteri, were driven by the Suebi across the Rhine near the sea. Caesar could not let the two remain in Gaul: not only were they displacing Gallic states, but some of the Gauls were urging them to attack the Romans. Caesar marched north to meet the Germans; in spite of a truce arranged through envoys, the Germanic cavalry attacked and routed the Roman. Knowing this defeat would incite the Gauls to rebellion, Caesar resolved to attack the Germans at once. Before he could do so, however, a deputation of leaders from the two states entered his camp; he detained them and then attacked theirs. Leaderless, the Germans panicked. The Romans cut down whichever Germans they could catch, even the women and children; many others drowned trying to cross a nearby river.

Caesar now resolved to cross the Rhine and strike such terror into the Germans that they would never again cross over into Gaul. Not trusting his Germanic allies, the Ubii, to ferry the Roman army across the river, he ordered a bridge built. Once over the Rhine, the Romans were able to compel some of the Germanic states to submit. The Suebi and other hostile states, however, withdrew deep into their forests; Caesar could do little else but set fire to their villages and cut down their corn. He then recrossed the Rhine and had the bridge destroyed.

The lesson he had taught the Germanic states, Caesar would now teach the British. British auxiliaries had joined the Gauls in battles against the Romans, and some of the more rebellious Gauls had taken refuge on the island. The world must be shown that no peoples could act with impunity against Rome, that even the Britons would feel its authority. Furthermore, it was said that the island was rich in gold, silver, iron, and pearls. The conquest of Britain might very well increase Caesar's wealth and give him another sphere for achievement.

Once one of his officers had reconnoitred the island, and the Romans received assurances from some of the British states that they would be well received (as well as hostages), on the night of August 26 Caesar with two legions crossed the channel. On arriving the following morning, the Romans found the natives lying in wait for them. As the Romans disembarked, the Britons fell upon them. The Romans fought from deep water, the Britons from shallow water or dry land, the Romans encumbered by their heavy weapons, the natives only lightly armed. Unused to this mode of fighting, the Romans panicked. On seeing this, Caesar ordered the warships to detach themselves from the transports and sail into the flank of the Britons. Frightened by the unfamiliar movement of oars and the hail of missiles, the natives fell back. Roman soldiers who had been frightened by the deep water now leapt from their ships. Recovering from their fright, the natives threw themselves upon the Romans, who soon could neither keep ranks nor find a foothold. British horsemen now joined in the attack. (The Roman cavalry had not yet crossed the channel.) Caesar sent vessels with soldiers to whichever points in the Roman line were in danger of giving way. Bit by bit, the Romans pressed toward the shore; on reaching land, they put the natives to flight.

The Britons at once sued for peace, a peace Caesar granted on condition he receive further hostages. A few days later, however, a gale damaged or destroyed much of the Roman fleet. The small Roman force was now cut off equally from reinforcements, supplies, and retreat, a vulnerability that heartened the natives quite as much as it disheartened the Romans. Caesar at once ordered one of the legions to repair the fleet, the other to gather corn. In spite of a lack of *materiel* and continuous attacks on the Roman foragers, within a short while the fleet was once again seaworthy, and other vessels brought from the Continent. All the while, however, the Britons had been gathering their forces; they now attacked the Romans by their camp. The Romans inflicted a further defeat, set fire to all the nearby farms, and then sailed for Gaul.

Though this expedition had achieved little, it delighted the Romans, to whom Britain was something of a mythic isle. The Senate, which Pompey and Crassus continued to hold well in hand, responded by ordaining a *supplicatio* of twenty days. Before leaving for Gallia Cisalpina and Illyria, Caesar ordered his men to construct a new fleet and refit the old in preparation for a second invasion of Britain. Now far better acquainted with its tides and shore, he designed ships that were lower, wider, and more manoeuvrable, outfitted with both sails and oars for swiftness. By the end of the winter, the soldiers, engineers, and workmen had built or refitted 600 transport ships and 28 warships.

In the spring of 54, with five legions and 2000 cavalry Caesar again crossed the channel. (To deter rebellion in Gaul, Caesar left behind three legions with cavalry and forced many of the Gallic leaders to go with him.)

So cowed were the Britons by the sight of the Roman fleet that they did not oppose the Roman landing. Caesar left ten cohorts by the beach to create a camp and with the others marched north in pursuit of the native force. On learning that a gale had damaged the fleet, however, Caesar returned to the Roman camp; he ordered the ships beached and included within the fortification works so that no further damage might be done, and ordered repairs to be made.

After ten days, Caesar once again marched inland. While he had been on the coast seeing to the camp and fleet, the Britons had appointed a supreme commander, Cassivellaunus, and collected a sizeable force. Cassivellaunus attacked the Romans continuously, while marching, constructing camps, and foraging. At first the natives got the better of the Romans through greater mobility: they would dash at the Romans on horses or chariots, inflict casualties, and ride off; if the Roman cavalry pursued them, they would fall upon the cavalry as soon as it was out of reach of the supporting infantry. When the natives once attacked the Romans in force, however, they were put to rout.

The Romans continued their northward march, soon crossing the Thames. Their sweeping the Britons from the opposite bank decided Cassivellaunus on a new tack: rather than fight the Romans openly, he would attack whichever soldiers or horsemen strayed from the main column and then withdraw into the forests. The Romans could now do little else but set fire to villages and fields. Soon, however, Cassivellaunus was forced to seek terms: the Romans were ruining his lands; some of the British states Cassivellaunus had himself tried to subjugate had gone over to the Romans; and, a native attack on the Roman coastal camp had failed. Caesar, too, was eager to come to terms: a bad harvest had made Gaul restive; the autumnal equinox was near, after which storms would make the crossing of the channel difficult; and, the Romans had found no riches. Caesar insisted on hostages and an annual tribute — the latter of which is unlikely ever to have been paid — and then returned to his coastal camp and thence to Gaul. Whether Caesar ever hoped to subjugate Britain is uncertain; if he did, he was quick to recognize that he could not do so while Gaul remained restive. One of his objects, however, Caesar most certainly did attain: the Britons would do little to aid the Gauls in the future.

While Caesar had been in Britain, many of the Gallic states had conspired to try once more to throw off the Roman yoke. Vassalage to Rome cost both their pride and their interests dear, as Rome directed their affairs and requisitioned troops and funds. That much of their country had been lost to the Romans without a fight, shamed the Gauls; only the Nervii and Veneti had resisted. If the Britons could prevent the Romans from conquering their country, why not the Gauls theirs?

In the winter of 54/53, a shortage of grain forced the Roman legions to disperse; they were thus isolated and vulnerable. In the territory of the Eburones were a newly raised legion and five cohorts, commanded by Lucius Cotta and Quintus Sabinus. The king of the Eburones, Ambiorix, visited the commanders. The Gauls were simultaneously attacking all the Roman camps, he told them, and Germanic states would soon arrive and join in the attack. Ambiorix promised the legions free passage should they wish to join another Roman camp two days' march away. He told them all this, he said, because of the favor Caesar had shown him.

Cotta and Sabinus held a council of war. Cotta argued that they should not trust an enemy's word; that, were they to be besieged by a host of Gauls and Germans, the other legions, or Caesar himself, would come to their aid; that their fortifications were sufficiently strong, and their corn sufficiently plentiful, to withstand a long siege. Sabinus argued that Ambiorix was indeed indebted to Caesar; that the Romans would not be able to withstand a siege by such a horde; that if indeed all of Gaul was rising up against the Romans, no one would be able to come to their aid. The debate continued until midnight, at which point Cotta yielded.

The following morning, the Romans marched out of their camp. Two miles from the camp, their march took them through a deep ravine. Once the Romans were well into the ravine, a mass of Eburones suddenly appeared on the heights; they barred both ends of the ravine and began to pour missiles down on the massed Romans. Sabinus panicked and could not command sensibly; Cotta, however, directed the soldiers as best he could given that the Roman column was stretched out the length of the ravine. Some of the soldiers in their terror fought poorly if at all, others valiantly.

Ambiorix instructed his men not to fight hand-to-hand with the Romans, but to hurl their missiles at them from a distance. Whenever a cohort sallied out against the Eburones, they simply withdrew. By early afternoon, many of the Romans had been killed or wounded. Sabinus now saw Ambiorix in the distance; he requested a parley, which Ambiorix granted. Once in their presence, Ambiorix had Sabinus and his companions cut down. The Eburones now redoubled their attack. Cotta fell fighting; leaderless, the Roman survivors now fought their way back to the camp; late that night, despairing of fighting such a host, the survivors committed suicide. A few of the soldiers had been able to escape from the ravine and make their way to Labienus's camp. Rarely had Rome suffered such a loss; Caesar vowed to cut neither his hair nor his beard until it was avenged.

This victory over the Romans electrified Gaul. State after state joined the rebellion; soon only the Aedui and Remi remained loyal to Rome. With the Nervii and the Atuatuci, the Eburones now besieged the Roman camp in the territory of the Nervii, employing techniques they had learned from the Romans. With only 7,000 men and 400 cavalry, Caesar set out for the besieged camp. Once near it, he exaggerated his weakness by having his men erect a small camp and run to and fro as if in panic, and by having the Roman cavalry fall back before that of the Gauls. So certain were the Gauls now of victory that they began to attack the camp. The Roman infantry and cavalry poured from the gates and fell upon the Gauls, killing a great many. On arriving at the Roman camp that had withstood the siege, Caesar found not one soldier in ten unwounded.

Certain the uprising would continue, Caesar ordered three further legions to be raised in Cisalpine Gaul. Though still winter, he made surprise attacks on the Nervii and other states, defeating all; he gave all the Nervii men and cattle he could catch to his soldiers as booty and ravaged their fields. When in the spring Caesar summoned the leaders of all the Gallic states, those of the Senones, Carnutes, and Treveri did not come. He now marched so swiftly into the territory of the Senones that both they and the Carnutes sued for peace.

Caesar resolved first to isolate the Eburones by attacking all those who might come to their aid, or to whom the Eburones might flee. He marched into the neighboring territory of the Menapii; when they withdrew into their marshes, Caesar had causeways built and pursued them. After the Romans had captured many of their men and cattle and set fire to their settlements, the Menapii sued for peace. Labienus, meanwhile, surprised the

Treveri and killed a great many, whereupon they, too, sued for peace. Caesar now crossed the Rhine to punish the Suebi for aiding the Gallic uprising, whereupon the Suebi again withdrew into their forests. Caesar returned to Gaul, leaving, however, a section of the bridge on the Gallic side standing as a permanent threat, guarded by 6,000 legionaries in strong fortifications.

Caesar now turned his attention to the Eburones. So that the Eburones could neither gather their forces nor flee, he sent his cavalry racing into their territory, he following swiftly with the infantry. The cavalry soon came upon a hut in which Ambiorix was meeting with his companions; as the companions fought the Romans, Ambiorix fled. The other Eburones now saved themselves as best they could, fleeing into woods and marshes. So as not to risk the lives of his soldiers in pursuing the Eburones, Caesar invited the neighboring states to join the Romans in plundering their territory. Soon, neither human structure nor crop remained: "The result was that any people at present in hiding seemed likely to die for lack of provisions when the army withdrew." (Caesar) Caesar then settled the Tungri on the lands of the Eburones. Though hunted by the whole of the Roman cavalry, Ambiorix with four horsemen was able to escape over the Rhine. In the autumn, Caesar held an inquiry into the rebellion and had its leader executed; he then sent most of the legions into winter quarters in the territory of the more rebellious states and returned to Gallia Cisalpina.

In Rome, Caesar's political position had grown weaker and more isolated. In the summer of 53, the Parthians had annihilated Crassus and his legions in the Syrian desert. Since Crassus was always more Caesar's ally than Pompey's — was, indeed, Pompey's ally only through Caesar's inducements — with Crassus Caesar lost a counterpoise to Pompey. (Indeed, it is unlikely the civil war would have come about at all had Crassus lived, because Pompey and the *optimates* would not have dared to fight both Caesar *and* Crassus.) Furthermore, a critical link between Caesar and Pompey had been lost: during Caesar's second summer in Britain, Julia, the daughter and wife both dearly loved, and who doubtless mediated between them, had died in childbirth, her child soon following.

Pompey was naturally drawn, would always be drawn, to the Senate because of his great desire for legitimacy, for its recognition of his primacy. Caesar had always been to him the less-preferred ally; indeed, he was Caesar's ally only because the Senate refused to grant him what he wished.

Hoping to force the Senate to declare him sole consul and dictator, and to earn its respect and esteem for bringing peace to the city, Pompey connived in gang violence and other disorder in Rome. In January 52, the Senate granted his request, first, because it found the anarchy so disquieting — at its culmination, a mob burned down the *Curia Hostilia*, the Senate House — second, because it had taken Pompey's measure and was thus far less afraid of him, and, third, because it recognized that Pompey might be of aid in bringing down Caesar. Pompey would try to maintain good relations with Caesar simply as a counterpoise to the Senate, but would now always side with the latter whenever the wishes of the two were in conflict.

Quite as much as Caesar's opponents in Rome, the Gauls were uniting bit by bit. In spite of six years of Roman victories, the Gauls were still far from reconciled to Roman rule. Through superior thinking and lightning surprise strikes, Caesar had continually defeated the Gallic states. But they were far from vanquished, far too well acquainted with life in Roman provinces to acquiesce to Roman rule. Caesar's waging war on all of Gaul had given the Gauls a sense of themselves as *Gauls*, rather than as individual states. They now saw their country as Caesar did, not as individual territories, but as a whole; the disunity that Caesar had exploited was now much reduced. And the Gauls were quite conscious of their vast superiority in numbers. Furthermore, if the native peoples of Mesopotamia could defeat the Romans, then so, too, might the Gauls.

A son of the chief of the Arverni had been visiting each state in turn, exhorting them to unite against the Romans. Vercingetorix was as intelligent as he was valiant, as gifted a general as he was skillful a politician. And he hated the Romans passionately. By the winter of 53/52, Vercingetorix had induced half the states of Gaul to join him in rebelling against Rome; some of those Caesar considered most loyal became Vercingetorix's allies. On being appointed supreme commander, from each state Vercingetorix requisitioned soldiers and especially cavalry, with which both the Britons and Mesopotamians had been able to defeat or check the Romans. He trained the Gauls in Roman tactics and entrenchment techniques, which he had studied with great care. At last the Gauls had a leader of great intelligence and courage.

Certain the situation in Rome would force Caesar to remain in northern Italy, Vercingetorix ordered the rebellion to begin. Its first act was the Carnutes' massacring all the Roman citizens of the town of Cenabum. Then, as one Gallic force cut the food supply of the legions in Gaul, another invaded Gallia Transalpina. So completely did the Gauls cut off their country that soon nothing could be learned of the legions there. So: as the Roman Senate declared Pompey dictator, all of Gaul rose up in revolt. Caesar's tribulations in Gaul emboldened his Roman opponents, and his tribulations in Rome emboldened the Gauls. It seemed as though all his work, in both Rome and Gaul, had come to nothing. He was as lost politically in Rome, as he was militarily in Gaul.

At first Caesar simply ignored the rebellion so that he might save what he could of his position in Rome. At the end of February, he crossed the Alps. He first levied twenty-two new cohorts in Gallia Transalpina and dispersed them throughout the province; they, the legionary recruits Caesar had brought with him, and local militias were to defend the province as best they could. He then crossed the Cevennes through deep snow — the Gauls had blocked all the roads — arriving in the territory of the Arverni before the Gauls knew he had set out. While his cavalry laid waste to the territory to draw Vercingetorix home, Caesar with a small group made his way with all speed to Vienna. There he joined some cavalry he had sent to the town and continued on into the territory of the Lingones, where two of the legions were stationed. He then ordered the other legions to join him.

Vercingetorix now laid siege to a tributary town of the Aedui, one of the few states still loyal to Rome. In spite of the great difficulty of obtaining supplies, Caesar had no choice but to relieve the siege: if Rome could not protect its allies, why be an ally of Rome? As he marched, he took, plundered, and set fire to Cenabum; his doing so forced Vercingetorix to raise his siege and march against him. From Cenabum Caesar went into the territory of the Bituriges, a state whose joining the rebellion had decided many other states to do so, and laid siege to the town of Noviodunum. The Gallic cavalry now attacked the Roman; the Romans put the Gauls to rout, and Noviodunum opened its gates to Caesar.

Vercingetorix now took a new tack: he would fight the Romans, not by taking the field against them, but by cutting them off from food and supplies. Since the Romans could not forage crops for themselves during the winter, but must take them from Gallic stores, the Gauls would set fire to all the farms and villages within reach of Roman foragers; it would be easy for them to do so, since they had far more cavalry than did the Romans. Any town the Gauls could not hold, they would destroy; only for their fortresses would they fight. Vercingetorix had many allies to supply his army from afar, Caesar none; whichever Romans sought stores from farther away would be killed. This new tactic would cost the Romans dear: the following day, the Gauls destroyed more than 20 towns of the Bituriges; they soon did much the same in other Gallic states.

As the Romans marched toward the capital of the Bituriges, Avaricum, the Gauls laid waste to the settlements along their route and attacked their foragers. The Romans soon arrived at the fortress, to which they at once laid siege. (Vercingetorix had argued that Avaricum should be destroyed, lest it fall to the Romans, but the Bituriges had beseeched him not to do so.) The inhabitants vigorously resisted the siege, showing as they did so that they were indeed learning how to counter Roman techniques: they snatched away the Roman grappling-hooks with nooses, created towers to match those of the Romans, undermined the Roman earthworks with tunnels, and made frequent sorties to harass the besiegers and set fire to the siegeworks. In the teeth of this resistance, and in spite of the cold and rain, the legionaries persevered. Caesar himself stayed by the earthworks, directing its construction and the fighting off of Gallic attacks. Since the Gauls had destroyed all the stores of food within reach of the Roman army, the Romans were soon without corn and living only on flesh. When Caesar offered to end the siege should the soldiers' privation be too great, they replied that they would rather die than suffer the dishonor of discontinuing the siege. Soon the Romans were fighting as much for the food within Avaricum, as for victory.

A month or so after the beginning of the siege, the earthwork was sufficiently high and broad for the Romans to bring a tower up to the wall. A fierce rainstorm now blew in. Caesar ordered the men on the siegeworks to do their work only fitfully; as they did so, he had two legions conceal themselves behind shelters. Once in place, the legionaries raced from behind the shelters, climbed the tower, and were upon the wall of Avaricum. Maddened by privation and the stout resistence with which they had met, the Romans "spared neither the elderly, nor the women, nor even the little children;" of the town's 40,000 inhabitants, only 800 survived. Rather than diminish Vercingetorix's prestige, however, the fall of Avaricum only increased it, as everyone remembered that he had been in favor of destroying the town so that it would not fall to the Romans. Even more Gallic states now sent him soldiers, archers, and cavalry.

As Labienus with four legions marched north for Lutetia (Paris), a fortress on an island in the Seine, to fight the Senones and Parisii, Caesar with six marched south toward the main fortress of the Arverni, Gergovia. When he arrived he found that Vercingetorix had occupied all the high points of a ridge overlooking the town. Gergovia stood on a high hill; it could not be taken by storm, and the Romans could not lay siege to it until the corn supply was secure. Caesar had his men construct a camp on a hillock at the foot of the hill.

A corps of Aedui auxiliaries marching to join Caesar now declared for the patriots. Caesar with four legions went out to meet the auxiliaries and force them to return to his standard. As he did so, Vercingetorix attacked the remaining two legions, who would have been lost had it not been for the swift return of their commander. As each day went by without a Roman success, more and more Gauls joined the rebellion; even the Aedui had begun to despoil and kill the Roman citizens in their territory. Their checking the Romans before both Gergovia and Lutetia — for Labienus, too, was without success — the Gauls took for victory. Caesar would soon be surrounded by warriors from perhaps all the states of Gaul; he must reunite his forces and put down the rebellion in some other way.

The Romans' departure must not, however, be taken for retreat. Caesar ordered his men to ascend the hill, breach a stone wall, and take some of the smaller Gallic camps — but *not* to pursue the fleeing Gauls to the walls of the town. Once the smaller camps were taken, Caesar, who was with the Tenth legion, sounded the retreat. As the Tenth descended the hill, the other legions, eager for glory and booty, and made confident by their earlier successes, raced to the walls of the town, which some of Romans even began scaling. From within and without the town, the Gauls now fell upon the Romans. Seeing that the Gauls would soon drive the greatly outnumbered Romans down the hill, Caesar hastened with the Tenth legion to its foot to attack the Gauls as they came. Bit by bit the Romans fell back before the Gauls, who themselves were attacked by the Tenth legion once they reached the foot of the hill. Having lost the advantage of both numbers and terrain,

Vercingetorix withdrew his men up the hill. The Romans had lost 700 soldiers, including 46 centurions.

The following day, Caesar ranged the legions in battle order at the foot of the hill; the Gallic and Roman cavalry met, and the Roman won. The next day, Caesar again had his men stand in battle order; the Gauls remained within their fortifications. The Romans now marched off for the territory of the Aedui. The Aedui had taken Noviodunum, where the Romans kept their stocks of grain and fresh horses, the treasury, most of their baggage, and the Gallic hostages (which the Aedui were using to induce other states, such as the Belgae, to join the rebellion). Now only the Remi and some of their allies remained loyal to Rome; many of Caesar's officers felt that Gaul was lost and urged him to return to Gallia Transalpina lest it, too, be lost. Caesar would agree to neither "the shame and disgrace of such a course" nor the destruction of Labienus and his army.

By forced marches Caesar soon reached the Loire. The Aedui assumed that the Romans would not be able to cross the river, as it was running high because of the melting snow. Caesar ordered the cavalry to form a barrier across the river to reduce its force, and the infantry to cross downstream. Once across, the Romans gathered stocks of corn and cattle — the Gauls had not yet destroyed the fields and settlements on the far side of the river — and then set out for the territory of the Senones. As they did so, they joined the army of Labenius, which a coalition of Gallic states had forced southward.

The Gauls now held a council of war at Bibracte. Here, they reconfirmed both Vercingetorix as their sole commander and his scorched-earth policy. His 15,000 cavalry would continue to cut the Romans off from supplies, and all the Gallic states to destroy their stocks of corn and storehouses should the Romans come near. Vercingetorix ordered the Aedui and other nearby states to invade Gallia Transalpina. Since Caesar could not levy further soldiers and cavalry from Italy or Gallia Transalpina — the Gauls occupied all the routes south — he did so from the subject German tribes. The Romans continued, however, to have far fewer infantry and cavalry than did the Gauls.

So that he might aid Gallia Transalpina, Caesar marched eastward to the territory of the Sequani. Vercingetorix assumed that the Romans would continue on into Gallia Transalpina, augment their forces, and then return;

he must destroy the Romans before they could do so. Vercingetorix ordered his cavalry to attack the Romans as they marched; in response, each Gallic horsemen vowed to ride through the Roman column twice. The Gallic cavalry soon attacked the Romans simultaneously from the front and both sides; in spite of the fierceness of the attack — Caesar himself had his sword snatched from him — not a single Gallic horseman passed through the Roman column. The German cavalry soon put the Gallic to rout. So shocked was Vercingetorix by this defeat that he hastened to the stronghold of Alesia. The Romans pursued him as he marched, killing 3,000 or so of the Gallic rearguard.

Alesia stood high upon a hill. To the west of the town was a plain, to the north, east, and south hills. To the north and south, between the hills and Alesia, were rivulets that flowed into the river Brenne in the plain to the west. Like Gergovia, Alesia could not be taken by storm, but only by blockade. Caesar at once began to lay siege to the town; before the Romans could draw the cordon tight, however, Vercingetorix sent our his cavalry with orders to ride throughout Gaul summoning the federated states. The 80,000 Gauls within Alesia had sufficient corn to hold out for one month.

Knowing the Romans would be besieged as they besieged Alesia, Caesar circumvallated the town with two siegewalls, one to defend themselves against the Gauls within, the other against the Gauls without. The inner wall was 10 miles in length, the outer 14. Both were earthworks with a rampart on top, to which a parapet and battlements were attached; to slow the enemy ascent, pointed stakes projected from the joint where the parapet touched the earthwork. Towers were placed at intervals of eighty feet. Here and there were a number of deep ditches 15 to 20 feet across; one of the ditches joined the two rivulets in the plain to the west, filling with water. Outside both siegewalls the Romans sunk tree-trunks and thick branches with sharpened ends; dug small ditches with five rows of interlinked, sharpened stakes; dug eight rows of pits, at three-foot intervals, filled with sharpened stakes and concealed by twigs and brushwood; and, in front of the pits, planted logs bristling with iron hooks into the earth. Caesar also had his infantry and cavalry create four camps each. Of those for the infantry, two were on the hill to the south (Mont de Flavigny), one on a hill to the northeast, and one half-way up a hill to the northwest (Mont Rea). Of those for the cavalry, three were in the plain to the west, one to the far north. Caesar also had the infantry and cavalry collect sufficient corn and fodder for one month.

A month or so after the beginning of the siege, food began to run short within Alesia. So that the remainder would go to the warriors who were fighting to free Gaul, Vercingetorix sent out all the women, children, and elderly men; so that the Gauls' food stores should be depleted before the relief force could arrive, Caesar refused to let them through the Roman lines. Most would die at the foot of Alesia's walls.

The Gallic relief force now arrived. The force was immense, 240,000 infantry and 8,000 cavalry; all the states of Gaul had contributed, even those allied to Rome. The force occupied a hill to the west of Alesia. The following day, the Gallic cavalry and infantry filled the plain. On seeing this, Vercingetorix led his rejoicing warriors out of the town and had them fill in the nearest Roman ditch with earth. Caesar had his soldiers occupy the tops of both siegewalls and then sent his cavalry out to engage that of the Gauls. The fighting, which continued from noon to sunset, was quite fierce; at first the Gallic horse, with its admixture of lightly armed men, held sway; at dusk, however, the Romans' German cavalry massed their squadrons, fell upon a single point in the Gallic line, and broke through, putting the Gauls to flight.

The following day, the Gauls occupied themselves with making wicker hurdles, ladders, and grappling-hooks. In the middle of the night, they crept up to the Roman fortifications and attacked. The Gauls and Romans hurled arrows, stones, pikes, and sharpened stakes at each other; since it was dark and so difficult to see, both sides suffered severe casualties. Caesar sent soldiers to whichever points of the ring were hardest pressed. While far from the Roman siegeworks, the Gauls had the advantage of a far greater number of missiles; but once near, they fell prey to the Roman ditches, pits, and other defenses. The Gauls within Alesia could not undo the Roman defense works in time to join in the attack. By morning, the Gallic attack was spent.

The Gauls now studied the Roman siegeworks with greater care. They soon discovered a weakness: since the peak of Mont Rea was too far from Alesia to be included in the siegeworks, the camp half-way up the hill was vulnerable to an attack from above. That night, 60,000 warriors from the most valiant of the Gallic states secretly marched to the north side of Mont Rea, where they then rested. At midday, at one and the same time, the 60,000 warriors raced over the crest of the hill and fell upon the Roman camp; the Gallic infantry elsewhere, joined by cavalry, threw themselves at the Roman fortifications; and, Vercingetorix sallied out from the town, covered the Roman defense works, and attacked the fortifications.

Recognizing that this would be the final battle, the Romans and Gauls fought with all their might. The Roman lines were so extensive that the soldiers had difficulty defending every point; the Gauls would flock to whichever point seemed weakest, and their numbers were such that they could continually send in fresh contingents. The Romans were frightened by the sounds of battle all round them, afraid that at any moment the Gauls would make a breach at some point in one or the other wall. Vercingetorix soon reached a point in the inner wall and began to tear down the parapet with grappling hooks. The Gallic attack on the camp on Mont Rea was especially fierce; the Gauls had the advantage of a downward slope, and by covering the ground with earth they not only covered the Roman defenses, but also formed a ramp to the Roman wall. A hail of missiles dislodged the Roman soldiers from the rampart. Everywhere the Romans began to run short of weapons and to tire.

At first Caesar took up a position from which he could observe the whole of the Roman ring; from here, he repositioned cohorts to whichever points were most in danger and shouted encouragement to his men. On seeing that the Gauls might soon take the camp on Mont Rea, he sent six cohorts under Labienus to its aid. He then led other cohorts to the point where Vercingetorix was pulling down the Roman wall and drove off the Gallic attackers. By this time, however, the six cohorts under Labienus were themselves beginning to fall back. Caesar ordered the cavalry to ride out from the Roman ring and take the Gallic force on Mont Rea in the rear and then with four cohorts made his way to the camp. At the sight of his distinctive cloak, the Gauls redoubled their attack. Soon, however, they spied the Roman cavalry to their rear, as well as 11 further cohorts summoned by Labienus converging on the camp. Seized with panic, the Gauls took flight, the cavalry hewing them down as they did so. As Vercingetorix withdrew his men into Alesia, the whole of the Gallic relief force fled. The Roman infantry was simply too exhausted to pursue them; the Roman cavalry did do so, however, killing a great many.

The following day, Vercingetorix surrendered. As Caesar sat in front of his camp within the Roman ring, the Gallic leaders filed by and laid down their weapons. In silence Vercingetorix alighted from his horse and knelt at Caesar's feet. So dignified was his carriage, and so courageous had his resistance been, that some of the Roman officers and men felt pity for him. Caesar did not: after excoriating Vercingetorix for having organized and led the rebellion, he had him bound in chains and taken to Rome. To each Roman soldier, Caesar gave a Gallic prisoner as booty (save those of the Aedui or Arverni, whom he restored to their states). Caesar then set out for the territory of the Aedui, whom, along with the Arverni, he "won back for Rome" and restored to their position of free allies (though he insisted on a great many hostages). With Alesia, the Gauls lost their unity. Though Gallic resistance to Roman rule would continue, it would not be a unified resistence, and since not unified, in vain.

In Rome, however, Caesar's position had continued to weaken throughout 52. The Senate had once again elected Pompey consul and renewed his command over the two Spanish provinces and their seven legions for a further five years, making it all but certain that his struggle with Caesar would be settled by military rather than political means. Pompey continued, however, to pursue his hopeless policy of trying to be the ally of both the Senate and Caesar. He passed a law permitting Caesar to stand for consul *in absentia* (a proconsul could not enter Rome without relinquishing his governorship). He passed another the effect of which was to permit the person whom the Senate appointed on March 1, 50 to succeed Caesar as governor of Gaul *to do so at once* rather than wait until 48. (Since an earlier law forbid the holding of a further consulship for 10 years, Caesar could not again become consul until 48.) But since Pompey omitted to make the law immune to tribunician veto, by paying off his debts Caesar induced one of the tribunes to veto it. Caesar tried to draw Pompey nearer by restoring the tie of marriage; he offered Pompey his nearest relative, his grandniece, or to marry Pompey's only daughter. But Pompey insisted that his daughter remain married to Sulla's son — during his dictatorship, Sulla had restored and strengthened the Senate — and he himself soon married the daughter of one of Caesar's bitterest enemies. And while the Senate granted Caesar a *supplicatio* of twenty days, it was more to suggest that Gaul was pacified — and thus that his successor could now be appointed — than to celebrate his victory at Alesia.

So restive was Gaul that Caesar was forced to winter there in 52/51. The Gallic states now resolved to defeat the Romans, not by uniting against them, but by each rising up within its own territory. The Romans, they felt, could not possibly quell a simultaneous rebellion in all of Gaul. Caesar's response was to march so swiftly from state to state that none could organize for war before he was upon it. Since the winter was so harsh, and since his men had been campaigning continuously for a year-and-a-half, he took different legions with him to each of the states. Now the Bituriges, now the Carnutes, now the Bellovaci succumbed to the Romans.

Since this would be Caesar's last year as governor, however, the Gauls continued to resist. Caesar became both more and less merciful; he must be certain of Gaul should he soon be forced to fight his fellow Romans. Toward those who continued to rebel, he was merciless. After taking Uxellodunum, a town in the territory of the Cadurci into which a great many of the rebels had withdrawn, he had the hands of all the Gallic warriors cut off. But to individuals and states inclined to loyalty and submission to Rome, Caesar showed every consideration, granting them honors, high position, money, and the confiscated property of rebels, and imposing no new taxes or requisitions. Thus would Rome rule Gaul; thus would Gaul benefit from Roman suzerainty.

In the autumn of 51, Caesar subjugated Aquitaine. While wintering at Nemetocenna in the territory of the Belgae, he created a constitution for the new province of Gallia Comata, defining the relationship between each state and Rome and the tribute to be paid by each state that was not a free ally. That Gaul would remain quiescent throughout the Roman civil war shows that Caesar had truly conquered it.

❦

Caesar felt that Roman society should honor him for his conquest of Gaul, that that conquest had won for him matchless *dignitas*. To the *optimates*, however, that conquest had simply made Caesar more frightening and hateful. The way in which he had conquered Gaul — directly and forcefully, without the pettiness, irresoluteness, and dubieties so characteristic of the Senate — terrified his opponents.

While in their own rule the *optimates* could not see reality for forms, in that of Caesar they could distinctly see the reality of monarchy behind the form of the republic. That his uncle by marriage was Marius, a Senate reformer, and that he would freely honor Marius in public; that he had once defied Sulla, the restorer of the senatorial regime; that he had prosecuted prominent Sullans following the dictator's death; that he had almost certainly been involved in the Cataline conspiracy to overthrow the government of the *optimates* and then, once the conspirators had been caught, had tried to induce the Senate to act irresolutely and not execute them; that he had as consul so undone Sulla's work, so vitiated the inherited order; that he himself, rather than a Senatorial commission, had organized Gaul; that he founded colonies and granted *de facto* Roman citizenship and Latin rights to certain Gallic communities; that he disposed of provinces, legions, and (whenever he might) consulships; that he was quite willing to use violence to attain his objects; that he had always shown such contempt for the inherited order — all clearly showed what lay in store should Caesar return to internal politics.

If Caesar was so monarchical *before* Gaul, what was he now, after nine years of sole rule? Caesar *was* alien; in a communal governing system such as Rome's, he was quite out of place. However was he to fit in, what position might he hold? Caesar simply could not be the equal of others of his class, could not be what the Roman order insisted he be, a mediocrity; he was too great. The pettifoggery of the Senate, once so hateful to him, he would now find quite impossible to put up with. And, as Pompey observed, Caesar would be far richer, and thus able to do far more (and to meet the many expectations of him among his supporters), as monarch than as a member of a communal government. The *optimates* still could not see that their very form of government was maladapted, and that Caesar was a natural outgrowth of that maladaption; they could explain him only as a tyrant.

The *optimates* asked whether Caesar would not seek to rule Rome as he had done Gaul, Caesar why Rome should *not* be ruled as it did its provinces. Rome was, after all, not unlike the Gallic states: in both, a hopelessly divided oligarchy that could not see its true interests ruled; in both, the mass of people were poor and disaffected. The Roman provinces were ruled by governors; why not Rome itself? And since Caesar was vastly superior to all others, should he not be Rome's governor? In Gaul, Caesar had come to see what a unified command could do; whatever veneration he might have felt for the inherited order, for rule by the oligarchy, died in Gaul. Unlike his fellow oligarchs, he was not dependent on the world of Rome; he could thus see it far more clearly, was far more willing to alter it. In Gaul, Caesar had become less and less a Roman aristocrat of the late republic, and more and more himself.

At the heart of the struggle between Pompey and Caesar lay this: while Pompey fancied himself the first man of Rome, Caesar *was* the first man, a military, political, and literary genius. A clash between the two was thus inevitable. And this: it was in the interests of neither Pompey nor the senators for Caesar to return to internal politics. Both recognized that Caesar, by far the most skillful Roman politician, would soon overwhelm Pompey. Pompey would very much have liked the *threat* of Caesar to continue; without it, the Senate would have much less need of him. But the end of Caesar's governorship now forced the issue.

While the senators did not wish to grant Pompey's request that his supremacy be recognized, did not wish to set such a precedent, they were willing to do so if need be, because they knew that at heart Pompey respected the inherited order, and that Caesar did not. But while the majority of senators preferred Pompey, they did not wish to displease Caesar — and thus risk civil war — by withdrawing his command. Caesar had eleven legions in Gaul, Pompey seven in Spain and two in Italy. Though the seven in Spain could attack Caesar's rear, it would take some time for them to do so, and the two legions in Italy had once been Caesar's and were thus of doubtful loyalty. Pompey and *optimates* could levy new legions, but doing so would take time and might provoke Caesar into marching on Rome.

The proximate cause of Caesar's launching the civil war would be his wishing to keep his opponents from arraigning him; the deeper cause would be his wishing to reform the Roman Empire. There was so much to do, and it simply could not be done under the present system. The coming civil war would be between two autocracies, one individual and functional, the other oligarchic and dysfunctional.

೧౨

Throughout the spring and summer of 51, the Senate continued to insist that the peoples of Gallia Cisalpina were not Roman citizens. At one point, an *optimate* consul had a magistrate (and thus Roman citizen) of Novum Comum — a colony Caesar had founded, and to which he had granted Latin rights — flogged; by doing so, the consul implied that the magistrate was not a citizen and that the colony did not hold Latin rights. This was not only an insult to Caesar as patron of the province, but struck at the heart of his power, since his support in the province rested on his ability to obtain citizenship for its peoples, and since he drew many of his soldiers from there.

While doing his utmost to increase his influence and popularity in Rome, Caesar — should that fail to win him an extension of his governorship — prepared for war. Early in the year, he published the seven books of *The Gallic War* to show how greatly he had served the republic; he also commissioned grand buildings in Rome and arranged for festivities and games in honor of his daughter, Julia. All the while, however, he continued to levy troops and collect munitions; granted his legions considerable rewards, including a doubling of their pay; and, commissioned buildings in cities and towns throughout the Empire and bestowed gifts on their leaders.

Afraid of Caesar, Pompey, and civil war, the Senate shilly-shallied throughout 50. The discussion on the succession in the two Gallic provinces began on March 1. Caesar offered to lay down his command if Pompey laid down his of Spain. (Without an army with which to influence politics in Rome, Pompey would be lost.) With Pompey ill, the majority of senators voted to let Caesar retain his command in Gaul until he should become consul in 48. When in early December Caesar's supporters forced a vote on whether to relieve Caesar or Pompey or both of their commands, the senators voted by 370 to 22 to relieve both. Though the consul Gaius Marcellus, a leading *optimate*, ignored the Senate's resolution — as was his right as consul — by so voting the Senate conferred legitimacy on Caesar, thus strengthening the side it least preferred.

The *optimates*, at heart no less authoritarian than Caesar, now forced the issue; Caesar *would* come to heel, even if it be through war. Seizing on rumors (he knew to be false) that Caesar was crossing the Alps with his legions, Marcellus beseeched Pompey to "defend Rome" by taking command of the two legions in Italy. At first Pompey simply did not decline — thus suggesting that he accepted — and then, within a week or so, openly took command of the legions. In response, Caesar secretly ordered two of the legions in Gallia Transalpina and the twenty-two cohorts of new Gallic recruits to join him in Gallia Cisalpina (where one further legion was at Ravenna) and three legions to Narbonensis in southern Gallia Transalpina (to secure himself against Pompey's Spanish legions).

At Cicero's behest, in early January 49 Caesar offered to retain only Illyricum and one legion until his consulship and to let Pompey's governorship of the two Spanish provinces continue. Pompey was inclined to accept this concession, if only because he felt Caesar's consulship to be less bad than civil war. So determined were the *optimates* to keep Caesar out of internal politics, so afraid were they of a new understanding between Caesar and Pompey, and so confident were they of military superiority, that on January 7 they induced the Senate to pass a *senatus consultum ultimum* commanding Caesar to "do what was best for the republic," that is, to lay down his command; it also appointed his enemy Domitius Ahenobarbus to succeed him at once. Only by imprisoning Caesar, the *optimates* felt, could they save the inherited order, and thus their position in Roman society. Pompey now began to recruit soldiers and requisition weapons and money throughout Italy.

Only by showing Roman society that his military prospects were not quite so hopeless as they seemed might Caesar force the Senate to reconsider. And he must not let Pompey continue to organize his forces in Italy. On the night of January 10/11, with a single legion Caesar crossed the frontier river of Gallia Cisalpina, the Rubicon.

The forces of Pompey and the *optimates* did indeed seem vastly superior to those of Caesar. Only in Gaul was Caesar strong; elsewhere, in the Roman Empire as a whole, Pompey was far more so. And the field of battle in the civil war would not be Italy, but the whole of the Roman world. Pompey had seven tried and valorous legions in Spain led by gifted officers. He could levy many more legions both there and in the East, whose Roman provinces were controlled by governors loyal to him. The rulers of most of the Roman client states supported the Pompeians; these rulers knew that they would be far freer under the indolent and imprudent rule of the *opti-mates* than under that of Caesar, knew, indeed, that Caesar would incorporate their states into the Empire. That which had so hobbled the Gauls — a weakness in organization and logistics, an inability to provision a large force — was Pompey's forte. Labienus, Caesar's most gifted subordinate, had defected to the Pompeians, whom he would teach Caesar's strategies and tactics. And while Pompey controlled all the ports and warships of the Mediterranean, Caesar had no fleet to speak of; more than anything else, it was Pompey's control of the sea that most convinced others he would be victorious.

But this was to consider the quantitative and not the qualitative, to consider that which matters little, and to ignore that which matters most: the commanders and their soldiers. As gifted and seasoned a general as he was, Pompey could not hold a candle to Caesar. Caesar's conquest of Gaul took far more brilliance and resolution than did Pompey's of the East. Pompey's conquest had been made far easier by the work of his gifted predecessor, Lucullus; no such Roman had preceded Caesar in Gaul. And while quite as factious as the peoples of the East, the Gauls were far better fighters. Pompey was good at organization, but little else; on campaign, he was quite timid and would attack only when possessed of far greater numbers than his adversary. Caesar was by his very nature versatile, Pompey rigid; his versatility would give him a great advantage over his opponent. (Tellingly, early in his career Pompey had been thrashed in Spain by a commander very much like Caesar, Quintus Sertorius.) The *optimates* were drawn to Pompey for the same reason all others, including the *populares* and the young Caesar, had been: he was pliable and controllable, a useful tool. As was their wont, the *optimates* hurt their interests in the selfish pursuit of them; they could indeed control a mediocrity far better than they could a man of distinction — but a mediocrity could not win against Caesar.

Caesar had had eight years in Gaul to organize his army as only he could; no army could march so swiftly, none was so disciplined or courageous. "Caesar's soldiers were, and felt themselves, a match for a ten-fold superior force." (Gelzer) Their great loyalty to their commander stemmed from their faith in his genius; his caring deeply about their welfare; his asking far more of himself than of them, and his being frequently found in the front ranks, fighting as did the best of the legionaries; his knowing almost all his soldiers (whom he would call on by name in the fiercest of engagements); and, the pride of victory. (Of all Caesar's officers and soldiers, only Labieus deserted.) To this was added the material inducements of doubled pay, booty, and so on and, for the majority (who were from *Gallia Transalpina*), the certainty that only Caesar would grant them citizenship. Furthermore, though both Caesar and Pompey had loyal clients throughout the empire, Caesar had in general treated the non-Roman communities better than had Pompey (and, certainly, had the *optimates*), since while he viewed the provinces as part of the Roman Empire, Pompey and the *optimates* did not.

Furthermore, the Caesarians had a unity of command quite lacking in the factious coalition of the Pompeians. Quite as much as the Gauls, the Pompeians would be weakened by their disunity, by the varying interests and distrust among the *optimates*, and between the *optimates* and Pompey. Until just before the civil war, Pompey had been Caesar's ally against the Senate; he had been a *populare* and quite unwilling to be seen as the equal of the senators. Indeed, the *optimates* felt that Pompey had "nurtured, aggrandized, and armed Caesar against the commonwealth." (Cicero) Both Pompey and the *optimates* knew full well they would turn on each other the moment they defeated Caesar. Pompey was far too weak a leader, and the *optimates* far too unruly, for him ever to control his forces. The *optimates* would be quite as bad at waging war as at ruling a state; but they could no more see this than that they could not govern and would thus insist on telling Pompey what to do. So greatly did Pompey wish to be popular, and so greatly did he dislike being unpopular, that he would often do as the *optimates* demanded, recognizing all the while that doing so was in neither his nor their interests.

Their selfishness caused Pompey and the *optimates* to miscalculate the degree to which the mass of Italians would resist Caesar. To Caesar, the civil war was simply between himself and his opponents; to Pompey and the *optimates*, it was between a revolutionary and Roman society. (This was why, while Caesar would ask only that all non-Pompeians remain neutral, Pompey would insist that all non-Caesarians join him.) "Anywhere in Italy," declared Pompey, "I have only to stamp my foot upon the ground, and there will rise up armies of infantry and cavalry." He would be quite disillusioned in this.

Like the vast majority of senators, most Roman citizens simply wished that civil war would not take place, as nothing good could come of it.

Levies of both soldiers and money were certain to come with the conflict, and confiscations and proscriptions afterwards. Whoever won could do just as he pleased. The citizens were deeply dissatisfied with the maladministration of the *optimates*, with the general insecurity in Italy and throughout the Empire; and they remembered all too well the proscriptions and confiscations under Sulla, an *optimate*, once he had defeated the *populares*. In spite of their great dissatisfaction with the ruling order, few Romans wished Caesar to oust that order through civil war. And Caesar, with his infantry of men from Gallia Cisalpina and Gallia Transalpina and his cavalry of Germans, seemed almost a foreign enemy. While the *equites* and municipal gentry feared Caesar would remit debts and restore exiles — or, at the very least, reform the financial system — some at least of the urban and rural poor might well have hoped to do better under him. The rustic poor felt as little allegiance to the state as did the legionaries — who, indeed, were drawn from the rustic poor. (Interestingly, the regions of Italy from which most of the legionaries were drawn were centers of peasant revolts in the late republic. Whyever would the rustic poor, legionaries or not, fight for an order that only took from them?) Though Cicero hoped his "army of the rich" would grow considerably during the war, he found that most of the municipal oligarchs cared "only for their farms, money-bags, and little country houses." (Brunt)

Both sides would have difficulty recruiting in Italy. Most Italians would simply follow necessity, joining whichever side controlled their region for the moment. While most Roman citizens *preferred* that the inherited order continue, only some were willing to fight for that order; most would naturally do what they thought best for themselves. (And, after all, there was no certainty Caesar *would* do away with the republic should he win.) "It will not escape you," wrote the *optimate* Marcus Caelius to his friend Cicero, "that in internal disputes, so long as they are conducted by civil and not military means, one must be on the more honorable side, but when it comes to war one must be on the stronger. Whatever is safest must then be considered best." Pompey and his allies "might still have the cause of the republic on their side, but not the republic itself." (Meier) It was quite clear that Roman society was no longer a citizens' republic; most Romans seemed to view the civil war as Caesar did, simply as a contest between Caesar and Pompey.

As Pompey drew up plans to attack Caesar in Gallia Cisalpina and Gallia Transalpina, Caesar with one legion stormed down the Adriatic coast road. He sent some cohorts farther down the coast road and others across the Apennines; he occupied several towns, threw the Pompeian levies into disarray, and scattered the new recruits.

Despairing of holding Rome, Pompey fled to Campania with half the senators. Here he received new concessions by Caesar: Caesar would relinquish his command at once and seek the consulship as a private citizen, *if* Pompey departed for Spain (the governorship of which he would retain) and the armies in Italy were disbanded. Caesar also requested a meeting with Pompey. Pompey and the *optimates* replied that Caesar was most certainly entitled to a triumph and second consulship; he must, however, first withdraw to Gallia Cisalpina (so that they might deliberate freely in Rome) and there dismiss his troops — *after* which Pompey would depart for Spain. Until Caesar did all that was asked of him, Pompey would continue to levy troops in Italy. And Pompey would not meet with him (the *optimates* were far too afraid of a new understanding between the two to let him do so). Caesar broke off negotiations.

In early February, Caesar occupied the region of Picenum. Now in possession of two legions — the Twelfth had by now reached him — Caesar marched for Corfinium. As he laid siege to the town, the Eighth legion and twenty-two cohorts joined him. The Pompeian commander of Corfinium, Domitius Ahenobarbus, so hated Caesar, and owned such large tracts of land in the region, that he ignored Pompey's order to evacuate, hoping to force Pompey to come to his aid. On receiving a letter from Pompey saying that he could not possibly do so with the slight forces at his disposal, Domitius tried secretly to escape with some of his officers. On being discovered by his soldiers, he and the town were surrendered to Caesar. Since it was night, Caesar waited until the next morning to occupy the town (lest his soldiers plunder it). All expected Caesar to put at least Domitius and the more vociferous *optimates* to the sword. Stating that he had come not to do injury, but simply to free the Roman people from oppression by the *optimates* and to protect himself from his enemies, Caesar merely reproached the *optimates* for their mistreatment of him. He permitted the Pompeians to retain the town's military fund, and he dismissed their officers without requiring that they vow not to take up arms against him.

Caesar's clemency toward Corfinium and, indeed, all the towns that fell to him, and his respecting private property, calmed the Italians, and particularly the propertied classes. And so it was calculated to do: "Let us try in this way, if we can," he wrote his officials in Rome, "to win back public opinion and gain a lasting victory." With "gain a lasting victory," Caesar quite clearly showed his colors: as in Gaul, he would not simply conquer, but retain his conquests.

While Caesar was besieging Corfinium, Pompey and the senators made their way to the Adriatic port of Brundisium, to which they summoned their two legions and whichever recruits they could collect. Caesar arrived in early March and laid siege to the town; with breakwaters and pontoons, he began to close the mouth of the harbor. Through emissaries, Caesar again asked Pompey to meet; Pompey again refused, saying he could do nothing without the consuls, who had crossed over to Greece with much of the army before Caesar arrived. In the middle of the month, the ships returned, and Pompey now set sail with the remaining soldiers. Caesar had no ships with which to follow.

Caesar's clemency at Corfinium and elsewhere did nothing to propitiate Pompey and the *optimates*. Caesar's pardons simply redoubled the fury of those who received them, as he had not only defeated them, but made them a gift of their lives. (A *Roman* did not receive clemency; he granted it.) The humiliation and ignomy he had visited on Pompey and the *optimates* by ejecting them from a country they viewed as little more than their property, made them all the more vicious and vindictive. As livid as they were powerless, they now threatened retribution against any who came to terms with Caesar and drew up lists of those to be proscribed on their return to Italy. (At this, one of the more sensible *optimates* declared that he was more afraid of the victory of his own party of that of Caesar. As the war continued, more and more did the Roman aristocracy face, in Cicero's words, "destruction or slavery.") All remembered that Pompey had been one of Sulla's officers, and that on gaining victory Sulla had slaughtered his opponents. The *optimates'* assurance that a reign of terror would follow their restoration further induced most of Italy to submit to Caesar.

Caesar could not permit the Pompeian forces to unite; were they to do so, they would be far stronger than the Caesarians. But which to attack first, the army in Spain, or that in Greece? To attack that in Spain would give

Pompey time to collect a large force in the East, to pursue him leave Gaul and Italy open to attack (or induce the Spanish legions to pursue *him* as he pursued Pompey). Since the Spanish army was at present far stronger than that in Greece, to defeat it would be not only be to dispirit the Pompeians, but also to weaken support for them and increase it for himself. Caesar could then unite his forces and attack those of the Pompeians in Greece.

On his way to Spain Caesar paid a flying visit to Rome. While he had been at Brundisium, his supporters had induced the senators still in Rome to grant citizenship to the freemen of Gallia Cisalpina, whose support he dearly needed. This was to be his only signal success. To the Senate, Caesar declared that he would prefer that it join him in governing the Empire, but that if it chose not to, he would do so himself. (Martial law was in force.) The Senate refused to grant his request that it proclaim him dictator and grant him full power to continue the war (and thus legitimize his position). When it also refused him the state's reserve treasure in the Temple of Saturn, he took it by force. Caesar also made certain dispositions to protect Italy while he was in Spain: he dispatched two legions to Illyricum should the Pompeians try to reach Italy by land, ordered fleets to be built in the Adriatic and Tyrrhenian Seas, and secured the corn supply by ordering the occupation of Sicily, Sardinia, and parts of North Africa.

Jesting, "I am off to meet an army without a leader; when I return I shall meet a leader without an army," Caesar set out for Spain. Forced on his way to lay siege to Massilia (Marseille), he sent six legions with 3,000 cavalry ahead to seize the passes through the Pyrenees. The commanders of the Pompeian forces in Spain, Lucius Afranius and Marcus Petreius, marched for the town of Ilerda with five of the seven legions. (The two least trustworthy were left behind in the province of Further Spain, which was more loyal to Caesar than to Pompey.) Augmenting these five were 18,000 native infantry and 5,000 cavalry.

Ilerda stood twenty miles to the north of the Ebro river on the western, or right, bank of one of its tributaries, the Segre. At Ilerda a single bridge crossed the Segre. The Caesarians, now joined by their commander and 900 further cavalry, took up a position just to the north of the town, to which they laid siege. As the two sides contested the town and its bridge, a great storm melted the mountain snow; both the Segre and the Cinca, thirty miles to the west, flooded. The two bridges the Caesarians had constructed 18 miles to the north on the Segre — the river was too wide at Ilerda — were swept away, confining the Caesarians to a narrow strip of land between the two rivers.

The Caesarians had by now run through their grain; that in the fields was not yet ripe, no cattle were to be had, and a convoy from Gaul with cavalry, archers, and supplies could not cross the Segre. Famine and disease soon wracked the Caesarian camp. Victory now seemed certain to go to the Pompeians, who had plentiful grain and fodder and — since the flood had not impaired the bridge by Ilerda — were receiving more each day from throughout the province. In Rome, cheering crowds gathered in front of Afranius's house; many of the senators who had remained in the city now joined Pompey in Thessalonica.

Caesar had his soldiers build boats of timber, wattles, and skins, similar to those they had seen in Britain. He then had them carry the boats on pairs of wagons at night to a point on the river 22 miles to the north. Because the Pompeians failed to guard the opposite bank, the Caesarians were able to cross the river and fortify a position. Once they did so, a legion crossed as well, and then the Caesarians began to build a bridge from both sides. Within two days, the bridge was completed. As the Gallic convoy crossed to the western bank, Caesar sent his cavalry to the eastern to harry the Pompeian foragers. With this change of fortune, many Spanish communities now came over to Caesar, supplying him with soldiers, grain, and draft animals.

Caesar now had his soldiers dig channels three miles to the north of Ilerda to divert part of the Segre (and thus to create a ford nearer the town). Afraid that Caesar's cavalry would cut them off from supplies, Afranius and Petreius set out late one night for central Spain, whose population was loyal to Pompey and Caesar little known, and where they might augment their forces with cavalry and auxiliaries. To slow their march, Caesar had his cavalry attack the rearguard. Seeing their cavalry fighting the Pompeians, and wishing to put an end to their labors, the infantry beseeched Caesar to let them cross the river. He was at first reluctant to do so — the channels had not yet done their work — but soon relented. He had pack animals placed above and below the ford to slow the current, and some of the cavalry downstream to catch any men who might be swept away; though the water was shoulder-high, not a single soldier was lost.

By mid-afternoon, the Caesarian infantry had caught up with their opponents. Exhausted by the march and by fighting off the Caesarian cavalry, the Pompeians pitched camp on a hill in the plain; Caesar made camp on a nearby hill. The following day, Caesar and the opposing commanders reconnoitred the country. Five miles to the south was a range of mountains; should the Pompeians reach its defiles first, while a small number of cohorts barred the way of the Caesarians, the mass of the army could cross the Ebro.

The following morning, the Caesarians marched out to the west. Taking their march for a retreat to Ilerda, the Pompeians jeered after them. As they watched, however, the Caesarians slowly turned to the south; realizing that Caesar hoped to reach the mountains first, they set out in all haste. The race began, the Pompeians hurrying along the plain, the Caesarians scrabbling over the gullies of the foothills. The Caesarian cavalry slowed the Pompeians' march as best it could. The Pompeians had started too late; just before they reached the mountains, the Caesarians dropped down into the valley in front of them.

Afranius and Petreius ordered four cohorts to try to seize the highest peak, thinking they might then cross the mountains along the ridge. In full sight of both armies, the Caesarian cavalry killed the Pompeians to a man. Senior commanders, centurions, and officers now beseeched Caesar to attack. The loss of the four cohorts had terrified the Pompeians; they were huddled about their standards, hardly fighting off the attacks of the Caesarian cavalry. Caesar refused to do so: he would neither risk the lives of his men nor take those of his opponents, when he could force the Pompeians to submit simply by cutting off their supplies. He moved his army a little away from the Pompeians, at which they retreated to their camp. Caesar posted detachments throughout the mountains to prevent the Pompeians from again trying to cross.

While Afranius and Petreius strengthened their fortifications, crowds of Pompeians crossed to the Caesarian camp seeking friends and fellow townsmen. They soon invited Caesarians to come into their camp, "so much so that the two camps seemed now to have become one." There was general rejoicing; a number of Pompeian officers and centurions went to Caesar to negotiate their surrender. On learning of this, however, Petreius with a cohort and some cavalry at once fell upon the Caesarians in his camp, killing any he could catch. The soldiers now ran each to his own camp. The Pompeians who remained in Caesar's camp and wished to join his army, he permitted to do so; all others he returned unharmed.

The Pompeians now retreated toward Ilerda, which was still held by a well-supplied Pompeian garrison. As they did so, the Caesarian cavalry attacked their rearguard continuously, and the Caesarian infantry followed close behind. The Pompeians pitched camp on unfavorable ground; Caesar again refrained from engaging them. Now without fodder, the Pompeians slaughtered their pack animals. When the Pompeians marched for a ford in the Segre, Caesar placed some light infantry and cavalry on the far side; the Pompeians returned to their camp. On the fourth day, short of food and water, Afranius and Petreius requested peace negotiations. Caesar insisted that these negotiations be held publicly, within hearing of both armies. He declared that he had fought the Pompeians as he had so as to spare their lives; he sought only to make peace as soon as possible. Not only would no Pompeian be killed or despoiled, but each would receive corn and the pay to which he was entitled. Caesar's sole stipulation was that the Pompeian army be disbanded so that it could not be used against him.

Caesar now summoned the leading citizens of all the Spanish communities, some to Cordoba, others to Tarraco. All came; with money and honors he rewarded the communities that had aided him. Finding the gates of all the cities and towns of the two Spanish provinces now closed to him, the commander of the Pompeian legions in Further Spain presented himself to Caesar at Cordoba.

While Caesar conquered Spain, Pompey organized. He collected eleven legions and (from client states) cavalry, archers, and slingers, as well as quite a lot of money and supplies, and several hundred warships. But he *did* very little: annihilated a small Caesarian force in Africa and the nascent fleet in the Adriatic, and occupied Illyria. His achievements were inconsiderable in comparison not only to those of Caesar, but also to what he might have done given his control of the Mediterranean: aided his forces in Spain; saved the Massiliots (who succumbed to the Caesarian siege); prevented the Caesarians from occupying Sardinia and Sicily; retaken Italy (which, tellingly, did not rise up against Caesar while he was in Spain). Pompey's party was now far less confident in their commander, who had neither the political skills to control the meddlesome *optimates* and fractious lieutenant-generals, nor the military skills to fight a Caesar. Pompey now planned to winter on the Illyrian coast and attack Caesar in Italy in the spring.

Following his victory in Spain, Caesar returned to Italy. On arriving in northern Italy, his soldiers, dissatisfied by the hardships and lack of booty, and certain of Caesar's reliance on them, mutinied. Much to their surprise, Caesar announced that he would decimate the ninth legion — that which had instigated the mutiny — and dismiss the survivors as unfit for service. The soldiers of the ninth legion now beseeched Caesar to forgive them. He did so, asking only for the names of the mutiny's leaders, one-tenth of whom he had executed. (This was done by lot; when a certain soldier was said to have been one of the leaders, but was later learned to have been away from camp when the mutiny broke out, Caesar had the officer who reported him executed instead.)

While Caesar had been in Spain, his representatives in Rome had had him appointed dictator. As dictator, Caesar in December conducted the elections; provincials recently admitted to citizenship by Caesar, and Romans proscribed by Sulla and Pompey whom Caesar pardoned, took part. Caesar was elected one of the consuls for 48 — at which point he laid down the dictatorship — an ally the other. He also celebrated the feast of the Latin league and its games (and in so doing obliquely criticized the consuls, who in their hurry to leave Rome had neglected to celebrate the feast and games). Since the Pompeians had levied a great many non-Italian troops, *they* now seemed the foreign power waging war on Rome. Bit by bit, the symbols of the republic were going over to Caesar.

Caesar also did what he could to revivify the Italian economy, which the cessation of credit had brought to a standstill. He appointed assessors to determine the pre-war value of the property of debtors and insisted that creditors honor those values; debtors could also deduct interest up to a quarter of the sum owed. Caesar also lowered the interest rate. While thus providing a measure of relief to debtors, Caesar also assured creditors that there would be no remission of debt and no despoliation of property. Though not to creditors' liking, these laws did much to revive the economy.

Caesar did not *await* attacks; he attacked. He could reach Greece either by crossing the Adriatic or by marching through Illyria. Since the Pompeians had 110 warships in the Adriatic to the Caesarians' twelve, it would have been far safer to take the Illyrian route. But since that would take more time, in early January Caesar set sail from Brundisium. With so few ships, he could take only seven legions; the ships must then return and ferry over the remaining five. The crossing took the Pompeians by surprise and was thus unopposed. Caesar sent the ships back that night; the Pompeian fleet, now lying in wait for the Caesarian vessels, burned them all with their crews.

Since Caesar could not risk coming upon Pompey's fleet, he must march from wherever he landed, a point a hundred or so miles south of Dyrrhachium. His object was that port, which stood astride the Via Egnatia and thus controlled the only land route from the Adriatic to Asia Minor, and which the Pompeians had filled with magazines of corn and military stores. Soon after landing, Caesar sent an emissary to Pompey with peace proposals calculated to please the mass of Romans. *Pompey* was not pleased by the proposals, but rather shocked at learning that Caesar had landed. He set out at once for Apollonia, hoping to keep it from falling to Caesar; the town, however, surrendered to Caesar on his arrival. On learning of this, Pompey marched with all speed for Dyrrhachium. His object now unattainable, Caesar decided to winter on the southern bank of the Apsus river by Apollonia and await the other legions. Pompey soon arrived and pitched camp on the opposite bank.

In spite of his great numerical superiority, Pompey did not attack, preferring instead to reduce the Caesarians by cutting off their supplies by both land and sea; once joined by his other legions in the early spring, he would annihilate the Caesarians. Caesar himself could not attack until his other legions had crossed the Adriatic. He did, however, hinder the resupplying of the Pompeian fleet, and increase the range of his foragers, by occupying much of the coast south of the Apsus. He also sent representatives to Greek towns well-disposed to him to seek their aid; quite a few of the towns joined his side. As in Spain, the two armies mingled. The Caesarians requested peace negotiations; the Pompeians acceded. The following day, as Labienus discussed terms with Caesar's representatives, a hail of missiles suddenly rained down on the latter. "Well, then," cried Labienus, "stop talking about peace. There can be no peace for us unless we get Caesar's head."

By late winter, Caesar seemed lost: the other legions had still not crossed, and he was wedged between an immense fleet and a land force three times the size of his own. So desperate was Caesar's situation that at one point he himself sailed for Brundisium in a small fishing-boat, disguised as a slave. A gail arose; when the helmsman began to turn back, Caesar made himself known and ordered him to continue. The wind and waves, however, soon forced the boat back. In the middle of April, a favorable wind enabled the Caesarian transports to cross the Adriatic. On reaching the Greek coast, however, the transports were propelled by the wind past first the Caesarian camp and then that of the Pompeians; the vessels landed well to the north of Dyrrhachium. (When a gale destroyed the sixteen Pompeian warships that were pursuing the transports, Caesar had all the survivors sent home.)

Caesar and Pompey set out at once, Caesar hoping to join his forces, Pompey to destroy the newly arrived legions; though his path was more roundabout and difficult, Caesar reached them first. On the joining of the Caesarian forces, Pompey marched for Dyrrhachium, Caesar in pursuit. Though his army was still far smaller than that of his opponent, Caesar offered battle; Pompey, however, still hoping to defeat Caesar through attrition, refused. Caesar now marched to the east, as if seeking supplies; he then secretly marched with all speed for Dyrrhachium. He arrived before Pompey and interposed himself between the town and his adversary. Though Caesar could not take Dyrrhachium — it stood on a peninsula, accessible only by a narrow strip of land between sea and marsh — at least Pompey could now not enter it.

Pompey encamped on a hill to the south of the town. Caesar at once began to circumvallate the Pompeian position with a line of fortification works along all the high points. By doing so he not only hemmed in the Pompeian cavalry — which outnumbered his six to one, and which now could not prevent Caesar's soldiers from gathering supplies — but also humiliated Pompey before the world, which was treated to the rare spectacle of the smaller army besieging the larger. (Caesar had sent some cohorts to collect supplies in Epirus and elsewhere, others to bar the way to Pompey's Syrian legions.) Pompey's response was to stretch Caesar's line as far as possible by first seizing as many of the high points as he could. His line of fortifications soon stretched fifteen miles, Caesar's seventeen.

While their fleet kept the Pompeians generally well provisioned, the Caesarians survived on meat, barley, and roots. Little could be had from the local region, which was mountainous, and which the Pompeians had plundered, and the fleet Caesar had ordered built in Gaul, Italy, and Sicily was slow in coming. (On being shown the bread the Caesarians had baked from roots, Pompey exclaimed, "I am fighting wild beasts!", and insisted it not be shown to his men.) Conditions within the Pompeian lines were, however, also unhealthy: the Pompeians had been forced by lack of grazing to kill their draft animals, whose stench now filled their camp, and Caesar had dammed or diverted all the rivers and streams flowing through the Pompeian lines. (The Pompeians could obtain fresh water only by digging wells in the marshes.)

After weeks of siege and inconclusive sallies by both sides, and with his horses now emaciated by lack of fodder, Pompey resolved to try to break out. Two Gallic deserters told him of a weakness in Caesar's lines: at the point farthest from Caesar's main camp, abutting the sea to the south, was a double line of fortifications the Caesarians had not yet had time to protect from the sea by a cross-wall. One night, Pompey had 60 cohorts, supported by slingers and archers, position themselves for attack: as some of the cohorts sailed to a point beyond the outer line and some to a point between the two lines, others marched up to the inner line.

At dawn, the Pompeians attacked simultaneously from within, without, and the sea. The ninth legion reeled back; Caesarian reinforcements could halt neither their panicked comrades nor the Pompeians. Only the arrival of twelve further cohorts checked the Pompeians. Caesar soon arrived, only to find that the Pompeians had built a fortified camp by the sea; the Caesarian line was broken. Caesar could do little else but fortify a camp next to that of the Pompeians.

Scouts now reported to Caesar that a single Pompeian legion was occupying an old camp nearby. Caesar secretly led thirty-three cohorts by a double line toward the camp; but as he with the left wing stormed the camp, the right lost its way. The lost cohorts came to a fortification joining the camp to a stream; they broke through and continued on, the cavalry following. As they did so, Pompey arrived with five legions and cavalry. Fearing their retreat would be cut off, first the cavalry and then the infantry retraced their steps along the narrow path through the fortification; in their panic, many Caesarians leapt or were pitched into the ditches on either side. The Caesarian cohorts within the camp, fearing they would be attacked by the Pompeians both within and without the camp, retreated in great panic. Caesar threw himself into the path of the fleeing soldiers, seized their standards, and cried out to them to halt, but they simply ignored him. (When Caesar caught hold of one legionary, in his panic the soldier raised his sword to strike his commander; Caesar's shield-bearer lopped off his arm at the shoulder.) Though he had encircled Caesar and his men, Pompey, afraid more Caesarians were lying in wait, withdrew; on this Caesar commented, "Today victory would have gone to our opponents, if they had had someone who knew how to win."

In their camp, the Pompeians celebrated their victory; 960 Caesarian soldiers and 32 centurions had been killed, most crushed to death. Labienus first taunted the Caesarian prisoners and then had all of them executed. Most of the Pompeians now felt certain of victory; Pompey himself, however, had far too much experience of war, and of Caesar, to share their certainty. Quite as shaken as his soldiers by this defeat, Caesar spent the whole of that night questioning his strategy. Only by land had he been able to provision his army; now, with the Pompeian cavalry once more free, he would no longer be able to do so. Furthermore, even *with* provisions he could neither storm nor reduce by privation Dyrrhachium and the Pompeian camp, since the Pompeians could resupply both by sea. And though Caesar had hoped his besieging Pompey would induce some of the *optimates* with commands elsewhere to go over to his side, none had. He could not attain his object here; as at Gergovia, he would raise the siege.

The following day, Caesar addressed his soldiers. He told them not to be downhearted or unduely disturbed by the events of the preceding day. He reminded them of their countless victories against the Pompeians, of their taking Italy and Spain with little loss and their crossing the Adriatic in spite of the colossal Pompeian fleet. A single defeat, particularly one that caused them so little harm, could easily be reversed with effort and courage. Caesar reprimanded and demoted only the standard-bearers, as they must *never* flee.

The following morning, Caesar marched for Apollonia, Pompey pursuing, but failing to catch, him. (To speed his march, Caesar had secretly sent the baggage and equipment on ahead the night before. And Pompey's soldiers slowed the pursuit by returning to camp to collect their baggage, showing as they did so that they had imbibed the irresolution of their commander.) After tending the wounded and garrisoning the coastal towns that he controlled, Caesar made for Macedonia, where he could link up with the legions he had sent there earlier and attack the Pompeian legions coming from Syria. Should Pompey do the same, Caesar would be able to fight him inland, far from his fleet and the supplies at Dyrrhachium.

Hoping to destroy the Caesarian legions in Macedonia just as Caesar hoped to destroy the Pompeian, Pompey marched inland with all speed. Though Caesar had farther to go — he was to the south of Pompey — and his way through mountains far more difficult, Caesar reached his legions first. Pompey had had messengers go throughout Greece reporting his victory at Dyrrhachium; a wild rumor had arisen that Caesar had been routed with the loss of most of his men. At this, many of the Greek communities once more sided with Pompey. One such town was Gomphi in Thessaly; within one and the same day, Caesar arrived, fortified a camp, erected the siegeworks, and took the town, though it had high, strong walls. Both to serve as a lesson to other Greek towns and to relieve his great shortage of provisions, Caesar let his men pillage Gomphi. On arriving before the walls of Metropolis, Caesar had the Gomphian prisoners relate what had happened to their town; Metropolis opened its gates to him, and Caesar forbid his men from harming or despoiling its people. With the examples of Gomphi and Metropolis before them, all the Thessalian towns save that occupied by the Pompeians now went over to Caesar.

In early August, Caesar pitched his camp in a plain near the town of Pharsalus, by the river Enipeus. Pompey arrived a few days later and made camp on a nearby hill. To increase the confidence of his men, each day Caesar would draw up his line a little closer to the Pompeian position. (Hoping Caesar would accept battle on disadvantageous ground, Pompey would draw up *his* at the bottom of the slope.) To increase the confidence of his cavalry, which was only one-seventh as numerous as the Pompeian, and to teach his light infantry how to support the cavalry, Caesar mixed the two.

Though Pompey preferred to continue his war of attrition, the *optimates* insisted he fight. Understanding little of war, they thought that victory was now, following Dyrrhachium, simply a matter of finishing off a fallen enemy. That they had failed in their pursuit of the Caesarians; that they were now far from their fleet and Dyrrhachium; that they had merely gone where Caesar wished them to go — all this was lost on the *optimates*. The *optimates* also suspected Pompey of wishing to retain supreme power for as long as possible, and they dearly wished to be rid of him. At length Pompey yielded.

On the morning of August 9th, the Pompeians descended onto the level ground at the foot of the hill. Pompey positioned his right wing on the Enipeus and massed his cavalry, with all the archers and slingers, on his left wing. His plan of battle was quite simple: his cavalry would sweep aside Caesar's, gallop round his right wing, and fall upon his rear. So confident was Pompey in this plan that he assured the *optimates* the cavalry attack alone would put the Caesarians to rout. Caesar initially drew his men up into three lines of battle; on seeing the cavalry massed on Pompey's left wing, however, he withdrew cohorts from his third line and formed a fourth opposite the cavalry. To the remaining cohorts of the third line, he gave instructions not to engage until he gave the signal by flag. Since this was where the battle would be won or lost, Caesar took up a position here.

Caesar had the trumpet sound the attack. The armies were far apart; the Caesarians charged. Thinking the Caesarians would be winded by their run and their line disarranged, Pompey ordered his soldiers to await the attack. Battle-tried as they were, however, the Caesarians checked their charge half-way to the Pompeian line, caught their breath, and then charged again. When in range, they hurled their spears, drew their swords, and fell upon the Pompeians. At the same time, the Pompeian cavalry brushed aside Caesar's and sprinted round his right wing, followed by the archers and slingers. As the cavalry outflanked his line, Caesar ordered his newly created fourth line to run forward and attack; coming upon this unorthodox line so shocked the Pompeians that they simply galloped off. At the flight of his cavalry, Pompey rode off to his camp.

The fourth line now fell upon the archers and slingers, slaughtering them where they stood, and then continued on, outflanking the Pompeian left wing and attacking from the rear. At it did so, Caesar raised the flag; the fresh troops of the third line threw themselves at the Pompeians. Attacked from both the front and rear, the Pompeian infantry fled to their camp. In spite of the midday heat and the difficulty of taking a fortified camp, Caesar ordered his men to storm the camp: they must take advantage of the

Pompeians' panic and demoralization. So fierce was the Caesarian attack that Pompey and the infantry soon fled the camp, Pompey to the coast, the infantry to some nearby hills.

With four cohorts Caesar pursued the infantry. When it halted upon a hill, Caesar had his men build a fortification between the Pompeians and their sole source of water. The following day, the Pompeians descended the hill and surrendered, weeping and beseeching Caesar to spare them. Caesar ordered that none be harmed or dispossessed, and he invited all who wished to join his army. Only those who had once before received his pardon did he put to the sword, permitting, however, each of his soldiers to save the life of one Pompeian. With some of his cavalry Caesar now set out in pursuit of Pompey.

15,000 Pompeians fell at Pharsalus, only 1,200 Caesarians. Almost all of the client states and cities allied to Pompey now made peace with the victor — signifying which they withdrew their naval and military contingents from Pompey — as did (at least outwardly) much of the Roman aristocracy. The Pompeian ultras, however, would never be reconciled to either Caesar or monarchy. Not recognizing the hopelessness of their situation following Pharsalus, they convinced themselves that they might still be victorious: their fleet still controlled the Mediterranean, their forces north Africa; much of Italy was still restive in its opposition to monarchy, as was much of Spain (where loyalty to Pompey, and hatred of Caesar's exploitative governor, were strong). Furthermore, while Caesar continued to show clemency to the less zealous of the Pompeians, he did not to the more; with execution all but certain, why not continue to fight?

In September, as Caesar was crossing the Hellespont in a skiff, a Pompeian flotilla hove into view. Rather than try to flee, Caesar ordered his men to row straight for the flagship. So frightened was the commander by Caesar's reputation that he leapt into the skiff and begged for mercy.

In the few days he was in Asia, Caesar reduced the ruinous taxes, tolls, and tributes the Pompeian commander, Metellus Scipio, had imposed, granted communities the power to collect taxes themselves (rather than have it done by the hated Roman tax farmers), and freed or otherwise rewarded the communities that had aided him. On learning that Pompey had sailed for Egypt, hoping to reorganize the war, Caesar set sail at once. When he arrived in Alexandria, courtiers at the Egyptian court presented him with

Pompey's head. Pompey had arrived three days before; thinking it would please Caesar, the courtiers had killed him as he was being taken to shore. Caesar is said to have turned away, and to have wept on being shown Pompey's ring. Pompey had once been his son-in-law, his colleague in rule, and his principal heir; Caesar would most certainly have pardoned him had he lived, and he treated his remains with great respect.

Egypt was the only sizeable state in the Mediterranean world other than Parthia not directly controlled by Rome. Caesar resolved to increase that control, at first by sorting out the royal succession to Rome's advantage. (Conquest might follow.) In spite of the terms of the late king's will, by which his son, Ptolemy XIII, and daughter, Cleopatra, were to rule jointly, the courtiers of the former had forced the latter to flee. Cleopatra had raised an army in Syria, which now confronted that of her brother on Egypt's eastern frontier. Caesar invited Cleopatra and Ptolemy to meet with him; while *he* could easily do so, however, *she* could not, as he controlled Alexandria.

One evening a small boat moored near the royal residence. A merchant disembarked carrying a long bag. Once in Caesar's presence, the merchant opened the bag, and out stepped Cleopatra. The queen apologized for her unorthodox arrival, but observed that she could come in no other way. Caesar was as taken with the plot as he was the plotter; indeed, he would soon fall in love with this precociously charming and shrewd young woman.

Livid that Cleopatra had won Caesar over, and certain that he would now favor her in the succession, Ptolemy's courtiers led the royal army of 20,000 veteran mercenaries in an attack on the palace and harbor. An island, Pharus, and a mole linking the island to the mainland divided the harbor into eastern and western halves. As the vastly outnumbered Caesarians held off the royal army in the streets of Alexandria, Caesar took and garrisoned the lighthouse at the eastern tip of the island. To control the lighthouse was to control the eastern half of the harbor; had the royal army taken the lighthouse, it would have cut the Caesarians off from supplies and reinforcements (which Caesar had summoned). The royal army did, however, occupy the rest of the island and the mole. To prevent the Egyptians from using their considerable fleet against him, Caesar had all their warships burned. (The conflagration spread to the city's celebrated library, the greatest in the ancient world; four hundred thousand papyrus scrolls were lost.)

The siege would continue for six months. The Caesarians could neither launch an attack without reinforcements nor withdraw from their fortifications (since the Egyptians would be upon them before they could reach their ships). The Caesarians and Egyptians continually augmented their fortifications both within the city and on the island and mole. At one point, the Egyptians diverted seawater into the conduits from which the Caesarians drew their water; Caesar ordered wells dug. At another, an attack by the reconstituted Egyptian fleet decided Caesar on taking the whole of the island and mole. The Caesarians did so; but as the legionaries were constructing a palisade across the southern end of the mole, Egyptian soldiers attacked the Caesarian sailors at the northern. Seeing the sailors flee for their ships, and the ships casting off lest they be caught by the Egyptians or sunk by the weight of the men, the legionaries panicked; soon all, infantry and sailors, were dashing for the ships. At first Caesar tried to stop them, but on seeing he could not leapt into his own vessel. So many others joined him that the ship could not move; Caesar now leapt into the water and swam to another. Over 800 Roman soldiers and sailors died in this *melee*.

In late March 47, a relief force of contingents from Cilicia, Israel, and Syria at last arrived. As Ptolemy sailed along the Nile to meet this force, Caesar sailed to the west of Alexandria and then marched in pursuit of the king. With Caesar almost upon him, Ptolemy fortified a camp on a plateau by the Nile. Caesar at once had the camp stormed from the front, flank, and rear; most of the Egyptians either fell to the Roman sword or drowned along with their king in the Nile. At the head of his cavalry, Caesar rode victorious into Alexandria, which threw itself on his mercy. Though now free to do as he liked with the Alexandrians, Caesar refrained from punishing them; he simply pointed out how little their resistence had achieved, and how much it had cost them. He placed Cleopatra and her younger brother on the thrown and installed a Roman garrison.

Caesar had not been in touch with Rome for over half a year; his interests suffered dearly from his absence. Following the battle of Pharsalus, Pompeians from throughout the Roman world had gone to north Africa; here, they appointed Scipio their supreme commander, reorganized and augmented their military forces, and reconstituted the Senate of three hundred at Utica. The Spanish legions that were to have gone to Africa to oppose the Pompeians were occupied by a revolt against the Caesarian governor. The king of the Cimmerian Bosporus (Crimea), Pharnaces, had taken much of Asia Minor. So impolitic were his legates in Rome that Italy was on the verge of revolt.

Caesar first settled affairs in Syria, Cilicia, and elsewhere in Asia. He then, within five days, marched into Asia Minor and annihilated Pharnaces's army. It is on the swiftness of this victory that Caesar commented, *Veni, vidi, vici,* "I came, I saw, I conquered." He also remarked that Pompey was fortunate to have been considered a great general for defeating such opponents. (Of Caesar's legionaries, fewer than 1,000 were veterans.) By October 47, Caesar was once more in Rome, continuing to mobilize his forces for the campaign in north Africa. There, the Pompeians and their African clients had collected ten Roman and four Numidian legions, 1,600 Celtic, German, and African heavy cavalry, innumerable Numidian light cavalry and mounted bowmen, masses of archers on foot, 120 elephants, 55 warships, and considerable stores. So long as such a force remained to them, the Pompeians would retain hope of victory, and the Roman world continue to be restive. Caesar must defeat this force, must make it clear to all that he was the victor in the civil war.

When Caesar commanded the veteran legions in Campania to sail for Sicily, whence they would sail for Africa, they refused. Pharsalus was a year earlier, and yet the war continued. How much longer must they fight? And when were they to receive their promised rewards? Because of Caesar's policy of clemency, the civil war had had far less booty than the Gallic; whyever were they fighting? Whichever representatives Caesar sent to them, the legions either stoned or killed; they then marched on Rome. As the legions neared the city, Caesar walked out to meet them. Touched by the sight of their aged and solitary commander, the soldiers deferentially requested that they be discharged and receive their reward. Addressing them as "citizens" rather than "comrades," Caesar at once granted their release. As for their reward, he would grant far more even than they had asked — once he had returned from Africa and celebrated his victory with other soldiers. Ashamed, the soldiers beseeched Caesar to take them with him. He relented, punishing only the ringleaders, and they only slightly. Caesar perhaps recognized that he had indeed asked too much of his veterans.

In early December, Caesar left Rome for Sicily. In part because of the delay caused by the mutiny, in part because the legions were dispersed throughout the Roman world, only six legions — one of veterans and five of new recruits — and 2,000 cavalry had arrived. To show the soldiers that he was resolved on assailing the Pompeians whatever his forces, Caesar pitched his tent on a spit of sand jutting out toward Africa. Unwilling to await the other legions, in late December Caesar set sail for Africa, hoping to elude the far-superior fleet of the Pompeians as he had in the Adriatic. The storm that kept the Pompeian fleet in a bay near Carthage, scattered much of Caesar's; he landed with only 3,000 infantry and 150 cavalry. Caesar at once sent ships to summon the remainder of his fleet and to requisition further troops and supplies; he then marched south and occupied the coastal plateau on which sat the town of Ruspina.

In early January 46, the other Caesarian ships landed at Ruspina. Caesar felt he could now venture out to collect grain. He did so with three legions, most of new recruits; as they crossed a plain, outriders reported that a large contingent of Pompeians was approaching. Caesar summoned his 400 cavalry and 150 archers from camp and drew up a single line of battle, the most he could do given his small numbers. The Pompeian force soon arrived: 1,600 Gallic and German cavalry, 8,000 Numidian cavalry, 1,600 further cavalry, more than 6,000 infantry, and many archers and slingers, some mounted; their commander was Labienus. As the Pompeian cavalry rode round the Caesarians and attacked from the flanks, their infantry and archers attacked the Caesarian line. The Caesarian infantry could retaliate against neither the cavalry nor infantry, since they would simply hurl their missiles and then take flight. The Caesarian cavalry, most of whose horses were soon wounded, could do little to fight off the innumerable Pompeian horsemen. At one point the fate of the Caesarians became so doubtful that the soldiers round Caesar began to flee. As one dashed by, Caesar caught him by the shoulder, turned him round, and shouted, "*That* is where the enemy is!"

The Pompeians soon formed a ring round the Caesarians. At this, Caesar ordered his men to stretch out their line as far as possible and for each cohort to stand with its rear to another cohort. The Caesarians soon cut the Pompeian line in two. Caesar now attacked a group of Pompeians who had become isolated, driving them back in panic; other Caesarian cohorts did the same. As the Caesarians slowly retreated to their camp, Numidian reinforcements arrived; the Pompeians took fresh courage and once more began to assail the Caesarians. Caesar ordered his infantry and cavalry to wheel about and drive the Pompeians beyond some nearby hills. The Caesarians remained on the hills a short while and then returned slowly to camp in the same formation, at which the Pompeians withdrew.

Caesar would not again leave the coastal plateau until reinforcements arrived. In the meantime, he augmented the fortifications of his camp, requisitioned archers and *materiel*, trained some of the sailors as light infantry, and set up smithies to manufacture missiles. Caesar also induced some of the north African kings to attack the lands of the Pompeians' African clients, their rivals, thus drawing off some of the forces of those clients. Caesar promised freedom and booty to whoever should join his side; these promises, the conviction among the Africans that the cause for which they were fighting was not theirs, but solely that of the Roman oligarchs, and the political maladroitness of the *optimates*, caused towns to submit to Caesar, and Africans to defect by the score. Caesar also gained quite a lot of Pompeian deserters by promising them freedom, respect for their property, and an equal share in the booty with his own soldiers. Scipio offered the legionaries and natives nothing, confining himself to declaring he would free the Roman Senate and people.

Within a few days of the battle in the plain, Scipio with eight legions, 3,000 cavalry, and scores of elephants had arrived and pitched camp three miles from Caesar's. Ignoring both the counsel of his fellow Pompeians and the disaffection of the coastal states, Scipio resolved to hold the coast. (A far better strategy would have been to retire inland, thus drawing Caesar into the open desert; there, the Caesarians would have been able to do little against the far more numerous Pompeian cavalry.) Kept from foraging far from their camp by the Pompeian cavalry, the Caesarians were soon short of both grain and grazing. Accustomed to dealing with such deprivation, the veterans began to feed the horses and draft animals seaweed they collected from the beach and washed in fresh water.

In late January, two Caesarian legions of veterans, 1,000 archers and slingers and 800 cavalry arrived, along with plentiful grain. Caesar now began to move about the plateau more freely. After the Caesarian cavalry routed his own, Scipio summoned his ally King Juba of Numidia, thinking the forces and prestige of the king would be of aid to him. Juba soon arrived with three legions, scores of cavalry, and 30 elephants. Caesar nonetheless continued his work of occupying the nearby hills and extending his fortifications. Quite as much to the surprise of the Caesarians as to the Pompeians, Caesar now engaged in a war of manoeuvring so that his soldiers could learn how to fight the swift Numidian infantry and cavalry. In March, Caesar began to march down the coast: the confidence and ability of his soldiers were much improved, he had difficulty obtaining provisions, and he must try to induce the Pompeians to engage in battle rather than continually assail him with their cavalry.

Though the Pompeian cavalry and light infantry continually attacked the Caesarians as they marched, Scipio refused to fight a decisive battle. To force him to do so, in the middle of the night Caesar marched for the coastal town of Thapsus, whose loyalty to Scipio would compel him to come to its defense. On learning of Caesar's march, Scipio followed by a higher route. The following morning, the Caesarians began to lay siege to Thapsus; as they did so, Scipio created twin camps eight miles south of the town. Two days later, Scipio began to fortify a camp by the sea a mile-and-a-half from Thapsus. On learning of this, Caesar at once took a force to attack the Pompeians as they worked. On arriving, he found Scipio's army drawn up in a battle-line in front of his camp, with the elephants on the right and left wings. Caesar drew his men up into three lines of battle, with a fourth line of infantry, archers, and slingers on either wing.

As Caesar went on foot from point to point in his line, reminding the veterans of their courage in previous battles, and urging the recruits to emulate the battle-tried and to covet their fame and status, the Caesarians noticed that the Pompeians still constructing the camp were running about as if in fright. They beseeched Caesar to give the signal for battle; replying that he did not believe in battle by sally, Caesar continually steadied the battle-line. Under pressure from the soldiers, however, a trumpeter on the right wing sounded the signal. Though their own centurions turned round and tried to hold them back, the soldiers began to move forward.

Seeing that he could not stop the soldiers, Caesar cried, "*Felicitas!*" A hail of missiles and stones rained down on the elephants; terrified, they wheeled round, trampled the soldiers behind them, and continued on into the camp. The Caesarians were soon upon the camp; while some of the Pompeians fought fiercely to hold it, most ran out by the back gates. All over the field, Caesarians pursued fleeing Pompeians. As the Pompeians reached the first of their southern camps, the Caesarians were upon them; when they reached the second, they found the Caesarians awaiting them. Their situation hopeless, the Pompeians laid down their arms and hailed Caesar as victor. The Caesarians would have none of it; Caesar had granted clemency throughout the civil war, and yet the war continued. As Caesar beseeched his men to show mercy, they butchered the Pompeians to a man. In their great fury, they then killed or wounded whichever *Caesarian* aristocrats and *equites* they viewed as responsible for the war.

At Thapsus, 5,000 Pompeians died, only 50 Caesarians. Following their defeat, the surviving Pompeians either capitulated or fled. When his ship was forced by a storm to land at an African port and then caught by Caesarian cruisers, Scipio committed suicide. So that they might "die like men," Juba and Petreius fought a duel; after killing Petreius, Juba ordered one of his slaves to kill him. Heeding the lesson of Thapsus, Caesar at once released most of his veterans and settled them on lands in Africa and elsewhere. He also rewarded the communities that had aided him, imposed fines on those that had aided the Pompeians, and united the most fertile land of Numidia with other lands to create the Roman province of Africa Nova.

In July, Caesar returned to Rome. To deter him from creating a monarchy, and to show that the inherited order continued to function and the Senate to be relevant, the senators conferred on Caesar numerous powers and honors. It appointed him dictator for ten consecutive years; there were precedents for a dictatorship, and it was exceptional, the dictator returning to the senatorial fold once he had fulfilled his duties. The Senate also appointed him "Overseer of Morals," a new position the duties of which included administering the Empire, conducting the elections, choosing who would be in the orders and classes of Roman society, and perhaps censoring what was written and said publicly. In addition, Caesar would have the right of speaking first in the Senate and of sitting in a special chair between the two consuls. The Senate also granted him a *supplicatio* of forty days. For his part, Caesar declared that he would hew to a policy of reconciliation and consult the Senate. Caesar's policy pleased neither the *optimates* (who hoped he would restore the inherited order) nor his own followers (who yearned to despoil the *optimates*). Caesar was growing more and more isolated.

Caesar occupied himself with administrative and social matters; there was much to be done, not only because of the three years of civil war — throughout which Italy and the provinces had suffered from ruinous taxes, spoilation, and retributions — but also because of decades of maladministration by the oligarchy. Caesar would achieve that which the oligarchs had been quite incapable of achieving, "tranquility for Italy, peace for the provinces, and security for the Empire." He introduced a law requiring praetors to govern a province for one year following their year in office, consuls for two (but no longer: a Caesar or Pompey must not arise in the future); placed imperial officials, reporting directly to him, in all the provinces as a counterpoise to the governors; stipulated that no Italian of marriageable age be out of Italy for more than three consecutive years except on military service, and that the sons of senators leave Italy only on public service (to reduce the outflow of Italians from Italy, and to lessen the exploitation of provincials); reduced taxes in most of the provinces, and granted the provincials a greater role in collecting them; laid down the qualifications for magistrates and councillors in the municipalities; imposed fines on aristocrats and others guilty of financial malfeasance or supporting Pompey or both (to defray the costs of the war and to reduce their colossal wealth, and thus their power; the proceeds went, not to Caesar, but to the state); increased the penalties for crimes, and introduced the confiscation of part or whole of the criminal's property (so that the rich whose penalty was exile would also suffer financially for their crimes); introduced a sumptuary law limiting the use or richness of litters, purple clothes, pearls, dishes, and funerary memorials (to limit extravagance by the rich); limited the interest rate that creditors could charge, forbid interest on arrears of interest, and stipulated that the interest owed could not exceed the principal owed and that an insolvent debtor could not become the slave of his creditor; insisted that at least a third of the employees of the *latifundia*, the large Roman farms, be free men (to force the owners to pay wages to at least some of their laborers, and to reduce brigandage in the countryside); took a census of Rome so that he might limit its corn ration (in part to relieve the public treasury, in part to dissuade the "work-shy" from flocking to Rome); settled 80,000 or so of the peoples of Rome in overseas colonies (to give them work and to further the Romanization of the Empire); granted citizenship to physicians and teachers from the provinces (to increase the educated of the city); introduced the Julian calendar (based on the solar rather than the lunar year, and far more functional than Rome's ancient calendar); rewarded his veterans with booty and land; and so on. Significantly, all laws and reforms not explicitly directed at Rome or Italy were to be applied to the Empire as a whole. Rather than submitting these resolutions for debate, which would have taken far too much time, Caesar either simply informed the Senate of their enactment or forged the signatures of senatorial initiators. Caesar was arranging the affairs of the Roman Empire much as he did those of his legions on campaign.

Caesar also celebrated his triumphs of Gaul, Egypt, Asia Minor, and Africa. He organized gladiatorial games, chariot races, wild-beast hunts, athletic contests, theatrical performances, and (in honor of Julia) public feasts at twenty-two thousand tables. Over five bloody days, men under sentence of death and other prisoners reenacted some of Caesar's more celebrated battles; for these he had had the circus enlarged and surrounded by a moat, and an artificial lake created. To shield the spectators from the sun, Caesar had silk awnings hung over the Forum Romanum, the Via Sacra, and the slope of the Capitol. The novelty and ingenuity of the staging and organization were quite beyond anything the Romans had ever seen; Caesar was as brilliant in celebrating his victories as he was in winning them. Following the Gallic triumph, Caesar had Vercingetorix, in Roman prisons for six years, executed.

After five months in Rome, Caesar in late November left for Further Spain, which was in open revolt under Pompey's elder son Gnaeus. Gnaeus had raised thirteen legions, some consisting of Pompeians who had succeeded in fleeing Africa, including Labienus. While Caesar had far more cavalry than did the Pompeians, he had far fewer infantry, and these consisted almost wholly of new recruits. (Most of the veterans either had been dismissed or were tied down in the provinces.) Caesar first lay siege to Corduba; since it could not be taken, and since Gnaeus would not be drawn into a pitched battle — Labienus having advised him to vitiate Caesar's forces through attrition as his father had done in Greece — Caesar set out for Gnaeus's strongest garrison, the town of Ategua, to which he laid siege. Once the town surrendered to Caesar in February, much of Spain, and even many of Gnaeus's own officers, crossed to his side, thus forcing Gnaeus to stake all on a decisive battle.

The battle took place near the town of Munda. So favorable was the Pompeians' position upon some heights, and so fiercely did they fight — Caesar was now executing captured Pompeians as rebels — that the Caesarians soon began to fall back. Caesar leapt from his horse, seized a shield, and forced his way to the front line. As his men continued to fall back, Caesar remained where he was, alone, under a hail of missiles, crying out,

I will not follow you! Remember this place, for this is my last day! Remember what kind of commander you deserted!

Ashamed, the soldiers turned back. An attack by Mauretanian auxiliaries on the enemy's flank soon decided the issue. 30,000 Pompeians died at Munda, Labienus among them. Within two months, Gnaeus had been killed in flight and the rebellion quelled.

Caesar remained in Spain until June to solidify Roman control over, and increase the Romanization of, the country. He created constitutions and imperial administrations; as in his colonies elsewhere, freedmen could be elected to town councils. Caesar also granted Latin rights or citizenship, further territory, and freedom from taxation to the cities and towns that had aided him, imposed taxes, tributes, and a loss of territory on those that had rebelled, and founded colonies for his veterans and Roman plebians. (All the colonies were to be fortified, and all male colonists to be subject to military service; Caesar wished the colonies to contribute significantly to preserving and defending the Empire.) He then did much the same in his old province of Gallia Transalpina. By such acts, Caesar continued to weaken the conception of the Roman world as a city state and its provinces.

Caesar returned to Rome at the beginning of October 45. The Senate granted him a *supplicatio* of fifty days and decreed that his victory at Munda be considered the refoundation of the city, to be celebrated each year with circus games.

❧

Caesar recognized that the solution to the dysfunctionality of the Roman state lay in the unification of the Empire and the creation of a fitting government. Just as an earlier social crisis had been solved by the merger of Rome and Italy, so, too, must this present crisis be solved by the merger of Italy and the provinces. Caesar *could not* revert to the inherited order; it did not work. The context had changed, and the structure of the Roman state and government must change with it. Monarchy would be the unifying political system of the Empire, Italo-Hellenic culture its unifying culture. Caesar also recognized, however, that most Romans were as opposed to the unification of the Empire as they were to the creation of a monarchy, that he simply could not declare his object. While retaining the forms of the inherited order, he would act as a monarch and continue to unify and better the Empire — all without saying a word about his object. Caesar would slowly suggest to men's minds the efficacy and propriety of monarchy and unification. On seeing the benefits of the two, the Romans would come round bit by bit, would come to value that which they now abhorred; in the contrast between Caesar's rule and that of the oligarchs, the Romans would come to see the superiority of monarchy. (*Caesar* seems to have seen the necessity of monarchy — and to have wished to persuade his countrymen of that necessity — even while quite young: in a speech at the age of 30, he remarked on the "venerability of kings, who are supreme among men.")

Caesar now continued his work of creating a government that fit the context, a hereditary monarchy possessed of an imperial civil service by which he and his successors might rule the Empire more efficiently. He had the Senate grant his degrees the power of laws, and him sole right of deciding on war and peace and disposing of Roman armies and treasures. Caesar transformed the Senate from a legislative body consisting solely of aristocrats into an advisory council of state consisting of a variety of classes and peoples of the Empire. He did so by increasing the number of senators from six to nine hundred and appointing (as he had sole power to do) both Italians and non-Italians of all classes, including freedmen. (By appointing provincials, Caesar also furthered the Romanization of the provinces.) He reformed the judiciary, the police, the Roman financial system, and the financial administration of the state (replacing the maladministration of the oligarchs with the competent management of his slaves; at his death, the public treasury would hold *ten times* as much cash as during the most flourishing period of the republic). He also stipulated that Roman law be unified and codified. By his will, Caesar adopted his eighteen-year-old grand-nephew Gaius Octavius (the future Augustus) and made him his chief heir.

To further unify the Empire, Caesar limited the jurisdiction of Roman magistrates to the city only (rather than, as formerly, to the Empire as a whole); conferred Latin rights on some provincial cities and towns, Roman citizenship on others (or at least on their Latin-speaking upper classes); restored Carthage and Corinth (whose destruction marked the transition from Roman protectorate to Roman tyranny); founded colonies for his veterans and others in Gaul, Spain, Africa, Greece, and Asia Minor (to reward the veterans and to Romanize the Empire); greatly increased the pay of the legionaries (to reduce pillaging; the soldiers would supplement the pittance they received from the state through plunder); augmented the frontier defenses (to protect the peoples of the provinces); directed that some of the dramas of the popular festivals be performed in the languages of the people of Rome, in Spanish, Hebrew, Syrian, and so on. To better Rome and Italy, Caesar directed: that a temple to Mars and theater be constructed, both to be the largest in the world; that a new Senate-house and bazaar be built; that a library housing the whole of Greek and Roman literature be constructed (the first in Rome); that new and better public baths be built in Rome (to improve public hygiene); that a high road be constructed from Rome to the Adriatic, over the Apennines, to stimulate commerce within Italy; that the Tiber be diverted to the sea at Tarracina, both to drain the Pontine marshes and to make a safe and easy passage for ships to Rome; that the harbor at Ostia be extended; that Rome be given a port near the mouth of the Tiber; that breakwaters be constructed on the sea nearest to Rome, to clear away obstructions to shipping; that a canal be dug through the Isthmus of Corinth (to improve sea communications between Italy and the East).

Rather than speak of monarchy, Caesar surrounded himself with its symbols. Since Romans and Italians constituted only a small minority of the peoples of the Empire — indeed, a considerable portion of the population of Rome itself was of oriental origin — Caesar's monarch would combine both Eastern and Western traits. Not only might such a monarchy appeal to both the Eastern and Western peoples of the Empire, but it would also be new, representing the new context. (Caesar adopted Eastern traits also because, while the Greeks and Romans had ruled only city-states, the peoples of the East had ruled empires.) Since their own regions were ruled by monarchs, the peoples of the East would be susceptible to such symbol-ism. But even the Romans and Italians *might* be susceptible to a ruler cult, since Hellenism, with its combination of Greek and oriental influences, had come to suffuse Roman society.

The Western symbols were generally more secular. Recognizing that, to the unintelligent, that which is least congenial is the unprecedented, Caesar sought remind his fellow Romans that monarchy *was* precedented, and that his would in a sense be hereditary, since his family was descended from the ancient Roman kings. He wore the purple toga of the ancient Roman kings, had his statue placed beside theirs in the Capitol, and had the kings referred to in many of his honors. The chair on which he sat in the Sen-ate was of gold and styled "imperial," his image was placed on coins (in antiquity the symbol of monarchy), and he could wear the gold wreath of the Etruscan kings and the red boots of the Alban. Caesar increased the number of patricians (which had not been done in over 400 years); by do-ing so he not only referred back to Roman antiquity, but also replaced the aristocracy of the oligarchs with the royalty of the patriciate (to which his family belonged).

The Eastern symbols were generally more religious. (Caesar would be far from the first Roman commander to be venerated as a god by the peoples of the East.) Following his victory in Africa, Caesar had commis-sioned a temple to Venus Genetrix, that is, to Venus the ancestress of the Julii (his family), rather than to Venus Victrix, "Bringer of Victory." He now accepted a host of religious honors: deification, the resolutions on which were inscribed in gold letters on silver tablets and placed at the feet of Jupiter; the right to wear the laurel wreath of Jupiter; the creation of a new god, *divus* Julius, to which a temple and priest would be dedicated, and to whom votive offerings would be made once each year; the inclusion of his statue (of ivory) in the procession of the circus (with those of the other gods, though his would have a special litter; his statue, like theirs, would have a holy resting-place); the placing of his statue in the temple of Quiri-nus, an old warrior god of the Quirinal district, with the inscription, "To the Unconquerable God" (Quirinus was also identified with Romulus, the founder of Rome, whom the senators had torn to pieces when he became a tyrant); the placing of his statue in all Italian cities and Roman temples; the placing of a gable over his house (as if it were a temple); the right to be buried within the walls of the city (which no mortal could be); the celebrating of his birthday as a public holiday and the renaming of the month of his birth "Julius" (July); the holding of games in his honor once every four years; the celebrating of the anniversaries of all his victories with annual sacrifices; and so on. (Was Caesar also trying to understand himself? He was vastly superior — in intelligence, understanding, courage, fortune — to other human beings. Why should this be so? The ancient world accounted for such superiority by supposing the individual a god. And Caesar often observed that his family was descended from Venus.)

And what would the title of this new monarch be? Not *rex*, or king: in Roman society, *rex* connoted the ancient Roman kings and, in Eastern, the despots of the East. On Caesar's return from Spain, the Senate bestowed on him the titles of *dictator perpetuo* (dictator for life), *imperator, liberator*, and *pater patriae*, "father of the fatherland" (the latter conferred only once before). Of these titles, Caesar seemed to favor that of *imperator* for his new monarch. During the republican period, *imperator* would be placed after a general's name *while he held military command*; Caesar was the first to retain the title following the celebration of his triumphs. *Imperator* made reference to the imperium, to the comprehensive powers of Roman governors. Caesar now included the title in all political oaths and placed it on all coins; perhaps most significant of all, he stipulated that *imperator* be conferred on his natural or adopted descendants.

In spite of all that Caesar did to better his society, the Roman aristocracy did not come round. The aristocrats continued to revere the republic above all else; they felt they "were living in a wretched time, as slaves, without a state, law-courts, or Senate." (Gelzer) In Roman thinking, societies subject to the will of one man were not free; the Romans viewed the Persians, for instance, as slaves of an absolute king. And to the Romans, to be a slave was to be of the lowest quality, immoral and debased. The aristocracy could not see Caesar's rule as fitting and functional government, but only as subjection. And that their *equal* — for so they continued to view Caesar, in spite of all his achievements — should treat them so, was particularly galling. Even many of Caesar's *followers* were dissatisfied at having so little say in governing. Cicero's remark on Caesar's reformation of the Roman calendar — that now even the stars must obey Caesar's commands — epitomized how the Roman aristocracy received Caesar's reforms. The aristocracy did not see that the calendar was now far better and more functional; they saw only that Caesar had done away with *their* calendar, a calendar with which they had been quite pleased, and which they had seen no need to reform. Caesar's policy of reconciliation — his issuing a general amnesty to all his political opponents, and his stipulating that the widows of fallen Pompeians whose estates had been confiscated receive their dowries and their children part of their patrimony — did nothing to reconcile the aristocracy to either Caesar or his policies. In private, the aristocrats referred to Caesar as *rex*, a word with the most hateful connotations in Roman society.

That their political and economic supremacy should now cease; that the Senate was to be no more than a council of state; that "semi-civilized Gauls," freedmen, and slaves now held positions once held by aristocrats; that Rome was no longer to be equated with the Roman state, but simply to be a municipal city (albeit a commercial and administrative center); that Caesar should remake the city as he saw fit; that the provinces could no longer be exploited with impunity; that Caesar should seek to improve the lot of the group rather than only that of Rome — shocked not only the Roman aristocracy, but also much of Roman society. So convinced were the aristocrats that "the good is what pleases the good," and that they were "the good," that they now felt certain what Caesar was doing *must* be wrong, since it displeased them so. And why must he show such disdain for the aristocracy and everything it held dear? His disregarding the laws on the ages of consuls and others and the timing of elections; his resigning his consulship and appointing two of his supporters (suggesting the consulship was simply booty); his celebrating his victory in Spain over "foreign" enemies (that is, over the Pompeians); his permitting two of his junior officers to receive a triumph (which the law did not condone) — all seemed calculated to show Caesar's scorn for the inherited order.

With Caesar's ascension, the Roman aristocracy lost what had been its for centuries, control of the state. Politics had been the domain of that class for over half a millennium; indeed, it was the sole career for the men of certain families. The *prestigio* and *dignitas* of such men rested on their political power; if they could now participate in politics only slightly, what was to be the basis of their position in society? What would become of their descendents (whom they wished to give what their ancestors had given them)? This loss of power, and with it the ability to arrange affairs so as to further their and their clients' interests, frightened and enraged them. And if this mainstay of Roman tradition should give way, which other traditions would not also go? Which could withstand the loss of the inherited order? Would a father cease to be the *patria potestas*, the sole authority in his family? Wild rumors, such as that Caesar would transfer the capitol of the empire to Alexandria (for love of Cleopatra) or to Troy (to honor his ancestors), now filled Rome.

That Caesar should suggest the world was not solely theirs, that others had rights as well, was as foreign to the oligarchic worldview as it was hateful to the oligarchs. They viewed themselves as masters of the world; his levelling of the peoples of the Empire was to them monstrous. The oligarchs were at heart *exclusive*; nothing was so dear to them as the distinctiveness of their property, privileges, and honors. This was to the oligarchs splendor: that no one but they should be rich, that no one but they should have any say in governing the Empire. (As Cicero acknowledged, the "liberty" of the mass of Romans was largely an illusion, albeit a useful one: it made the masses feel more significant, distinguished them from slaves and provincials. The value of liberty lay not in the actual benefits it conferred, which were slight, but in flattering the vanity of those who possessed it.) The oligarchs valued, not the most functional government, but simply that in which they were preeminent. That they themselves had been tyrants to countless city states, more ancient even than Rome, that under their rule the mass of peoples of the Empire lived "in a wretched time, as slaves," the oligarchs cared not a fig.

The inherited order was doomed, not by Caesar, but by its not fitting the context; it was not Caesar, but maladaption that destroyed the order. And by their great selfishness and ridigity, by scotching any reform — that is, by ensuring that the Roman political system could not possibly not fit the context — the *optimates* ensured that the order would die. In Mommsen's words, the *optimates* "conserved the order to death." (In truth, the *optimates* were only imperfectly conservative: while stamping out whichever novelties did not serve their interests, they were quite willing to accept those — such as the exploitation of the provinces — that did. Any change that furthered their short-term interests was permissible.) Rail as they might against "dictators" with "extraordinary powers," it was the *optimates'* misrule that had made such dictators necessary; they were the sole cause of the decomposition of the Roman state.

The inherited order was superannuated and dysfunctional; it would soon have succumbed to economic collapse or slave revolt or barbarian invasion — or perhaps all three — and with it the Roman state. Mommsen observes that, had the rule of the oligarchs continued, the irruption of barbarians into Italy "would have occurred four hundred years sooner than it did, and would have occurred at a time when the Italian civilization had not become naturalized either in Gaul, or on the Danube, or in Africa and Spain." Cicero held that "freedom consists not in having a just master, but in having none;" but without a master, the *optimates* would have ruined the Roman state. And as it weakened, the barbarians would have conquered Italy; once they did so, whichever *optimates* survived would hardly have been free (and the barbarians would have been far crueler than Caesar). The Romans were exceedingly fortunate that a Caesar should arise during the late republic; but they did not understand that they were so.

The inherited order was no longer functional; it was quite that simple. Orthodoxy was not possible; a policy could either be orthodox or functional, but not both. In trying to combine respect for the inherited order with competent imperial administration, Pompey had shown the impossibility of doing so. One could either respect the order or rule the Empire efficiently, but not both. Only a monarch could create the sort of state Cicero envisages in his *de republica*; but in that work he writes that "no one man should have more power than the commonwealth" — but then the state he wishes for could never come into being. (Indeed, it would be the *monarch* Augustus who would create a society most like that in Cicero's work.) Caesar was indeed willing to destroy the inherited order; but his doing so was simply an *ancillary* purpose, his principal purpose being the creation of a great state. Caesar represents less the transition of Roman government from republic to monarchy, than the transition of the Roman state from city-state to empire, less a change in form of government, than a change in context.

Both Caesar and the *optimates* spoke of Roman virtue and honor. But to the *optimates* virtue and honor consisted of maintaining the forms of government, to Caesar ruling as sensibly and prudently as did the ancestors (whether or not the organs of government resembled theirs). Whereas his fellow aristocrats revered the old Roman *forms*, Caesar revered the old Roman *traits*, such as service to the state and achievement. (Indeed, so taken was Roman society with forms that even Augustus would have to pretend that the inherited order rather than a monarchy ruled the Empire.) To Caesar, all *systems* were provisional; none was hallowed. To Caesar, not tradition, but context, was authoritative. To Caesar, legitimacy flowed, not from age, but from functionality. To Caesar, the most natural system was that which best fit the context. Caesar's worldview is clearly shown by his writings: he sees what needs to be done and does it. What needs to be done is not conditioned by politics, feelings, or ideology: *it is*. Caesar was the context speaking and acting through a human being. In seeking to preserve the inherited order, the *optimates* were immoral; in seeking to overthrow that order, Caesar was moral. In the late republic, a political act gained legitimacy by its proposer persuading "the good" to adopt it; but since "the good" were so only in name, and cared not one whit for the group, most legitimate acts were immoral, and many illegitimate ones moral.

What made Caesar so rare — perhaps unique, at least among the Roman upper classes — was his caring more about the interests of the group than about individual, class, or party interests. "As a result of his victory," writes Gelzer, "the Empire had at last passed into the hands of a man of genuine political ability, who no longer followed selfish party or class interests, but who intended to shape the Empire as a whole in the way that circumstances required." (By not hewing to this or that party or interest, however, Caesar pleased no one; what is done for the group as a whole, wins the heart of few of its individual members.) Over against the paltry ambition of the *optimates* was the sublime ambition of Caesar: to create a great empire in which Italo-Hellenic civilization might flourish. His "aim was the highest which man is allowed to propose to himself — the political, military, intellectual, and moral regeneration of his own deeply decayed nation, and of the still more deeply decayed Hellenic nation intimately akin to his own." (Mommsen) In the Caesarian environment of the late republic, the Roman aristocracy was immoral; in that which followed the civil war, Caesar was moral. Without limits, the aristocracy was dissolute, Caesar great — thus the chief distinction between the two. (That Caesar could still wish to serve a society that had shown itself so foolish, cruel, spiteful, and little, shows a rare and great nature.) Only very rarely do we find such an example in history, that of a great force, in perfect accord with reality, wholly refashioning his society for the better — much as we suppose a god would do.

Caesar was in the invidious position of reforming a society against its will. But what was he to do? He saw what few of his compatriots saw; how could he possibly convince his society of what it could not see, that it must change if it was not to be doomed? And if he could not get his society to see reality, to go with (as he did) the upper rather than the lower realms of the human brain, should he not do what he knew must be done? Like Cicero as senator, Caesar "had regard rather to the interests than to the will" of the Romans. Roman society was on the verge of destroying itself; Caesar would not let it do so. If his society viewed that restraint as an infringement of its liberty, so be it. (Would the destruction of the Roman state not have been a far greater infringement?) Caesar could not do what needed to be done *and* be politic; he could be civil, gracious, charming — but not politic. Caesar simply could not flatter Roman conceits.

When all is said and done, Roman society simply could not understand Caesar; he was too superior. Cicero said that Caesar was a *teras*, "a wonderful, frightening, monstrous, and inscrutable phenomenon of a higher order." The animus of Roman society must have been quite intelligible to Caesar: others simply did not understand why he was doing what he was doing, did not understand necessity. He must have recognized that that which benefits society is often received with hatred, and that which harms it with gratitude. He must also have recognized — and it was perhaps of some consolation to him — that posterity appreciates far more what is done to better a group, than does the group itself. "Like every genuine statesman he served the people not for reward — not even for the reward of their love — but sacrificed the favor of his contemporaries for the blessing of posterity, and above all for the permission to save and renew his nation." (Mommsen) In a speech to the Senate, Cicero declared that Caesar would ensure his fame by "discharging his obligations to the commonwealth" — that is, by restoring the republic. Had Caesar done so, we might well remember him as little as we do Sulla. "Great men are necessary for our life," said the historian Jacob Burckhardt, "in order that the movement of world history can free itself sporadically, by fits and starts, from obsolete ways of living and inconsequential talk." Unfortunately, humanity is apt to hate those who do away with its "obsolete ways of living," to hate those who do the necessary rather than the possible.

∾

Relations between Caesar and Roman society grew worse by the day. No one cheered when Caesar's statue was carried with that of Victory in a triumphal procession; when one of his consuls entered the theater, the cry went up that he was not truly a consul; on the walls of the city were posted placards saying, "A fine deed! No one is to show a new senator the way to the Council-house!" While much of Roman society seethed, Caesar planned a campaign against Parthia, the empire that stretched from the eastern border of the Roman province of Syria to Persia. The Parthians had annihilated the Roman army under Crassus and were now making incursions into Syria, which was itself controlled by a Pompeian. Caesar had done what he could in Rome; rather than remain and confront the hatred of Roman society, he would continue to round out the borders of the Empire, would continue to achieve.

Some time before, sixty or so men had resolved to assassinate Caesar. The chief conspirators, including their leader, Marcus Brutus, were all Caesar's confidants. Understanding nothing of the context, of the conditions that had permitted Caesar's rise, they assumed that to kill Caesar was to restore the republic, to kill the monarch to kill the monarchy. Fifteen years of civil war would follow Caesar's assassination. "Very few, indeed, of the assassins outlived Caesar for more than three years," writes Suetonius, "or died naturally." What the *optimates* had been unwilling to grant, would be taken from them in the coming war. Twenty years hence, the Roman aristocracy would side with Augustus, because to be conservative — that is, to conserve what little remained to them — was to support the monarch. The aristocrats "were to find that the price they had been unwilling to pay for retaining their liberties had to be paid, after those liberties had been lost, to preserve order and stability. In refusing to satisfy the needs even of those 'miseri' whom they were obliged to arm, the republic ruling class had displayed not only a lack of social sympathy which is conspicuous in their policy as a whole, but also a lack of prudence that was fatal to their power and privileges." (Brunt) The assassination would take place at the Senate meeting of March 15 in Pompey's curia, a few days before Caesar was to depart for the Parthian campaign.

On the morning of the meeting, Caesar felt unwell; he would not go. One of the conspirators called on Caesar and induced him to attend the meeting. As Caesar stepped out of his carriage, a Greek scholar who knew of the conspiracy handed him a scroll; when Caesar turned to hand it to his servant, the scholar cried, "Caesar, you must read it, alone and quickly! It contains important matters of special concern to you." Caesar continued on into the curia, walked past the standing senators, and sat down. Some of the conspirators stood behind his chair; others approached as with a petition. As they spoke, one of the conspirators tore the toga from Caesar's neck, the signal to begin the attack; each of the twenty-three conspirators present had vowed to strike a blow. The first stabbed Caesar in the neck; the wound was not deep, and Caesar was able to seize the dagger. The others now fell upon him. At first Caesar dodged this way and that, deflecting the blows as best he could. Then, mortally wounded, he stood still and drew his toga over his head.

THINK

In antiquity, a hunter would kill a wild boar thus. On seeing the hunter, the boar would charge; as it did so, the hunter would kneel, plant one end of his pike into the ground, and point the other at the boar's chest. Running full tilt, the boar would impale itself on the pike and, still no less resolved on goring the hunter, run along it until stopped by a crossbar. Courage *of itself* availed the boar of nothing. In antiquity, wild boars rarely ever did, and almost always died.

Wild resolution of itself rarely brings victory. The legionaries who climbed the steep hill of Gergovia and attacked the town showed great courage; their doing so, however, achieved only the loss of 700 Roman lives and the emboldening of the Gauls. That Vercingetorix remained within Alesia rather than rode off with his horsemen showed much courage, but little intelligence; with the loss of Vercingetorix, the Gallic nation lost its rebellion. In her introduction to *The Gallic War*, Carolyn Hammond writes that, throughout his commentary, "Caesar stresses the relationship between himself and his men as one of co-operation and above all *control*. Uncontrolled aggression poses a threat to strategic planning and careful tactics. The proof of this comes from the Gauls and Germans, whose random aggression is highlighted to form a contrast with the channelled, organized sort displayed by the Romans." Once he recognized at Gergovia and Dyrrhachium that he could not win, Caesar marched off. He was no less willing to die if he could not do; it is simply that he was far more likely to do than die elsewhere. Caesar was not a wild boar. (So inspired were his soldiers by his speech following their defeat at Dyrrhachium that they wished to attack the Pompeians at once; while this spoke well of their courage and zeal, it did not of their thinking.) Richelieu insisted that one must always fight as a rational being, *never* like a goaded animal. It is quite simple: the more you think, the further you are from the beasts; the less you think, the closer.

"Nothing is attained in war except by calculation," said Napoleon. "During a campaign whatever is not profoundly considered in all its details is without result." He likened planning a campaign to giving birth: "I am like a woman in labor." Of Napoleon's brilliant defense of Dresden against the Allies, the Prussian field marshall Yorck von Wartenburg said, "I know of no example in war that furnishes clearer evidence of how the numbers and morale of troops, important features as they are, may be so overmatched by the weight of one person of genius." The Prussian General Von Bulow called Napoleon's victory at Marengo "a succession of marvels." "The true general's duty," said Caesar, "is to secure victory as much by strategy as by the sword." Caesar's victories were due quite as much to his thinking as to his resolve; much of his self-confidence was due to his confidence in reason. When, before their first battle against Germanic tribes renowned for their fierceness and valor, Caesar's soldiers panicked, he called their officers together and calmly explained *why* they were certain to win.

The victories of Caesar, Richelieu, and Napoleon were due quite as much to their opponents' *not* thinking well, as to their own thinking. "The intelligence that [Caesar] brought to the waging of war," writes Meier, "made him far superior to the Gauls, who had great courage, but lacked cunning and were not sufficiently detached from events to appreciate the multitude of possibilities and so avoid being taken in by the first impression that Caesar conveyed to them." The poorer you think, the more likely it is you will make a mistake, a mistake any opponent worth his salt will exploit. Of Napoleon Wellington said: "There certainly never existed a man in whose presence it was so little safe to make what is called a false movement." The less you think, the more false movements you will make.

The more passion you feel, the better you think; intelligence stoked by passion is far keener than intelligence that is not. In civilization, however, the more reason rules, rather than emotions, the better. Emotions cause creatures to react to stimuli in ways that are roughly adaptive; each emotion developed for, and is adaptive in, certain contexts. But the context in which our emotions evolved no longer exists; what our emotions would have us do is far more apt to hurt than further our interests. In the wildly complex societies of today, thinking is far more adaptive than emotion; *its* responses benefit the individual far more. It is the neocortex that is fitted to civilization. (Observe that Caesar, Richelieu, and Talleyrand were all supremely intelligent. Because the world is a complex system, a leader must have high intelligence if he is to be great; the simpleton cannot be a great leader.) Socrates would often simply stop where he was and *think*; he once did so, for a day-and-a-half, during a siege.

By far the best process humanity has discovered for thinking, for seeing reality, is the synthetic scientific method: study the world, classify and then interpret with theories what you find, and verify your theories with further study. *The scientific method is by far the most adaptive mode of thinking, that which most increases the survival chances of a survival machine.* In spite of its great functionality, however, only a minority of human beings follow the scientific method. "Today the greatest divide within humanity," writes Wilson, "is not between races, or religions, or...the literate and illiterate. It is the chasm that separates scientific from prescientific cultures." And the cognitive traits of prescientific cultures, he continues, "are commonplace in citizens of modern industrial societies... Systematic logico-deductive thought...is still rare." Life has certain natural traits that make us draw away from scientific thinking, that obscure reality.

All life is heliotropic. Life leans toward light and warmth, away from dark and cold; it leans toward the pleasurable and pleasing, toward (because it is vulnerable) that which makes it feel safe. Life is naturally inclined *not* to see reality. "As I go on in this life, day by day," said Robert Louis Stevenson, "I become more of a bewildered child.... The prim, obliterated, polite surface of life, and the broad, bawdy, and orgiastic foundations, form a spectacle to which no habit reconciles me." We soften whatever comes to us in too harsh, exacting, or disagreeable a form; when presented with natural selection, for instance, we posited the "good of the species." We soften our religions: "Religious precepts are easily obeyed," said Gibbon, "which indulge and sanctify the natural inclinations of their votaries;" the precepts that do not, the votaries simply ignore. The less late-republic politics was to his liking, the more Cicero wrote tracts on the ideal statesman. That Aurelius could write his *Meditations* while waging war shows the degree to which our species is able to disregard reality.

Most of humanity seeks in its thoughts and beliefs the very same qualities it seeks in its houses, clothes, and chairs: comfort and warmth, a general pleasingness. But thoughts and beliefs are not clothes or chairs; they should be selected for their truth, *not for how they make you feel.* You should be *exceedingly* suspicious of any belief that makes you feel good; such beliefs are almost always heliotropisms, and almost always wrong. The sweetest of all heliotropisms is perhaps that which we ourselves create, fantasy; it is so because its wellspring is self-love. Fantasies are will-o'-the-wisps, delusional hopes or plans where necessity is suspended; but necessity is never suspended. Nothing is easier than to create wondrous worlds in our mind. Creating such worlds is the most primitive form of human thought; it is what all early human beings did. Imagination is to simulate what might happen or be in the world of reality, *not* to create a world that is not. The worlds we create are simply worlds we create; in *this* world, said Tolkien, "Hobbits would not have survived even as slaves."

Most of humanity would seem still to believe in magic, though the beliefs take such varied forms that they may not at first be discernible as magic. Words and thoughts are not magical; saying or thinking a thing a certain way does not make it so. To suppose that things will work out of themselves, just as you wish, is to believe in magic. Of Richelieu Burckhardt said, "...what must strike us most of all is that Richelieu, though he felt the sublime compulsion which carried him irresistibly on, never subsided for a moment into a passive reliance on his star, into an irrational blind sense of his mission, but at every point of his work relied on the full employment of the human reason." (Rely on your star rather than your reason, and life will give you a thrashing.) If magic is what you seek, *think*; the creation of new thoughts and ideas out of the raw material of learning is little short of miraculous. That which you seek to do through magic — manipulate the external environment to your advantage — you can do best through thinking.

One of the more dangerous heliotropisms is supposing our species to be of higher quality than it is. "In the mass of mankind, I fear," said Lord Chesterfield, "there is too great a majority of fools and knaves... And a man who will show every knave or fool that he thinks him such, will engage in a most ruinous war, against numbers much superior to those that he and his allies can bring into the field." *The general human quality is low*; in wisdom, understanding, intelligence, morality, compassion, and benevolence, the human median is low. But natural selection has sovereignty over even the high-quality. "I perceive," said Montaigne, "that in the strife that is tearing France to pieces and dividing us into factions, each man labors to defend his cause — but even the best of them resort to dissimulation and lying. The justest party is still a member of a worm-eaten and maggoty body." (Do not think as a child does, that, if of two rivals one is bad, the other must be good; they may very well both be bad. Rarely is a contest between good and evil, but most often simply a rivalry of interests.) "Men must be very bad," said Napoleon, "to be as bad as I think they are." (Ours is the only species sufficiently developed to despise itself.) Montaigne quotes Juvenal:

If I discern a man in holiness and virtue rare,
To a two-headed child this freak of nature I compare...

To see clearly, you must be quite as dispassionate about our species as you are the others. You must not be prejudiced; you must be objective. "Man towers above the rest of creation so long as he recognizes his own nature," said Boethius; "when he forgets it, he sinks lower than the beasts." Whatever their ideals, you would do well to view others as primates; that which is inexplicable when considered from ideals, is easily understood when considered from natural selection. "That Caesar was murdered by twenty-three conspirators," said Chesterfield, "I make no doubt; but I very much doubt, that their love of liberty, and of their country, was their sole, or even principal motive; ...many other motives at least concurred...such as pride, envy, personal pique, and disappointment." On "liberating" a village in Franconia, Napoleon's Marshal Lefebvre addressed it thus: "We have come to bring you liberty and equality, but don't lose your heads about it: the first one of you who moves without my leave will be shot." Beethoven dedicated his *Eroica* symphony to Napoleon; when the latter had a member of the Bourbon family executed purely for reasons of statecraft, Beethoven struck out the dedication, crying, "So he is also nothing more than an ordinary man!" What, perchance, did Beethoven think he was? In society, you will see every species of folly and perversity. Do not rail against what you see; study it: it will tell you much about our species.

"The result," said Thoreau of heliotropisms, "is dullness of sight, a stagnation of the vital circulations, and a general delinquium and sloughing off of all the intellectual faculties." Soften reality, and you will infinitely increase your suffering. *You must see things as they are, not as you wish them to be.* "[I]f history and science have taught us anything," writes Wilson, "it is that passion and desire are not the same as truth." We try to fashion life as we wish it to be, to dictate its characteristics; but life has its own characteristics. We suppose the world to be as we would have created it; but we created neither ourselves nor the world. Perhaps nothing has ever been so misunderstood, or caused more suffering, bitterness, cruelty, and rage, than this: *we do* not dictate the rules to life; *life* dictates the rules to us. The truly religious person so loves and respects God's creation that he studies it so that he might understand it; the truly irreligious person ignores what God has created and supposes creation to be as *he* wishes it. The religious person is scientific, the irreligious hubristic; the religious person acknowledges, the irreligious denies, limits. (Said the French-Russian philosopher and novelist Vladimir Volkoff, "Any distortion of reality is an act of Lucifer.") *This is the revolution in thinking that science wrought: reality is *discovered*, not dictated; the world, reality, is revelation. Science bows to God, and in doing so slights human self-love, continually offends human sensibilities.

∽

Just as selfishness distorts moral thinking, so, too, does it distort all of thinking. (Particularism or tribalism is simply an extension of selfishness and distorts quite as much.) Selfishness limits how much we walk round an object; we peer at it from one point only. In considering why the *optimates* could not conceive of alternatives to the inherited order, Meier writes, "Only outsiders could do this. It had nothing to do with [the *optimates*'] capacity for abstract thought, but with the place from which their thought proceeded, their viewpoint — in other words, the position that the thinker occupied." We think well of all that benefits us in the short term and flatters our self-love; we think vile all that hurts our interests in the short term and depreciates our significance. Nothing benights like the self.

It was selfishness that caused the *optimates* to make that fatal miscalculation at the beginning of the civil war, to suppose that the mass of Romans would join them. Their accusation against Caesar — that he sought to do away with political liberty — ignored a certain reality: only *they* had ever had such a thing; the mass of Romans had very little say in politics — the tribunes of the people notwithstanding — and provincials and slaves none at all. The Gallic nobles who cried out that Caesar was depriving the Gauls of their liberty themselves sought dominion over their own and neighboring tribes. When a young member of the opposition, Richelieu wrote, "Honest people receive new hope when they see how discontented the *parlement* of Paris is and how courageously it speaks up." But in 1638, as First Minister, he said, "We must deal firmly with the *parlement*, not negotiate with it." And whenever it resisted his edicts, he called its members "a pack of rebels."

When Alexander laid siege to Thebes, the Thebans beseeched the neighboring city-states to come to their aid, to "free the Greeks from their tyrant." But Thebes had itself created a local empire, had imposed its rule on and cruelly exploited the very city-states it now implored to aid it. Quite politicly, Alexander asked Thebes's neighbors to decide its fate; they voted for its destruction. After taking the city, Alexander permitted the city-states to pillage it, which they did with great brutality. Thebes was destroyed, all its lands were given to its neighbors, and 30,000 Theban men, women, and children were sold into slavery.

Yet another natural trait that obscures reality is a preference for the familiar. A deer or fox prefers a familiar territory; we prefer familiar thoughts and views. We are exceedingly reluctant to "accompany the intellect on its narrow and tortuous path of philosophical inquiry and logical deduction," said Clausewitz, because by doing so we will arrive "in unfamiliar surroundings where all the usual landmarks seem to have disappeared." Not surprisingly has a preference for the familiar been one of the teachings of evolution: we know the dangers of, and the escapes offered by, a particular place. But "territorial thinking" is fundamentally unlike physical territoriality and should be resisted: not to think, simply to the play the same thoughts over and over, can be quite as dangerous as straying from one's home. Our traits evolved under conditions wildly dissimilar from those pertaining today; some of those traits — such as clinging to the familiar — are now *highly* maladaptive. One reason we recoil from thought is that it requires courage — indeed, quite as much as does fighting. Be intrepid; think.

Few things warp perception quite so much as persisting in a certain view simply because we have always held it. Much of Roman society thought the young Caesar effeminate; some *optimates* persisted in thinking him so even after he had conquered Gaul, simply because they had once thought it. "Speak what you think now in hard words," said Emerson, "and tomorrow speak what tomorrow thinks in hard words again, though it contradict everything you said today." You should be as unfeeling toward your thoughts as toward your opponent; flay each thought with thinking. (It is as difficult to criticize our thoughts as it is to criticize ourselves. "If my mind is of high quality," we think, "its thoughts must be valid." But our thoughts are more chaff than wheat, and the truth is far dearer than self-love.) Play with a thought; have fun with it; recognize that it is fleeting and protean. Love, not individual thoughts, but the process of thinking. If you come to see that a certain thought, a certain approximation of reality, is false, discard it; do not let your conception of the world keep you from seeing the world. If you see something today you did not see yesterday, or think silly today something you thought wise yesterday, do not be cross with yourself, but rather be pleased that you have refined your thinking.

Of a piece with versatility in thinking, is acknowledging your mistakes. When in 56 BC Caesar proposed to Pompey that Pompey receive the governorship of Spain for Caesar's of Gaul, Pompey readily agreed, so certain was he that Caesar could never become his rival in power. This is perhaps why Pompey was so slow to act on the eve of the civil war: "What harmed Pompey most," surmised Montesquieu, "was the shame he felt on reflecting that he had lacked foresight when he helped Caesar to power. He...failed to go on to the defensive because he did not want to have to admit that he had put himself in danger." By refusing to admit his mistake, Pompey made it far worse. Caesar, to the contrary, "knew well that a great commander is never so great as when he recognizes his own failure and prepares calmly to retrieve it." (Fowler)

∾

In Greek literature, Dionysus represents the life force, the "force that through the green fuse drives the flower;" his *thyrsus* blesses with honey those who see, but kills those who do not. Just so with reality: it will reward those who see it and destroy those who do not. "The traditional [Roman] order had been grounded in reality and always derived its efficacy from the sense of reality possessed by its supporters." (Meier) That of the late republic did not see reality and, in not seeing it, destroyed itself. *Only by first seeing reality can you influence it as you would wish.* Meier observes that Caesar's risk-taking was "nourished by the experience of how little resistance reality often offered if one took a firm grip on the facts of a situation." Richelieu had a certain enemy, Berulle. As a young man, Berulle was so little of this world that he could not distinguish one coin from another and had the administration of his estates taken from him by his mother. Berulle's great dream was to unite the Christian world; he achieved nothing. Richelieu, to the contrary, achieved great things by "working within the bounds of an actuality that seemed narrow and trivial in the world's eyes." (Burckhardt) Like a portraitist, you must observe carefully if you are to represent a thing well; the portraitist who does not observe well, does not depict well. A scientist is a discerner of reality; be like a scientist: love reality, and learn how to ferret it out. (If reality could speak, what would it say?) To be moral, to do what is best for the group, you must see reality, the context, as it is.

All scientific thinking is in truth this: seeing the fundamentals. To understand a thing — bread, a society, our species — you must understand its fundamentals, the substances of which it consists and the processes by which it was made. Only by discovering the constituent elements of matter could we understand it; just so with anything. Understand biology, and you shall understand life; understand life, and you shall understand us. The fundamentals constitute the context; this is where all understanding begins. Caesar begins his *Gallic War* with a description of the context, of the geography, politics, and social conditions of Gaul. Your touchstones should be, not the creations of the human mind — religion, ideology, fantasy — but biology, natural selection, and the natural sciences. Caesar, said Mommsen, "stood aloof from all ideology and everything fanciful." *You must understand how things work.*

৩৩

Thinking well requires time. It has been said that a different point of view is worth 80 IQ points; so, too, is considering a thing over time. Intelligence is thus partly a function of time: we are far more intelligent over the long term than the short; that which we do not see today, we may very well see tomorrow. A concept is like a creature: it evolves from more to less primitive over time; to think briefly is to think badly. Consider a complex matter; put it aside without having understood it. Now consider other, ancillary matters. Go deep here, go deep there, all round the initial matter. As you come to understand the related matters, you will understand the initial matter, just as, to dislodge a large stone, you must first dislodge the smaller stones round it. Once presented with a topic by the conscious mind, the unconscious mind continues to mull it over after the conscious has occupied itself with other things; the contribution of the unconscious mind is often far greater than that of the conscious. (In truth, what the mind is doing is this: forming new neural pathways.) What we struggle to understand today, becomes as nothing, a simple matter, over the long term.

Nothing is as critical to thinking, to seeing, as is questioning. Indeed, seek far more to formulate questions than to arrive at answers; answers will come with time and thought, once the questions have been posed. Hold a Socratic dialogue with yourself, with one interlocutor questioning the other. (This method is so efficacious because it flatters our self-love: if either our questions or answers are good, we are pleased with ourselves.) One of the better questions is a quite simple one: *why*; when presented with a fact, ask *why*. Pompey sailed from Brindisi to Greece; *why*? Combine asking *why* with a consideration of alternatives: not simply, why did he do such-and-such, but also, why did he *not* do such-and-such? Why did Pompey *not* sail to Spain? (He had, after all, seven tried legions in Spain, and none in Greece.) And why did Caesar not pursue him? To understand an act, you must consider what else the person might have done. And once you have arrived at an answer, ask: is this the only possible answer? An answer is like a swordsman's thrust: it is quite as possible to thrust at other points as at this one.

Do not think in *idees recues*: "Democracy is good." "Monarchy is bad." Study the nature of the *particular* society and monarch; in certain contexts, where a society is ignorant or corrupt or both, and the monarch wise and strong, monarchy is far better than democracy. (And *which* democracy do you think best? There are as many forms of democratic government as there are democratic states.) The best government is that which best suits a particular society. If Caesar's life has taught us anything, it is that our fidelity should be, not to forms, but to what is most functional. Caesar did not care a fig how long the Roman republic had existed; he cared only that it no longer fit the context, that a new structure was needed. A leading *optimate*, Cato, insisted that Metellus Scipio command the republican forces in north Africa, even though Cato was the better commander, simply because Scipio had once been consul, and Cato only praetor. There is a far higher authority than forms: it is what is best now, what most functional; it is abstract, it lacks legitimacy — but it is nonetheless higher. Adaptability is a far greater virtue than venerating what is. Do adhere to principle, but to that which is higher: adaptation to the context.

Draw distinctions. You will never understand a thing if you judge it by standards appropriate to another; take each thing on its own terms. Go about with a single or a few models for things, and the world will confound you. Ever since Aristotle deemed Sophocles's plays the ideal, critics have viewed those of Euripides (which are quite different from Sophocles's) as "broken" and "botched." But Euripides's plays are works of the purest genius; of his *Bacchae* Arrowsmith writes, "[T]he reader who is not willing to follow where the play, rather than his prejudice, leads him forfeits his quarry." Impose criteria fitting to one thing upon another, and you shall never understand the other. How Caesar bound a Gallic tribe to Rome depended on the tribe itself; while he installed kings in some, he strengthened the aristocracy against the monarch in others. Do not think in categories; always remember the great variation in our world and species, the infinity of modes.

Be chary of terms: there may be wild variation within any group of people or objects designated by a single term. We speak of the *optimates* — but within the *optimates* were some open to suasion and some not, some willing to compromise and some not, some concerned about society as a whole and some not. We speak of the *equites* — but in the civil war, some of the *equites* fought on the side of Pompey, some on that of Caesar, and most not at all; and within the *equites* were the publicans, who received (and were greatly enriched by) the public contracts, and whose interests were often quite different from those of the other *equites*. We speak of the Pompeians — but the Pompeians were a factious group of *optimates*, *equites*, the urban and rustic poor, Gauls and Germans, Orientals and North Africans. We speak of the Caesarians — but perhaps half of Caesar's assassins were Caesarians. We speak of the Roman infantry and cavalry — but both also consisted of non-Romans, of Gauls, Germans, Spaniards, Numidians, and so on. The Oxford historian P.A. Brunt observes that when historians speak of Greek and Roman conceptions of liberty, they in truth mean the conceptions held by the *Athenians* and the Roman *aristocracy*. The conceptions held by other towns and classes — and indeed even *within* Athens and *among* the Roman aristocrats — were almost certainly different. Within every group of people or objects to which we refer by a single term, are infinite differences; while the term is unitary, the group is not. Everything admits of degrees.

(Indeed, since we are apt to present ourselves — and the organizations with which we are affiliated — "in two aspects, the actions in one fashion and the speeches in another," you would do well to ignore the term and go by the thing itself. The *optimates* were hardly so…)

A simple, elegant relationship exists between thinking and chance: the better you think, the less you leave to chance. And nothing, said Clausewitz, so lessens our self-confidence as that which we do not anticipate. On Sabinus's reaction to the Eburones' surprise attack, Caesar writes, "Because he had anticipated nothing of the kind, it was only then that Sabinus finally showed some anxiety, and ran about arranging his cohorts. Even this he did fearfully, and as if all presence of mind were seen to fail him. This generally tends to happen to men who are obliged to make decisions in the midst of action." This is why Pompey lost his head at Pharsalus: that which he had anticipated — that his cavalry would put the Caesarians to rout — did not come to pass. As you think, continually ask yourself, *What is it I do not see?* Our view of reality is in truth a highly simplistic simulation; true reality is far more complex than we shall ever know. How much each of us sees varies with intelligence; the world is as simple or complex as the mind that considers it. As with all other species, our ability to perceive, to reason, and to judge is limited and imperfect; our measurements are always a bit off. All is approximation; all that can be hoped for is good approximation. We only ever see a bit of reality; always remember that you are not omniscient.

To lessen chance, you must anticipate, must simulate what is likely to happen. Meier observes that Caesar was "able to foresee the host of possibilities inherent in any situation and to arm himself against them… It was one of his maxims that not the slightest scope should be allowed to chance." (And you must be mindful of *all* your rivals, not simply the one you are now fighting. "Even when Caesar was dealing with single tribes," writes Meier, "he had to secure his operations on all sides and keep an eye on large parts of Gaul.") "Military science," said Napoleon, "consists in carefully weighing all possible eventualities, and then, almost mathematically, eliminating chance. It is here that no error must be made, for a decimal more or less may change everything." Months before a campaign, Napoleon would devise a master plan based on the forces and propensities of his opponent and the "worst conceivable situation;" he would then devise alternative plans (which he would continue to do well into the campaign). (Indeed, much of thinking is simply this: a consideration of alternatives.) In 1807, Napoleon wrote his Chief of Staff, Berthier:

> What will the enemy do, once our army is cantoned around Ratisbon? Will he move on Cham? We shall be able to assemble all our strength against him, so as to hold him fast in the positions which we shall have reconnoitered on the Regen. Will he move on Nuremberg? He will in that case be cut off from Bohemia. Will he move on Bamberg? He will be cut off there, too. Will he resolve to march towards Dresden? In this case we shall enter Bohemia and pursue him into Germany. Will he operate against the Tyrol and at the same time break out from Bohemia? In this case he will undoubtedly reach Innsbruck; but the ten or twelve regiments which he would have in Innsbruck could not take up a position near the issues from Bohemia, and these troops would only learn the defeat of their army in Bohemia by our appearance at Salzburg. Finally, if it should appear as if the enemy intended to take our extreme right or left wing as the goal of his operations, we shall have to choose the central line by a retreat to the Lech, while holding Augsburg occupied, so as to be certain of being able to make use of this town at any moment.

Napoleon's secretary, Louis-Antoine Fauvelet de Bourienne, tells us that, early in the Italian campaign of 1800, the First Consul lay on the floor, pushing pins into maps, and said, "I shall fight him here — on the plain of the Scrivia." Napoleon considered all that the Austrian Melas might do, and eliminated each in turn. On June 14, Napoleon met Melas on the field of Marengo, which lies by the river Scrivia.

You must adapt your strategies and tactics to the context. The Parthians attacked Crassus and his five legions in the desert; the horse-mounted archers of the Parthians suited the desert perfectly, the Roman infantry, which could neither construct fortifications nor strike at their opponents, not at all. Simply because of context, the Parthians were able to annihilate legions that were elsewhere invincible. Crassus had but one mode of fighting, whatever the context. Contrast Crassus with Caesar, who recognized that strategies and tactics appropriate elsewhere were not so in the desert.

The author of *The African War* writes: "Caesar trained his men not like the commander-in-chief of a triumphant veteran army with great achievements to its credit, but like a manager of gladiators training raw recruits... He told them how many feet to retreat from the enemy, in what way and in how small a space to turn and resist their opponents, how to alternate running forward with drawing back and threatening to charge, and almost where and how to throw their weapons." Caesar would march his men out of camp with no other purpose than to practice warding off the attacks of the Pompeians; he also brought elephants over from Italy so that the soldiers might learn where best to strike them. Teaching his men so, Caesar not only made them far better fighters, but also greatly increased their confidence.

While fighting, you must continually alter your strategies and tactics to fit alterations in the context; you must always conceive afresh. Said Napoleon: "A great general must say several times a day to himself, 'What should I do if the enemy appeared in my front, or on my right or left flank?' If he finds it difficult to answer such questions, he is not in a good position, or all is not as it should be, and he must alter it." On learning that on march each Roman legion was followed by its baggage, the Nervii resolved on attacking the legions one by one as they came up. Once the Nervii saw that Caesar had altered the legions' order of march so that the baggage followed the first six legions, they should have altered their tactics; rather than fighting one legion, they found themselves fighting first six and then, as the two guarding the baggage arrived, eight. When the far more numerous Pompeian cavalry, archers, and infantry attacked Caesar on a plain in North Africa, he ordered his men in succession to: form a single line of battle with the cavalry on their flanks; remain in line rather than pursue the fleeing cavalry and Numidian infantry (so as not to disarrange the line); lengthen their line and face each cohort back-to-back (on being encircled by the Pompeians); attack isolated groups of Pompeians; retreat slowly toward their camp; wheel about (on the arrival of Pompeian reinforcements) and drive the Pompeians beyond the furthest hills. Whatever occurred, whatever change took place in the context, Caesar adapted. A Microsoft programmer said of Gates: "If he really believed in something, he would have this intense zeal and support it and push it through the organization and talk it up, and whenever he met with people talk about how great it was. But if that particular thing was no longer great, he'd walk away from it and it was forgotten."

Understand the Thinker

Perhaps nothing is so critical as understanding the self, because this is where an understanding of reality begins. "In order to judge of the inside of others," said Chesterfield, "study your own... Observe with the utmost attention, all the operations of your own mind, the nature of your passions, and the various motives that determine your will; and you may in a great degree, know all mankind." Understand yourself, and you shall understand the world; misunderstand yourself, and you shall always misjudge "the inside of others." You are a creature like other creatures and can be studied just as other creatures are studied; analyze yourself as dispassionately, objectively, and coolly as you would another. If you succeed at understanding yourself, understanding your opponent will be as nothing, a very simple thing.

One of the great peculiarities in life is that we do not, simply by being ourselves, understand ourselves. "Understanding oneself," said Cervantes, "is the most difficult task conceivable." Three things determine our mode: genes, childhood, and later growth. The will is both formed by and influences these three; all are then affected by context. Each of us has two selves, a genetic self and a childhood self; which predominates is largely determined by context.

Human childhood is far longer than the childhood of any other primate. At one year of age, the brain of the human child is only half or so as large as the adult brain; by that age, the brain of the other primates is four-fifths or so the size of the adult brain. By retaining its plasticity over a far longer period, the human brain is able to shape itself to its environment (which is why human beings are able to learn, for instance, complex languages and social arrangements). Childhood experience greatly affects the size of the elements of the brain; the shape and production of its neurons; its molecular organization; its microstructure; its wiring and circuitry; its blood flow; the production and release of its neurotransmitters; its electrical activity; and, which hemisphere is apt to be used. *The sculpting done in childhood remains throughout life.* To understand your childhood is to understand the formation of your brain, to understand how your brain is apt to react and respond to particular stimuli, how you are apt to think and feel in particular situations. Study not only your childhood, but also your siblings, your parents, your parents' parents, and so on; study the environments, that is, of those who formed *your* environment. To study your family is to study yourself.

Such is our selfishness that we are rarely conscious of the gulf between our ideals and our operative values, that is, how we actually live. *We must feel that we are good*, and so we are apt simply not to see whatever bad we do. "The slaughter-houses and indecencies without end on which our life is founded are huddled out of sight and never mentioned," said William James, "so that the world we recognize officially…is a poetic fiction far handsomer and cleaner and better than the world that really is." You must be conscious of what you do and why you do it; not to see what you do, or not to understand your motives, is to obscure reality. "A man always has two reasons for doing what he does," said J. Pierpont Morgan: "a good reason, and the real reason." To confound your pretext and your motive is to deceive yourself, which is to say, is to muddle your understanding of yourself. Just as "by their fruits you shall know them," so, too, by *your* fruits shall you know yourself. And just as you would do well to view others as primates, so, too, would you do well to view yourself as such.

The variation in intelligence within each individual is quite as great as that within our species. *All intelligence is of a kind.* Our intellect is as uneven as the seabed; each of us is here shallow, there deep — perhaps shallow in mathematics, perhaps deep in understanding of humanity. And the higher the intelligence, the greater the variability. Of Caesar's officer Labienus Mommsen said, "To all appearance Labienus was one of those persons who combine with military efficiency utter incapacity as statesmen, and who in consequence, if they unhappily choose or are compelled to take part in politics, are exposed to those strange paroxysms of giddiness, of which the history of Napoleon's marshals supplies so many tragi-comic examples." Though Richelieu was the most systematic and precise of thinkers, his *Le Testament politique* has an "unsystematic and fortuitous organization."

At a certain soiree, the duc d'Enghien remarked that a man who speaks poetically of his love does not truly love. His remark excited much comment in society. Intrigued, Richelieu invited all those who had been at the soiree to his chateau at Rueil; he had the chairs arranged in a circle, asked the Princesse Palatine to act as president, and conducted the meeting with great dignity. The duc d'Enghien repeated his view, his sister dissented, and then all the others expressed their views. Following the "debate," Richelieu took a vote; he was delighted to find that the majority agreed with the duc d'Enghien, his own view. Of this proceeding the Princesse Palatine wrote: "The sublime genius which could balance the destinies of empires, which could cast an eagle eye over all of Europe, which could make such bold decisions and follow them up with such persistence, deserted Richelieu the moment it came to private discussion. Then he showed himself pedantic and formalistic." In such matters, Richelieu was simply silly.

You must take your own measure, must learn what you are good at and what bad. *You must understand your mode, your genetic and life attributes.* To be ignorant of, or to ignore, your distinctive limits is to be hubristic, and to be hubristic is to court destruction. You must not let your wishing to be good at a certain thing — almost always something society values — delude you into thinking you *are* good at it. Socrates pointed out to Alcibiades that he was no better at governing than he was at flying, but that while he did not try to fly because he knew he could not, he did try to govern because he did not know he could not. (The degree to which you can *grow* into that which you wish to be, acquire a trait you wish to have, is limited; like all else in life, growth has its limits.) Do not be vainglorious; heed the great Arab philosopher al-Ghazali: "Beware of making yourself the ultimate perfection." You must be certain of yourself, if you are to fight well.

Caesar could do away with the Roman republic and establish a monarchy; *Pompey* could not — but Pompey could not see this. Once when Napoleon withheld the Imperial Guard from a certain battle, some of its soldiers muttered, "Forward!" "What is that?", cried Napoleon. "Only a beardless youth would presume to judge in advance what I should do. Let him wait until he has commanded in thirty pitched battles before he dares to give me advice!" In October 1806, the young officers of the Prussian Noble Guard marched in front of the French Embassy in Berlin, shouting that they would crush Napoleon. Three weeks later, Napoleon marched the officers down the very same street, as prisoners; that they were far less gifted than Napoleon in the military arts, only now did they see. Of the ex-revolutionaries whom he appointed to his government Napoleon said, "There were good workmen among them; the trouble was that they all wanted to be architects." Just so.

In *The Red and the Black*, Julien Sorel tells himself once each hour for many years that Napoleon, "an obscure and penniless lieutenant, had made himself master of the world by his sword." This is quite true; *Napoleon* had done this. But to suppose that *he*, Julien, might rise in the same fashion is perhaps to commit a fatal mistake. The military art was Napoleon's peculiar gift. Julien is not Napoleon; he is Julien, and he must find *his* means of rising.

Let us consider another fictional character. So many young men in Russia in the 1800s fancied themselves Napoleons that Dostoevsky created such a young man in *Crime and Punishment*. Here, our putative Napoleon is the student Raskolnikov. He, like Napoleon, will live by his own code and decide who will live and who die; he will be beyond good and evil. Raskolnikov concludes that the money a certain old shrew has gotten through usury could be put to much better use. With very little planning — quite unlike Napoleon — he enters the harridan's home, kills her, and begins to rifle through her drawers. As he does so, her saintly younger sister enters; she gapes in horror at her sister's body and at Raskolnikov, whom she knows. Raskolnikov has no choice: he must kill her, too. Someone comes to the door; Raskolnikov is almost caught. He is just able to escape, and he hides the valuables underneath a stone. Raskolnikov then begins, much against his will, to feel remorse for what he has done. Napoleon would never have felt such a thing, but then Raskolnikov is not Napoleon: he is Raskolnikov. Bit by bit, his conscience begins to torment him; he cannot bring himself to touch the valuables. A detective, suspecting Raskolnikov of the murders, begins to play upon his remorse. After a year or so of pure torment, Raskolnikov confesses.

"When I was young," said a certain Russian composer, "in my mind there was only me. As I grew older, I reluctantly conceded that there was me and Mozart. In middle age, there was Mozart and me. Now that I am elderly, I see there is only Mozart." To those who had conferred on him full command, the Roman soldier Saturninus said, "Comrades, you have lost a good captain to make a bad general." After being savaged by Napoleon for mistakes he had made in battle, one of Napoleon's generals remarked, "What the Emperor does not understand is that his generals are not Napoleons." In 1588, as the Spanish fleet was preparing to attack England, its admiral, Santa Cruz, died. King Philip II appointed Medina Sidonia his successor; at this, Sidonia wrote the King:

Since I have not the slightest experience of either seafaring or naval war it is impossible for me to take command of such an important enterprise. I know nothing of the disposition made by the Marques of Santa Cruz nor of the information he had regarding England. Consequently I feel that I am duty bound to submit a negative assessment of my suitability for this post. If I were to command the fleet without knowledge I would have to rely on the opinions of others, in which case I would be unable to distinguish between good and bad advice and would not know which of my advisers were misleading me. The Mayor of Castile is far better suited for this post than I. He is a man of extensive knowledge of military and nautical affairs...

As Burckhardt observes, Sidonia's reply "could not have been less Castilian in spirit" — which speaks even more highly of this garden that knew he was a garden. Caring only that Sidonia was of such high rank that no one would object to serving under him, and certain of God's favor, Philip ignored Sidonia's objections. Sidonia set sail; though he might easily have caught the English fleet in Plymouth harbor, he simply sailed by. The swift English ships caught and attacked the Spanish ships that night. Sidonia retreated to the harbor of Calais; English fire-ships sailed in among the Spanish vessels, setting fire to many. The Spanish fleet took to the open sea, where the next morning it met with a hurricane; many more Spanish ships were lost on the reefs. When Sidonia returned to Spain, he had no fleet to speak of. Spanish supremacy at sea was no more; that of England would now begin.

Our gifts may not be what they seem. What many have is not skill in doing a certain thing, but *understanding*. Of Clausewitz one of his fellow officers said, "On the battle-field he would have been quite out of place. He lacked the art of carrying the troops along with him... If one saw him among the troops, one noticed in him a certain want of ease, which disappeared as soon as he left them." For half a millennium, wise people have bowed down before Montaigne's essays; and yet, in his introduction, Montaigne humbly says that we may object to reading his work because he has achieved nothing great. And many of those who *do* cannot quite say how. Alexander wrote no military treatises; Napoleon's memoirs are a muddle. Great pianists are rarely great teachers, and great teachers rarely great pianists.

If you cannot do a certain task, it is far better, for both yourself and the group, to stand down. Napoleon continually promoted Andoche Junot because of his courage; Junot was, however, equally incompetent as commandant of Paris, ambassador to Lisbon, and military governor of Paris. He lost Portugal to Wellington; he made a hash of the Battle of Smolensk. A series of appointments to positions for which he was not qualified was too much for the poor man; he lost his mind and, as governor of the Illyrian Provinces, took to strolling about Venice wearing only his epaulettes and sword. He committed suicide in 1813. "Of all pitiful parts," said Mommsen, "there is none more pitiful than that of passing for more than one really is." Pitiful, and dangerous...

Our intelligence varies greatly from day to day. Just as a landscape is now light, now dark, now luxuriant, now denuded, over time, so, too, does the mind vary wildly. One day our mind is the Critic, the next the Thinker, the following the Poet, and the following, it must be said, the Simpleton. Our mind is by turns frivolous and deep.

We also vary greatly with context. In this, we are rather like our genes: "The effect of the gene," writes Dawkins, "depends on its environment, and this includes other genes. Sometimes a gene has one effect in the presence of a particular other gene, and a completely different effect in the presence of another set of companion genes." *Each of us is a gallimaufry.* In this context we are shy, in that voluble; in this courageous, in that fearful; in this determined, in that irresolute. As a teacher we teach, as an architect we design, as a soldier we kill; we are like the publishing house of which Montaigne speaks, publishing now Bibles, now pornography. *The Brothers Karamozov* is said to be autobiographical, and that Dostoevsky is not one, but all three of the wildly dissimilar brothers. Each of us thinks better in some contexts than in others; we may think far better while reading a book, for instance, than while speaking with others.

Following his abdication, Napoleon was taken to the south coast of France via Provence, where royalist sentiment was strong. At Avignon, a crowd stopped his carriage and almost lynched him; at Orgon, he saw himself hanged in effigy. Napoleon broke; he disguised himself in an Austrian uniform and refused to eat any food at the inns. An English representative remarked, "He certainly exhibited more timidity than one would have expected from a man of his calibre." To the Austrian Commissioner, Napoleon said, "As you know, my dear General, I showed myself at my very worst." Napoleon! who at Arcola had charged the Austrians across a bridge and been pitched into the river, who had retreated from Russia with such calmness, who at Bautzen had sat calmly as bullets and shells filled the air about him. When young, Napoleon had once been thrashed by a mob; what battles could not make him feel, a mob quite easily could.

Since understanding yourself is in your interests, and not understanding yourselves perhaps fatal, you should be exceedingly thankful to anyone who helps you to see yourself. But we are far more apt to hate — and to wish to hurt — whoever does so. Just as we are apt to think *morally* good that which is good for us, and morally bad that which is bad for us, so, too, are we apt to think those who flatter our conceits good and those who criticize us bad. But often quite the contrary is true. When asked by the Athenian *democracy* which punishment he himself would propose for his "crimes," Socrates replied with perfect sincerity, "Feed me at the House of Councilors for the rest of my life." That his teachings would further their interests, would they but listen, few Athenians could see.

Our natural inclination is to critique others rather than ourselves, to weigh and consider others' acts rather than our own. But it is far more adaptive to see our own faults than others'. Critique others only if by doing so you learn something that will better yourself or — by revealing how best to deal with them — further your interests. Whenever you find yourself critiquing another to no purpose, force yourself instead to think how you might improve yourself.

Quite as critical as thinking in fighting, is volition. "I place the will on a level with reason," said Richelieu. "A military leader must possess as much character as intellect," said Napoleon; "the base must equal the height."

Be Self-Controlled

Just as Richelieu and Napoleon recognized that France could fight well only once unified and well-organized, so, too, can you fight well only once fully in command of yourself. Of Oliver Cromwell John Milton said, "He first acquired the government of himself, and over himself acquired the most signal victories, so that on the first day he took the field against the external enemy, he was a veteran in arms, consummately practised in the toils and exigencies of war." "Caesar had immense inner resources," writes Meier, "and the strength and skill to organize them." A survival machine only in poor control of itself, does not serve its genes well.

Why must we control ourselves? Our brain is "a patchwork of make-shifts," a hodgepodge of fish, amphibian, reptile, primitive mammal, and hominid brains, adapted to wildly different environments over millions upon millions of years. "We are complicated machines," said Chesterfield; "and though we have one main spring that gives motion to the whole, we have an infinity of little wheels, which, in their turns, retard, precipitate, and sometimes stop that motion." You must control the "infinity of little wheels" within yourself. The brain is a factious, unruly populace; what Gibbon said of society — "Without government is anarchy" — is quite as true of ourselves. Each of us is a dystopia; each of us has dysfunctional, maladaptive traits to which we give the name weaknesses. We cannot hope to be rid of them; we can only hope to control them. "When [Richelieu] was tired," Burckhardt tells us, "it sometimes happened that...he seemed to act against his essential nature, with its almost painful clarity, elevation, freedom, and genuine humanity; but...occasionally there appeared for a moment, only to be burned up again in the pure fire of his genius, something low in his bearing, composed of uncertainty and anger...[in his portrait] one can remark a touch of weakness, even of malice, about the mouth...but these traits never predominate; the minor qualities remain subordinate, fully mastered by the higher ones." Richelieu was emotionally unstable, subject to mood swings and depression, and wracked by migraines, lesions, and hemorrhoids; that he could do all that he did with such afflictions, shows great self-control. Recognize the corruptions within yourself, and control them; resist dissolution.

You must follow your interests rather than your feelings. When Talleyrand was once said to be "at heart" with a certain cause, the rejoinder was: "It's too funny to hear you talking about his heart. If you were to say his head, I should probably agree with you." Following the dictates of the reptilian and amphibian brains, of emotion and instinct, is ruinous to your interests. Understand the promptings of these earlier brains, suppress them, and then *think*. Go not with your inclinations, but with your reason. "So various and inconsistent is human nature," said Chesterfield, "so strong and so changeable are our passions, so fluctuating are our wills, and so much are our minds influenced by the accidents of our bodies, that every man is more the man of the day, than a regular and consequential character." Do not be influenced by the accidents of your body; be "a regular and consequential character." Caesar would doubtless have liked to put many of his enemies to the sword once they fell into his hands; but, preferring his object to his feelings, and knowing that clemency might bring him closer to victory, he did not. Avoid the "poetico-sensual ebullitions" Mommsen sees in Alexander (in, for instance, his burning Persepolis). You should be a force in pursuit of an object, not an emotional being vacillating this way and that. You should be like Caesar.

No matter how much is riding on a fight, or how tempestuous or hopeless the situation, *you must remain calm*. Panic is ruinous to reason and resolve (as it is to learning, which the stress hormone corticosteroid suppresses). Only once was Alexander ever recorded to have sacrificed to the God of Fear: before his last battle with the Persian King Darius, whose army was six times the size of his own. *Alexander* was not afraid: he knew how greatly fear would weaken his soldier's resolve. While natural selection laid down the general policies by which we live, it left day-to-day decision making to the neocortex; in a crisis, however, natural selection has the more primitive regions of the brain take over. What was sensible and in our interests in the earlier environments in which these regions evolved, may very well doom us in this. Remaining calm requires courage, is of a piece with do or die. "Few people realize," said Napoleon, "the strength of mind required to conduct, with a full realization of its consequences, one of these great battles on which depends the fate of an army, a nation, the possession of a throne." Knowing you have planned, and thus thought, well will help you to remain calm. So, too, will practicing being calm; it is far easier to remain cool and collected during a fight if you are practiced at being so in everyday life.

In the most desperate situations, when all seemed lost, Caesar would be perfectly serene, even cheerful. Richelieu would sometimes panic, but would always wait until quite in possession of himself to make decisions.

At one point during the battle of Eylau, Russian cavalry attacked the hill on which Napoleon stood. Though all those round him panicked, and though he himself was almost "trodden under foot," Napoleon remained perfectly calm, exclaiming simply, "What boldness! What boldness!" At Aspern and Essling, after his attack on the Austrians had failed, Napoleon was perfectly calm and composed as he withdrew his men to the island of Lobau.

You must, in short, follow your reason rather than your emotions. Emotions jounce us out of the plane in which we sit and help us to see that which we did not. But you must not let emotions muddle your thinking; you must apprise things coolly. "In politics, as in everything else," said Talleyrand, "one must not invest one's heart, or love too passionately; it causes confusion, clouds the mind, and is not always appreciated." Of Richelieu Auchincloss said, "In an age of violent emotion, he was always dispassionate. In a time of muddy thinking, he was always clear." (Passionately hating your opponent is in itself neither good nor bad; if it increases your resolve, it is good, if it muddles your thinking, bad.) Caesar criticized the Gauls as impulsive, fickle, and emotional and felt their being so weakened them greatly. "In the [Gallic] towns," he writes, "a crowd surrounds traders and forces them to declare every place they have come from and every matter they learned there. These facts and rumors often prompt them to take decisions on matters of great importance, which they are instantly made to think better of. For they are slaves to vacillating rumors, and most men give them answers made up to suit Gallic wishes." The Furies are the weakest of the Greek gods, because the least cerebral.

Be Self-Reliant

To be objective, you must be self-reliant; self-reliance contributes greatly to clarity of vision. The more you require of others, the less clearly you will think; the more you draw your sense of self-worth from others, the less good will your observation and analysis be. Only if you are self-reliant can you follow the scientific method; you cannot see clearly that which you need. Once while in Greece, Alexander visited the philosopher Diogenes, who so little valued the things of this world that he lived in a wooden tub.

They spoke for a while, and then the most powerful Western monarch of his day asked Diogenes if he might do anything for him. "Could you move a bit?", asked Diogenes. "You're blocking the sun." You should ask as little of others as Diogenes did of Alexander.

To be self-reliant is to recognize that life is selfish, and that that self-ishness sets you free. To be self-reliant is to recognize that life is a general instance of *sauve qui peut*, of each man for himself. To be self-reliant is to seek nothing from others but learning; to be free of others is to ask nothing of them. To be self-reliant is to accept that no one will take care of you. To be self-reliant is to be affected little or not at all by the context. To be self-reliant is to eschew others' heliotropisms. To be self-reliant is to recognize that your significance has nothing to do with the attention of others.

So highly does Christianity esteem self-reliance that it terms it "righteousness," the conviction that God is with us, thus freeing us from our fellows. "Self-existence is the attribute of the Supreme Cause," said Emerson, "and it constitutes the measure of good by the degree in which it enters into all lower forms." Always remember your mode; always remember that you are mortal. Think as though you will die tomorrow; this will help you to see yourself as distinct from others, to think your own thoughts. (This is why being in the wilderness is the best teacher of self-reliance: it is very much like death; in the wilderness, shorn of title and possessions, you have no one's esteem but your own.) Recede, emotionally and psychologically, from the world; let it touch you as little as possible. Hold yourself psychologically aloof; withdraw inwardly. Recede, recede…

We are not naturally self-reliant; natural selection crafted us so. In general, a mammal increases its chances of survival by doing as the other members of its group do; when one deer bolts, all bolt. And by crafting us to care what others think of us, to seek the esteem of our fellows, natural selection induces us to live within a group and contribute to its welfare. (So greatly does Sophocles's Ajax care what others think of him that he goes mad when they proclaim Achilles the greater warrior.) *Social life is a contrivance to enhance personal survival and reproductive success.* So we should view it. Survival machines think little about other survival machines; we rarely excite much feeling in our fellows. You *should* care what others think of you: *not* because your sense of self-worth requires it, but because what they think of you affects your interests.

All too often self-love is gratified at the expense of self-interest. "Most men," said Jean de La Bruyere, "…seek less to be instructed, and even to be amused, than to be praised and applauded." Seek to be instructed rather than applauded; doing so will serve your interests far better. Do not, for the sake of your *prestigio*, hurt your interests. Your object — which is consonant with your interests — *should always take precedence.* On the eve of the civil war, Pompey fell ill while in Naples; on recovering, he traveled to Rome. Wherever Pompey went, people held festivals of thanksgiving; there were feasts and sacrifices, escorts by torchlight, and flowers strewn upon him. All this quite turned Pompey's head; he was now certain of victory. But feasts and flowers had nothing to do with military reality.

Others were surprised that Richelieu should sit for hours with a young cleric in the service of the Nuncio of Turin. Whyever should *Richelieu* waste his time on someone with no title to speak of? Richelieu did not care a fig about the man's title; he cared only about the man himself. "The finest intellectual equipment that could be conceived," Richelieu later wrote of him, "a gifted mind, which can master with ease the nature of political affairs and the arts of negotiation." Had Richelieu's self-love required that he speak only with his peers, France would not have had his brilliant successor, Mazarin. Before the battle of Austerlitz, Napoleon questioned local peasants on the topography of the region. He did not care that they were paupers and he Emperor of France; he cared only that they had information he very much needed. And Caesar treated his soldiers as comrades…

Of self-dependency, self-trust, and self-sufficiency, we can have no better model than Caesar. Meier speaks of his "immense self-sufficiency," of an almost preternatural *soleness.* Caesar's recognition that he was vastly superior to others contributed to this self-sufficiency; who other than him should be his touchstone, if he himself was superior to all? Caesar's self-sufficiency took him to Gaul, and his life in Gaul increased his self-sufficiency; the longer he was away from Rome, the more alien its codes and principles seemed to him. And his self-sufficiency contributed to his ability to see fundamentals and question the inherited order. "Caesar's brilliance and superiority," writes Meier, "his serenity and charm, were closely linked with his detachment from the petty, stolid, ineffectual world of contemporary Rome, a detachment that he deliberately cultivated. His freedom and assurance, and the flowering of his talents, became possible only because he stood aloof from the Roman world, at first inwardly, then outwardly." Pompey wished to be *considered* the first man of Rome, Caesar *to be* the first man of Rome. Pompey fought Caesar in part to force him to recognize his primacy; Caesar did not care a fig whether Pompey (or anyone else) recognized *his*.

Time and again, Caesar's officers and men would beseech him to do this or that; he would consider their requests and then do what he thought best. When, following their unsuccessful siege of Gergovia, some of his officers counseled him to abandon Gaul, Caesar marched to join Labienus. When at Dyrrhachium the soldiers were ashamed of the cowardice that had led to their defeat, and begged Caesar to give the order to attack, he marched off to Apollonia. Many other such instances could be cited. Pompey, in contrast, would often do what others asked him to do, though he disagreed with them — and this in spite of his frequently saying that a doctor should never follow the advice of his patient. "Such weakness would have been disgraceful enough in a master of a ship," observes Plutarch; "it was much more so in the case of a general in supreme command of so many nations and so many armies."

To be self-reliant is to ignore that which does not touch your interests. Your purpose is to attain a certain object; ignore all else. Do not be touchy; ignore trifles. Do not be like the Roman consul of whom Mommsen speaks, who "avenged every pinprick with a dagger-blow." Indeed, do not avenge pinpricks at all; simply ignore them. You should be intellectually, rather than emotionally, sensitive. With any act taken against you, consider only the injury, and ignore the insult. (Ignoring is distinct from forgiving. To forgive is to resent a thing done to you and then pardon the doer, who in most instances could not care a fig whether you pardon him or not; to ignore is to take notice of neither the thing nor the doer. Forgiving takes far more time, and brings far more angst, than does ignoring.) Natural selection instilled in us the feeling that we must appear invulnerable. That is why we so dislike others' mistreating us: it signals our bestial self that they view us as powerless and that more, and worse, is to come. But only rarely does more come.

Few skills are as contributive to health, happiness, and efficacy as is that of ignoring. A thing that would be vexatious were we to take notice of it, is as nothing if we do not. *You must ignore much of what is said and done round you.* Richelieu hoped that by attaining great wealth and power he would keep others ever from being unkind to him; no one has ever had that much wealth and power. It will help you, in this, to remember that human beings are fitted to life in small kin groups rather than in gargantuan, atomistic societies; that most act on their "jarring passions, ...variable humours, ...[and a] greater or lesser degree of health and spirits;" that most simply do not know what they are doing. No one would choose to be unintelligent, foolish, weak, little, frivolous, incompetent, tactless, or emotional; no one would choose to hurt his own interests. *We might just as well quarrel with a stone for falling to the ground.* All that is simply disagreeable, treat as you would a dog's barking.

Of Caesar Suetonius writes, "When given the chance, he would always cheerfully come to terms with his bitterest enemies." He was not, Suetonius tells us, vindictive: "My researches show that not a single Pompeian was killed at Pharsalus, once the fighting had ended." Caesar "also preferred to discourage rather than punish any plots against his life, or any slanders on his name." The poet Catullus once vilified Caesar in a poem; Caesar was a sybarite, gambler, and glutton who slept with one of his officers: "Schooled in one bed, two lechers equally lustful, companions and rivals with the girls." Caesar complained to Catullus's father, who insisted his son apologize. Catullus did so; Caesar invited him to dinner that very day, and he continued to have the best of relations with the father. Mommsen observes that Caesar "was too much of a ruler to be sensitive." On becoming dictator, Sulla massacred his opponents; on becoming dictator, Caesar bettered the empire. Caesar was self-reliant, Sulla not.

Caesar, Richelieu, Napoleon, Talleyrand, and Gates fought only those who got in the way; all others they simply ignored. Caesar, writes Cassius Dio, "would pardon many of those, even, who had vexed him greatly, or pursue them only to a limited extent, because he believed they would do no further injury; whereas upon many others he took vengeance, even beyond what was fitting, with an eye to his own safety." Caesar disbanded the Pompeian legions in Spain with the words, "I will continue to ignore mistreatment by the *optimates*, but I must deprive them of the means to injure me." Richelieu ignored agnosticism, though he despised it, because it had nothing to say about his policies; Jansenism, however, he fought, because it opposed them.

To be self-reliant is *not* to be free of all need and constraint. You can never be so; that is not the human mode. You will always face necessity. To be self-reliant is *not* to be without others; to the contrary, a strong community, and particularly a strong family, can make you more self-reliant. (Indeed, most objects require that you form relationships with many others; you should, however, arrange these relationships so that they serve as a counterpoise to one another, so that you are psychologically free among them all.) It is also quite impossible to be wholly untouched by others' views of us; evolution fitted us so. But you must not let those views muddle your thinking, or only very briefly. Once while marching through a snowstorm in the Alps, French soldiers vilified Richelieu as his carriage passed by. "Do you hear the impudent devils?" he cried to their commander. "It must be stopped!" The soldiers' insults did not touch Richelieu's interests in the least; he should simply have ignored them. *But Richelieu let such things affect neither his thinking nor his actions.*

Focus

Not only was the world in which we evolved far simpler than that of today, but the tasks it required of us were also far more concrete; we were rarely required to think about one (abstract) task while ignoring multitudinous others. Thus focusing does not come naturally to us. You must not let yourself be distracted, though there is much to be distracted by; address each task as Plutarch said a certain Roman tribune did, "as if it were the only one." When the brain is required to do two complex tasks at once, it applies only half as many voxels, or units of brain tissue, to each as it would were it to do each task in turn. To multitask is to see only in halves. Focusing takes a certain degree of self-confidence, the certainty that you will be a match for the other matters once you take them up. It is also in proportion to resolve; the more the resolve, the more the focus on the object. Indeed, it is very much of a piece with do or die: the more thought you give to what might befall you, the less able you will be to focus on what you must do to prevail.

Meier observes that in Caesar's writing, "every sentence is trained on a target." He quotes Klingner: "Whatever does not pertain to the planning and action of the commander and the politician is excluded.... No half-distinct background elements obtrude. We see nothing but the matter Caesar has in hand at any given time." As Caesar wrote, so, too, did he think. That he could ignore the uprising in Gaul during the winter of 53/52 while seeking to salvage his position in Rome, shows the degree to which he could focus "on the matter at hand." Caesar could *simultaneously* dictate four important letters to his scribes, and perhaps seven unimportant ones, Napoleon (whose ability to focus rivaled that of Caesar) five memos to five secretaries. To Chaptal, his Minister of the Interior, the First Consul once dictated, without the use of notes, military dispositions consisting of 517 articles. "Different subjects and different affairs," said Napoleon, "are arranged in my head as in a cupboard. When I wish to interrupt one train of thought, I shut that drawer and open another. Do I wish to sleep? I simply close all the drawers and there I am — asleep." Once while imprisoned in the Chateau d'Antibes, his life in danger, Napoleon intently studied *The Campaigns of Marshall de Maillebois*.

It is a natural human inclination to think about ourselves; our mind is drawn to that which flatters our self-love — *not* to that which it is most critical we think about. Our interests are far better served, however, by our thinking about the context, that is, about others. We tend, for instance, to consider how *we* feel about a certain event; we would do far better to consider how others feel about it, because their reaction may very well affect us. Rather than study the Parthians, Germans, or others whose territory bordered the Roman Empire, the *optimates* concerned themselves solely with Italian affairs; but the objects and power of these other peoples were independent of events in Italy. Control what you think about, exercise a strict governance over your mind, and you will be far more adaptive.

So certain were the *optimates* of victory at Pharsalus that they spent the days before bickering over which of them would receive which office, which would despoil which Caesarian, and who should be proscribed. Three *optimates* quarreled fiercely over which of them would receive the supreme pontificate and abused one another in public. To Pompey, one *optimate* accused

Afranius of being a "traitor to his army;" another complained that Pompey was keeping them from the "figs of Tusculum." Some of the *optimates* took glee in designing the court that would try those who had fought either against the Pompeians or too little with them. Some rented houses in Rome suitable for a consul or praetor. Much of the final council of war was taken up with debating whether a certain *optimate* could be elected to a praetorship while in Parthia. "In short," comments Caesar, "all of them were concerned with either office, or monetary reward, or pursuit of their private enemies, and thought not about how they could achieve victory, but how they ought to use it." So focused were the Caesarians on their object that, rather than pillage the Pompeian camp following their victory, they pursued the Pompeian infantry and cavalry.

Learn

Learning is the foundation of thinking: you simply cannot think about that which you do not know. (In such situations, you think about what you *do* know, which may have very little to do with what is taking place.) Only by learning much can you think well. Because the world is a complex system, and because all intelligence is of a kind, you must have help in seeing the world clearly, in understanding it. The more you learn, the better you understand the world and its fundamentals; and the better that understanding, the better your adaptation. *Only through learning can you adapt to a world for which evolution did not fit you.* Take an instrumental view of yourself: value not your *self*, but your fitness as a survival machine, your ability to learn and to adapt. "Caesar was so observant, so versatile, so quick to learn," writes Meier, "that he constantly reviewed the course of events and made fundamental changes in his strategy and tactics... He seems to have raised Roman military technique, tactics, and strategy to a new plane." Early in his reign, Napoleon knew little of administration, finance, or legislation. To learn about these things, he would call meetings of the State Council, listen to the reports of his ministers, and question both the ministers and those who had worked on the reports. "From report to report," writes a historian, "he underwent such changes that his ministers failed to recognise him.

During the first report it still was possible to deceive him, during the second it was harder, during the third — dangerous." And, the more you learn, the better you will understand yourself, the better you will see your mode.

It is not our technology or our training that distinguishes us from barbarians, but our *learning*; a Visigoth with a modem is a Visigoth still. To be learned is elegant, ignorant inelegant; ignorance is brutish and bestial. Fowler observes that the Romans were in no way fitted to ruling an empire, so ignorant were they. Ignorance worsens the ESS. Of learning there are two kinds, general and specific; to fight well, you must acquire both. You should learn many things well, and one thing exceedingly well. By specializing, you will know what it is to know a thing exceedingly well; it will show you how much there is to be learned on any matter. But to know *only* one thing well is never to see the context; and if you do not understand the context, only by chance will you do anything of worth (and indeed are far more likely to do harm).

Learning helps you to be versatile, to be enterprising and resourceful, because it gives you so very much on which to draw. When flooding confined the Caesarians to a narrow strip of land between the Sege and Cinga rivers, Caesar and his men were saved by their familiarity with British boats, by their having learned how to construct such craft. The Roman soldier could fight, row, and build siegeworks, earthworks, fortifications, ships, and bridges. Learning also helps you to be creative. The fount of creativity is not the blank slate, but that on which much is written; learning, not ignorance, is the grist of creativity. That which is new comes from a synthesis of that which is known.

Nothing so impedes learning as does thinking we know. "Humility," said Thoreau, "like darkness reveals the heavenly lights." St. Augustine and Ibn Khaldun, two of the more learned members of our species, said when elderly, "I know nothing." "Human knowledge," said William James, "is a drop in the sea of knowledge." We have only to look round us to see that this is so. The highboy: why is it designed so? What is its provenance? What were its antecedents? The carpet: on which traditions does it draw? Whence its arabesques? The chair, why *that* curvature to its arms, the clock, *that* ornamentation, the chandelier, *those* pendants? The very objects among which we sit testify to our ignorance. Just so with everything. Nothing, said Socrates, is so critical as knowing what we do not know. When Plato's half-brother Glaucon proposed entering politics, Socrates asked him a series of questions. What were the sources of Athen's revenue? What were its income and expenditure? Its naval and military strength? The state of its garrisons? How dependent was the city on imports? Glaucon could answer none of these. Apply the Socratic method to yourself; show yourself that, whereas you thought you knew a certain thing, you do not. Eschew the infinitely pleasing, learning-killing *I know*.

By far the best medium for expressing thoughts and ideas — as well as for calling forth our own thoughts and ideas — is the book. The other media cannot hold a candle to the written word's ability to instruct; you will learn far more from a good book than, say, a good film. (Indeed, a book is deeper even than its author, as it is drawn from the mind over a very long time.) Genius is rare; but we are now blessed with 3,000 or so years of civilization, and thus quite a lot of geniuses, on which to draw. Not to do so is to forsake a treasure. The great thinkers saw more than we see; their analyses of human beings, of various characters and temperaments in assorted situations, are so very useful to us. "If I see further," said Sir Isaac Newton famously, "it is by standing on the shoulders of giants." Where would you rather be, when you fight: on the shoulders of giants, or the ground?

At the Royal School of Brienne, Napoleon poured over books on history and mathematics. He devised games based on the wars of antiquity; he once designed and built fortifications out of snow, from which he and his classmates sallied forth to inflict a defeat on the besieging upper classmen. At the Artillery Training School at Auxonne, Napoleon was, said one of his instructors, "a devourer of books," reading countless works on the military art: *The New Artillery in Practice, Reflexions on the Principles of Warfare, The Art of War, Reflexions on the Profession of War, Essay on Tactics, Frederick II's Instructions to his Generals, The Campaigns of Hannibal, The Warfare of Invasion, Systematic Warfare...* "Consequently," writes Chandler, "it was from books rather than from actual experience in the field that Napoleon initially drew his major military ideas." Napoleon took Guibert's writings and Bourcet's *Principes de la Guerre des Montagnes* with him to Italy. "It would not be far wrong to say," writes Markham, "that Napoleon's Italian campaigns were Guibert and Bourcet in action." While at Harvard, Gates read innumerable books on corporate law, finance, and programming. A Microsoft CFO once conceded that Gates knew more about finance than he did, a General Counsel, law, a programmer, programming.

A misconception as common as it is lamentable is that reading softens the reader; nothing could be further from the truth. "We are told," writes Gibbon, "that in the sack of Athens the Goths had collected all the libraries and were on the point of setting fire to this funeral pile of Grecian learning, had not one of their chiefs...dissuaded them...by the profound observation that as long as the Greeks were addicted to the study of books they would never apply themselves to the exercise of arms. The sagacious counsellor...reasoned like an ignorant barbarian. In the most polite and powerful nations, genius of every kind has displayed itself about the same period; and the age of science has generally been the age of military virtue and success." Caesar studied philosophy, rhetoric, and the arts; he could hardly be said to have been soft.

Reading can turn even the most arid periods of life to account. In the spring of 1618, Richelieu was exiled to Avignon. The King hated him; he was poor; his brother and brother-in-law were exiled with him; his sister-in-law died in childbirth, as did the child, far from Richelieu and his brother; he had little prospect of ever returning to power. Richelieu fell ill; certain he would soon die, he made out a will. And yet throughout the whole of this period, Richelieu read; of it Burckhardt observes, "His great political conceptions grew clearer during this time of solitude."

Reading inspires. At one point during the siege of La Rochelle, Richelieu lay in his tent, reading of Alexander's siege of Tyre in Quintus Curtius's *Life of Alexander the Great*. His own siege was going rather badly. It was the dead of winter; the French army was sitting in a bog round the city; the sea kept breaking through the dike Richelieu hoped would seal the city's harbor; the English were mounting a fleet to relieve the siege. The King had returned to Versailles and his hunting; the Queen, the Queen-Mother, and most of his court were beseeching him to lift the siege. Richelieu himself was wretchedly ill. And so Richelieu, febrile, trembling, lay on his bed, reading of Alexander's siege of Tyre... (Learning from others' lives is also a form of simulation, of trial and error. The consequences of Pompey's timidity, for instance, teach us why we must not be timid.) Whatever challenges or difficulties you face, they are as nothing compared to what Caesar faced at Alesia.

One of the better ways of learning how to think, is to study the methods of fine thinkers. An instance of this is Brunt's critique of a point by Syme. Syme argued that the *optimate* Cato's political influence stemmed from his aristocratic connections; to support his theory, Syme constructed a family tree showing that Cato was indeed related to many *optimate* ultras. Brunt offers two criticisms of Syme's theory: first, a family tree of *any* Roman aristocrat of the time would show such relationships and, second, if Cato's tree were enlarged only slightly, it would include Caesarians, those who had gone back and forth between the two parties, and neutrals. Furthermore, the more you learn, the better able you are to draw distinctions (simply because, the less you know, the more you suppose groups and objects to be simple and uniform). And reading gives you practice in considering things disinterestedly. In our own affairs, self-interest distorts our thinking, makes us intellectually dishonest; in reading about the affairs of others, we consider those affairs more honestly, because more disinterestedly.

You must be very careful in choosing your reading; your diversions should also instruct. Shallow writing takes us to our shallow points, deep writing to our deep points. "I confess," said Thoreau, "I do not make any very broad distinction between the illiterateness of my townsmen who cannot read at all, and the illiterateness of him who has learned to read only what is for children and feeble intellects." Thoreau draws the following distinction between news and gossip: "If we read of one man robbed, or murdered, or killed by accident, or one house burned, or one vessel wrecked, or one steamboat blown up, or one cow run over on the Western Railroad, or one mad dog killed, or one lot of grasshoppers in the winter — we never need read of another. One is enough. If you are acquainted with the principle, what do you care for a myriad instances and applications? To a philosopher all *news*, as it is called, is gossip." Of each book you consider reading ask, will it make me a better survival machine?

You must be self-reliant in your reading; *you* must decide what is wise and what foolish. You must not rely on certifications; what Arrowsmith said of textbooks — that they are "tidy morgues of leached opinion" — is true of much else that is "certified." "A goose is a goose still," said Thoreau, "dress it as you will." *You* must see that it is a goose, or that that which is not dressed up at all, is worthy of attention. (During the late Roman republic, the corrupt Senate always held its meetings in hallowed precincts, in the Senate House, the curia, or a temple.) In spite of all our science and all our technology, we still cannot measure wisdom or understanding. Gibbon was at Oxford only one year; Jane Austen left school at the age of nine; Darwin and Hume took no high degrees; Edith Wharton received no formal schooling — one could go on and on. And yet these *uncertified* human beings produced works of the greatest wisdom and understanding. *Their work certified their work*; no degree or title did so. (All were, however, supremely well educated; all learned from books, tutors, and life.) Judge by the statement itself, rather than by the speaker. The more you learn, the more you acquaint yourself with the best our species has ever produced, the better able you will be to distinguish wisdom from simulacrum.

You must think critically about what you read. "Many great readers load their memories," said Chesterfield, "without exercising their judgments; and make lumber-rooms of their heads, instead of furnishing them usefully; facts are heaped upon facts, without order or distinction." A work of genius is uneven; not everything in it is true. Here, too, you must distinguish. Foolishness may come from a genius, and wisdom from a fool; it is simply that you will find far more wisdom in a work by a genius than by a fool. The reason the wise are considered so, is that *most* of what they said is wise. If you think about and question what you read — and you *must* do so, since there is so much each writer does not see — learning will hone your thinking skills.

In your reading, do not range only along the dimension of space; range along that of time as well. Go in both dimensions. "Not to know the events that happened before one was born," said Cicero, "that is to remain always a child." Neither human biology nor the modes of human existence have changed one whit since the beginning of civilization; to read Aristotle's description of young men is to read of young men today. To study only the present is never to understand it; only a study of the past makes the present intelligible. And only by peering into the past can one peer into the future; think ahistorically, and you suppose that what is, *should* be, and that what is, will always be. Natural selection crafted us so; the study of history is perhaps the best way of ridding ourselves of this natural supposition. "Within a historical perspective," writes Meier, "every state of affairs is transitional..." As changeable was the past, will be the future.

We place far too much value on being *au courant*; natural selection made us so, both because a creature survives by being particularly attentive to the *now*, and because studying a period other than the present requires abstract thinking. Far too much is made of things simply because they occur now. Why study the conceptions of one of our politicians, simply because he lives today, when we can study those of a Caesar, Richelieu, or Talleyrand? Acquaint yourself with the greatest human beings who have ever lived, and you will be far less apt to celebrate those who live now. These figures give us a standard by which to judge; next to them our contemporaries seem quite small.

To study history is to see the great variation in our species and in contexts; it is also to become far less heliotropic about our species, to see its folly, perversity, and selfishness. The moral deny the turpitude of the immoral, the intelligent the stupidity of the unintelligent; both would be far less apt to do so, were they to study history. To study history is to see that human beings who care for neither the group nor the long-term come to power, what they are apt to do once there, and the consequences of their actions. (The more one studies history, the less susceptible one is to the heliotropism that one's leaders are moral and beneficent.) One of the great lessons of history is this: whenever a society ignores reality, whether because of heliotropisms, selfishness, or a clinging to the familiar, some force other than the society itself — other societies, the environment, economics — will force that society to realign itself with reality. A realignment caused by an outside force is far more violent and painful than is self-realignment. (God is that power societies hope will undo their botching of things.)

You must be able to see the connections among elements and events in disparate societies at different times. The *optimates* were not unique to Roman society; at every time and in every place are human beings who care nothing about either the group or the long term; who are hubristic, who fancy themselves exempt, that the ordinary rules and conditions of human existence do not apply to them; who think they are not "a piece of the continent, a part of the main;" who view others simply as "scum;" who think all within the world should be theirs, and nothing others'; who, no matter how much they have, want still more; who have the most paltry ambitions conceivable (to vie with others in the acquisition of luxuries rather than to relieve distress or better society); who arrogate to themselves even goodness (*optimate, boni,* Christian); who do not understand the context; who do what is in no one's long-term interests, even their own. There are many worlds: that of Alexander, that of Caesar, that of 17th-century France, that of the French revolution; the more worlds with which you are acquainted, the better you will understand your own. (But, as we shall see with Napoleon, you must be careful to see the distinctions between their context and your own.) And to acquaint yourself with these other worlds is to become more self-reliant, as you will learn conceptions and notions wholly different from those of the people round you.

Quite as critical as the study of history, is that of literature. Literature shows the world as it is, rather than "as it is said to be;" literature is truthful. In his plays, for instance, Euripides "preserves the disorder of actual experience, measuring its horror against the unrequited illusion of order which sustains human beings." (Arrowsmith) Literature confirms that what we see in the world — but which we doubt because no one speaks of it — is truly there. Literature is mithridatism, not to poison, but to reality; it accustoms us bit by bit to seeing the world as it is. Literature shames us, shows us the folly and littleness of our conceptions and acts, shows us the conceits that spring from self-love, shows us that we do indeed "present ourselves in two aspects, the actions in one fashion and the speeches in another."

Quite as essential to wisdom and understanding as books, is first-hand experience of the world. "The speculative, cloistered pedant in his solitary cell, forms systems of things as they should be, not as they are; and writes as decisively and absurdly upon war, politics, manners, and characters, as that pedant talked who was so kind as to instruct Hannibal in the art of war." (Chesterfield) Books help us understand the world, the world books. Know books, but not the world, and you shall understand very little; and if you know the world, but not books, you shall understand quite as little. Only very rarely does a human being attain high *sophia* without both, only very rarely come to see the fundamentals. Learning from both books and life makes us far less susceptible to heliotropisms, far less guileless and naïve. Learning and experience are toxic to ideology, to preferred and preconceived notions of the world; dip a pleasing notion in the solution of learning and experience, and it will dissolve. (Aurelius's hopeful view of human relations could not survive incessant warfare.) It is by viewing the world from different points of view that we come to understand it: from that of the natural sciences; from that of anthropology; from that of genetics; from that of the ancient Greeks; from that of literature; from that of history; from that of economics and commerce; from that of *diverse* experience...

In conversation, we should do as Socrates did: rather than seek to overthrow our interlocutor, we should "try to engage him in a common search for the truth." (Forde) One of our more amusing traits is this: while we are quite willing to sit quietly for hours reading a wise book, we are generally quite *unwilling* to sit quietly even for a few minutes listening to a wise person (save when he is lecturing). And while we do not begrudge a writer his far greater understanding and knowledge — that is, after all, why we read him — we very much begrudge these things in our interlocutor. While natural selection prompts us to assert ourselves with a person, it has nothing to say about books.

怔

The object of all learning is growth. To grow is to rise to a higher mode, to go from a lower to a higher quality, to extend the base and the height. Learning is distinct from growing; one can learn, and yet not grow. The ability to grow, to better one's habitual way of thinking, feeling, and being, is rare. Just as we prefer familiar thoughts and ideas, so, too, do we prefer the familiar in ourselves; but the more intelligent the creature, the more plastic it should be. Immutable instinct governs less intelligent creatures; more intelligent creatures should be ever-changing, protean. You should seek always to be in the ascendant. Perfection, said Chesterfield, "ought to be every body's object, though in some particulars unattainable; those who strive and labour the most, will come the nearest to it." The more you grow, the better a survival machine you will be.

FORMULATE AND PURSUE
A SENSIBLE OBJECT

One does not, of course, fight simply to fight; one must have something to gain, some object in view. The goal is not to fight, but to attain an object. Fighting is so costly, and entails such risks, that it must be worth the candle. "What!", cried Napoleon after a particularly bloody battle. "No results from such carnage? Not a gun? Not a prisoner?" The object itself is usually quite simple, attaining it far less so.

To be sensible, an object must enhance your long-term *interests. To formulate your object, you must see clearly where your interests lie. How well we do what is best for ourselves, how well we perceive our long-term interests, depends on the quality of our brain and how well we use it. (The greater the object, and the longer the term, the more difficult it is to determine whether it is in our interests. It interacts with so many other acts, and so much new is done. Was it in Caesar's long-term interests to conquer Gaul? Was it in Rome's? Was it in Gaul's, Europe's, or the world's?) Of Caesar Gelzer writes, "In constructing his policies he never laid a stone on which he could not build further: as a result, a retrospective view gives the impression that everything was actually planned in advance in full detail, as if by an architect." We see Caesar, for instance, even as a young man using Pompey to vitiate the inherited order. You must consider whether eliminating a certain rival will not benefit your other rivals, which it may well do if the rival you eliminate is also* their *rival. You must also be careful not to create new rivals as you fight.*

To be sensible, an object must fit the context; an ESS presupposes an understanding of the context. Just as no creature is generally adaptive, but rather to a particular environment, so, too, is each object adapted to a particular context. An object that fits the context is attainable; an object that does not, is not. (This is not a tautology, i.e., the object was attained, hence it fit the context; the object was not attained, hence it did not. If an object is attained, it fit the context. If it is not attained, it may or may not have fit the context; other things, such as a lack of intelligence or resolution, may have been the cause of its not being attained. And you must distinguish between an object's attainability *and its* desirability; *an object may fit the context, and thus be attainable, but not be in your long-term interest.) If your object does not fit the context, and thus you do not attain it, you show others that you can be defeated, that you are vulnerable. "Nothing attracts a serious duel as does an inconclusive one," declares Monsieur de Chateau-Renaud in* The Count of Monte Cristo. *Such signaling is most decidedly* not *in your interest.*

120

Once you have formulated a sensible object, one that enhances your long-term interests and fits the context, do not permit yourself to be turned aside. Your strategies and tactics may change; your object will not. Caesar marched away from Gergovia because his object was to put down the Gallic uprising, not to take the town; he could attain his object better elsewhere. "With its mass of vivid impressions and the doubts which characterize all information and opinion," said Clausewitz, "there is no activity like war to rob men of confidence in themselves and in others, and to divert them from their original course of action." You must not be diverted from your object. The feeling of do or die rests largely on there being an object you feel you must attain. Caesar, Richelieu, Napoleon, and Talleyrand risked their lives for the sake of their object; any might have been killed innumerable times. They cared only for their object, nothing for their self-love or comfort. At Pharsalus, the camp of the optimates *was filled with luxuries, while Caesar lived as his men did, eating bread made of roots: the* optimates *cared about preening their self-love, Caesar attaining his object. Following the battle of Austerlitz, Napoleon wrote Josephine, "I am a little weary. I have camped in the open for eight days and as many freezing nights."*

You should cease fighting the moment you attain your object. Fighting is taxing, others may attack you, and it may be in your interest to form an alliance with your erstwhile foe.

In the early 17th century, two Habsburg sovereigns related by marriage ruled over much of Europe. Philip IV, king of the Spanish branch of the Habsburg dynasty, governed the Iberian peninsula, Portugal and its colonies round Africa and the Indian Ocean, the Netherlands, Franche-Comte, Milan, Naples, Sicily and Sardinia, and part of the New World. The Holy Roman Emperor Ferdinand II, of the Austrian branch, governed Austria, Hungary, and (to a lesser extent) the German states. Philip IV and his Prime Minister, the Count-Duke Gaspar de Guzmán Olivares, wished to restore Catholicism to Germany and felt the preservation of Christendom, the Catholic religion, and the royal house demanded unity with Vienna. Ferdinand II wished to create religious unity in the German-speaking lands, to root out Protestantism, restore the Roman Catholic faith, and establish the rule of one sovereign house above all the others. Ferdinand felt, indeed, that all Christian sovereigns were his to rule, and he insisted that all Church lands, no matter how anciently expropriated, be restored. The Imperial armies, joined by those of the Catholic League, the German Catholic states, had conquered much of Germany, and Ferdinand was now on the verge of wresting control of the Baltic from Sweden, Denmark, and Holland.

Fighting the Spanish and Austrian Habsburgs and their Catholic Bavarian and Rhenish allies for control of central Europe were the Protestant states of Germany, Holland, Denmark, and England.

That successive French governments had vacillated between an alliance with and opposition to the Habsburgs mattered little: France was an inconsequential state, weak and divided. During the 16th century, the country had been torn by *eight* religious and civil wars. Law and order were still rare; the French national debt was elephantine, the country's financial system in disarray. France had no fighting fleet or merchant navy to speak of; other European countries and the Barbary states could block the French coastline, make landings, capture French commercial vessels and sell their crews into slavery, and aid opposition groups within France, as they pleased. Other states would sell France goods at whatever price they pleased, and pay whatever they pleased for French goods. France could neither aid its allies nor enrich itself through trade and the acquisition of colonies (as Spain, England, Venice, and other European states did). The English disdainfully referred to the French naval commanders as "fresh-water admirals." Indeed, so weak was France at sea that England refused it permission to sail under its own flag.

France was little else but a collection of factions, of self-seeking communities and classes. The country was a patchwork of regional dialects and cultures. Each region had fiscal and administrative autonomy; the country had, for instance, *four* admiralties, each acting independently of the other; many provinces had their own navies. Since every coast had its "High Officer of the Crown" who claimed maritime rights, it was quite impossible to move naval forces from one province to another. The regions to the north of the Loire followed customary law, to the south Roman law. French loyalties were feudal, regional, or religious rather than national; the country wholly lacked a sense of community, a sense of the common good.

Many within France were opposed to a strong monarchy, reasoning the weaker the king, the stronger themselves. Most opposed were the great nobles, *les grands*, and the Huguenots. *Les grands* were territorial princes who insisted on the feudal rights of sovereignty; they acted in virtual independence of the crown, fortifying their domains, levying imports, raising private armies, and carrying on private feuds. (These territorial sovereigns would rebel simply to induce the king to pay them *not* to do so.) *Les grands* viewed the King simply as first among equals and felt it their right to take part in his councils. In the south, a Huguenot Protestant minority held two hundred fortified towns in virtual independence of the crown. La Rochelle on the west coast was more their capital than was Paris, the province of Languedoc in the southeast all but its own country. Other states, particularly Spain and England, supported the Huguenots. The lower bourgeoisie and farmers also wished the royal government to be weak. All these groups took an internationalistic rather than nationalistic view; their affiliations were to their own classes and religious groups *throughout Europe* rather than within France. They denied the supremacy of the French King, investing other entities, such as the Church, with authority.

The French king, Louis XIII, was of the Bourbon family. On the assassination of his father, Henry IV, in 1610, the Queen-Mother, Marie de Medici, had become Regent over her son, who was then eight years old. The Queen-Mother was Habsburg through her mother, Archduchess Johanna of Austria, the daughter of the Holy Roman Emperor Ferdinand I. As Regent, the Queen-Mother — in contradistinction to the policy of her late husband — had sided with the upper and lower classes against the upper bourgeoisie, that is, with the internationalistic groups who favored a weak monarchy. Louis had married Anne of Austria, the daughter of the Habsburgs Philip III of Spain and Margaret of Austria, and the niece of the Austrian Emperor Maximilian II. Since the King and Queen were childless, the King's brother, Gaston d'Orleans, would become king were Louis to die. The Queen-Mother, Queen, and Gaston formed the core of the Catholic Party, or *devots*; the party favored alliances with the Habsburgs and supported its Counter-Reformation against the Protestants within and without France. Most of *les grands* were of the Catholic Party, since they often sought support from the Habsburgs in their opposition to the monarchy. Though most of what Henry IV and his great Finance Minister, the duc de Sully, had done to improve France's internal and external situation was undone by the Queen-Mother during her Regency, they at least showed what could be done through prudent policies.

Though France and its monarchy were both quite feeble, there were certain countervailing forces. France was the most fertile, densely populated, and homogeneous state of Europe. A feeling of nationalism was slowly suffusing the whole of the country; the French were beginning to view themselves as *French* rather than as Catholic or Protestant. While continuing to feel an ancient piety, the French were heartily sick of the religious wars; both townsfolk and countryfolk desired unity and security. The upper bourgeoisie, who were growing wealthy through trade, marrying into the old aristocracy, and acquiring high position in government, found the feudal social arrangements, which impeded their rise, odious. The upper bourgeoisie were quite nationalistic; they viewed themselves as French, and their affiliation was to the state. The upper bourgeoisie felt the King held sole supremacy, a supremacy invested by God; they wished him to be strong. Joining the upper bourgeoisie was the provincial nobility, which was growing poorer and weaker and viewed the King as its protector.

And the Habsburg imperium had certain weaknesses. Spain was itself factious and decentralized, was indeed even more feudal than France. Like France, the country had a colossal national debt. Between 1600 and 1630, the tonnage of Spanish shipping to the New World fell by 75 per cent, the number of sheep in Spain by 60 per cent, and the number of its textile manufacturers by 75 per cent. The Catholic states of Germany were rather uncertain allies; while some of the German Catholic princes did indeed view themselves as subjects of the House of Austria, others felt they were simply independent allies of that House. Even the Elector of Bavaria, Duke Maximilian I, the leader of the Catholic League, preferred that Germany remain divided, convinced as he was that Austria wished to subject his country to its rule and Spain the whole of Europe to *its*. Furthermore, the trade barriers erected by the religious schisms of the 16th century had greatly displeased the German states, as the barriers had been ruinous to their economies. To the Protestant states of Europe, the Habsburgs were synonymous with Roman Catholicism; they viewed the Counter-Reformation simply as a pretext for Spain and Austria to extend their political power. Protestant Europe — and, indeed, even much of *Catholic* Europe — disliked the cruel and intolerant Christianity of Spain. Not only because it was itself Protestant, but also because it vied with Spain for colonies, England supported Protestant Europe in its opposition to the Habsburgs. And the Pope, Urban VIII, was quite opposed to the extension of Spanish power in Italy.

∞

On April 29, 1624, Cardinal Armand-Jean du Plessis Richelieu joined the French Council of State. Richelieu would soon come to be the foremost advisor to Louis XIII. Richelieu had earlier, as advisor to the Queen-Mother, been closely involved in affairs of state but, to his great frustration, not directing them; now, the affairs were his to direct. Richelieu recognized that the organizing principle of France — that of religious and family cantons — no longer fit the context. He saw that Europe was slowly coalescing into national, autonomous states, and that the rise of the nation-state dictated that each state be strong. Richelieu recognized the criticality of unity, that a unified France could achieve so very much, a disunified France little; a particularist state such as France was weak and vulnerable. To Richelieu, the division of Europe was political rather than religious; Europe was not, to him, Catholic and Protestant, but rather France and the other states. Europe was not a *corpus christianum*, but a *corpus politicus*; religious affiliation was to be subordinate to political affiliation. His was the view of the upper bourgeoisie and the provincial nobility. Far more than others, Richelieu considered the Pope to the spiritual sovereign, but the French King to be the secular sovereign. The demarcation between the secular and the sacred, if muddy in early 17th-century Europe, was not at all so in Richelieu's mind. "The one thing on which everybody, friend or enemy of Richelieu, seemed to agree," writes Auchincloss, "was that he had a clear view."

Thus Richelieu's object: he would first unite France under a strong, absolute monarchy by breaking the power of the Huguenots and *les grands*, and then vitiate the Habsburg imperium. Richelieu's childhood in a France rent by civil war, plague, and famine made him value order above all else. He had seen ungoverned humanity and understood with Gibbon that "without government is anarchy." Richelieu knew the virtue of strictness; indeed, this is why he preferred Catholicism to Protestantism: Catholicism was paternalistic, Protestantism individualistic. Richelieu sought to make France what he conceived heaven as being, ordered and harmonious. (His own life was as ordered and harmonious as he could possibly make it.) "So long as the Huguenots in France are a State within a State," wrote Richelieu, "the King cannot be master within his realm, or achieve great things outside it." Richelieu would do away with all vestiges of feudalism, all remaining medieval privileges; he would centralize the administrative and financial control of the state. In Richelieu's view, France had it quite backwards, with strong internal fortifications, and weak external ones; he would rid the country of its internal fortifications while constructing fortifications on its borders.

Richelieu considered all non-Habsburg states to be France's natural allies; he would maintain good relations with all the Catholic states *save* those of the Habsburgs. (He would so in part to satisfy Louis and the *devots*, to show them that his was a political rather than religious war.) In Germany, Richelieu would aid the Protestant states in their opposition to Austria and separate the Catholic states from the Emperor and then neutralize them. He hoped to unite, on purely political grounds, the German Protestant and Catholic states in opposition to the Habsburgs. France must also create a strong navy and create or improve its harbors. It must also extend its borders to impregnable areas and there create assault bases from which French forces might defend neighboring countries against the Habsburgs.

The *devots* would staunchly oppose Richelieu's policies. Favoring an alliance with their co-religionists the Habsburgs, the Catholic party did not recognize, as Richelieu did, that to be the Habsburgs' ally was to be their satellite. Neither did the *devots* understand the changes taking place in Europe and thus the necessity of Richelieu's policies. "It is quite evident," observes Burckhardt, "that Richelieu was...no more than the energetic executor of centralizing tendencies that had been present long before he himself began to direct French national policy." "We have seldom an opportunity," said Gibbon, "of observing...what effect may be produced, or what obstacles may be surmounted, by the force of a single mind, when it is inflexibly applied to the pursuit of a single object." We have this opportunity with Richelieu.

∽

Much of Richelieu's first two years in office was taken up with centralizing power in Paris. He increased the power of the *intendants*, administrative and financial commissioners whom he sent to the provinces (and who reported directly to him). Since the *intendants* could suspend the sovereign jurisdiction of the provincial *parlements* and their courts, through them Richelieu could direct administrative and financial affairs in the provinces. He also transferred certain matters, such as the upkeep of the roads, from regional authorities to officers of the crown. Richelieu induced Louis to create the office of Controller-General of Navigation and Trade, of which he himself would be the first holder. Through the buying out of offices or *force majeur,* Richelieu did away with all the feudal rights of sovereignty over France's maritime affairs and centralized control over the French navy in his office. He ordered eighty warships, galleys, and galleons to be built or bought; he saw to the construction of arsenals and the recruitment and training of sailors and gunners. (So defective were the cannon and powder provided by the Controller-General of Artillery that Richelieu created his own commissariat to procure the two.) He created specialty posts in admiralty administration, shipping, colonial affairs, and maritime law. He ordered French coasts and harbors to be inspected frequently, and he set about creating harbors at Le Havre, Brest, and Brouage.

Richelieu knew that nothing would show *les grands* that a new order prevailed as would his *strictly* enforcing a new edict against dueling. (Louis's father had issued such edicts, but all had been roundly ignored.) *Les grands* considered these "affairs of honor" a prescriptive right; lives were theirs to take with impunity. (On the wild popularity of dueling among *les grands,* Burckhardt speculates that they sensed the obsolescence of their way of life, of the feudal world, and sought to kill themselves off.) Dueling greatly increased disorder throughout the country as "the streets of the towns were... used as fields of combat." (Richelieu) Dueling was emblematic of the lawlessness and lack of central control endemic to France. By strictly enforcing the edict, the crown would proclaim its authority, would excise some of the rebellious *grands.* "Either the duels must be done away with," Richelieu wrote his King, "or Your Majesty's edicts." A monarch who would not or could not enforce his edicts invited contempt.

On May 12, 1627, Count Francois de Bouteville-Montmorency, of a house inferior only to that of the Bourbons, showed his disdain for the King's edict by fighting the Baron de Beuvron at midday in the Place Royale, in the heart of Paris. The duel was inconclusive, and both fled; de Bouteville was caught, de Beuvon not. Though "the whole of France spoke for the accused," Richelieu insisted that de Bouteville be executed. "Every single quarrel which has arisen at Court over the past six years," Richelieu pointed out to his King, "was instigated or caused by" de Bouteville and his opponent. By the age of twenty-seven, de Bouteville had fought twenty-two duels, had "spurned the edicts twenty-two times." To spare his life would be to give "full license to duels and to every kind of offence," would "endanger the lives of many others." Richelieu quoted Tacitus: "The most effective way of strengthening the law is by punishing persons whose social rank is as exalted as their crimes are grave." Furthermore, Richelieu felt that a reprieve would be misunderstood, "that those who had tried to save de Bouteville would be inclined to ascribe an act of clemency to their own influence and not to the King's kindness," thus further convincing them of their own power and the King's weakness. The King, whose "love for his state was greater than his compassion for these two gentlemen" (as Richelieu commented in his Memoirs), consented to de Bouteville's execution.

Richelieu used this occasion, as he would many others, to show *les grands* that while he did not seek to fight them, he would do so if they rebelled; his object was not to fight *les grands*, but simply to obtain their submission. To the head of the Montmorency family, Henri II, Richelieu wrote, "In all other matters that do not involve the welfare of the State, you will undoubtedly receive tokens of His Majesty's goodwill towards you. As for myself, I would ask you to place your trust in the love to which my future actions will testify and which will show you more clearly than words that I am, as far as is humanly possible, your affectionate and sincere servant." To a nobleman related to the Montmorencys by marriage, he wrote, "I beg you to assure the Countess de Bouteville that in future I shall take all measures calculated to contribute to her welfare." Richelieu's point was not to be missed: Be obedient to the crown, and you will be shown every courtesy; disobey, and you will die. Whatever Richelieu might have *felt* toward the Montmorency family — which considered itself, not subjects, but peers of the Bourbons — his object demanded that he try to be reconciled to them so that he might free himself to fight others.

❧

The port of La Rochelle, on the Atlantic Ocean, was one of the more powerful and flourishing cities in France, accessible to the largest ships. La Rochelle was a city-state; the loyalty of the Rochellois was to their polis rather than to France, and they paid no taxes to the crown. The port was guarded by three islands, Rhe, Aix, and Oleron. Its fortifications were modern and unassailable; watch-towers and chains made any attack from the sea hopeless. To the west lay the sea, to the north and south salt marshes. The mayor of La Rochelle was its military commander, all its men soldiers.

Of all the Huguenot cities, why strike La Rochelle first? The seaport was the proudest and strongest of the Huguenot cities, their capital, and it was England's gateway to France. (There was still some debate to which of the two states La Rochelle belonged; for half a millennium it had been under the control of, now France, now England.) Whenever at sixes and sevens with the French King, the Rochellois would instinctively turn to their co-religionists, the English, for support. Richelieu was, however, in a rather ticklish position: he must suppress the Huguenots without upsetting the Protestant states he hoped would later become his allies against the Habsburgs. The state he least wished to upset was England; but its king, James I, was guided by George Villiers, the First Duke of Buckingham, a foolish and frivolous fop who could not quite see where English interests lay (indeed, saw them lying precisely where they did not). Like the French *devots*, the King and Buckingham did not understand Richelieu's policies in the slightest; the two were convinced that Richelieu sought Protestant alliances *not* to strike at the Habsburgs, but simply to suppress the Huguenots. They assumed that Richelieu viewed the world as they did, that to the Cardinal religion was paramount, politics secondary. Buckingham induced his King to support the Huguenots in their struggle against France; both Parliament and English public opinion were with Buckingham, and the King was weak. In vain did Richelieu try to get the English government to see sense, that their common enemy was the Habsburgs and their confessional differences a matter of indifference.

All the while, however, Richelieu organized for the siege he knew would come. He acquired vessels from Spain and the Low Countries, strengthened the fortifications and garrisons of the island forts, and procured equipment, clothing, housing, and food for the King's army, contributing the whole of his private income so that he might do so. To lessen corruption, and thus discontent, he insisted the soldiers be paid directly, rather than through their officers; he also took measures to ensure their camp would be hygienic — rarely would French troops be so well treated. Once the English government and public were hopelessly with the Huguenot cause, and relations between Spain and Holland so strained that France could break with

England without alienating the other Protestant states, Richelieu laid siege to La Rochelle.

In July 1627, Buckingham took the initiative by attacking the island of Rhe and its fortress of St. Martin. He had preferred to assault Fort Louis, the mainland fort from which the French might bombard La Rochelle, but the temporizing and vacillation of the Rochellois — who were not yet prepared to break fully with the French crown — forced him to consider his line of retreat; so Buckingham chose as his object a fort the taking of which would matter little. Richelieu did not at first respond: beyond considerations of relations with other states, he hoped by waiting to increase discord among the Rochellois. (The factiousness of the Huguenots here and elsewhere in France, their characteristic autonomy and individualism, would be their undoing; their would-be leader, Henri de Rohan, once cried in vexation, "I would rather preside over a gathering of wolves than a gathering of [Huguenot] ministers!") To sharpen these divisions, Richelieu in August ordered the King's army to tighten its cordon round La Rochelle: no food was to be brought in or harvests gathered. He then had the King declare in a letter to the Rochellois that all good Frenchmen must oppose the English assault and that loyal Huguenots would receive the protection of the crown. Most of the high magistrates now left La Rochelle; the Rochellois revolt would largely be a revolt of its masses.

On September 10, work on the fortifications of Fort St. Louis provoked the Rochellois into firing on the fortress; Richelieu could now justly say to the Protestant states that the Rochellois had initiated hostilities. He soon arrived at La Rochelle, followed by the King in mid-October. Since the fleet Richelieu had created was too weak to blockade the harbor, he ordered the harbor to be sealed. Ships were sunk in line at the mouth of the harbor, and a stone dike was laid upon them; an opening was left in the middle to let the tide through. Richelieu personally supervised the building of this dike, once toiling himself in the icy waters to encourage the workers. Richelieu also ordered a further 250 ships to be built to guard the dike, the coast, and the approach from the open sea. On failing to prevent the reprovisioning of Fort St. Martin, and on being savaged by a French force, in early November Buckingham withdrew. His siege of the fort had only weakened La Rochelle: the Rochellois had sold him food they could not replace, and the city was forced to take in a thousand sick English soldiers.

Throughout the siege of La Rochelle, Richelieu engaged in diplomacy to keep the other states quiescent, to prevent their aiding the Rochellois or launching attacks on France while it was weakened by its internal conflict. To Catholic Spain, he insisted that France was exterminating heresy, that is, Protestantism; to Protestant Germany, Scandinavia, and Holland, he pointed out that a weak France was a strong Spain. (This was characteristic of Richelieu's foreign policy: when speaking to Catholic rulers, he would speak as a Catholic, to Protestant rulers, as a minister of state.) To show the Protestant states that this was purely a political conflict, Richelieu recruited Protestants into the King's army. In attacking La Rochelle, Richelieu weakened the Spanish monopoly on the Counter-Reformation, thus gaining him the support of the Vatican. To occupy the Imperial forces, Richelieu subsidized the King of Denmark, Christian IV, in his war against the Imperialists and Catholic League in Germany.

In February, Louis, sick of the bog and the tedium of the siege, and missing his fox- and stag-hunting, returned to Paris; no one, least of all Richelieu, believed his assurances that he would return the following month. The world took Louis's departure as opposition to Richelieu's policies; all thought the siege would soon be lifted. The Rochellois took heart, the Protestant states considered supporting the Huguenots once more, and the King's troops became demoralized. At the King's departure, *les grands* became wildly disobedient; Louis himself had remarked on leaving that his marshals were "as likely to obey Richelieu as to obey the kitchen boy." *Les grands* did as little as possible to contribute to the success of the siege; one, Francois de Bassompierre, declared that "we nobles would be fools to take La Rochelle." (Richelieu would long remember this and other such remarks by *les grands*.) Food began to run short, and the health of the King's troops to fail, in the cold marsh, and the tide continually broke through the dike. Richelieu himself now fell ill. The Queen-Mother, who judged the sensibility of an object by its degree of difficulty, suddenly announced herself quite opposed to the siege; soon, the whole of the Catholic Party joined her in opposition. So discouraged was Richelieu that he considered following the King to Paris.

But La Rochelle must fall. If the city did not, it would remain a state within a state, forever a weakness in the French state, potentially an ally to both other states and rebellious *grands* within France. With such a state, Richelieu could never hope to strike at the Habsburgs; the whole of his policy would die on the vine. As an elderly officer now wrote the King, "Your France, Sire, has so many great nobles who are never quiet, that only a green prince of the blood is needed as a pretender, for them all to pin their hopes again on this town of La Rochelle." A certain Capuchin monk, Father Joseph, whom history would style Richelieu's *Eminence Gris*, bucked the Cardinal up: pursue your object in spite of all difficulties, this confidant urged him; otherwise, you will be lost. As difficult as the situation was in the French camp and court, it was far worse in La Rochelle itself. By late winter, the siege had begun to tell; hunger and malnutrition had become acute within the town. The Rochellois began to make desperate sorties, and desertions increased; attempts were made on the lives of the mayor and town councilors. The English garrison within the town became restive. The mayor of La Rochelle requested that the women and children be permitted to leave; Richelieu refused.

On learning that the English planned to send a second fleet to aid the Rochellois, in late March the King rejoined his army. The fleet arrived in mid-May, but was so disheartened by the strong dike and now-fine state of the French troops that it soon departed. By early fall, the Rochellois were dying by the score, the survivors living on grass, hats, boots — whatever might be turned into sustenance. The Rochellois would send their women and children out, the King's troops drive them back. Richelieu had pamphlets circulated in La Rochelle falsely stating that "food profiteers" within the city were hoarding stores of food. In early October, another English fleet appeared. Its officers, however, simply refused orders to attack, so little did they agree with the purpose of their mission; this would be the last of the half-hearted English attempts to aid the Rochellois.

In late October 1628, with no further hope of English aid, La Rochelle capitulated; less than one-fifth of its population remained. The royal council met to discuss how the Rochellois should be treated. Caring only to further the Counter-Reformation, the Catholic Party argued that they should be severely punished. Not wishing to fight the Huguenots elsewhere in France, and wishing to form alliances with Protestant states, Richelieu countered that the Rochellois should be forgiven as Caesar had done his opponents in the civil war. (La Rochelle, he felt, should serve as an example of how the crown would treat Huguenot towns should they submit.) So as not to reveal his future policy to the Catholic Party, however, Richelieu spoke simply of mercy, pity, and the monarch's "greatness of heart." Louis sided with Richelieu; the Rochellois were granted their lives, goods, and liberty of worship. Fewer than a dozen of their leaders were exiled, and that only for six months; only their mayor was driven from the city forever. All forms of self-governance were lost to them; state officials would now govern La Rochelle, and the town's walls and towers were demolished.

❧

The Valtelline valley in the southern Alps was critical to Habsburg interests. The valley offered the only means by which the Spanish territories in Italy could communicate with those on the Rhine and Danube. Through the Valtelline, Spanish troops could march to Germany to assist Austria, and Austrian troops to Italy to assist Spain. Near the Valtelline was the fief of Mantua. During the siege of La Rochelle, the childless Duke of Mantua had died; he had left his fief, an Imperial possession, to his French cousin the duc de Nevers. That a French fief should come into being near both the vital corridor of the Valtelline and Spain's northern Italian dominions alarmed that state, which soon laid siege to the Mantuan fortress of Casale.

Though Richelieu wished to avoid open conflict until France was stronger, he recognized that the siege of Casale must be relieved. Were Mantua to fall, France would not only lose all influence in Italy, but it would also show the now-quite-weak and demoralized German Protestant States that it simply could not be depended on to protect its allies. The Queen-Mother, her chief councilor Michel de Marillac, and others of the Catholic Party argued that France should not fight its Spanish coreligionists, and that anyhow the religious duty of crushing the Huguenots in the south of France was far more important than relieving Casale. They charged that Richelieu had taken La Rochelle, not to further the Counter-Reformation as they had hoped, but simply to strengthen France so that it might attack the Habsburgs. Richelieu knew that he and the King could not be away from Paris while the Catholic Party remained restive; were the party to unite with other *grands* and Huguenots while he and Louis were in Italy, the King, and thus Richelieu, might very well fall. To mollify the Catholic Party (and calm the King's own misgivings about attacking his co-religionists), the Cardinal stressed that they would indeed reduce the Huguenot towns of southern France, but only once French possession of Mantua was assured.

He also induced the King to make the Queen-Mother Vice-Regent over all the provinces beyond the Loire and to give other nobles in a position to hurt Richelieu dukedoms or abbacies. Richelieu hoped that these beneficies would keep the Queen-Mother and nobles quiescent, at least until he and the King could return from Italy.

The greatest threat to Richelieu and his work, however, was not the opposition at court, but rather the King himself. The Cardinal now took a great risk: he showed his sovereign to himself. Nothing could stand in Richelieu's way, not even the King; he simply could not be away from France while uncertain of his sovereign. On January 13, 1629, in the presence of the King, the Queen-Mother, and the King's confessor, Richelieu critiqued his monarch. Some excerpts from that critique:

> The King is good, virtuous, discreet, courageous, and intent on acquiring fame, but it is equally true to say that he is precipitate, suspicious, envious, and susceptible to sudden antipathies and first impressions to the detriment of all and sundry.
>
> Many think, and not without reason, that His Majesty is naturally disinclined to apply himself to affairs of state and quickly tires of those that call for protracted effort... The King pays so little attention to his affairs, and disapproves so readily of the expedients proposed to him in order to ensure the success of those he does undertake, that in future it may well prove difficult to serve him... There have been princes who wanted the ends but not the means, which is to say that they wished their affairs to prosper, but did not want to take the necessary steps to that end.
>
> A man must be strong by virtue of reason and not passion... Many, when fired by passion, speak and act with force and vigor, but when the fire has gone out of them, they let everything go... The King will please take care to guard against this kind of failing.
>
> It is so very dangerous for the State when the application of the law is treated with indifference that I feel bound to observe that His Majesty appears to show a lack of firmness and zeal regarding the observance of his own laws... A Christian can never forget a wrong or forgive an offence quickly enough, but a King, a governor, or a magistrate can never punish them quickly enough when they

concern the State... Without examples and without punishments all manner of injustice and violence would be committed with impunity and to the detriment of public order.

Justice must be administered dispassionately, and a Prince who dispensed it by persecuting those whom he disliked and excusing and exempting those fortunate enough to enjoy his favor [would cause great harm to his State].

His Majesty must try to master a certain tendency towards a [false] sense of goodness, which prompts many Princes to accede to all requests made to them in person, even though they be bad, and prevents them from saying anything they think will displease the other person, even though they be mistaken... Those who do not know the King's nature attribute this tendency, which stems from pure goodness of heart, to weakness.

His Majesty must avoid like death itself a certain tendency towards envy, which has prompted many a Prince to find it intolerable that his subjects should be dealing with affairs on his behalf that the ruler himself is neither willing nor able to deal with... In this connection I wish to say quite openly that His Majesty must either decide to pursue the affairs of state with persistency and force or must delegate his authority to some other person, in order that he may act for him... Otherwise he will never be well served and his affairs will come to grief.

Princes who wish to receive true service must choose ministers who are guided by reason alone and who spare no man [for subjective reasons]... Many Princes, although strong in themselves, lack the strength to resist the representations that are made to them to the detriment of those who serve them best and to whom they owe greater protection. [The King must] silence all those who speak badly of others in his presence [a reference to the King's allowing his retinue to speak ill of Richelieu, which all took to mean that Louis was quite willing to have Richelieu removed, a source of endless conspiracies against the Cardinal].

That Louis took his Minister's critique without a murmur speaks well of him.

∾

At the end of January 1629, Louis and Richelieu set out for Italy at the head of the French army. Richelieu drove them all on, through mist, snow, and frost, seeing to everything. By early March, they were on the border of Savoy; the King asked to be allowed to pass through, the Duke of Savoy, a Spanish ally, refused. The French stormed the mountain-pass and town of Suze, whereupon the Duke sought terms; since he had fought Louis, the King could now easily have taken possession of Savoy. But Richelieu had attained his object, free transit through Savoy; acquiring Savoy itself would simply have involved France in diplomatic complications. Alarmed by the successes of the French army, the Spanish raised their siege of Casale, which Louis and Richelieu promptly occupied.

It was now time to take the remaining Huguenot towns in the south of France. As with the siege of La Rochelle and the operations in Italy, Richelieu planned this campaign in minutest detail. At first he remained in Italy, seeing to affairs; the King, meeting with no success without Richelieu, summoned his First Minister, and soon Languedoc, Vivarais, and Provence fell. The French were quite merciless in their attacks; their situation hopeless, the Huguenots sued for peace. At Alais in June, a Huguenot assembly ratified the Peace of Alais, which was striking in its moderation. Of the Huguenots, the peace demanded only that they live as loyal subjects of the crown and raze their fortifications; it confirmed the Edict of Nantes, which provided for religious toleration. Here again, Richelieu sought through his moderation to reassure the Protestant states of Europe, with whom he hoped to form alliances. He also wished to free himself of the restraint of further conflict within France, so that he might devote French resources to external affairs.

Richelieu now rode from one Huguenot town to another, offering counsel and providing aid. All were amazed that this man who "waged war in all its severity" should be so conciliatory, solicitous, and helpful (but then, that is what Richelieu *would* do, once he attained his object). In all circles but one, that of the court, Richelieu was now held in the highest esteem; he had defeated England, made the Habsburgs feel the power of France, and pacified his country. The King spoke of his First Minister in the warmest of terms, declaring that "all our successes inside and outside the kingdom are due to his wise and bold counsel."

At court, however, in spite of his successes against the French Protestants, opposition to Richelieu and his policies continued to grow. That he should increase the power of the crown *vis-à-vis* their own; that he rather than they, to whom the right to govern was theirs by birth or marriage, should be directing affairs; that he should be victorious — all made the Cardinal hateful to *les grands*. The Queen-Mother, far too simple to understand Richelieu's policies, seeing only her Habsburg family ties, loving comfort and luxury (and not perceiving that such things do not procure themselves), now came out in open opposition. She, the Queen, Marillac, and *les grands* declared that the party strife within France, the conflict with the Habsburgs, and the weakness of France's frontiers, were all due to Richelieu and his policies. To the King, the Queen-Mother insisted that Richelieu was the cause of all her unhappiness, the Queen their estrangement. Torn between his filial duty to his mother and his dependence on his First Minister, the King tried to reconcile the two, but in vain. While Richelieu, seeing his interests clearly, treated the Queen-Mother with every courtesy, she, seeing her interests not at all, spurned him. Richelieu's greatest source of anxiety, however, continued to be the King himself, in whom the Cardinal's achievements intensified the feelings of both appreciation and resentment.

Well aware of Richelieu's uncertain position at court, and hoping perhaps to bring about his fall, Spain now once again laid siege to Casale; the Austrians contributed their finest troops. It now seemed certain the Habsburgs would retake Mantua; and if Spain were simultaneously to attack France from the Pyrenees and (with its German allies) from the north, France might itself fall. All of Richelieu's work now seemed to have come to nothing; all viewed his foreign policy as a miscalculation. Sensing Richelieu's weakened position, *les grands*, hoping to replace the King with his brother Gaston, became more restive still.

In late December, Richelieu once again marched for Italy as Commander-in-Chief of the French army, continuing to work out the coming campaign as he went. In the middle of March, the French forces entered Savoy and laid siege to its capital, Turin. Leaving a small force to carry on the siege, Richelieu besieged and soon took Pignerolo, a critical city the possession of which secured Richelieu's lines of communications to Paris. In early May,

Louis joined Richelieu in Grenoble. His court had followed him to Lyons, beseeching him the whole of the way to repudiate his First Minister and his policies; so tormented was the King by the opposition of his family and *les grands* that he soon returned to Lyons. By doing so, he increased the confidence of the Imperial forces and decreased that of his own — six thousand French soldiers deserted at once — and made Richelieu wretched: "Never before have I been in such a horrid position. How gladly would I be out of this world and upraised into the mercy of my Lord."

A plague now broke out in Piedmont and upper Italy; as it was reducing the French army by a third, the Habsburgs stormed the fortress of Mantua. As at La Rochelle, *les grands* did not fight, but simply disputed among themselves over precedence; for Richelieu, to rule against a certain *grand* was to add him to the opposition. The Duke of Savoy declared that the war was solely of Richelieu's making; in France, the people rioted and the *parlement* murmured against the King and his First Minister. In August, fresh troops arrived, but soon succumbed to the plague; Richelieu implored the redoubtable French commander inside Casale, Jean de Toiras, to continue to hold out. Not willing to risk his great Minister's dying, the King now summoned him to Lyons. Without Richelieu's presence, the French operations were certain to fail.

Two French representatives, Pere Joseph and the French ambassador to Switzerland, Brulart de Leon, now arrived in Regensburg to negotiate with the Holy Roman Emperor. All assumed the mission of Pere Joseph and Brulart to be the negotiation of peace in Italy; in truth, their mission had nothing to do with Italy. Indeed, Richelieu had said nothing of that country in his instructions; his representatives could do there just as they pleased. What Richelieu cared about was the situation in Germany; it was imperative that the French representatives weaken Austrian influence over the German states and increase that of France, that they prevent the German states from unifying with one another or with Austria. With his incorruptible sense of proportion, Richelieu saw that Italy, for all its open conflict, mattered far less to French interests than did Germany. Even now, when he might fall because of the Italian imbroglio, when only peace in Italy could save him, he continued to focus on French interests: not because he was selfless, but rather because he was unwilling to relinquish his object. While Pere Joseph and Brulart were negotiating in Regensburg, Richelieu in early September arranged an armistice in Italy; the Spanish would withdraw from Casale, the French from Savoy.

At the end of September, the King fell ill with a fever and dysentery. The Queen-Mother nursed him, and mother and son grew closer. She continued to work on the weakened King, beseeching him to renounce his First Minister. Were Louis to die, or were he and his mother to be reconciled, Richelieu would be lost. Neutral *grands* now joined the party of the Queen-Mother, the Queen, and Marillac; they laid plans for Richelieu's execution once the King died. On learning of this, Richelieu made arrangements to flee to Avignon, to place himself under the protection of the Pope. In early October, Louis was sufficiently well to make the journey to Paris; he asked Richelieu to accompany him. In Roanne, they learned that Pere Joseph and Brulart had signed a treaty of peace with the Emperor; the treaty provided that France would remain neutral in Germany and respect the neutrality of the Duchy of Lorraine. The treaty was the work of Pere Joseph, who recognized the tenuousness of his friend's position, that Richelieu could ill-withstand the fury a conflict in Germany would bring. All, Richelieu's opponents and the French people, were elated by this treaty; no war would take place in Germany. Richelieu, it seemed, was saved.

In a rage, Richelieu tore the document to pieces. Were the treaty ratified, all would be lost: France would be forced to give back everything it had won, and alliances with other states would be forsaken for dependency on the Habsburgs. Pere Joseph and Brulart were to negotiate a separate peace in Italy, only; a general peace between France and Austria would alienate Venice, Holland, and Sweden and prevent France from continuing to work against Austria. However could France occupy Lorraine, which was to be a launching point for future attacks on Germany, once it had recognized Lothringian neutrality? Declaring that de Leon had exceeded his powers, Richelieu refused to ratify the treaty. Louis, recognizing that he was still too weak to oppose the general desire for peace, ordered Richelieu to defend his views before the King's Council. In the teeth of violent opposition by the Queen-Mother and Marillac, the Council voted to repudiate the treaty.

Now that Richelieu was in Paris, his enemies began to conspire in earnest. Unpopular in court circles and throughout France before rejecting peace, the Cardinal was now wildly so; no one, friend or enemy, doubted he would fall. The King was cold to Richelieu and, indeed, would only rarely see him. Richelieu fell into a deep depression; it was thought he would soon die. His friends begged him to discontinue his policy of opposition to the Habsburgs, but in vain: Richelieu could no more forsake his object than forsake himself; he was possessed by it. The King had withdrawn not only from Richelieu, but from society; he slept only fitfully and would go for long rides in the woods, debating within himself whether to dismiss his First Minister. When at the beginning of November Richelieu beseeched the King to receive him so that they might discuss the intrigues against him, Louis refused. Louis resolved to come to a decision following a private discussion with his mother.

The discussion took place on November 10, in the Queen-Mother's apartments; to be certain of their privacy, she ordered all the doors bolted. The Queen-Mother, half a Habsburg, implored the King to rid himself of this enemy of her house. Bit by bit, Louis became once more the timid and weak child of an unloving and selfish mother. The Queen bore in on him; he was on the verge of succumbing, of renouncing his First Minister. Suddenly, a little-used door opened, and Richelieu stood before them: he had disobeyed his sovereign's command that they not be disturbed. The Queen-Mother lost control of herself — or, rather, now became herself. She shrieked; she insulted Richelieu roundly: he was "a liar" and "a traitor," the ruin of both France and her class. "You have cost me millions," she cried. She became wildly illogical; Richelieu wished to overthrow her son and replace him, now with this noble, now with that one. She would have nothing more to do with him; indeed, she would extirpate him and all his appointees. The King must choose between Richelieu and herself; either he or she must go.

Richelieu, weeping, knelt before his King. He begged for mercy, that Louis forgive whatever wrongs he might have committed; he offered to re-sign. All the while, the Queen-Mother continued to shriek "like a fish-monger's wife." The King tried to speak; she would not let him. Treating the monarch so was simply unthinkable. "What are you doing?", cried Louis. "You offend, you insult me!" She had wounded his touchiest sen-sibility, his dignity. She was treating him as she had when he was a child, dismissively; she sought to undo all his growth, to make him once more her miserable, insignificant creature. Her love, both for her son and her country, was shot through with cruelty; it was a "love" that sought only to make the world conducive to herself. She neither cared about nor knew how to serve her son's or France's interests. Louis stood, commanded Richelieu to rise, and strode from the room; though Richelieu followed, Louis did not say another word to him.

By reminding Louis of his childhood, by being so completely her illogical and emotional self, the Queen-Mother doomed herself. The King now saw clearly: his mother was the antithesis of Richelieu; Richelieu was a worthy though toilsome object, his mother only fickle and selfish heliotropism. Only sentiment attached her son to her, and she had killed it. She had made a hash of his childhood; he would not let her make a hash of his monarchy. Richelieu and the court, however, knew nothing of these reflections; all thought Louis would now dismiss his First Minister. The Queen-Mother and Marillac spent the rest of the day receiving *les grands*, who congratulated them and sought high office. Richelieu made arrangements to flee France.

To Richelieu's great surprise, the King summoned him. Richelieu again knelt, weeping; Louis took him by the hand and raised him. The King assured Richelieu of his esteem, that he had nothing to fear from either Louis or his enemies. The King spoke with unusual candor: too many of his ancestors had made the mistake of dismissing worthy ministers because of mindless cabals; Louis would not commit such a mistake. It was quite simple: Richelieu could help with affairs of state, the Queen-Mother not. "I honor my mother, but my obligations to the State are greater than towards her." The King's object had won out over his weaknesses, and Richelieu was saved. To dismiss Richelieu would be to replace a brilliant reign with a mediocre one.

The King now commanded Marillac to proceed to a certain village near Versailles. Marillac did so to the congratulations of his supporters; all were now certain of his triumph. That evening, the King called a meeting of his Ministerial Council, Marillac, however, remaining in the village. Louis declared that the intrigues that had for a year muddled the affairs of state and the Italian campaign were at an end; Michel de Marillac would be stripped of his office and interred in the castle of Chateaudun, far from Paris. Richelieu's policy, reflective of the transition from medievalism to nationalism, now became the recognized policy of France.

Now began the "great storm," the reduction in earnest of *les grands*. Marillac's brother, one of the commanders of the French force in Italy, was seized, returned to Paris, and beheaded. One of the conspirators, Bassompierre, was stripped of his possessions and immured in the Bastille. Castles, walls, and fortifications throughout France would soon be razed. Even the Queen-Mother was not untouchable. Louis first had her interred in the town of Compiegne; Richelieu ordered the guard withdrawn, whereupon the Queen-Mother "escaped." She intended to ensconce herself in the fortress of La Chapelle, near the frontier, and thence, with the support of Spain, negotiate with the King; Richelieu ordered the fortress closed to her. She now had no choice but to cross the frontier; she did so, and made for Brussels. She and Louis would never again see each other; all her possessions in France were confiscated. She from Brussels and elsewhere, and her son Gaston within France, both supported by the Habsburgs, would continue to be a center of nettlesome opposition to Richelieu and his policies.

༄

Freed for the present from fighting the Huguenots and *les grands* in France and the Imperialists in Italy, Richelieu now stepped up his "masked war" against the Imperialists in Germany. While France had been occupied with the siege of La Rochelle, the conflict in Italy, and the suppression of the Huguenots in southern France, the Imperialists and Catholic League had defeated Christian IV, the leader of the German Protestant states. All of northern Germany now stood open to the Imperial and League forces, and Richelieu's nightmare of Imperial power reaching to the Baltic, linking it with Spain to the north, was all but realized. France could not itself fight the Habsburgs until its forces were sufficiently strong, and until it was in possession of certain critical territories and strongholds; all Richelieu could do for the present was increase his subsidies to other states to induce them to fight, or to continue fighting, the Habsburgs. (Fortunately for France and its allies, in March 1629 the Imperial Emperor Ferdinand, who preferred the claims of religion to those of state interests, had proclaimed the Edict of Restitution, which ordered the German Protestants to restore to the Church the bishoprics, abbeys, and monasteries lost to it 100 years earlier. The German Protestant states would respond to this ill-considered edict by denying the Imperial and League armies transit rights, contributions, and quarters.)

In Sweden lay Richelieu's main hope of checking the Imperial advances. Richelieu reconciled Sweden with Russia and Poland to free its king, Gustavus Adolphus, for a German campaign, which began in the summer of 1630. (Richelieu's subsidizing a Protestant state to fight Catholic states would both unify and disunify France: while pleasing and reassuring the Huguenots, it quite enraged the *devots*.) Richelieu intended Gustavus simply to weaken the Imperialists and Catholic League; so gifted a warrior was Gustavus, however, that he took city after city and soon reached the Rhine. Even though Richelieu had obtained from Gustavus a promise not to attack the Catholic states (which the Cardinal hoped to separate from the Imperialists through diplomacy), he was now threatening to do so. Such a threat undid Richelieu's diplomacy, since the Catholic states, knowing that France would be unwilling to help them *militarily*, would seek their salvation from the Emperor. Furthermore, once victorious Gustavus would combine the states of Germany with those of Scandanavia, thus creating a great Protestant power in Central Europe. Such a power might very well attack France itself; at the very least, it would make the Huguenots restive and perhaps even encourage and support a new Huguenot revolt. The *devots* cried that Richelieu was indeed waging a religious war: how else to explain his fathering such a strong Protestant state? In truth, Richelieu wished neither the Protestant states nor the Habsburgs to be strong.

Richelieu tried valiantly to keep the Catholic League from throwing itself at the feet of the Emperor. The League insisted that France either force Gustavus to restore the territories he had annexed from League states or break with him. Richelieu insisted that the League first break with Austria; this, he said, would mollify Gustavus. Not willing to be wholly isolated, with no guarantees of support from France, the League refused. France was now faced with the possibility of ruptured relations with both the Catholic League and the Swedes.

In the spring of 1632, Gustavus took Munich, the capital of Bavaria, the leader of the Catholic League. Richelieu was now saved, not by his work, but by fortune: the Imperialists counterattacked, and in November Gustavus was killed. In the chaos that was now Germany, Richelieu was in his element. To prevent the Imperialists from winning over any of the

Protestant states, Richelieu paid bribes to influential individuals in those
states. He then induced the German Protestant states to form the League
of Heilbronn, the members of which vowed to continue the war against the
Imperialists (but not against the Catholic League, whose neutrality was to
be respected), to contribute subsidies for troops, and to reject any offers of
separate (and thus neutralizing) peace from the Habsburgs or the League.
Richelieu also occupied Lorraine (which the Imperialists were too weakened by Gustavus's victories to defend) and, to keep Spanish troops bogged
down, scotched armistice talks between Spain and the Netherlands.

In late 1633, the two Habsburg houses began negotiating a grand coali-
tion that would include the German Catholic Princes, most of the Italian
Princes, the now-dispossessed Duke of Lorraine, and the French opposition,
led by Louis's brother, Gaston. The coalition would attack France from
Germany, the Spanish Netherlands, and (through the Spanish navy) the sea.
These negotiations resolved Richelieu on making France so powerful on the
Rhine that the Spanish would no longer be able to march southwards along
it, or the Imperialists to cross it. French dominance on the Rhine would
also permit France itself to enter the war in Germany when propitious.

In the spring of 1634, the Imperialists launched their offensive. Since
Sweden and the Heilbronn League were at sixes and sevens — because Sweden was no less imperious than Austria — they were unable to arrange con-
certed resistance to the offensive. By the fall of 1634, the Imperialists were
once more in possession of the whole of southern Germany; the Heilbronn
League might well now disintegrate, and Sweden sign a peace treaty with
the Emperor. In September, Alsace obtained French "protection" from the
Imperialists by ceding control of the state to France; Richelieu also induced
Sweden to cede France certain strongholds along France's eastern frontier,
the most critical of which was Philippsburg. France was now in possession
of the whole of the upper Rhine. In October, Richelieu induced Sweden
and the Heilbronn League to renew their alliance. To satisfy the *devots* and
his King, he obtained the restitution of the Catholic religion in the territories conquered by the Swedes. He also offered neutrality to any state
that placed itself under the protection of France (in contradistinction to
Austria, which insisted that all states were either its allies or its enemies).
Throughout the winter of 1634-1635, the Imperialists continued their offensive, taking Philippsburg and, across the Rhine, the fortress of Speier.

In May 1635, the Emperor, the Elector of Saxony (the leader of the German Protestant states), and other German states not allied with Sweden and France signed the Peace of Prague. The Peace suspended the Edict of Restitution for 40 years and provided that the Swedes would be paid to withdraw from Germany; should they refuse to do so, the Imperialists and Saxony would drive both the Swedes and the French from German territory. The signers became quite bellicose: they would march on Paris, "show no quarter" to French troops, divide the French provinces among themselves, and place the Duke of Lorraine upon the French throne. The bellicosity of the signers of the Peace of Prague was met with bellicosity in France; since the context now required that France itself enter the war, this served Richelieu's ends perfectly. Given the Habsburg victories in Germany, Richelieu would have preferred to wait further still to break openly with Spain. He recognized, however, that subsidies were no longer a sufficient inducement to the Protestant states to maintain their coalition. The states demanded that France itself now enter the war; were France to lose its allies, it would face the combined Habsburg forces alone. Before declaring war, however, Richelieu did all he could to aid France diplomatically. He concluded an alliance with the Dutch with the aim of dividing the Spanish Netherlands between the States General and France. In the spring of 1635, Louis and Queen Christina of Sweden signed the Treaty of Compiegne, which provided that neither would agree to a separate peace or to cede strongholds.

On May 19, 1635, France declared war on Spain. Cardinal de La Valette commanded the French army on the eastern frontier, Marshal de La Force, Conde, and others the armies in Lorraine. To please France's Protestant allies, Richelieu appointed Chatillon, a Protestant, to command the French forces in the Netherlands. Much to the surprise of the other European states, France was able to put into the field six armies with a total strength of 134,000 infantry and 26,000 cavalry, the result of Richelieu's rearming since 1624.

In October, 1635, Richelieu reached agreement with Bernhard of Saxe-Weimar whereby Saxe-Weimar would fight on behalf of France in close collaboration with La Valette. (Saxe-Weimar, a Protestant, had been Commander of the Swedish Body Guards under Gustavus.) France agreed to provide Saxe-Weimar with supplies and an annual subsidy of 4,000,000 livres. The Duke was given the title of Landgrave of Alsace: all Habsburg territories within Alsace, save the strongholds France had wrested from Austria, would be his; he also received guarantees that the Duchy of Franconia — his own — and the fief of Hagenau would be assigned to him upon the conclusion of peace. Richelieu insisted that Saxe-Weimar promise to protect the Catholic religion in his future sovereign territories — an insistence Richelieu made of all Protestant princes with whom he formed alliances, to please the *devots*. In April 1636, Richelieu arranged a further treaty with Sweden providing that that state, in exchange for French subsidies, carry the war into Silesia and Bohemia, thus drawing Imperial troops away from France.

(Richelieu would dearly also have liked to form an alliance with England. He ignored English support for their fellow Protestants of La Rochelle, as well as other English provocations such as the capturing of French ships, because he needed English support against the Habsburgs, particularly English help in shutting off the English Channel to Spanish shipping. Richelieu ignored popular opinion in France, which was not only against an alliance with England — which was, after all, Protestant — but indeed for retaliation. He instructed the French ambassador to England not to be over-sensitive where French honor was concerned. Rather than lead to a *rapprochement*, the marriage between Louise XIII's sister and the Prince of Wales merely complicated relations between the two countries, in large part because of Henrietta's loyalty to her mother and her policies. French and English competition in the New World contributed further to a worsening of relations between the two states. But pre-revolutionary discord within England made an alliance quite impossible; the English revolution and rise of Cromwell caused England to withdraw itself temporarily from Continental affairs.)

By early 1636, the French and Habsburgs were crossing swords in Germany, Alsace, Lorraine, Franche-Comte, Burgundy, Holland, and Italy. By late summer, the Habsburgs had gotten the better of France; Charles of Lorraine had fought his way between the armies of La Valette and La Force and was soon to be upon the towns of the lower Rhine. The King took command of one of the French armies — Richelieu was too ill to join him — but was forced to retreat upon the fall of St. Mihiel. The Habsburgs then took La Capelle and Le Catelet and crossed the Somme, laying waste to the countryside as they went. With the fall of Corbie, the road to Paris lay open to the enemy. Habsburg cavalry soon reached Clermont, 20 miles to the east of Paris. The King called up the *noblesse d'epee*, but most, not wishing to displease the Habsburgs who now occupied their lands, did not respond. Parisians fled for Lyons, Orleans, and Tours.

All this was laid at Richelieu's feet. Had he not ordered the main French force to Lorraine and thus emptied the northern frontier of troops? His very declaration of war on Spain was now viewed as folly (as was his breaching the wall of Paris so that his Palais-Cardinal might have a sizeable garden). The *parlement* now insisted on its right to question all the King's decisions; throughout France, people began to call for Richelieu's death. The Cardinal went to pieces; he issued nonsensical orders, countermanded them, savaged those about him, and then did nothing. His friend and counselor Pere Joseph soon restored to Richelieu his calm and confidence; he found soldiers and money, arranged the French forces brilliantly, organized a *levee en masse* (an emergency tax of the guilds, tradesmen, and farmers), and drove through the streets of Paris in an open carriage, unguarded, his calmness calming all who saw him. Because of Richelieu, the King now found himself commanding a new army of 20,000 men.

As the Habsburgs disagreed among themselves whether to continue on to Paris, Saxe-Weimar pounced. Both because of Saxe-Weimer's assaults and the unreliability of the "allies" they had gained through the Peace of Prague, the Habsburgs could not remain where they were. They began to withdraw; France was saved, and Saxe-Weimar, all recognized, was its savior. The French successes continued. In November, Chatillon retook Corbie. The fortress of Breda in the Netherlands fell to Holland, a French ally, forcing the Spanish to withdraw troops from Franche-Comte. Hunger and disease slowly vitiated the Habsburg forces. Saxe-Weimar now went on the offensive by invading the Bishopric of Basle, a member of the Catholic League. From Basle, he proceeded to the Upper Rhine, where he took stronghold after stronghold. All France celebrated Saxe-Weimar's victories; he was honored with festivities and accolades, and Louis himself wrote the Duke to thank him for his victories and to assure him of his support. Only Richelieu continued to regard Saxe-Weimar coolly. When Saxe-Weimar pleaded for troops and money, he sent none; when the Duke asked that he be given title to the Alsatian fortresses he had taken — as his agreement with France intimated — Richelieu replied that these matters would be discussed in the future.

In spite of this, in the late spring of 1638 Saxe-Weimar laid siege to the most important of the Imperial fortresses, that of Breisach on the Rhine. Breisach was one of two key positions on the route linking Italy with the Netherlands; to take it would be to cut Habsburg communications between the Low Countries and the Alps. Saxe-Weimar constructed a fortress round Breisach, cutting it off; he would starve its defenders into submission. To the Habsburgs, nothing was more critical than relieving Breisach; three Imperial armies converged on the stronghold. Saxe-Weimar beseeched France for reinforcements, but was at first simply ignored. Though two of the Imperial armies soon united, disagreements between the generals weakened the combined force. In July, French reinforcements arrived, though far fewer than Saxe-Weimar had sought. Marching at night, he fell upon the Imperialists at the village of Freisenheim and defeated them.

On learning of this victory, Louis wrote Richelieu, "With only a small force the Duke of Saxe-Weimar has achieved great things that other generals with large forces are unable to achieve," to which Richelieu replied coolly, "We have no Duke of Saxe-Weimar in France." Through von Erlach, his representative in Paris, Saxe-Weimar was assured he would come into possession of all the territories he had conquered. Saxe-Weimar again pleaded for troops and money; with them, he might achieve great things in Germany. The King assured him that more of both would come soon. Richelieu made certain that neither did: Saxe-Weimar had almost achieved what he wished him to; it simply would not do for the Duke to grow too powerful. The Cardinal would not have a second Gustavus. It was not until October that Richelieu sent the troops for which Saxe-Weimar had been pleading, and these far fewer than he had requested. Richelieu also appointed the Secretary of State, De Noyers, who roundly disliked Saxe-Weimar, as his negotiator with von Erlach.

All the while, Saxe-Weimar's siege of Breisach continued, as did his sallying out to meet and defeat each Imperial army in turn. One of the armies was able for a short while to besiege the besiegers, but then it, too, was driven off. In early December 1638, the commander of Breisach, his troops on the verge of starvation, capitulated. To the vexation of France, Saxe-Weimar installed a German rather than a French garrison, said nothing of France, Sweden, or the Heilbronn League in the capitulation agreement, and appointed von Erlach governor of the stronghold, as well as of all the other fortresses he had taken. The Duke was gradually taking possession of that which France had promised him. France and its allies had, however, benefited greatly from Saxe-Weimar's victories. The Austrians had all but lost their dominions in Switzerland and Alsace; in all likelihood, Lorraine, Strassburg, and Franche-Comte would also soon be wrested from them. The Emperor repeatedly sought to be reconciled with Saxe-Weimar; through various intermediaries, such as Christian IV, the King of Denmark, he assured the Duke of his utmost esteem, promised to protect his family's domains in Weimar, and intimated that the post of Commander-in-Chief of the Imperial armies could be his. To all these feelers — of which he would promptly inform Paris — Saxe-Weimar replied simply that he was not empowered to sign a separate peace, that France and Austria must reach a general peace. All the while, in spite of his many complaints the Duke received little or no further support from France.

In the winter of 1639, Saxe-Weimar occupied Upper Burgundy and Franche-Comte. Relations between France and its "sword" were now *distinctly* strained. Saxe-Weimar would refuse to discuss his intentions with representatives of the French crown; the King and Richelieu would send the Duke fulsome letters, but say nothing substantive. An alliance between France and Saxe-Weimar was simply unworkable; Saxe-Weimar was set on his object, Richelieu on his. Saxe-Weimar's dream was to acquire sovereign territories of his own — Alsace and the strongholds of Upper Burgundy — ally them with the German Protestant states, and lead the combined force against the Emperor. Once he had acquired those territories with French aid, he required of France only that it remain neutral, that it not interfere. But it was simply not in France's interest to have a new sovereign territory, a Protestant one at that, spring up on the country's eastern frontier. Furthermore, as Richelieu observed, "Saxe-Weimar will make it quite impossible for France to force the Emperor to accept peace terms, for if he retains his power he alone will be in a position to do so." Richelieu was quite willing to provide Saxe-Weimar with a considerable annual income and arrange a marriage with some princess or other, perhaps even with his own niece; but he was quite *unwilling* to harm his own interests. While France viewed Saxe-Weimar as a general under its ultimate command, he viewed himself as an independent sovereign receiving French subsidies (much like Gustavus). Saxe-Weimar supposed that because he had saved France and behaved honorably, out of gratitude Richelieu would grant him what he asked. The Cardinal was unmoved by such considerations; sentiment had no place in Richelieu's thinking. Saxe-Weimar did not understand Richelieu, did not understand that nothing but his interests would sway Richelieu.

Saxe-Weimar was now invited to the French court. Quite distrusting the French, he declined the invitation, saying that circumstances required that he remain in the field. He sent von Erlach; the King and Queen received him warmly, showing him their first child, the future Louis XIV, and declaring that Saxe-Weimar would teach the Dauphin the art of war. Von Erlach received assurances that France would provide Saxe-Weimar with the most generous subsidies — *if* he allowed the French to take possession of all the territories and strongholds he had conquered and would conquer. France argued that none of these conquests would have been possible without French subsidies, von Erlach that they had been won by the valor and blood of Saxe-Weimar and his men and that, anyhow, Saxe-Weimar was quite willing to cede Franche-Comte to France to repay its subsidies and other aid. All the while, Saxe-Weimar continued to be courted on all sides. The Emperor offered his niece in marriage and considerable territory, and would consider restoring to the Duke the Duchy of Franconia. Both the English and Swedes assured him of support should he retain the strongholds he had taken, especially Breisach. Saxe-Weimar rejected all these offers; when Spain tried to negotiate with him, he refused to meet with its emissary.

Wishing to consolidate his gains in southern Germany, Saxe-Weimar once again asked for French support. Rather than provide that support, Richelieu simply encouraged the Duke to continue his campaign in Germany. After crossing the Rhine, however, Saxe-Weimar fell ill and, on the morning of July 8, 1639, died. In October, in violation of Saxe-Weimar's will, which stipulated that all territories he had conquered be returned to the Holy Roman Emperor, France took possession of all his conquests.

⁓

Richelieu now wished to join the States General in an attack on what he considered Spain's weakest point, the Flemish front, to cut the Spanish domains in the Netherlands off from Austria. But the year 1639 saw only siege following inconclusive siege, now the Habsburgs victorious, now the Bourbons. Thwarted at present in the Netherlands, Richelieu took the war to the Iberian peninsula (for which he had laid plans since at least 1635). The conflict with France and its allies had greatly weakened the Spanish economy; shipping volume and commodity prices had both fallen, and Holland had wrested northern Brazil from Spain, greatly reducing Spain's imports of precious metals. Spain was thus far less able to resist an attack. Throughout the conflict, Portugal and Catalonia had been at sixes and sevens with Spain over their rights and liberties *vis-a-vis* the Spanish crown. The two states were willing to be part of Spain so long as nothing was asked of them; the moment they were inconvenienced, they rebelled. Quite as in need of funds as France, Spain attempted to impose the Quint, a tax of one-fifth of municipal income, on the Portugal and Catalonia; this attempt enraged the Portuguese and Catalans — owing to reduced Mediterranean trade and poor harvests, both economies had been in decline since the early 1620s — as did Spain's insistence that Portugal and Catalonia provide troops (which neither did).

Richelieu sought through *provocateurs* to incite the Portuguese and Catalans to rebel. (One of the *provocateurs*, a certain Saint-Aunais, posing as a traitor to France induced Spain to besiege the Catalan capital of Barcelona, provoking great anti-Spanish sentiment in the province.) Richelieu assured the Portuguese and Catalans of French support should they proclaim their independence from Spain; both did in late 1640 and early 1641, whereupon France signed treaties of alliance with both. Barcelona proclaimed Louis XIII its Count and Protector, and a French Viceroy took up residence there. Rather than serve as a launching point for the Spanish into France, as Madrid had hoped, Catalonia might very well now serve as a launching point for the French into Spain. These two secessions, won by diplomacy, were more beneficial to France and hurtful to Spain than any of the military contests between the two.

In 1641, Richelieu sought to take some of the coastal strongholds of Catalonia still loyal to Spain. To draw Spanish troops inland, the

French laid siege to the fortress of Tarragona; though neither the coastal strongholds nor Tarragona fell to them, in 1642 the French met with rather more success, taking certain fortresses in the county of Rousillon. As the French campaign continued, in late November 1642 Richelieu fell ill with pleurisy; with his own hands Louis fed the dying man the yolks of eggs. Richelieu asked that Giulio Mazarini, Jules Mazarin, the brilliant papal nuncio he had discovered and initiated into French and European politics, be appointed his successor, to which the King acceded. In the late afternoon of December 4, Richelieu died.

∾

Richelieu's objects were attained following his death. Under the regency of Queen Anne and ministry of Mazarin, *les grands* rebelled once again against the crown; the rebellion was suppressed, and monarchical absolutism flowered. In 1648, France, Sweden, the German princes, and the Holy Roman Emperor signed the Peace of Westphalia; not only did the Peace win for France most of the territories and fortresses Richelieu had sought, but it also, by conferring territorial sovereignty on the German principalities, broke the Holy Roman Empire into a multitude of weak states. Since the Peace made the western frontier of the Empire virtually indefensible, France and Sweden could now interfere as they pleased in the Empire's internal affairs. (The Holy Roman Empire would dissolve in 1806.) And though France and Spain would continue to fight intermittently until 1815, France would grow ever-stronger, Spain ever-weaker.

A century after Richelieu's death, Lord Chesterfield wrote that he disliked "the treaty of Hanover, in 1725, between France and England…for it was made upon the apprehensions…that the marriage of Don Carlos [of Spain] with the eldest archduchess [of the Holy Roman Empire]…would revive in Europe the exorbitant power of Charles V. I am sure I heartily wish it had, as in that case there had been what there certainly is not now — one power in Europe to counterbalance that of France…"

STUDY THE OPPONENT

Just as siegeworks must be tailored to the stronghold under siege, so, too, must your strikes be fitted to your opponent. "One must know the genius, character, and talents of the enemy general," said the military strategist Turpin de Crisse; "it is on this knowledge that one can develop plans." Caesar would always try to engage the enemy commander in lengthy negotiations, not only so that he might avoid battle, but also to give him a chance to study the commander should he not be able to do so. The moment France seemed likely to go to war with another European state, Napoleon would ask his librarian to bring him all manner of books on that state, on its history, geography, political life, and leaders. Study your opponent as you do yourself; to do so is to learn how best to strike and demoralize him.

The opponents of Caesar, Richelieu, Napoleon, Talleyrand, and Gates misunderstood them, and in misunderstanding, lost. The Pompeians' jeering at the Caesarians as they marched away from the Ebro shows how little they understood their opponent. In 49, Pompey drew up plans for attacking Caesar in Italy; following Caesar's lightning attacks on Italy and Spain, however could he think Caesar would await his attack, rather than attack him in Greece? With so much evidence of what his opponent was likely to do, why did Pompey continue to misunderstand him so? In bickering over consulships and praetorships before the battle of Pharsalus, the *optimates*, said Plutarch, were "behaving as though their adversary was Tigranes the Armenian or some king of the Nabataeans, when in fact it was Caesar — Caesar and that army of his with which he had stormed 1,000 cities and subdued more than 300 nations..." It was folly for Pompey's successors to continue the war against Caesar; if *Pompey* could not defeat him, how could they? So certain was Pompey of his superiority to Caesar that he was quite willing to agree to any augmentation in Caesar's power; so certain was Caesar of *his* that he was quite as willing to agree to any augmentation in Pompey's. One understood himself and his opponent far better than did the other. Caesar knew that his conquest of Gaul took far more brilliance and resolution than did Pompey's of the East; he also knew how greatly the discord and rivalry of interests among the *optimates* would weaken the Pompeians.

Never, ever suppose that a particular rival cannot hurt you. History is littered with people whose dismissal of an opponent was soon followed by their succumbing to that opponent; self-love all too often results in the depreciation of the opponent. In the early 1990s, WordPerfect refused to develop a version of its software for Windows 3.0, simply because its market share was so much greater than that of Microsoft Word. Windows 3.0 was wildly successful, and Word soon surpassed WordPerfect in popularity. The founder of Powersoft, Mitchell Kertzman, said, "Bill Gates was still [in the mid-1990s] thinking about OS/2 [once a rival to Microsoft's Windows operating system]. You would think, 'Does Bill Gates think about OS/2? Hell no. That war has been won.' But he was still thinking about it. When Microsoft displaces an OS/2 customer in a corporation, Bill knows about it. That's amazing. This is the least complacent company you have ever seen." (Wallace) Microsoft has spent billions of dollars countering threats that later turned out to be of little consequence. You simply do not know which rival can overthrow you and which will not; you are not omniscient. Do not be like the *optimates*; do not think your defeat inconceivable.

Study the Opponent before Fighting

Study your opponent as a scientist would a photon or gene: coolly and dispassionately, shorn of all obscuring hopes and wishes. See him as he is, not as you wish him to be. Take him on his own terms, not on terms appropriate to another; draw distinctions between him and all others. Of the *optimates* Meier observes, "Their conviction that the old republic was the only true order may have made it impossible for them to imagine that its opponent could be so strong." The trueness of the republic had nothing at all to do with Caesar, with his military and political skills. Why did Pompey misunderstand Caesar so? It may be that he could not fight Caesar as he was, and so psychologically must suppose him to be the sort of opponent he *could* fight. As with all thinking, so, too, with studying the opponent: certain natural tendencies obscure our view.

Do not gauge your opponent by his position. Position is a highly inexact indicator of human quality; a person may be far more or less than his title would suggest. No one who studied Caesar and Pompey, who analyzed their merits and campaigns, would have been in the least doubt which of the two would be victorious in the civil war — though Pompey held the higher position. Judge, not by position, but by nature.

Do not gauge your opponent by his manner. His manner is one thing, he another; manner is not the man. Life evolved to judge other life chiefly by its behavior, by how it presents itself; to judge so is to judge concretely rather than abstractly. *You judge so at your peril; you must resist this tendency at all costs.* Sallust remarked that Pompey's "honest face" hid his "shameless intentions;" ignore the face, and discover the intentions. Richelieu frequently wept and wore a "tormented" expression; yet it would have been the height of folly to conclude from this that he could not fight well. And much of Roman society thought Caesar effeminate. Similarly, do not take your opponent at his own estimation; that estimation may be quite a bit low or high of the mark, may have little to do with his true quality.

Do not assume your opponent is like you. One of the more difficult things to do is to imagine a greater or lesser ability than that which we ourselves possess. It is, for instance, quite difficult to know what a person who is less or more intelligent or educated than we are sees or does not see. The *optimates* assumed that Caesar was like them, that in seeking sole rule he sought only to further his own interests; they did not understand his work, what he hoped to achieve, in the least. As Pharnaces crossed the valley between them, Caesar assumed he would not be so imprudent as to attack the Caesarians upon their steep hill (because Caesar himself would not do such a thing); when Pharnaces *did* attack, the Caesarians were so taken by surprise that they very nearly lost. Early in his career, Napoleon would sometimes make the mistake of assuming his opponent would do what *he* would do in such a situation; since the opponent was not a military genius, however, he would always do something quite different.

Ask certain questions about your opponent. Is he of low or high quality? (One indicator of his quality: whom does he value, people of high quality, or of low?) Does the base equal the height? The Holy Roman Emperor Ferdinand II once consulted a commission of twenty-four priests on the propriety of signing a treaty with a Protestant sovereign; this told Richelieu much about the sensibleness of his opponent. (Richelieu himself was quite willing to form an alliance with any state, Catholic or Protestant, that might be of use to France.) Does he know himself, know his mode? Is he self-ignorant? Does he think himself quite good at that which he is in truth quite bad? Is he complacent and self-satisfied? Does he think himself invulnerable, that you cannot hurt him? In Euripides's *Bacchae*, "it is by playing upon Pentheus's vulnerability, his deep ignorance of his own nature, that [the god Dionysus] is able to possess him, humiliate him, and finally to destroy him." (Arrowsmith)

Is your opponent intelligent? Is he creative and versatile? What does he read? To know what a person reads is to know the person; books give an almost perfect measure of the mind. Like attracts like: the great mind is attracted to great books, the little mind to little books, or to no book at all. If your opponent reads "only what is for children and feeble intellects," rejoice. To an allied city the Parthian vizier showed the romances found in Crassus's camp and asked, "Do you still think the Romans formidable?" Nothing should please you quite so much as learning that your opponent is unintelligent or — that which is similar in its effects — full of himself.

How resolute is your opponent? How willing is he to fight, and to continue fighting? Where are his vital points? One of the vital points of the Veneti were the halyards of their ships. Under Richelieu, writes Burckhardt, "the task of France was to spy out the vulnerable spots in the greatest power in Europe of the sixteenth century, to estimate in Madrid and in Vienna the weaknesses of the Habsburgs, to search for the Empire's hidden, self-generated poisons..." (Vital points can be quite idiosyncratic. "Alexander was only defeated once," quipped the Cynic philosophers, "and that was by Hephaistion's thighs." Hephaistion was Alexander's male lover.) How will he react to each strike you contemplate? If you miscalculate here, all may be lost. Napoleon assumed that once he took Moscow, Tsar Alexander would sue for peace; Alexander did not.

It is well to remember that your opponent is likely to be "more the man of the day, than a regular and consequential character," to be wildly variable. In early 1800, as the French army engaged that of the Austrians in northern Italy, the Austrian general Melas did something quite uncharacteristic: he kept his army compactly massed and took it over bridges Napoleon had been told were destroyed. Faced on an open plain by 30,000 Austrian soldiers to his 22,000, and 92 artillery pieces to his 15, Napoleon very nearly lost. Fighting creates quite a different context; in such a context, your opponent may be quite a different person.

Continue to Study the Opponent while Fighting

In Gaul, Caesar would continually interrogate prisoners, and have his cavalry do reconnaissance, to learn the whereabouts and strategy of his opponents. Which vital points does your opponent leave undefended? Have new ones come into being, or been exposed, through his reaction to your strikes, or his striking in turn? What is his true state? It is quite natural to see one's own wounds and not the opponent's, to see one's own state and not the other's; but the opponent's may be far worse than one's own. "In war you see your own troubles," said Napoleon; "those of the enemy you cannot see." Though the condition of the French army round La Rochelle was quite bad, that of the Rochellois was far worse. Condition is always relative.

If you gain a victory or suffer a defeat, consider — rationally rather than emotionally — why you did so. The Pompeians' victory at Dyrrhachium greatly stoked their confidence. "They failed to consider," comments Caesar, "that the fighting had taken place neither when line had fiercely charged line, nor in pitched battle, and that our men had inflicted more harm on themselves because of their numbers combined with the lack of room than they had suffered at the hands of the enemy." The Pompeians had won, not by skill or courage, but by chance; but they did not understand the reasons for their victory, and in not understanding miscalculated their strength vis-à-vis the Caesarians.

Do not *think* yourself victorious; be certain of it. On that open plain in northern Italy, by 2:00 the Austrians had put the French to rout. Victory his, Melas formed his center into a column of route and handed over command to his chief of staff. A French division now arrived; Napoleon hurriedly drew up a new plan of battle and then hurled his soldiers at the Austrians. Within a very short while, the Austrians were dead, captured, or in flight. "The victor is not victorious," said the Roman dramatist Ennius, "if the vanquished does not consider himself so." Of Caesar Suetonius said, "It was his rule never to let enemy troops rally when he had routed them, and always therefore to assault their camp at once." Until certain of the enemy's submission, Napoleon's object was quite simply to annihilate him. "I congratulate you on the successes you have gained," he once wrote one of his officers. "But do not give yourself any rest; pursue the enemy, with your sword at his ribs, and cut all his communications."

STRIKE A VITAL
POINT STRONGLY

"The principles of war," said Napoleon, "are the same as those of a siege. Fire must be concentrated on a single point, and as soon as the breach is made the equilibrium is broken and the rest is nothing — the place is taken." Strike a vital point with great force, and you will make a breach. "There are in Europe many good generals," he continued, "but they see too many things at once; as for me, I see only one thing, namely the enemy's main body. I try to crush it, confident that secondary matters will then settle themselves." Secondary matters do settle themselves, once the main body is crushed.

You strike strongly by striking with a strong point. Napoleon's "highest rule of war" was this: "Try to put your strong points as to time and space against the enemy's weak points." (To do so, you must understand yourself and your opponent.) Though Napoleon would often have far fewer men than did his opponent, he would always have more at the decisive point of attack: "Strategy consists in always having, in spite of an army of inferior strength, a larger force than the enemy at the point attacked..."

You should try to strike your opponent in such a way as to place him between a Scylla and Charybdis. In Greek mythology, the Scylla was a sea-monster, the Charybdis a whirl-pool; the avoidance of one increased the risk from the other. No matter what the opponent might do, he is lost. Should he be corrupt, his corruption may offer a fine Scylla and Charybdis. By striking him with his own villainy, you will make it deuced difficult for him to strike back. Your opponent will be as in a bog: the more he fights, the deeper he will sink. Strike so that he hoists himself with his own petard.

Strike creatively. Of Caesar Meier writes, "One is struck by his rich imagination, his immense technical and tactical inventiveness..." (An instance of this is Caesar's having his men cut the halyards of the Venetic ships with sickles.) You must also strike with precision: "It is not sufficient that the soldier should shoot," said Napoleon. "He must shoot well."

Following a series of French victories over Austria in Italy, on April 18, 1797 General Napoleon Bonaparte and the Austrian plenipotentiary, Louis Cobenzl, signed the preliminaries of peace at Leoben. During the negotiations, Napoleon said:

Bonaparte considers himself superior to any king.

If I had a hundred thousand peasants in Russia, I would turn them into soldiers and organize them. I would then declare war on the sovereign and seize the throne.

France looks upon the Mediterranean as part of her own waters and intends to be predominant there.

That summer, the Directory, the committee of five that ruled France, appointed Charles-Maurice de Talleyrand-Perigord Foreign Minister. Though he had joined in the Revolution, detesting the maladministration of the Bourbons, Talleyrand was quite as put out with what followed. "I admit," he said, "that I should not be at all sorry if the details of this great calamity were lost for ever. What lesson could mankind possibly learn from such aimless and unpreconceived actions, the spontaneous results of unrestrained passions?" Talleyrand was heartily sick of the corruption, imprudent policies, and bellicosity of the Directory; but however were its members to be ousted, and who would take their place? The popular young victor of Italy might very well be able to do both.

Their alliance began through correspondence. Talleyrand wrote Napoleon to tell him of his appointment; Napoleon soon replied. Both made clear they wished to do away with the Directory, which Napoleon felt was "fit only to piss on." Napoleon arrived in Paris on December 5th; he and Talleyrand now met for the first time. The two were quite taken with each other, and their conspiracy against the Directory now began in earnest. They far preferred that Napoleon come to power through popularity than by the sword; much to their delight — and much to the discomfiture of the Directory — Napoleon was received by cheering crowds wherever he went. Napoleon and Talleyrand soon recognized, however, that "the pear is not yet ripe," that it was not yet time for them to overthrow the Directory. Napoleon also recognized that much of his popularity would be lost were he to remain idle: "In Paris, nothing is remembered for long. If I remain doing nothing, I am lost." And it was not in his nature to be without command; to a companion he remarked, "I've done with obedience. If I can't be supreme, I shall leave France."

The idea of conquering Egypt had come to Napoleon while still in Italy. The occupation of Egypt, he felt, would strengthen French commercial interests (and weaken those of England) not only in the

Middle East, but also — should France be able to reopen the ancient Suez Canal — in the East. France might even come to control India, which the English could reach only by sailing round the Cape of Good Hope. At the very least, French officers would be able to infiltrate the country and stiffen Indian resistance. The object of controlling Egypt was not, however, sensible. The French fleet was of far lower quality than the English, in part owing to the emigration of so many French naval officers during the Revolution. With the English in control of the Mediterranean, however could France supply its army in Egypt? Indeed, only a few months before Napoleon himself had rejected an invasion of England as too risky given the quality of the English fleet; as he wrote the Directory, "Whatever efforts we may make, we shall not attain naval supremacy for several years. To carry out a descent on England without mastery of the sea would be the boldest and most difficult operation ever undertaken." Would it not be equally difficult to descend upon Egypt, a vital English interest that country was certain to defend with might and main? That the English fleet was not in the Mediterranean at present was of no consequence; it would come the moment English interests were threatened. Moreover, it was one thing for the Mamelukes or Turks, both Muslim, to control Egypt, quite another for a Christian power to try to do so. And should another European state choose to attack France while its best generals and army were in Egypt, however could the country withstand that attack? As Markham observes, "there is an air of grandiose fantasy about the whole expedition."

Though Talleyrand had long advocated the creation of French colonies, this preternaturally far-sighted statesman recognized that the expedition to Egypt must fail. He may not, however, have been opposed to it: he preferred that France direct its warring passions toward a non-European state, and he recognized that the failure of the expedition would further weaken the teetering Directory. And though Talleyrand wished to create a constitutional monarchy in France, the monarch might be Napoleon or some other; if Napoleon were to be killed in Egypt, so be it. Napoleon asked Talleyrand to go to Constantinople to negotiate with the Turks; somehow or other, neither Talleyrand nor the envoy nominated in his place ever quite set out. The Turks were certain to disapprove of France's occupation of Egypt, and they might very well express that disapproval by executing French representatives.

On May 19, 1798, Napoleon set sail from Toulon. Though the English fleet under Admiral Horatio Nelson was sailing just off the coast, it was not able to intercept the French armada. On July 2, Napoleon landed at Alexandria; within a few hours the city was his. He then set out for Cairo, which he also soon took. On August 1, Nelson caught the French fleet in Aboukir Bay. Recognizing that their fleet was no match for that of the English, the French officers anchored their ships close to shore and placed all their cannon on the seaward side. So skilled were the English seamen, however, that they were able to sail between the French ships and the shore and annihilate the French fleet. The French army could now neither return to France nor be supplied; the squalor of Egypt, the continuous Egyptian resistance, and the isolation from Europe soon demoralized the French troops. To forestall a Turkish attack, Napoleon marched to Syria, where he met with little success; half the French army was lost in this campaign. Rather than come by land, in July the Turks did so by sea. Napoleon met and defeated them near Alexandria.

By the end of 1799, the Directory was as unpopular as it was vulnerable. Infuriated and alarmed by the French attempt to dominate both the East and the Mediterranean — Napoleon had taken Malta on his way to Egypt — and encouraged by the loss of the French fleet, Russia, Austria, Turkey, and Naples had formed the Second Coalition and declared war on France. Uprisings in Italy had forced the French army to withdraw from Naples and Rome — two of the cities that the first brilliant victories of Napoleon's career had obtained for France. Government finances had fallen into disrepair; the government could, for instance, no longer pay its armies. And so dysfunctional was the structure of government that conflict between the Directory and the legislative Councils, the Council of Five Hundred and the Council of Elders, could be resolved only through unconstitutional purges, greatly lessening the regime's legitimacy.

In October 1799, Napoleon secretly sailed for France, his army remaining in Egypt. At once, he, his brother Lucien (President of the Council of Five Hundred), Talleyrand, and others began to conspire to supplant the Directors — and particularly their leader, Vicomte Paul de Barras — with Napoleon, Emmanuel-Joseph Sieyes (one of the fathers of the Revolution and a constitutional reformer), and Pierre-Roger Ducos (a rather inconsequential figure). The French Constitution granted the legislative Councils the right to elect the Directors. The conspirators induced the Councils to move to St. Cloud so that they might "deliberate freely," and Napoleon was appointed commander of both the garrison of Paris and the guards of the Directory and the Councils. Talleyrand had kept Barras quiescent by making him think he was part of the conspiracy; once the Councils were in St. Cloud and Napoleon well in control of the garrison and guards, Talleyrand compelled Barras to "resign."

Rather than simply appoint Napoleon, Sieyes, and Ducos to the Directory, as Napoleon and the others wished, the Councils insisted on following Constitutional protocols. By mid-afternoon, Napoleon had lost all patience. He strode into the hall of Elders and, to the hooting of the members, delivered a speech as injudicious as it was provocative. Incensed by their continuing resistance, Napoleon turned to his aides and said, "If there is talk of declaring me *hors la loi*, I shall appeal to you, my brave companions in arms. Remember that I march accompanied by the god of victory and the god of fortune." This hint at the sword was not well received. Napoleon's secretary, Louis-Antoine Fauvelet de Bourrienne, tugged him out of the hall with the words, "General, you don't know what you are saying."

Napoleon now marched into the Council of Five Hundred, alone. Before he could speak, members of the Council set upon him; he was rescued by some grenadiers and taken outside. Sieyes and others urged Napoleon to enter the hall with troops. Though at first reluctant to do so, Napoleon changed his mind on hearing cries of "*hors la loi*" from within. He and Lucien addressed the guards; they told them that "brigands" in the pay of England were terrorizing the Council and had attacked Napoleon; officers spread the rumor that there had been an attempt on Napoleon's life. This was too much for the grenadiers; they rushed into the hall, the terrified members of the Council fleeing however they could, many through windows. Now seeing the judiciousness of acquiescence, at 7:00 p.m. the Council of Elders decreed the nomination of Napoleon, Sieyes, and Ducos as provisional Directors, or Consuls. By 9:00, a quorum of the Council of Five Hundred ratified the decision of the Elders. It was the 19th *Brumaire*.

Sieyes assumed that he would be the true leader of the Directory and Napoleon simply his "sword." Over the following months, however, through brilliant maneuvering and his popularity with the French people, Napoleon increased his, and lessened Sieyes's, power and reconfigured the government to strengthen the executive. Napoleon insisted a new constitution be drawn up and submitted to plebiscite as quickly as possible. ("A constitution," he later remarked, "should be short — and obscure.") This constitution was largely of Napoleon's making; there would be a First, Second, and Third Consul, the Second and Third simply "consultative" to the First. (The position of First Consul was to rotate among the Directors, but would not.) Consuls would hold office for ten years and could be reelected. In February 1800, the constitution was ratified by plebiscite.

Though not yet officially First Consul, Napoleon was by now well in control of governmental affairs. To strengthen the central government and weaken the governments of local communities (which had grown in power following the Revolution), Napoleon did away with the cantons of the Directory and strengthened the Departments, *arrondissements*, and communes, the leaders of which were to be appointed by the First Consul. He also created a Council of State to aid in the making of policy; so that he might rely on its advice, and to vitiate the many factions into which France was divided, Napoleon appointed the most gifted men he could find to the Council, regardless of party. (Of the Council Stendhal, one of his administrative officials, remarked, "Napoleon has assembled fifty of the least stupid Frenchmen.") To gain the support of the aristocracy, he revoked both a special tax on the rich and the law of hostages (which permitted the imprisonment of *emigre* relatives in France), let some of the *émigrés* return to France, and invited the aristocracy to balls and receptions. (Talleyrand, the sole member of the aristocracy in government, was responsible for most of these acts.) Napoleon also set about restoring the finances of the country. With funds confiscated from a French war contractor, he created the private Bank of France to aid in financing the government. He appointed Martin-Michel-Charles Gaudin, a brilliant Treasury official of the *ancien regime*, Minister of Finance. In strengthening the Departments, *arrondissements*, and communes, Napoleon also made the collection of taxes far more efficient. Like Richelieu, Napoleon was unifying France and giving it a strong central government; unlike Richelieu, he did so simply to give himself a strong instrument of conquest, the core of his Grand Empire.

Soon after the 19th *Brumaire*, George Washington died. Talleyrand delivered a speech praising Washington for having given his country liberty, peace, prosperity, and enduring institutions: "Washington was a man whose courage and genius did most to free his country from bondage and elevate it to the ranks of independent sovereign nations." Talleyrand proposed that a statue of Washington be erected in a Parisian square, and that the square be dedicated to him. Napoleon rejected the proposal.

∾

In one of his letters to Talleyrand from Italy, Napoleon stated that, were he a member of the Directory, he would reduce the legislature to a Council of State "possessed of no status in the Republic" and wholly subservient to the Directory. The legislature would have little say in either domestic or foreign affairs. "Why should the right to declare war, or maybe peace, really be considered a prerogative of the legislature?... Why include among the prerogatives of the legislature matters that are foreign to it?" He belittled the English Constitution, the spirit of which was quite lost on him. Napoleon drew little distinction between a society and an army; in neither, he felt, was liberty compatible with order. To his brother Joseph he would later write, "I haven't been able to understand yet what good there is in an opposition. Whatever it may say, its only result is to diminish the prestige of authority in the eyes of the people."

Talleyrand's views were quite different. As a member of the Constitutional Committee of 1789, he had composed the celebrated Article VI of its Declaration of the Rights of Man: "Law is the expression of the general will. All citizens have the right to participate personally or through their representatives in formulating it... All citizens are equal in its eyes and therefore eligible for any public honor, rank, and occupation according to their abilities." Talleyrand insisted the Declaration be taught in French elementary schools, that it become "the new catechism." In a letter to a fellow member of the French Institute in 1799, Talleyrand averred that only the legislature has the right to declare war and ratify treaties of peace and alliance, that the executive is entitled only to negotiate, and that only if it keeps the legislature well informed as it does so.

Talleyrand was in favor of a constitutional monarchy like that of England, not only because he wished to introduce political liberty into France, but also because such a monarchy would calm the other states of Europe, as they themselves were governed by monarchies. Talleyrand recognized that these states were as frightened by the French Revolution as by the Directory's immoderation, recklessness, and insistence on "revolutionizing" France's neighbors (which is to say, conquering and exploiting them). "What foreign nations need," he once wrote, "is to be reassured as to their independence, to be confronted with a settled constitution, and to be shown a firmly established government with whom they can treat." Talleyrand was also strongly opposed to the conquest of other states:

> True primacy, the only useful and rational kind, the only kind worthy of free and enlightened men, is to govern ourselves and not entertain the absurd desire to govern others... We have learned that all territorial expansion, all seizures by force or by cunning...are merely the cruel workings of political madness and abused power, the effect of which is to increase administrative expense and confusion and to diminish the comfort and security of the governed merely to indulge the whim or vanity of their governors.

In early 1800, Napoleon offered peace negotiations to the Second Coalition, but only to please the French people: he knew the Coalition would not accept the terms he offered. By late May, Napoleon was in northern Italy with 30,000 men and on June 14 inflicted a defeat on the Austrians at Marengo. Further French victories induced Austria in early 1801 to sign a separate peace at Luneville; the country recognized French possession of Belgium and Luxembourg, the French claim to the left bank of the Rhine, and France's "Italian Republic" (consisting of Lombardy, Emilia, Modena, and Bologna). Austria also ceded some of its Venetian territories and, to a French ally, Tuscany. In drawing up the terms of this treaty, Napoleon consulted neither his own Foreign Minister, Talleyrand, nor Austria. (When Talleyrand presented Cobenzl, now Austrian Foreign Minister, to the First Consul in one of the Tuileries drawing rooms, Napoleon remained sitting on the only chair in the room. After a while, he looked up from his work and motioned them to go.) "I know what the First Consul ought to do," Talleyrand later said to a friend, "what his interests demand, as well as the interests of France and of Europe: [institute a] federal system, which leaves each conquered ruler master of his own land under conditions favorable to the conqueror... [But] what if he chooses to incorporate and unite? Then he faces an endless task."

With Austria's separate peace at Luneville, the Second Coalition collapsed. Disheartened by the Austrian defeats and a failed English landing in Holland, Tsar Paul withdrew his armies. To draw Russia to the side of France, Napoleon returned the Russian prisoners of war unconditionally and intimated that he would cede it Malta. (Napoleon was ever weakening coalitions by proffering this or that to its members.) Paul was, however, soon assassinated and replaced by his son, Alexander. In early 1802, England, as war-weary as it was alone, signed the Peace of Amiens with France. On this treaty, too, Napoleon did not consult Talleyrand.

In spite of Napoleon's penchant for imposing treaties of his own making, his relationship with Talleyrand was at this time quite good. His secretary and archivist, Agathon-Jean-Francois Fain, recorded that "Talleyrand and [Secretary of State Hugues-Bernard] Maret were the only people allowed to witness the innermost workings of [Napoleon's] mind." Unlike Foreign Ministers under the Directory, Talleyrand worked and corresponded with Napoleon directly. The two were truly fond of each other; on Talleyrand's recovering from an illness in the summer of 1804, Napoleon wrote him, "I am glad to hear of your recovery. I need you and hope your life will be a long one." "The feelings that bind me to you," responded Talleyrand, "my conviction that by devoting my life to your career and to the great aims by which you are inspired I shall contribute to their fruition, have caused me to take an interest in my health that I had hitherto never felt." On another occasion, on the eve of his departure from Paris, Talleyrand wrote Napoleon, "Your ideas, your sayings, and the nature of the work that I see you engaged in, have made me realize the loss my impending absence will be to me..."

In their flattery and obeisance, Talleyrand's letters to Napoleon bear a striking resemblance to those of Richelieu to Louis XIII. Talleyrand seems to have hoped that his relationship to Napoleon would be like that of Richelieu to Louis XIII, that he would guide Napoleon as Richelieu did his monarch. "I was fond of Napoleon," Talleyrand would later write. "I had even become attached to him personally in spite of his faults; at the outset I felt myself drawn towards him by the irresistible attraction inherent in a great genius; I felt sincerely grateful to him for his kindnesses... I had delighted in his glory, some of which was reflected upon those who were helping him in this noble task." But while Talleyrand was possessed of Richelieu's political genius, Napoleon had none of Louis XIII's tractability.

In spite of the amity between the two, in 1802 Napoleon induced Talleyrand to marry his, Talleyrand's, mistress, a woman as stupid as she was vain. Napoleon hoped that by forcing Talleyrand, an unfrocked priest, to marry a divorced *demi-mondaine*, he would further Talleyrand's break with the Bourbons and the church and thus further bind Talleyrand to himself. So mortifying was this marriage to Talleyrand that he refused ever to speak of it, even to his dearest friend.

Through a plebiscite drafted by the Council of State rather than by the Legislature, in 1803 Napoleon altered the Constitution to make himself First Consul for life. He then induced the Senate, a creation of his new Constitution, to modify that Constitution through a *senatus-consultum* to let the First Consul nominate both his successor and the two other Consuls. In future, the First Consul was to preside in the Senate and nominate new Senators; he would also control the Electoral College. (One of Napoleon's first acts under the altered Constitution was to oust the twenty leading members of the opposition from the legislature.) Napoleon also created a Privy Council of eleven members that could issue *senatus-consulta* and sanction treaties and declarations of war. "With the constitution of the Life Consulate," notes Markham, "Napoleon held power far more absolute than any Bourbon monarch..."

Napoleon also created the position of *auditeur*, a sort of higher civil servant attached to a committee of the Council of State. "There is no conquest I could not undertake," he would later say on St. Helena, "because with the help of my soldiers and *auditeurs* I could conquer and rule the whole world... Having finished their education and reached the right age, the *auditeurs* would one fine day have filled all the posts of the Empire."

❧

Napoleon was quite as acquisitive following the Peace of Amiens as he was before it. While withdrawing from Holland (as the Peace required) only slowly, he forced Austria out of the Rhineland and south German states, took control of the Alpine passes, imposed an alliance on Switzerland, and acquired Piedmont, Elba, and Parma and new colonies such as Louisiana. While England was quite willing to let France expand to its "natural boundaries" — which were greater than its pre-Revolution boundaries — it would not accept French hegemony on the Continent. With the resources of the whole of Europe at its command, France would be able to create a colossal fleet that would threaten English sea power and export markets. The Continental view at the time was expressed by the Prussian Foreign Minister, Count von Haugwitz: "The arbitrary behavior of the English at sea is very inconvenient to be sure, but the Continental despotism [of the French] is infinitely more dangerous." In retaliation for the slowness of the French withdraw from Holland, England refused to evacuate its forces from Malta.

Since the French fleet would not be a match for the English for quite some time, Napoleon did not yet wish to go to war with England. He was, however, quite willing to hector the English: "Let it be understood that the first shot fired may mean the sudden creation of the Empire of the Gauls… The First Consul is only thirty-three and has hitherto only destroyed states of the second rank; who knows how long he would need, should he be compelled to do so, to change once more the face of Europe and revive the Empire of the West." One observer commented that Napoleon was obsessed with the idea of taking London, another that he could not resign himself to being the first man in Europe and the second on the seas.

In vain did Talleyrand try to preserve the peace, in vain did he counsel Napoleon that annexing other territories and attacking English interests were not in France's interests. Talleyrand's opinion was not well received; at a sitting of the Privy Council, Napoleon railed at him for being in favor of peace. To Lord Whitworth, the English Ambassador to France, a member of the English foreign staff wrote, "As for M. de Talleyrand, my lord, you must be well aware that he is so interested both as Minister and as an individual in the maintenance of peace that his assistance can be counted upon in the event of any occurrence which might lead to his influence securing the upper hand..." Talleyrand knew the Peace of Amiens could be lasting, if only Napoleon would let it be.

So antipodean were Talleyrand's and Napoleon's views that a rift between them was inevitable. Talleyrand continued to feel responsible for Napoleon's government, to consider it his own creation; if he were to resign, he would have no say in the conduct of affairs and would give up what little influence he now had over Napoleon. And by whom was Napoleon to be replaced? The return of the Bourbons or the Directory was unthinkable. As injudicious as Napoleon was, he was far better than his predecessors.

In March 1803, in the presence of all the ambassadors to France, Napoleon savaged Lord Whitworth for English actions. So rattled were the English by this outburst that they insisted France at once withdraw from Holland and Switzerland and declared they would retain Malta for a further ten years. Napoleon suggested Russian mediation, England refused, and Lord Whitworth left Paris in May, as did the French Ambassador London.

Since France was supreme on land and England supreme at sea — the war between them would be likened to that between an elephant and a whale — they could not at first quite come to grips. Both did what little they could: England seized French ships, and France interned English civilians of military age. Napoleon once again prepared an invasion of England at Boulogne.

In August 1803, the English landed Georges Cadoudal and other royalists on the Channel coast of France; Cadoudal and his men were to make their way to Paris and assassinate Napoleon. The First Consul soon learned of this plot, as well as that "a Bourbon prince" was to take his place once he was assassinated (though which prince remained a mystery). In early 1804, Cadoudal and the others were arrested in Paris. At the same time, Napoleon was told that the duc d'Enghien, the last of the Conde line of the Bourbons and the leader of a corps of *émigrés* in the Prussian invasion of France in 1792, was meeting with an English government official and exiled royalist at Ettenheim in the neutral territory of Baden.

Napoleon felt certain d'Enghien was the Bourbon prince who was to replace him and ordered that he be seized. Once d'Enghien was in Paris, however, it became clear that he had met with neither the English official nor the royalist exile and indeed was innocent of any connection to the Cadoudal plot. In spite of this, early in the morning of March 21, 1804, in the prison of Vincennes d'Enghien was tried by a military commission and shot by firing-squad. That an innocent Bourbon prince should be seized in neutral territory and shot horrified all of Europe, and particularly its royal houses. Only Russia, however, protested formally; Talleyrand responded simply that France had not asked for an explanation of Tsar Paul's death. (Alexander almost certainly conspired in his father's assassination; so guilty did he feel at his father's death that he once walked out of a performance of *Hamlet*.)

Why did Napoleon have d'Enghien shot? He wished to put an end to the royalist plots on his life; he also wished to make clear to the Bourbons, the royalists (both within and without France), the other European states, *and* the French people that the Bourbons were *not* to return. He may also have wished to incite the other states to war. But why had Talleyrand urged him on? He, too, wished to put an end to the plots and destroy Bourbon hopes of returning; but he also hoped that Europe, in its revulsion against the execution, would unite against Napoleon. (Talleyrand's reference to the assassination of Tsar Paul thoroughly embittered Alexander against the First Consul.) Talleyrand at once let it be understood throughout Europe that the execution of the duc d'Enghien was wholly Napoleon's doing, that he himself had had nothing to do with it.

Provoked by the royalist plots on his life, in May 1804 Napoleon finally consented to proclaim a hereditary French Empire in the dynasty of the Bonapartes. Talleyrand, Lucien, and others had long tried to induce Napoleon to do so, to reintroduce the hereditary form of government. Though Napoleon was in general quite averse to considering who might succeed him were he to be killed, Talleyrand and others recognized that he would be less so were the successor to be his son, the beginning of a Bonaparte dynasty. Furthermore, Napoleon came to see that a hereditary dynasty would simultaneously reassure the peasantry and others that they would retain the lands taken from the Church and *emigres* and make clear to the Bourbons and other royalists that they would not return. Much to Talleyrand's discomfiture, however, Napoleon insisted on taking the title of Emperor; Talleyrand beseeched him to take that of King instead, since the imperial title would greatly alarm the other states of Europe. Ignoring Talleyrand's counsel, Napoleon crowned himself Emperor on December 2 in the Cathedral of Notre-Dame, following an anointment by the Pope.

Talleyrand dearly hoped Napoleon would now appoint him Archchancellor, one of the Grand Dignitaries of the Empire. Should Napoleon die before formally appointing a successor, or should his heir still be a child, the Grand Dignitaries would be called upon to choose his successor or act as regents. Napoleon chose one of the consuls instead, greatly embittering Talleyrand against him.

In an address to the Senate in March 1805, Talleyrand tried to get Napoleon to see sense. The comparisons being made between Napoleon and Charlemagne and Alexander were, he said, "frivolous and deceptive. Charlemagne was a mere conqueror who founded nothing. Builders of states govern not only in their lifetime but for centuries to come... Alexander merely prepared a bloody end for himself by perpetually extending his conquests... Can it be said, however, that [Your Majesty has]' been led astray by a vague and indefinite passion for domination and aggression? The contrary is the case... Your Majesty's aim is to restore order in France and peace in Europe." In May 1805, Napoleon converted the Italian Republic into a hereditary kingdom, crowned himself king, and annexed Genoa to France, all in violation of the Treaty of Luneville. By August, the Third Coalition of Russia, Austria, and England had formed.

By now Napoleon recognized the futility of trying to cross the English Channel in force. He told Talleyrand of his new plan: "I mean to attack the Austrians before next November in order to have a free hand to deal with the Russians." The Prussian Ambassador to France reported that "M. de Talleyrand is in despair." In October, Talleyrand submitted an official memorandum to Napoleon suggesting how he might "turn his victories to account." Once Napoleon had defeated Austria, he should offer the country generous terms to induce it to form an alliance: France would withdraw to within its natural boundaries and renounce Italy; both France and Austria would agree not to acquire new territories. An alliance between France and Austria would redirect Russian imperialism from Europe toward Asia, which would ruin relations between Russia and England. (Talleyrand had advocated an alliance with Austria from the beginning of Napoleon's reign, and he would continue to do so until 1814.) But Napoleon, Talleyrand later wrote, was too taken with the thought of "marching on Vienna, gaining fresh victories, and dating his decrees from the Imperial Palace of Schoenbrunn to think of anything else."

In late October, Talleyrand learned that Admiral Nelson had annihilated the French fleet at Trafalgar. Royalist spies, perhaps within the French Foreign Ministry, had informed Russia of the movements of the fleet, and Russia had shared this information with England. It is uncertain whether Talleyrand colluded in the leaking of this information; he may have done so to weaken Napoleon and protect the England he so admired. Rather than view the loss of his fleet as a restraint, however, Napoleon took it to mean he could get at England only by subduing all of Europe and Asia.

Also in late October, Napoleon surrounded the isolated Austrian General Mack at Ulm and forced him to surrender with 50,000 men. In early December, Napoleon crushed the Austro-Russian army at Austerlitz. Talleyrand beseeched him once again not to weaken Austria: "I rejoice in Your Majesty's success as one whose thoughts and affections are closely concerned with Your Majesty's happiness and renown... Your Majesty may now crush the Austrian monarchy or raise it up. Once crushed, it will be beyond even Your Majesty's power to reassemble the fragments and re-create a single body. Yet the existence of this single body is essential. It is indispensable to the future security of civilized nations." An alliance with Austria would be far preferable; nothing would ensure peace, Talleyrand felt, as would an alliance between the two great states of Europe. A weakened Austria would only draw Russia into Hungary and thus Europe.

Ignoring Talleyrand's advice, Napoleon ordered him to wrest German and Italian territory and a sizeable war indemnity from Austria. In negotiating the Treaty of Pressburg with Count Louis Cobenzl — Talleyrand's schoolfellow at the College d'Harcourt and his "comrade" — Talleyrand did all he could to obtain better terms for the country. Though Austria was forced to cede Venetia, Istria, Dalmatia, the Tyrol, and Vorarlberg to France and to recognize Bavaria, Wurtemberg, and Baden as independent kingdoms (thus evicting it from both Italy and Germany), Talleyrand took it upon himself to reduce the indemnity by 10 percent and defer its payment. (Napoleon insisted it be paid immediately.) These concessions displeased Napoleon greatly: "You made a treaty for me in Pressburg that annoys me considerably." While Talleyrand and Cobenzl were negotiating the treaty, Napoleon announced that "the dynasty of Naples has ceased to reign;" he would soon crown his brother Joseph king of the principality.

Treaties such as that of Pressburg would only bring more wars, only force Napoleon to continue fighting. Austria would quietly rearm until it could fight him once more. Following the signing — or rather imposition — of the treaty, the Austrian Ambassador to Paris, Prince von Metternich, wrote, "During the campaign of 1805, M. de Talleyrand determined to bring all his influence to bear against Napoleon's ruinous projects… We are indebted to him for the slight, more or less favorable modifications in the Pressburg negotiations." (Some years later, Talleyrand would refuse to have his name engraved on a monument commemorating the treaty.) As he told the Austrian emissaries and others, Talleyrand now resolved to resign his post at the first suitable opportunity.

In June 1806, under its new Prime Minister, Charles James Fox, England issued peace feelers to France. Concessions were to be made by all sides. General Anne-Jean-Marie-Rene Savary wrote that Talleyrand "would have made any sacrifice to have peace with England. He told everyone who cared to listen to him that otherwise the Emperor's problem would be insoluble, that his position would be consolidated by a series of victories, the first of which would be A and the last Y or zero." In the negotiations that followed, Talleyrand made certain territorial concessions in hopes of forcing Napoleon to agree to what his Foreign Minister had promised. Napoleon, however, would have nothing to do with these concessions. Talleyrand also now began to perfect his slothfulness; he would slow Napoleon's acquisitions by sitting on his work, by simply not getting round to it. All this strained relations between the two.

That Talleyrand took every opportunity to induce Napoleon to make peace was well understood by the foreign diplomats in Paris. One, the Austrian Counselor of Legation, de Floret, wrote, "He takes skilful advantage of every circumstance to restrain his master's ardor by representing to him the paramount importance of making peace, the eagerness for which, in view of the general distress and the outcry in the provinces, can no longer be concealed." Talleyrand even tried to divert Napoleon's attention from conquest by procuring him women; to his dismay, he found that "sexual satisfaction was rarely a need and perhaps scarcely an enjoyment" for the Emperor.

On the 5th of June, Napoleon made Talleyrand Prince de Benevent. Since Benevento, an enclave of the Kingdom of Naples, belonged to the

Holy See, making Talleyrand its prince would, like his forced marriage, worsen his relations with the church and thus, Napoleon hoped, bind him even more to himself. Napoleon made his brother Louis King of Holland and awarded the duchy of Pontecorvo to one of his marshals, Jean-baptiste Bernadotte. On July 26, Napoleon created the Confederation of the Rhine, reorganizing and consolidating the German states under French suzerainty; the Holy Roman Empire now ceased to exist. Europe was informed of, rather than consulted on, these annexations. "A French news dispatch announces a new king," said the wife of an Austrian diplomat, "and princes of Benevento and Pontecorvo. It seems like a dream; one wonders whether all this can actually be happening in a civilized universe ordered by God. Here no one talks about it, or rather they keep silent, crushed by a sense of helplessness."

Throughout 1805 and 1806, Napoleon had secured Prussian neutrality by hinting that he might give the country a free hand in north Germany and grant it Hanover. On learning that the terms of peace required France to restore Hanover to England, the Prussian king, Frederick William III, became more bellicose, a bellicosity that encouraged Tsar Alexander to refuse to ratify a new treaty with France. Far from agreeing to an alliance with France, on October 7 Prussia issued France an ultimatum (that France withdraw beyond the Rhine by the following day); the result was war.

In battles at Auerstadt and Jena on October 14 and in the following pursuit, Napoleon annihilated the Prussian forces. In the space of three weeks, the renowned Prussian army — of which even Napoleon himself had been apprehensive — ceased to exist. By late October, the French were in Berlin; Frederick William sued for peace and on November 6 agreed to Napoleon's terms. Talleyrand presented Napoleon with a memorandum that, though lost, was doubtless similar to that which he submitted the year before, laying out how France might secure a general peace through an alliance with Austria. Once in Berlin, however, Napoleon learned through Prussian documents that Frederick William had been secretly negotiating with England and Russia throughout the previous year and that Russia intended to fight him in Poland. He now resolved on retaining Prussia as a base of operations.

Now in control of the northern German ports, Napoleon decreed the "Continental System," a boycott of English exports. England had a colossal national debt; by constraining its exports, Napoleon might force the country to default on its obligations; at the very least, he would make it far more difficult for England to subsidize its allies on the Continent. Indeed, so impoverished were the mass of English people that a constriction of the country's economy might very well lead to revolution. Only through such a system, Napoleon declared, could the Continent free itself from "the English tyranny of the seas" and commercial domination. It would, however, soon become clear that France itself was not to suffer as were the other states of the Continent. Furthermore, all recognized that the logic of the Continental System dictated that Napoleon control the whole of the Continental coast. Talleyrand was bitterly opposed to this decree.

Also in 1806, Napoleon induced the French Bishops to introduce a new catechism into French elementary schools. Question: "What should one think of those who would fail in their duties to our Emperor?" Answer: "According to the Apostle St. Paul, they would resist the order established by God Himself, and would make themselves deserving of eternal damnation." The contrast between Napoleon's catechism and that of Talleyrand, the Declaration of the Rights of Man, could not be more stark.

On February 8, 1807, Napoleon defeated the Russian army in a snowstorm at Eylau. The slightness of the victory electrified Europe; Napoleon had won, but only just. On the 14th of June, the French and Russian armies met again at the town of Friedland. The Russian commander, Count von Bennigsen, inexplicably placed his army in front of the town with a river to its rear. Napoleon forced the army back into the town and onto one or two of its bridges, where the French artillery annihilated it. Following Friedland, Talleyrand wrote Napoleon that the victory

> will go down as one of history's great events. But I see it not in terms of glory alone; I like to imagine it as a harbinger, a pledge of peace, the security which Your Majesty, after ceaseless effort, privations, and perils, has wrested for his subjects; I like to think of it as the final victory Your Majesty need win. That is why I cherish it, for despite its splendor, I must confess that its value would shrink immeasurably if Your Majesty were to march on to fresh battles exposing himself to fresh perils, the thought of which alarms me the more readily in view of Your Majesty's known scorn for them.

At once Tsar Alexander sued for peace; he and Napoleon met on a raft in the river Niemen. Dearly wishing to form an alliance with Russia to force England to make peace and free him to attack India, Napoleon did his utmost to charm the Tsar. He proposed that France and Russia divide Europe between them; Russia could do as it liked in Finland, Sweden, and Turkey, France as it pleased elsewhere. Alexander was as taken with Napoleon as he was his proposals. By the terms of the Treaty of Tilsit, the result of their meeting, Prussia lost half its population and revenue and would remain occupied until it paid France a colossal war indemnity. For their collaboration with Prussia, the Duke of Brunswick and the Elector of Hesse-Kassel would be deposed and their territories combined with others to form the kingdom of Westphalia, of which Napoleon's youngest brother, Jerome, would be king. Russia, Denmark, Sweden, and Portugal were to close their ports to England.

The Treaty of Tilsit was to Talleyrand an abomination. In his view, Europe must have a strong Austria in the East and a strong England in the West, the first as a buffer between Russia and France, the second for the cultural and social life of Europe. "If the English Constitution is destroyed," he once remarked to Madame de Remusat, "you may be certain that the earth will be shaken to its very foundations." Talleyrand was concerned less with the boundaries of individual states than with that between western Europe, which he viewed as enlightened, and eastern Europe, which he felt to be far less so.

Within a month of the treaty's signing, Talleyrand resigned as Foreign Minister, as he had resolved to do a year-and-a-half earlier. "For some time Napoleon adhered to the views that I felt it my duty to submit to him," he later wrote in his memoirs. "They were framed with the two-fold object of providing France with monarchical institutions...and of reconciling Europe to our good fortune and glory by our self-restraint. I freely admit that by 1807 Napoleon had long since strayed from the path that I had done my best to induce him to follow, but this was the first opportunity afforded me of resigning the post I held." Talleyrand's views on European affairs and the governing of France had not changed one whit from the time of the Directory through that of the Consulate and Empire: France must have a constitutional monarch who would restore order within the country and bring peace to Europe. *Napoleon* was not that monarch; *he* had restored order within France simply to make war more efficiently. Talleyrand had consistently advocated the relinquishing of conquered territory and an alliance with Austria; Napoleon had instead taken territory as far as the Russian border, and he was now poised, through alliances with Russia and Persia, to acquire further territory in the East.

When asked why he had resigned, with Napoleon's power at its height, Talleyrand replied, "It is quite simple. I do not wish to become the executioner of Europe." Napoleon accepted Talleyrand's resignation, made on grounds of ill-health, with the greatest reluctance. All of Europe recognized that Talleyrand was an advocate of peace; so long as he was Foreign Minister, Europe would continue to hope that Napoleon might one day make peace. Furthermore, so skilled was Talleyrand at politics that Napoleon supposed he could persuade the other states to accept whatever France might do. On August 14, Napoleon made Talleyrand a Vice-Grand Elector; as a Grand Dignitary of the Empire, Talleyrand would have a say in the governance of France should Napoleon be killed or ousted.

Talleyrand's relations with Napoleon cooled considerably after his resignation. Napoleon could not, however, exclude him entirely, as all of Europe viewed him as representing peace. "While treating M. de Talleyrand with the utmost consideration," reported the Duke de Pasquier, "[Napoleon] confined his interviews with him to a minimum and took particular care to prevent him interfering in matters of state without special permission..."

Following the Treaty of Tilsit and Talleyrand's resignation, Napoleon became far more peremptory. In 1807, he abolished the Tribunate, like the Senate a legislative body created by his Constitution. In 1808, he had the inscription *Republique Francaise* removed from the coinage and revived the Great Seal of the Bourbons (though he replaced the royal rooster with an eagle with a lightning bolt in its beak, round which were bees, a reference to the Merovigian kings of France). He created the University of France, a sort of Ministry of Education, to license the country's teachers; of it he said, "My principal aim in the establishment of an official body of teachers is to have the means of directing political and moral opinion." Higher education would become increasingly vocational, and the teaching of art, literature, and politics would be discouraged. By 1810, Napoleon would strengthen the Ministry of Police, greatly limit trial by jury, create "special courts" and political prisons, and permit detention without trial. By 1811, the government would control all the major newspapers of France. In vain would Talleyrand counsel Napoleon, "Frenchmen of any class whatever cannot remain assembled in silence," and, "We must have representation in France in order to levy taxes." The government of the Empire would become far more repressive than that of the *ancien regime*.

In July 1801, Napoleon and Pope Pius VII had negotiated a Concordat recognizing the Roman Catholic religion as "the religion of the great majority of the citizens." Napoleon had come to see that the principles of the Revolution were lost on the mass of French peasants, that their loyalty continued to lie with their priests. With the Concordat, he hoped to control the Pope and Bishops and, through them, the peasantry. In 1806, Napoleon had reported to the Council of State that "the Catholic priests behave well and are a great help. They have contributed to the fact that the call-up this year has been much better than in previous years... As a corporate body, they are foremost in speaking well of the government." By early 1808, however, relations between Napoleon and the Pope had deteriorated to such a degree that Napoleon felt no qualms in ordering French soldiers to occupy Rome (whereupon the Pope retreated into the Quirinal, or papal residence). A year later, he would annex the Papal States to the Empire.

In the spring of 1808, Napoleon dethroned the Spanish Bourbons. He did so not only to give his brother Joseph a throne, but also to acquire the country's financial and naval resources — which were far slighter than he supposed — and to extend the Continental System. Though Talleyrand felt that France should be certain of Spain and Portugal, and though he wished to divert Napoleon's attention from Austria and elsewhere and assure him of his loyalty by yet again favoring an attack on the Bourbons, he opposed the French occupation of Spain. While negotiating with the Spanish royal family in Bayonne, Napoleon learned that Talleyrand was criticizing his Spanish policy within the diplomatic community in Paris, worsening relations between the two.

To make it seem as though Talleyrand were in favor of the deposition of the Spanish royal family, Napoleon interned Ferdinand, the Prince of Asturias and heir to the throne, along with his brother and uncle at Talleyrand's estate of Valencay. He ordered Talleyrand to take up residence there so that he might act as host to the royal family. Hoping to impoverish

Talleyrand and thus increase his dependence, Napoleon refused to give him a stipend with which to support his guests.

On learning that their royal family had been dethroned, the Spanish people rose in revolt. By mid-summer, the French were at war in Spain; Spanish guerrillas, supported by an English expeditionary force soon to be commanded by the Duke of Wellington, began to wage a war of attrition. Only by transferring most of the *Grande Armée* from Germany to Spain could Napoleon drive out the English and pacify the country; and only by first inducing Russia to guarantee Austrian quiescence could he transfer the army. Napoleon now proposed to Alexander that they hold a "Congress" at Erfurt in the fall; he confided to Talleyrand that, once he had formed an alliance with Russia, he would pacify Spain, crush Austria, and then impose his will on Russia. The future of Europe would hold nothing but more wars.

Talleyrand's quiet and persistent opposition to Napoleon and his policies had achieved nothing. It was now time to fight.

The Context

Talleyrand's opposition to Napoleon's conquests was rooted in his recognition that a balance of power among the European states would be far more stable and conducive to civilization than any one state's expansion at the expense of other states. All the countries round France were either its clients or allies; a war of conquest would provoke Austria, Russia, and Prussia into acquiring the territory of these clients and allies, hopelessly upsetting the balance of power on the Continent.

Peace was in France's interest. The country was the richest, most populous, most homogeneous, and most centralized state on the Continent. In 1789, France had a population of 27 million, the Habsburg monarchy 25 million, Prussia 7 million, the British Isles 12 million, and Spain 10 million; Italy and Germany consisted of countless little states. While living in London following the Revolution, Talleyrand had written the Directory a memorandum denouncing French aggression: "The territory of the Republic is adequate to the needs of its inhabitants and the huge industrial combinations to which the spirit of liberty will give birth. France must remain confined within her own boundaries." Rather than invade the other states of Europe, he argued, France should form alliances and trade partnerships with them. (Talleyrand's policies differed radically from those of Richelieu, but were quite as sensible. The policies of both fit the context; each pursued an ESS appropriate to his period. At the time of Richelieu, the Habsburg Empire was strong, France weak; at that of Talleyrand, France was strong, the other states of Europe less so.)

The harsh and humiliating terms Napoleon imposed on defeated states deprived the states of their pride and self-respect and would only lead to more wars. Burckhardt observes that foreign policy must be "in accord with the principle of moderation, which alone can ensure that new international orders established by the conclusion of peace treaties are afforded some degree of durability." As Talleyrand recognized, Napoleon's treaties had no durability, because no moderation. The defeated states became nominal allies only; they would secretly rearm and then, once sufficiently strong, fight to regain their territories and subjects. *France did not have a single reliable ally.* Burckhardt also observes that "positions that are acquired by force can be maintained only if they are based on an arguable and enduring legal premise…" Richelieu was always quite careful to lay out the legal premises on which his forcibly acquired positions were based. (These premises may have been nothing more than pretexts, but at least Richelieu recognized the need for such pretexts.) Napoleon did not see the need for such premises.

The Continental System was clearly unworkable. States such as Holland lived by their trade with England; to cease that trade would be to die. And since England had deprived many of these states of their colonies, the states could obtain colonial raw materials only through England. England controlled the seas and thus much of the world's trade; prices for coffee, cocoa, sugar, pepper, spices, indigo dyes, and raw cotton rose to five or ten times their pre-System prices, even for French manufacturers. Money now flowed, not to producers or consumers, but to corrupt customs officials (or Napoleon's generals). The credit system, without which commerce withers, was disrupted and distorted. The moment a country fell under French sway, and was thus drawn into the Continental System, the value of its currency collapsed. "In view of the enforced suppression of the productive powers of the conquered lands," observes one historian, "one must conclude that the gigantic Napoleonic empire inevitably would have crumbled..."

To ensure that France itself should not suffer under the Continental System, Napoleon bled the other states of Europe. "My policy," he declared, "is France before all." Napoleon viewed the "new departments" — that is, vassal states — simply as markets for French goods or sources of raw materials; they were *not* to be competitors to the French industrial and commercial bourgeoisie. He imposed tariffs, special taxes, and bans to restrain and exploit the new departments. (Napoleon would, however, soon be hoisted by his own economic petard: the consumers of the new departments would be deprived of their purchasing power, making it quite impossible for them to purchase the goods of the old.) But it was one thing to exploit colonies, which were weak, quite another to exploit modern European states — as Talleyrand quite clearly recognized. Napoleon's policy provoked the most violent opposition and simply could not be sustained.

And not only Napoleon, but also his officers and soldiers viewed the new departments simply as territories to be plundered. In her memoirs, Madame de Remusat writes that

> the conquered countries saw themselves exposed to the rapacity of the conqueror, and many Austrian magnates and princes paid with the complete plunder of their castles for the obligation, forced upon them, of entertaining a general for a single night... They could not prevent this or that marshal taking what he liked with him at his departure from the castle. I heard, after the return from this campaign, the wife of [a certain marshal] relate laughingly that her husband, knowing her taste for music, had sent her an enormous collection, which he had found at the castle of, I forget what German prince; and in the same ingenuous manner she related to us that he had forwarded to her such a number of boxes full of Viennese candelabra and glassware, which he had laid violent hands on in all sorts of quarters, that she did not know what to do with them all.

Not only was bleeding the vassal states unsustainable, but the English economy was far more resilient than the French. Between 1785 and 1800, while the Revolution retarded French technological development, England experienced a technological leap. By 1800, the steam engine was the chief motive force in most English factories — but not in the French. And the English system of banking and credit was far more sophisticated than the French. Furthermore, most of England's exports went, not to the Continent, but to its colonies and the New World. In the upshot, the Continent — including France — would suffer far more under the Continental System than would England. "French overseas commerce," writes Markham, "was completely ruined as the System tightened: the great ports like Marseilles and Bordeaux seethed with discontent and latent royalism." Within three years of creating the System, Napoleon would begin to undo it.

Napoleon wished to create an empire in Europe as Caesar had done. But the Europe of the first century BC was not the Europe of the early 1800s; it was one thing to conquer Gaul, a land of factious tribes, quite another to conquer states with strong national identities. Even in Richelieu's time, when the borders of the European states were somewhat fluid — France was able to incorporate Lorraine, for instance — no country could create an empire on the Continent; even the Habsburgs with all their riches and might could not hope to do so. By the time of Napoleon, nationalist sentiment had been growing for centuries in Europe; the industrial revolution greatly stoked this sentiment, as it created a colossal middle class that insisted on representative government and national self-determination. Napoleon was not pursuing an ESS; in 1813, Metternich would say to him, "Between Europe and the aims you have hitherto pursued there is an absolute contradiction." "[O]nce an ESS is achieved," writes Dawkins, "it will stay: selection will penalize deviation from it." Napoleon was deviating from the recognized ESS of Europe: one European state shall not conquer another. Caesar himself could not have created an empire in early 19th-century Europe — nor would he have tried.

In spite of their present disunity and distrust, *a coalition of European powers was certain to win over the long term*. The resources of France, in men, material, and specie, were limited; and by 1805 or so, both the French people and Napoleon's generals were heartily sick of war. Furthermore, the Napoleonic Empire was the creation of a single military genius; no such genius would follow to hold that Empire together. "My poor little mind," said Talleyrand, "fails to comprehend that what we are doing beyond the Rhine will last any longer than the great man who is ordering it...."

The Object

Talleyrand did not care a fig about individual rulers. France was to be the preeminent state of a civilized Europe; civilization was all. So long as France's ruler governed well, Talleyrand would support him; once he began to govern badly, Talleyrand would oppose him (why he also opposed the Bourbons and the Directory). "Regimes pass," observed Talleyrand, "France remains." Talleyrand was not so simple as to equate the ruler with the state, or morality with authority: "Sometimes by serving a regime zealously, one can betray all the interests of one's country, but by serving the latter, one is sure to betray no more than intermittencies." Napoleon was simply an "intermittency." Had Talleyrand lived during the late Roman republic, he would have fought the *optimates*, so greatly did they maladminister the Empire; he would also have fought Caesar, had he, too, done so. Just as "Caesar was general not of the senate, but of the state," (Mommsen), so, too, was Talleyrand the adherent not of Napoleon, but of France, Europe, and civilization.

Napoleon would never make peace so long as he could do as he pleased; he must be hemmed in and hedged about, but *not* deposed — a very difficult thing to do. "You must realize," wrote Talleyrand to Madame de Remusat, "that in spite of all his faults the Emperor is still indispensable to France, which would otherwise collapse, and we must do our best to prevent this..."

The Self

Talleyrand was peerless in his understanding of politics. Like Richelieu, he had a clear view; he understood the context, always considered the long term, and had preternatural foresight. What Talleyrand valued most was the doable, the attainable, the possible, a political realism he learned in part from the Revolution. Talleyrand's god was reality. He also understood economics and finance. As a young man he was a friend of Panchaud's, a Geneva banker who created England's flourishing fiscal system. In 1789, Talleyrand submitted a paper to the Estates-General calling for the creation of a National Bank — which Napoleon later instituted as the Bank of France — a sensible and fair system of taxation, a new system of land distribution, and the freeing up of church property. (The church owned one-fifth of all the land of France, and most of its arable land; much of this land was simply stagnant capital.)

Talleyrand was brilliant. He was also supremely well-educated. (He was so unhappy while in seminary as a young man that he spent most of his time in its library reading.) Talleyrand was always learning and growing, was quite plastic and adaptable. He had almost perfect self-control; he was calm and deliberate and hated impulsivity. He was always rational, always guided by his long-term self-interest, never by emotion; he never let his emotions muddle his thinking. Only rarely was he spiteful or vengeful. He had an exquisite manner, a rare and pleasing grace, poise, and refinement. He loved risk, loved to gamble in both games and life; his niece and lover, Dorothee, remarked that he had "a kind of courage marked by coolness and presence of mind, a bold temperament, an instinctive bravery that instills an irresistible craving for danger in all its forms, which makes perils alluring and hazards inviting." Talleyrand had a passion for living well and so was always after money; but he never let this passion alter his objects.

Like Caesar, Talleyrand was preternaturally self-reliant. His biographer Orieux observes that "the train of insults and threats following him about all his life altered his conduct and thinking no more than the trail of dust from a thoroughbred's hooves slows its race." He was sphinx-like, revealing as little of his thoughts as possible. Whatever he did, he did quietly, without calling attention to himself. Whence came this self-reliance? Talleyrand knew who he was, a Perigord, one of the older aristocratic families of France, advisors to its kings. He had had a wretched childhood; in her novel *Delphine*, Germaine de Stael represents Talleyrand as Madame Vernon, whom she has say, "No one took care of me when I was a child. I bottled up my feelings, acquiring at an early age the art of dissimulation, stifling my natural sensitivity... I grew up imbued with profound contempt for people." His parents never once hugged him, and he never once spent a night under their roof. (The horrid woman with whom they placed him once left him unattended atop a chest of drawers; the fall broke his foot, maiming him for life.) And Talleyrand had been in the wilderness, both literally and figuratively: while in exile following the Revolution, he had bought and sold tracts of land in the wilds of the United States. Nothing so contributes to self-reliance as does being in the wilderness.

Talleyrand was profoundly resolute; he would rather have died than succumbed. With Talleyrand, one could do only one of two things: what Talleyrand wished one to do, or have Talleyrand shot. The wilderness held no terrors for him; he had been there, and he had learned that it is not to be feared. Talleyrand's only vital point was his life.

Talleyrand valued civilization, high culture, and the arts above all else; he supported whatever furthered civilization and opposed whatever impaired it. His friend Aimee de Coigny once said of him that he was "interested solely in curbing violence." Talleyrand deplored the ignorance of the mass of Frenchmen and proposed providing each child with a free elementary education. (His princedom of Benevento was the only European state to provide free public education.) Talleyrand felt that women contribute greatly to civilization and that they should attend school: "Educating women is one of the best ways to refine and uplift morals." His female friends, of which he had a great many, were exceedingly dear to him. (Talleyrand also recognized the contribution women make to political affairs, that they were a source of both information and influence; indeed, he felt that "women *are* politics.") Quite as much as Napoleon, Talleyrand lived at the wrong time; he loved tranquility, order, and the arts, but lived at a time of war, instability, and ignorance.

And perhaps most important of all, Talleyrand understood all this, understood himself.

The Opponent

Napoleon's object, that of creating an empire in early 19th-century Europe, tells us much about him. That object was nonsensical. Napoleon simply did not understand the context.

Napoleon fancied his fighting the ancient monarchies of Europe to be quite like Caesar's fighting the *optimates*. It could not have been less so. Caesar's doing away with a superannuated, corrupt republic and creating a monarchy fit the context of the Roman Empire of the first century BC.

Napoleon's doing away with incipient constitutional monarchies and creating an autocracy did not fit the context of early 19th-century Europe. Caesar's monarchy fit the context and benefited the ruled, Napoleon's did not. (Compulsion, absolutism, is in itself neither good nor bad; the nature of the society and autocrat make it so. The supplanting of the kings of ancient Rome by a Senate of aristocrats was sensible and functional; so, too, was the supplanting of the Senate by a monarch far later.) "Where [Caesarianism] appears under other conditions of development," said Mommsen, almost certainly thinking of Napoleon, "it is at once a caricature and a usurpation." History, he continues, "cannot any more than the Bible hinder the fool from misunderstanding and the devil from quoting her..." (Thus the conundrum of government: A low-quality person can do far more evil as a monarch, a high-quality person far more good; a low-quality person can do far less evil as a democratic ruler, a high-quality person far less good.) In truth, Napoleon was far more like the *optimates* than like Caesar; he maladministered his empire quite as much as they did theirs, exploited his "provinces" — the other states of Europe — quite as much as they did theirs. (Napoleon's policy of "France before all" echoed that of the *optimates*, Rome before all.) Caesar was civilization, Napoleon anti-civilization.

Napoleon was quite right in thinking that the monarchies of early 19th-century Europe no longer fit the context; he was quite wrong in thinking the solution was a Caesar. Napoleon assumed that, just as for the Romans the alternative had been "Caesar or the republic," it was for the Europeans "Napoleon or the old monarchies." Napoleon did not wish to do away with the rotten old monarchies of Europe and replace them with new, functional republics; he wished to do away with the rotten old monarchies and replace them with himself. In 1796 he wrote to the Italian Count Melzi, "Do you think I am conquering Italy...to establish a Republic? What an idea! It is an illusion that infatuates the French, but it will pass like all the others." Napoleon could not see that the monarchies were slowly falling away of themselves through an economic and political process, and that their being supplanted by constitutional monarchies (proto-democracies) was far more adaptive, and far better, than their being supplanted by himself.

Two hundred years before Napoleon, Richelieu recognized that the peoples of Europe were coalescing into collective entities with a sense of national identity. Though this process was well advanced by the early 1800s,

Napoleon perceived neither nationalist sentiment nor the historical and cultural differences from which that sentiment sprang. To his brother Eugene he once wrote, "You will come to see that the states of Europe are very much alike." And to one of his marshals, Joachim Murat: "The climate of Europe is the same everywhere." Napoleon's not seeing the distinctions among states was one of the causes of the Spanish debacle: he thought the Spanish middle class would support the French, not recognizing that Spain had only a very small middle class and was "predominantly a country of priest-ridden peasants." (Markham) Caesar recognized that Gaul was semi-civilized and could be appended to the Empire and Romanized, that Germany was barbarous and could not.

It was not simply that Napoleon did not understand the context; he seemed to think it of no consequence. Napoleon was the perfect solipsist; he proceeded as if in a vacuum, as if he did not live in a world of circumstances. When one of his admirals protested that the roughness of the sea made a naval demonstration in honor of his birthday impossible, Napoleon exiled him on the spot and insisted the demonstration proceed; as he paced the beach, livid, 2,000 sailors died. Caesar could subjugate the Gallic tribes, but not the British or Germanic; indeed, even *within* Gaul Caesar had to content himself with *de facto* armistices with the more resolutely independent tribes. Caesar recognized limits, that the context bounded and circumscribed what he might do; Napoleon did not. Talleyrand once wrote Madame de Remusat that Napoleon "grows suspicious whenever I mention the word 'moderation.'" To Napoleon, Talleyrand's recognition of limits was simply an indication of his inferiority, of his narrowness of vision.

Napoleon understood politics quite as poorly as he did the context. In military affairs, he was a genius, in political, whether on a small or large scale, a simpleton. He was as obtuse in politics as he was brilliant in war; only in military affairs did the base equal the height. In politics, he was witless; he simply could not do statecraft, was not in the least a political realist. What Mommsen says of Pompey is quite as true of Napoleon: "For nothing was he less qualified than for a statesman." Napoleon was far too asymmetrical to be the ruler of a state. (Since Napoleon simply went about parroting him, it was quite a while before Talleyrand realized that Napoleon did not understand politics; Talleyrand was at first quite taken in.) Napoleon believed in palmistry — in *political* affairs; he would *not* consult the palms of others when engaged in military affairs, that is, when engaged in that which he understood. Nothing shows incompetence in a thing as does resorting to magic.

Napoleon's conception of international affairs is shown by his remark to his Minister of Police, Joseph Fouché: "Europe is no more than a rotten old whore whom I shall use as I please with 800,000 men." To Napoleon, politics was neither more nor less than throwing dust in others' eyes; it was dissemblance and obfuscation, simply a way to buy time. (An instance of this is his retaining Talleyrand to make the peoples of Europe think he preferred peace.) Talleyrand appointed Persian and Turkish specialists to the college de France to train French diplomats for posts in the Near East; Napoleon preferred to appoint his generals ambassadors.

Caesar was both a general *and* a politician. In Gaul, observes Gelzer, *Caesar augmented the power of his legions through diplomacy* — here appointing a trusted individual king, there strengthening the aristocracy against an un-reliable king, or consolidating the position of certain tribes *vis-à-vis* others. In Caesar, writes Mommsen, "the officer was thoroughly subordinate to the statesman... A regularly trained officer would hardly have been prepared... to set aside the best-founded military scruples in the way in which Caesar did on several occasions... Several of his acts are therefore censurable in a military point of view; but what the general loses, the statesman gains." One might say that, in Napoleon, the statesman was thoroughly subordinate to the officer. Why did Caesar not march on Rome far earlier than he did? Certainly he did not do so in part because Gaul was not yet pacified; but he also did not do so because he had confidence in his diplomatic and political skills, that they, too, might enable him to attain his objects. Battle was the sole means by which Napoleon could attain *his*. Lacking political sense, he never appreciated Caesar's, which was immense. Napoleon admired Caesar without ever understanding him.

That a revolution should have swept away the monarchy of the richest, most populous, and most homogenous state of Europe, and that a reckless, pugnacious government should have taken its place, frightened the other states of Europe considerably. Talleyrand argued that France must there-fore seek to calm and reassure the other states. So poorly did Napoleon understand politics, however, that he drew quite the opposite conclusion: "Between old monarchies and a young republic the spirit of hostility must always exist. In the existing situation every treaty of peace means to me no more than a brief armistice; and I believe that, while I fill my present office, my destiny is to be fighting almost continually." (Not for Napoleon was an *entente cordiale*.) Napoleon's unilateralism and militarism did not make him respected as he hoped; they simply made him hated.

As without France, so within it. Napoleon did much to vitiate the French governmental institutions Richelieu had done so much to strengthen. He simply did not understand the need for such institutions; he sought to make France like the late Roman republic, in which individuals were strong and institutions weak. And, unlike Caesar and Talleyrand, Napoleon never sought the aid of women in attaining his objects; to Madame de Remusat he declared that "he would have no women ruling at his court: they had injured Henry IV and Louis XIV."

Napoleon did not understand politics in its most elemental sense: how to please others, how to discern their wishes and desires. He once asked the duchesse de Fleury, a woman renowned for her love affairs, "Well, Madam, do you still love men?" ("Yes, Sire," came the reply, "especially polite ones.") To Dorothee he said in the presence of his court, "Those wretched Perigords ceased to be of any concern to me a long while ago." Germaine de Stael wished to cut a figure in the world; when she asked Napoleon, "Who is the greatest woman, alive or dead?", he replied, "The one who has had the most children." Such remarks served no purpose whatsoever and only turned others against him. Napoleon would savage French aristocrats and foreign diplomats quite as freely as he would his own administrators. His continual belittlement and humiliation of Talleyrand served only to increase the latter's disaffection. (Josephine's daughter, Hortense, once remarked that "Napoleon would do better to humiliate less and punish more.") Napoleon was truly unsociable; as Bourrienne said while dragging him from the Council of Elders, "General, you don't know what you are saying."

As with other elements of the context, Napoleon simply did not see others' interests. Of him Madame de Stael said, "He treats men like things, never as his equals. Hate is as non-existent as love. For him there is only one person, himself; all others are mere ciphers." That Napoleon supposed his object not only attainable but *desirable* shows how very solipsistic he was. Of the French Stendhal would say, "In January 1814 the most vital people in Europe were, as a nation, nothing better than a corpse." (Napoleon took a rather novel approach to independence movements: rather than free Corsica, he enslaved France.) Had Napoleon been able to expand his Empire over the whole of Europe, the latter would have become a police state. *The pride of one man requires the submission of the multitude.* Napoleon did not understand that human beings dislike submission, that they wish to order their world, *not* to have it ordered by another. (Even many of Caesar's *followers* disliked his autocracy and wished to influence the world as they saw Caesar doing.) Talleyrand appreciated the interests of the social group, Europe; Napoleon did not.

Napoleon understood economics and naval matters as little as he did politics. His economic views were pre-Adam Smith, that prosperity comes, not from commerce and industry, but from territorial conquest. (The significance of the industrial revolution was quite lost on him.) No one with the slightest understanding of economics could have supposed the Continental System might work, or that the vassal states might be bled indefinitely. Though Talleyrand continually pointed out to him the commercial value of colonies, Napoleon sought none. To Napoleon, said the financier Ouvrard, credit was "an abstract idea, in which he saw merely the dreams of ideologists, and the empty notions of economists." Though nothing was more critical to Napoleon's plans than creating a fleet with which to strike England, and though France had superb natural harbors and was rich in the raw materials of shipbuilding, unlike Richelieu Napoleon never drew up a systematic plan for creating a navy. And it was Napoleon who ordered the French Admiral Villeneuve, over the latter's objections, to set sail from Cadiz to face Nelson at Trafalgar.

Understanding neither the context nor politics, economics, and naval affairs, Napoleon could not possibly know what he was doing. Following his victories over Prussia in the fall of 1806, he wrote Talleyrand, "Things here have turned out exactly as I calculated they would do two months ago in Paris, march after march, event after event, one might almost say; I was right in everything." But what did this matter? It was all to no purpose, as Talleyrand recognized. When during the negotiations of the Treaty of Tilsit Savary said to Talleyrand, "If peace is not made within a fortnight, Napoleon will cross the Niemen [into Poland]," Talleyrand rejoined, "And what will he do when he gets there?" As was said of such generals in antiquity, Napoleon knew how to win victories, but not what to do with them.

Richelieu recognized that France, rich and fertile, had only to see to its own security, and that by creating a strong navy and extending its territory to its natural borders. Why did Richelieu fight? To bring about a balance of power in Europe. And Napoleon? To destroy that balance. When Louis XIV went beyond the boundaries laid down by Richelieu, and expanded into Germany, the Low Countries, and Spain, all of Europe united against him; Louis then faced invasion and had to melt down his silver to pay his troops. Napoleon learned from neither Richelieu's example nor Louis's folly.[3]

Napoleon did indeed contribute to freeing Europe from "obsolete ways of living and inconsequential talk." The continual French victories forced the other states of Europe to make long-needed reforms; if they were to be capable of opposing France, they must reorganize not only their armies, but also their governments and societies. The ruling aristocrats were gardens that fancied themselves jungles; their being continually worsted by a "Corsican squireen" did much to lessen the veneration in which they were held, to hasten the decline of their rule. Unlike Caesar, however, Napoleon did not sweep away rotten old structures and create vital new ones; he simply swept. "Barely once in a thousand years," said Mommsen, "does there arise among the people a man who is a king not merely in name, but in reality." Caesar was a king in reality, Napoleon an Emperor "merely in name."

❧

Why was Napoleon as he was? Socrates observes in the *Protagoras* that politics is a craft like any other, architecture, shipbuilding, or shoemaking: it requires certain natural gifts and study. A politician with neither is no more suited to govern than is a shipbuilder without talent or training to build ships. Napoleon's genius lay in war, not in politics; genetically, he was

---

3 The *Code Napoleon* is often cited as evidence of Napoleon's statesmanship. But Napoleon contributed little to the *Code*, which was begun well before he became First Consul and until 1807 referred to as the *Civil Code*. Napoleon was the midwife, not the mother, of the *Code*. As "interesting as his observations occasionally are," writes the French legal historian Esmein, "he cannot be considered a serious collaborator in the great work." But does his promoting the *Code* in France and the vassal states not show a concern for the group? Napoleon once urged his brother Joseph to adopt the *Code* by saying it would "fortify your power, since by it all entails are cancelled, and there will no longer be any great estates apart from those you create yourself. This is the motive that has led me to recommend a civil code and establish it everywhere."

a warrior. He could not have been a great statesman, even had he wished to be. Napoleon did not understand this, did not understand himself (as his fancying himself like Caesar clearly shows, and his once remarking, "I am a man who can be told anything"). He supposed that since he was a genius in military affairs, he was a genius in all else.

Napoleon was enrolled in French military schools from the age of nine; he learned little of politics in these schools, and he seems to have read little of politics later in life. While a student in Paris, Talleyrand would visit Richelieu's tomb and "hold conversations" with him; Napoleon's "conversations" were with ancient and modern generals. "The soldier," said Mommsen, "played in [Caesar] altogether an accessory part, and it is one of the principal peculiarities by which he is distinguished from Alexander, Hannibal, and Napoleon, that he began his political activity not as an officer, but as a demagogue." And certainly Napoleon's family could teach him little about ruling an empire. Neither his father nor his mother seems to have been a realist; his father joined the quixotic Corsican struggle against the French occupation, and his mother would counsel him on Elba, "Go, my son, fulfill your destiny. You were not made to die on this island." (In 1832 she would tell a friend of the Duke of Reichstadt's, Napoleon's son, "You will tell him that above all else he must respect his father's wishes. His hour will come. He will ascend the throne of France.")

Napoleon also learned little of literature or the arts either in school or later. "It is a pity," said Talleyrand, "that so great a man should be so ill-bred." Napoleon learned the traditions of neither his native nor his adoptive country. "Napoleon had no political or religious principles...of any kind," observes the French historian Emile Dard. "He lacked tradition, a guide more essential to a man of genius than to ordinary mortals." Being uncultivated, Napoleon did not know to what use to put money and power; conquest was his sole interest. A single trait, military genius, propelled Napoleon to the summit; he was rather like the ancient Romans: military brilliance had gained him an empire, but he was in no way fitted to ruling that empire.

Indeed, this is why Napoleon did not perceive nationalism: he himself did not feel it. "Wherever his charger carries him and his Roman eagles force their way," commented the French historian Albert Sorel, "there for him will be France." It is unlikely that Napoleon felt a strong affinity for his adoptive country: he was named after an uncle who died fighting the French on Corsica; he may well have been mistreated by his French schoolfellows; while garrisoned at Valence as a young man, he wrote *Lettres sur la Corse*, a paean to his native land; and, he himself felt great admiration for, and indeed supported, the Corsican independence leader, Pasquale Paoli. In 1813, Napoleon would declare to the Legislature, "France has more need of me than I have need of France." Only a foreigner could have said this.

On becoming First Consul — which is to say King — Napoleon was a *young man*, only 30, to the ancient Romans still an *adulescens*. When Caesar became governor of Gaul, Richelieu First Minister, and Talleyrand Foreign Minister, all were in their early 40s; had they been ten years younger, they would almost certainly have governed far less well. The mode of the young man is to think himself unique, exempt from necessity, superior to one and all, and certain to do great deeds. Of young men Aristotle said:

> They are eager for honor, but more eager for victory; for youth wants superiority, and victory is a kind of superiority… They have exalted ideas because they have not yet been humbled by life or learned the power of necessity. Moreover, their hopeful disposition makes them think they are equal to great things… They would rather do noble deeds than useful ones… All their mistakes lie in the direction of doing things excessively and vehemently. They disobey Chilon's precept by overdoing everything; they love too much and they hate too much and the same with everything else…. But if they do wrong, it is because of hubris, not wickedness.

To Goethe Napoleon said, "The world should be shown how happy Caesar would have made it, how different everything would have been, had he been given time to bring his lofty designs to fruition." It is quite like a young man to suppose such a thing, that a "great man" (himself) will come and make the world happy. To Goethe Napoleon also vilified Tacitus, who hated tyranny, and extolled Corneille, of whom Auchincloss said, "He worshipped glory while understanding that it led only to the grave."

Richelieu, Talleyrand, and perhaps Caesar had been in the wilderness; Napoleon had not. In the wilderness, we learn that the gods will allow us to fail and to suffer, that success is not ordained us (we come to think "human thoughts" and to be *exceedingly* careful); we cease striving for others to view us as favored by the gods, as fortunate and exempt from necessity (we learn self-reliance, because we have only ourself; we live in oblivion; humanity has simply ceased thinking of us). Napoleon's great success from an early age seemed to confirm the supposition of his youth — that he was exempt from necessity, not bound by the context. To the people of Madrid he would soon declare, "God has given me the will and the force to overcome all obstacles."

Napoleon was only in poor control of himself; he often went with his passions rather than his reason. After savaging Lord Whitworth, the English Ambassador, Napoleon confessed to his stepdaughter, Hortense, "Talleyrand told me something that put me in a temper, and this great gawk of an ambassador came and put himself in front of my nose." Following the imbroglios in the Council of Elders and Council of Five Hundred in 1799, Napoleon confessed that he had lost control of himself. "The Emperor," said Talleyrand, "exposed himself to danger the moment he was able to do a quarter of an hour sooner what I obliged him to do a quarter of an hour later." On appointing Jean-Baptiste Nompere de Champagny Foreign Minister, Napoleon advised him, "You ought to keep my letters under your pillow for three or four days before sending them."

But why did Napoleon not come to understand the context over time, to alter his object? Nothing becomes so clear from a prolonged study of Napoleon as this: *Napoleon could not grow.* The commander of the French forces in Italy in 1796 was the farmer on St. Helena in 1820: a martial genius, imperious, and impolitic. The political philosophy he laid out in his letter to Talleyrand in 1797 was precisely that which he held on St. Helena. His conception of economics was quite as fixed and immutable: "From the first year of his rule," observes one historian, "Napoleon had at hand a complete set of economic rules, to which he adhered, without the slightest deviation, until the end of his reign." Even in the wilderness Napoleon could not grow; on St. Helena he would write, "I would have been the greatest man in history had I succeeded. I should have controlled the religious as well as the political world, and summoned Church Councils like Constantine."

"Napoleon," said Talleyrand, "is the least easily influenced and the most obstinate man God ever created." Napoleon's brother Lucien once reproached him for not being open to new ideas. (Lucien was perhaps the most politically astute member of the Bonaparte family, but Napoleon

197

heeded him as little as he did others.) Napoleon could learn, but he could not grow; he studied not to determine *what* he should do, but to do better that which he had set out to do. Knowledge did not alter Napoleon. When he arranged for Napoleon to be made First Consul, Talleyrand overlooked some rather worrisome traits because he assumed Napoleon would grow; he could not know that Napoleon was immutable.

And why could Napoleon not grow? The great resolve that contributed so to Napoleon's victories in the field was present in all else he did; but while his military objects were always sensible, his political and economic objects rarely were. (His Spanish policy is a perfect example of this, as would be his invading Russia.) But he would no more let go of a political or economic object than he would a military object; he would see it through, no matter how ill-advised it might be.

Napoleon was not self-reliant. When he learned that the French aristocracy was belittling his victories of Ulm and Austerlitz, he cried, "So they think they are better than I, those gentlemen of the Faubourg Saint-Germain! We shall see, we shall see!" Not being self-reliant, Napoleon was susceptible to the adulation of the French people, the mass of whom were taken with a "sentiment of the most spurious kind, a need for servility and wonder, a craving to be intoxicated by an impression of greatness and to fantasize about it." (Jacob Burckhardt) (Thus was Gibbon's observation yet again confirmed: "As long as mankind shall continue to bestow more liberal applause on their destroyers than on their benefactors, the thirst of military glory will ever be the vice of the most exalted characters.") The Austrian ambassador to France, prince zu Schwarzenberg, would say of Napoleon in 1813, "He seemed like a man afraid of being deprived in other people's opinion of the prestige surrounding him." Napoleon's rise was too swift; one should make mistakes, and learn, in obscurity. All Napoleon's mistakes were made on the world stage, and on the world stage it is deuced difficult to admit one has been wrong.

Napoleon was insecure, quite uncertain of his place in French and European society. "What!," he once shouted at a Ministry of Finance official. "You're making mock of me, is that it? You think that a man who was not born on a throne and who walked the streets on foot will allow you to bring him such absurd arguments?" Dard suggests that Napoleon's incivility and truculence toward aristocrats were due in part to his insecurity, to his feeling their inferior. Caesar's family was of the patriciate (the original aristocracy of Rome), Richelieu's and Talleyrand's of the French aristocracy. Napoleon had no such roots, no such sense of place.

One senses in Napoleon a feeling of great vulnerability. This feeling may have come from his having been so vulnerable as a child: from the age of nine he was far from his parents, and thus the feeling of being protected by them (and even had he been with them, it is unlikely he would have felt secure, as they were themselves quite vulnerable); he was quite a bit smaller than his peers; his schoolfellows mocked his queer accent; and, he was quite poor until early adulthood. This is perhaps why Napoleon sought to control the world: never again would he be mistreated as he was as a child.

In military affairs, Napoleon could see; in most other affairs, he could not. In those affairs, he should have consulted those who *could* see; but he did not, in part because he was insecure, in part because he understood these things so poorly he did not see that he did not understand them. Of naval matters Napoleon would confess on St. Helena, "There is a specialization in this profession that blocked all my ideas." If this was so — and could not the same be said of politics and economics? — why did Napoleon not entrust naval matters to someone who *had* specialized in that profession? Where weak, such as in finance and administration, Richelieu appointed brilliant men to critical posts. And the more Napoleon sensed that he would not be able to attain his object, the less he wished to be told he would not. The *auditeurs* of his early reign were far superior to the men he would later appoint, nullities who could teach him nothing. "Napoleon had no men of ability," remarked Stendhal, "because he wanted none."

Indeed, Napoleon was trained *not* to consult others. "General Bonaparte was exceedingly ignorant of the art of government," said Stendhal. "Bred on military ideas, to him discussion always seemed insubordination." Said another observer: "The First Consul handles political matters the same way he handles military ones. Everything must yield to his will in the end..." And others learned — from the exiling of the admiral and other such acts — that they would do well to depict the context, not as it was, but as Napoleon wished it to be.

Napoleon may have reasoned so: "Have I not attained my objects through battle till now? Has battle not answered? If so, why should I not continue to do so, why should battle not continue to answer, in the future?"

If so, he reasoned falsely: his many battles had changed the context. (In a campaign, Napoleon was exquisitely sensitive to any change in the context, and would swiftly change his own dispositions in response; in politics and economics, he was oblivious to changes in the context.) In truth, Napoleon fought simply because it is what he did best; he could no more have stopped fighting than Mozart could have stopped composing or Pushkin stopped writing. In a sense, Napoleon drew his object from his skill. What does one do, when one can fight better than anyone else? Create an empire.

Napoleon's martial genius created a Caesarian environment in which his "ticks and follies" could flower. His success in the field removed the limits that would have hedged his flaws about; and in this removal of limits was his doom. It was with Napoleon in mind that Talleyrand said, "True greatness sets its own limits; true strength restrains itself." Napoleon's Waterloo would not be Waterloo; it would be his pursuing an object that was unattainable, and his inability to recognize that it was so.[4]

---

4 It is not inconceivable that some at least of Napoleon's defects were due to his gestation. While Letizia Buonaparte was pregnant with her second son, the French were forcibly occupying Corsica. Napoleon's father, Carlo, was with the Corsican resistance; the last few months of Letizia's pregnancy were spent in the mountains of Corsica fleeing the victorious French. One can only imagine the stress the young woman felt, pregnant, with one child, and with a husband being hunted by an increasingly successful invader.

High levels of the stress hormone cortisol disarrange the brain of the fetus. Excessive cortisol reduces the size of the hippocampus and suppresses the production of, alters the shape of, or kills its neurons. (The hippocampus has an exceedingly high density of receptors for cortisol.) The hippocampus controls our ability to distinguish fantasy from reality; it is where dreams are thought to originate. One of Napoleon's ministers, Count Mole, said: "It is strange that though Napoleon's common sense amounted to genius, he could never see where the possible left off." In 1806, his Minister of the Marine, Decres, cried, "The Emperor is mad and will destroy us all."

If excessive, cortisol also disarranges the amygdala and cerebellar vermis. The amygdala creates the emotional content of memory. High levels of cortisol disorder the structure of gamma aminobutyric acid receptors in the amygdala; less able to receive this acid, an inhibitory neurotransmitter, the amygdala is subject to overstimulation and electrical storms (which may result in seizures, which Napoleon indeed suffered). The cerebellar vermis, which like the hippocampus has a very high density of receptors for cortisol, produces and releases the neurotransmitters norepinephrine and dopamine. A lessening of these neurotransmitters can result in electrical excitability in the limbic system, in the hippocampus and amygdala. (A disarranged cerebellar vermis is also associated with psychiatric disorders.) Limbic electrical excitability is associated with aggression and exasperation — both quite pronounced in Napoleon. His solipsism and unsociability may also have been due to a disordering of his limbic system and cerebellar

The Vital Point

Talleyrand's great strength was Napoleon's great weakness: politics. Only in battles could Napoleon fight well; in politics, he could not do so at all. Talleyrand would put his strong point against Napoleon's weak point. He could not fight Napoleon within France; here, Napoleon was far too strong. To strike Napoleon strongly, he must strike with other states.

Talleyrand recognized that the chief weakness of the states opposed to Napoleon was their disunity. Whenever an individual, organization, or state becomes too strong, others naturally seek to create a counterpoise to that individual, organization, or state; but these others are also rivals of one another. A union of states, observes Chesterfield, "has, besides the common and declared object of their alliance, some separate and concealed view to which they often sacrifice the general one, which makes them either directly or indirectly, pull different ways… Suppose, any four or five powers, who all together shall be equal, or even a little superior, in riches and strength, to that one power against which they are united; the advantage will still be greater on the side of that single power, because it is but one." Or, as Napoleon said, "One bad general is better than two good ones."

Even the subjugation of other states may not induce the surviving states to unite for their own preservation. "The nations of antiquity," writes Gibbon, "careless of each other's safety, were separately vanquished and enslaved by the Romans. This awful lesson might have instructed the Barbarians of the West to oppose, with timely counsels and confederate arms, the unbounded ambition of Justinian. Yet the same error was repeated, the same consequences were felt, and the Goths, both of Italy and Spain, insensible of their approaching danger, beheld with indifference, and even with joy, the rapid downfall of the Vandals [of North Africa]." Caesar's conquest

---

vermis. "Under the Empire," said Chateaubriand, "we disappeared; there was no longer any mention of us, and everything belonged to Bonaparte."

Markham suggests that Napoleon is simply unintelligible: "The irrational, the unlimited, the daemonic is as fundamental to the nature of Napoleon as it is to the character of Mozart's *Don Giovanni*." But "the irrational, the unlimited, the daemonic" also bespeak a malformed limbic system and cerebellar vermis. One must take care, however, in positing such a thing, because Napoleon was wildly complex. He could, for instance, perceive certain aspects of reality quite well — indeed, far better than could others — and at times be quite charming. That Napoleon was a military genius is certain; what is less certain is the healthiness of the brain in which that genius lay.

of Gaul was made possible quite as much by Gallic disunity as by his own brilliance and resolve. And as dysfunctional as the rule of the *optimates* was, their opponents (before Caesar) were far too factious to overthrow them.

If Talleyrand could not be the Foreign Minister of France, he would be that of Europe. He would become a sort of "supra-Foreign Minister," would unite the states opposed to France and guide them in vitiating Napoleon.

❧

Before the Congress at Erfurt, Napoleon ordered Talleyrand to compose a draft Convention. He urged him to invoke principles wherever possible: "Principles are fine; they entail no commitment." The draft promised Russia Moldavia and Wallachia, "but with the mediation of France." "That clause is good," said Napoleon, thinking that he would simply refuse to mediate. Without informing Talleyrand, Napoleon added two further articles: that he would decide under which conditions Russia would declare war on Austria, and that Russian troops were to be placed at once on the Austrian frontier. When Napoleon refused to let either the Emperor Francis or Metternich attend the Congress, Talleyrand secretly pledged them his support. Talleyrand, wrote Metternich, "now professes his devotion to the Austrian Court and has recently given me sincere pledges of his desire to establish the closest relations between us and France."

So critical were the negotiations at Erfurt to the future of his Grand Empire that Napoleon insisted on Talleyrand's joining him. (Napoleon felt he had so compromised Talleyrand that he could be certain of his fidelity.) Napoleon was received at Erfurt with flattery and obeisance; Talleyrand, too, insisted on being treated as if he were a sovereign. Through the Princess of Thurn and Taxis, the Tsar and Talleyrand arranged to meet late each evening at her home. And each morning, Talleyrand would meet with M. de Vincent, the Austrian envoy. Napoleon would not be told of these meetings.

Alexander arrived at Erfurt thinking he and Napoleon would form an alliance and divide Europe between them. At their first meeting, Talleyrand revealed Napoleon's intentions to the Tsar: he would conquer Spain while Russia kept Austria quiescent; once he had done so, he would occupy

Austria and then impose his will on an isolated Russia. Talleyrand told Alexander that Napoleon must be compelled to make peace. "Sir, what are you doing here?," he asked. "It is your duty to save Europe, and you can do so only by standing out against Napoleon. The French people, unlike their sovereign, are civilized, whereas the Russian people, unlike their sovereign, are uncivilized. The Russian sovereign must therefore ally himself with the French nation." At a later meeting, Talleyrand would say, "The Rhine, the Alps, and the Pyrenees are the conquests of the French people, and the Emperor is responsible for the remainder: France does not want them." And to Vincent: "The cause of Napoleon is no longer that of France; Europe itself can be saved only by the closest cooperation between Austria and Russia."

Napoleon had copied Talleyrand's draft Convention by hand, inserting his two articles. He shared this Convention with Alexander with the request that he not show it to any of his, Napoleon's, ministers (that is, to Talleyrand). The first evening Alexander and Talleyrand met, Alexander handed Talleyrand Napoleon's hand-written Convention. Talleyrand persuaded Alexander to strike out the two articles added by Napoleon. The following morning, Talleyrand told Vincent that Alexander had done so; Vincent and his government were elated. Napoleon could now neither be certain of Austrian passivity nor have a free hand in Spain.

At their evening meetings, Talleyrand and the Tsar would discuss the negotiations that had taken place during the day, Talleyrand suggesting fresh proposals and arguments for the following day. As the Congress went on, Alexander became less and less tractable. Napoleon was mystified; the Tsar was usually quite easy to browbeat. In his private meetings with Talleyrand, Napoleon would ask why Alexander should be so unlike himself, so unwontedly firm. When Napoleon asked Talleyrand why the Tsar would not simply sign the treaty, Talleyrand replied, "He believes that his word and his affection for you are more binding than treaties." The negotiations became more and more difficult. At one point, Napoleon threw his hat to the floor. "You are violent," said Alexander calmly, "but I am stubborn. Your rage will get you nowhere. Either we talk like reasonable men, or we shall not talk at all."

On Napoleon's acquiescing to Russia's occupation of Finland and the Danubian provinces, Alexander agreed to attack Austria should it attack France. Talleyrand, however, induced Alexander to write the Emperor Francis assuring him that he had no intention of complying with the treaty. Alexander arrived at Erfurt hostile to Austria and left its ally.

Napoleon went to Erfurt with one further hope: that of marrying one of the Tsar's sisters. His doing so would not only strengthen their alliance, but also enable him to father a dynasty. Though adamantly opposed to such a marriage, Talleyrand recognized that marriage *negotiations* would stay Napoleon's hand for a few months at least, and he persuaded Alexander to tell Napoleon he would consider his request. Three months later, the Grand Duchess Catherine would be engaged to the Duke of Oldenburg and the Tsar's youngest sister, the Grand Duchess Anne, pronounced, at fourteen, too young to marry.

At Erfurt, Talleyrand showed Russia and Austria that he was quite willing to betray Napoleon. "I had done everything in my power to win the confidence of the Tsar Alexander," he later remarked, "and I succeeded." Talleyrand had induced the French ambassador to Russia, Armand Caulaincourt, to aid him in gaining the Tsar's trust. (He did so by convincing this rather simple soldier that Napoleon himself desired peace; Caulaincourt would never have knowingly betrayed Napoleon.) On his return to Paris, Talleyrand wrote Metternich, "Alexander will no longer let himself be dragged in against you," and he urged Austria to rearm so that it might meet a French attack. "The time has come at last," said Metternich, "when allies are apparently offering us their cooperation within the Grand Empire." Talleyrand would later view the Congress of Erfurt as the most glorious work of his career and would take joy in reading his account of it to his friends. "Every day," he once remarked to a friend, "you hear people claiming that they are saving the monarchy. Well, at Erfurt I saved Europe."

In December 1808, while Napoleon was in Spain, Talleyrand held a reception to which he invited Fouche, the Minister of Police and his bitter enemy. The two had agreed to be reconciled so that they might collaborate on choosing a successor to Napoleon should he be killed in Spain. Talleyrand ostentatiously linked his arm through that of Fouche and promenaded up and down before the other guests, to their utter astonishment. So public a reconciliation reassured Russia and Austria of Talleyrand's independence from Napoleon.

On learning of this reconciliation and its purpose, Napoleon returned to Paris in high dudgeon. He summoned Fouche, Talleyrand, and the other Grand Dignitaries and ministers to his palace. He was indignant that "certain individuals" should have had the temerity to consider who might succeed him. "Those whom I have made great dignitaries or ministers cease to be free in thought or word and must remain my instruments... For them, treason has begun when they permit themselves to doubt; it is complete if they go from doubt to dissent." He savaged Talleyrand: "You are a thief, a coward who has no respect for anything. You don't believe in God. You've never in your life performed any duty faithfully. You have betrayed and deceived everyone. Nothing is sacred to you. You would give away your own father." He insisted that the policy he was following in Spain was of Talleyrand's making, that Talleyrand thus had no right to criticize that policy, that the Treaty of Pressburg was an abomination, and so on. As Napoleon excoriated him, Talleyrand leaned against a mantle — he could not sit in the Emperor's presence, and could not stand because of his infirmity — seemingly cool and composed. This serenity drove Napoleon to fury: "You are nothing," he shrieked in conclusion, "but shit in a silk stocking!"

That evening, Talleyrand suffered a seizure. Napoleon's only retribution, however, was to remove him from the office of Grand Chamberlain. Talleyrand returned its symbolic key with a note saying, "My consolation is that I belong to Your Majesty, strengthened as I am by two feelings that no sorrow can overcome or lessen, gratitude and devotion, which shall end only with my life." (Within a month, Napoleon would again be speaking to Talleyrand.) Talleyrand soon called on Metternich: "He told me...that the time had come and that he felt it his duty to get into direct touch with Austria... The fact that he held so important an appointment accounted, he said, for his previous refusal. I am free now, he went on, and our cause is the same." Talleyrand asked the Austrian government for funds, as he had now lost his salary and was being ruined by his hosting of the Spanish princes.

On February I, Metternich composed a report to his government on his conversations with Talleyrand. "Talleyrand has just warned me that General Oudinot has received orders to march on Augsburg and Ingolstadt... Great importance attaches to any movement on the part of Oudinot's corps, as the Emperor rates its fighting value very highly. [Talleyrand] considers that we ought to make the next move on the part of Oudinot a pretext for bringing our forces up to war strength." Metternich reviewed this report with Talleyrand, who recommended that it be shared with Russia so that the latter would have no doubt who was the aggressor. In early March, Metternich wrote, "My relations with [Talleyrand] are very continuous. It is owing to him, to a great extent, that I am constantly in receipt of information that concerns us... I have obtained...two memoranda of immense importance as regards the present situation... As Russia is let off in them no more lightly than Austria I have sent them to St. Petersburg. They reveal the secret of Napoleon's policy, which is to destroy everything that does not depend upon the founder of the new dynasty." Later that month, Talleyrand gave Metternich a report from the French Ministry of War on the latest dispositions of the French army and the strength of each of its corps.

Rather than simply make itself strong so that it might resist a French attack, as Talleyrand advised, Austria resolved on striking first. Though it hoped to catch the French forces while they were still dispersed, within a few days of Austria's declaring war on April 9 Napoleon had concentrated his forces. In a series of brilliant battles at Abensberg, Landshut, and Eckmuhl, he defeated the Austrian army under the Archduke Charles. As Napoleon occupied Vienna, Charles reorganized his army on the left bank of the Danube at the villages of Aspern and Essling. On the 20th, Napoleon occupied the island of Lobau, which was joined by a bridge to the two villages.

Once 36,000 French soldiers had crossed to the left bank of the Danube the following morning, Charles had barges floated down the river, destroying the bridge. The French force, facing 100,000 Austrians, could now neither retreat nor be reinforced. Throughout that day and night, Napoleon had the bridge repaired; the following morning, he sent reinforcements across to the villages. Just as the French were striking at the Austrian center, barges again broke through the bridge; the bridge was again repaired, and the mauled French force retreated onto the island. Napoleon now fortified Lobau, arranged a string of boats to protect the bridge, and brought up reinforcements. By early July, he had 170,000 men to Charles's 135,000. On the 5th, Napoleon crossed the Danube in force; Charles fell back on the village of Wagram. On perceiving that the Austrian line was overextended, Napoleon concentrated his forces and broke through its center. (During the whole of this campaign, the Tsar, following Talleyrand's advice, simply moved his forces from place to place along the Austrian frontier. "This is not much of an alliance," commented Napoleon dryly.)

On October 14, Metternich, now Austrian Foreign Minister, was forced to sign the harsh Peace of Schonbrunn. By the terms of the treaty, Austria lost the three and a half million subjects of Salzberg, the Illyrian Provinces, and parts of Galicia; it was also forced to pay a colossal indemnity, limit the size of its army to 150,000 soldiers, and rejoin the Continental System. While in Schonbrunn negotiating the treaty, Napoleon narrowly escaped assassination by a young German student. The Emperor could not understand why an educated young man of the middle class, the son of a Lutheran minister, should wish to kill him, should refuse to save himself by renouncing his deed, should go to his death crying, "Long live Germany; death to the tyrant!" Why should such a person wish to kill the liberator and modernizer of Europe?

While on campaign in May, 1809, Napoleon had decreed the annexation of the Papal States to the Empire. When the Pope excommunicated the "aggressors against the Holy See" in response, Napoleon ordered one of his generals, Radet, to arrest some of the Pope's advisors; Radet, however, took it upon himself to arrest the Pope as well. Deeming "what is done is done," Napoleon interned the Pope at Savona, where he would remain until January 1812. Though Napoleon would continue to try to compel the Pope to do as he wished, the Pope would have none of it.

Talleyrand was not the slightest bit disheartened by the Austrian defeat; he continued to work to weaken Napoleon and unite his opponents. Napoleon had Talleyrand spied upon and his mail opened, but such measures revealed nothing. To make Napoleon think he knew the extent of his intrigues, Talleyrand would openly speak out against Napoleon's policies. And to suggest that he was not involved in politics, on occasion Talleyrand would retreat to his country house at Saint-Germain. Napoleon would still occasionally seek his advice, both because he recognized that public opinion in both France and the other countries of Europe still favored Talleyrand, and because Talleyrand understood European politics far better than did anyone else; Napoleon could not wholly do without him. Napoleon also seemed to miss the pleasure of conversing with Talleyrand, as well as the piquancy of being told what he did not wish to hear. ("What a devil you are!" Napoleon once said to him. "I cannot avoid discussing my affairs with you or stop myself from liking you.") But these conversations invariably left Napoleon enraged.

So disastrous had the Peace of Schonbrunn been for Austria that the Emperor Francis and Metternich recognized that they must accept French domination for the present. To strengthen the relationship between France and Austria, and to forestall a strengthening of that between France and Russia, in early 1810 Talleyrand and Metternich proposed to Napoleon that he marry the eldest daughter of the Emperor Francis, the Archduchess Marie-Louise. Napoleon was quite taken with this idea, both because such a marriage would enable him to father a dynasty, and because he was convinced the Emperor Francis would never intrigue against his son-in-law. Napoleon so appreciated Talleyrand's aid in arranging this marriage that he once more treated him with his former cordiality and openness.

Soon after the Congress at Erfurt, the Russian Count Charles de Nesselrode had presented himself to Talleyrand with the words, "I have just come from St. Petersburg. I hold an official position with [Russian Ambassador to France] Prince Kurakin, but it is to you that I am really accredited. I am responsible for maintaining a private correspondence with the Tsar, and I bring you now one of his letters." Talleyrand now told Nesselrode that Napoleon was secretly negotiating an alliance with Sweden and assisting Turkey in its war against Russia. And once Napoleon had suppressed the Spanish insurrection, Talleyrand continued, he would further weaken Russia by restoring Polish independence. Talleyrand also told Nesselrode that Napoleon had ordered a study of Russian military preparations and fortifications. Russia's only hope, Talleyrand concluded, was to make peace with Turkey, regain English subsidies, strengthen its forces while Napoleon was occupied with Spain, and draw closer to Austria. (The royal marriage, he assured Nesselrode, had not increased Austrian loyalty to Napoleon in the slightest.)

So startled was Nesselrode by this information that he organized a system of espionage to draw out further French state secrets. He also shared the information with the Chevalier de Floret, who had taken Metternich's place as the Austrian representative to France. On receiving this information, Metternich wrote Nesselrode that "friendly and confidential relations between Austria and Russia [are] the only possible basis of a conservative and peaceful policy in Europe." Talleyrand continued to hold sway over Caulaincourt, the French ambassador to Russia, who continued (unwittingly) to work against Napoleon.

In early 1810, Napoleon dismissed Fouche as Minister of Police on learning that Fouche had joined Talleyrand in secret peace negotiations with England. As he had Talleyrand a year earlier, Napoleon savaged Fouche for his actions: "You think yourself very smart, but you're not. Talleyrand is smart, and this time he has played with you as if you were a child; he has used you as his tool." Napoleon appointed Savary in Fouche's place. To punish Talleyrand for his involvement in the Fouche affair, Napoleon sought to ruin him financially. Talleyrand was soon forced to sell his library and one of his houses and to cede control of his financial affairs to his many creditors. Fouche's dismissal showed Europe that Napoleon had no intention of making peace, that he considered the mere discussion of peace or moderation to be treason. What Talleyrand lost by Fouche's dismissal, however, he gained by the Emperor's vanity. Following his marriage to Marie-Louise, Napoleon had insisted the greatest families of France attend them. So pleased was Napoleon with this arrangement that he soon placed these aristocrats throughout his government. They soon began supplying Talleyrand, one of their own, with information as considerable as it was invaluable.

So alarmed was Russia by the information Talleyrand shared with Nesselrode that it now prepared an offensive against France. On learning through his Polish supporters that Russia was concentrating its forces on its frontier and assisting the anti-French party in Poland, Napoleon annexed Holland, the Hanseatic towns, and the canton of Valais and called up 120,000 conscripts. Through Nesselrode, Talleyrand beseeched Alexander not to initiate hostilities. Public opinion would be against whichever country did so, and Russia had yet to make itself strong, make peace with Turkey, establish an alliance with Austria, or regain English subsidies. Talleyrand proposed that Russia and Austria agree on a "defensive line" beyond which Napoleon would not be permitted to go; if he marched beyond that line, the two countries would combine against him. Talleyrand also urged the Tsar to impose high tariffs on French imports and renounce the Continental System. (In October, Napoleon had ordered the seizure and burning of English manufactured goods throughout Europe.) Alexander followed

Talleyrand's advice; his imposing tariffs on French goods and renouncing the System in December, 1810 convinced Napoleon that Russia would soon reestablish its alliance with England.

On the 20th of March 1811, Napoleon's first legitimate son, the King of Rome, was born. The Empire now had an heir.

One evening during the summer of 1811, an officer arrived at Talleyrand's home with a letter from Savary stating that, by Napoleon's order, Talleyrand and his wife were to live at her estate at Pont-de-Sains. Talleyrand induced Savary to rescind the order, which Napoleon had issued simply to remind Talleyrand that he could do with him as he pleased.

On August 15, 1811, Napoleon violently upbraided Kurakin in the presence of the entire diplomatic corps. He did so not so much because he was upset with Russia as to show Kurakin and the other diplomats that the concession to come did not indicate French weakness. Napoleon first touted French military might, and then he made the concession: he would agree to an Austrian guarantee that he would not seek to restore Polish independence. This guarantee was the work of Talleyrand and would draw Russia and Austria closer together.

By this time, however, Napoleon had so wounded Russian sensibilities and interests that Alexander would not consider negotiating further. Napoleon had threatened Russia with Polish independence for far too long; he had refused to grant Russia Constantinople and the Straits following Tilsit (Napoleon did not wish to have a rival in the Mediterranean); in May 1810, he had approved the Swedish Diet's nomination of Bernadotte to be King of Sweden (Alexander viewed Sweden as a Russian vassal state); he had annexed the Grand Duchy of Oldenburg, the heir to which was Alexander's brother-in-law; he had married the daughter of the Austrian Emperor. Most of the aristocrats at Alexander's court were hostile to France, in part because the Continental System had been ruinous to their interests. (Alexander was exceedingly sensitive to the views of the Russian aristocracy, which, when dissatisfied with his father's rule, had assassinated him.) Alexander's German advisors were quite as hostile to France as was the aristocracy. Furthermore, a rather fatuous Russian diplomat in Paris, Tchernichef, so disliked Napoleon that he conveyed only his threats. Most galling of all, however, were Alexander's own losses to Napoleon, losses he was determined to avenge. The French difficulties in Spain, and the certainty of a resumption of English subsidies, further encouraged Alexander.

On April 8, 1812, Alexander sent Napoleon an ultimatum. Far from displeasing Napoleon, the ultimatum suited his wishes perfectly: the defeat of Russia would show Europe that resistance was useless and so strengthen the Continental System that England would be hobbled. To the Comte de Narbonne he remarked, "Alexander was as far as I am from Moscow when he marched to the Ganges" (of which Narbonne later said, "It was halfway between Bedlam and the Pantheon.").

Napoleon appointed Talleyrand his High Commissioner to Warsaw; no one but Talleyrand could keep Austria and Prussia quiescent, gain Polish cooperation, and negotiate peace with Alexander following the war. And Napoleon could not feel safe so long as Talleyrand remained in Paris; Napoleon had permitted Fouche to return, and he and Talleyrand would doubtless once again conspire against him. But Talleyrand's opening an account in Vienna (on the pretext that Warsaw had no French exchange), and the spreading of a canard by his enemies that he had boasted of his appointment, led Napoleon to rescind it. Napoleon ordered Savary to keep Talleyrand under surveillance. While away from France, Napoleon would continue to wound Talleyrand, instructing Marie-Louis not to invite him to any of her affairs, and refusing to let Talleyrand assign his pension to his adopted child, Charlotte. Though Talleyrand would remain hidden from public view throughout the Russian campaign, he would closely follow the course of events within his circle of dear female friends.

In April 1812, having suffered privations under the Continental System, and incensed by the French occupation of Swedish Pomerania three months before, Sweden allied itself to Russia. In May of that year, Russia signed the Peace of Bucharest with Turkey; Alexander could now focus on France. Napoleon had, however, been able to compel Austria and Prussia to provide auxiliaries to the *Grande Armee*.

On June 25, 1812, Napoleon crossed the Niemen River with 450,000 men. Half or so were of allied or vassal states, and most were of indifferent quality; 80,000 were, however, of the elite Imperial Guard. Though no one could control the movements of half a million men, Napoleon insisted on being the sole source of authority; Caulaincourt observed that "as the Emperor wanted to do everything himself and give every order, no one, not even the general staff, dared to assume the responsibility of giving the most trifling order." In spite of the slow movement of the French army, its supply system broke down within a few days of its crossing the Niemen. Napoleon had hoped the Poles would furnish the French with supplies; but pillaging by the French army, and Napoleon's refusal to restore the Kingdom of Poland, made the Poles quite unwilling to do so. Soon discipline of all but the Guard broke down, and countless soldiers deserted.

So colossal was the French army that the Russian commanders, Prince Barclay de Tolly and Prince Bagration, had no choice but to retreat. At Vitebsk, Napoleon's officers beseeched him to call a halt to the campaign, which was being hobbled by a lack of supplies and desertion. Though he at first assented, two days later Napoleon ordered a continuation with the words, "Victory will justify and save us." In mid-August, he almost caught Barclay at Smolensk, but the dilatoriness of General Junot permitted Barclay to escape. Though he now had only 160,000 men, Napoleon was only 200 miles from Moscow; to retreat would be to concede that his strategy was ill-conceived. Napoleon pressed on.

On August 20, Alexander appointed Prince Mikhail Kutuzov Commander-in-Chief. Kutuzov was not only the shrewdest of the Russian commanders, but also the one who understood Napoleon best. (He had commanded the Russian forces at Austerlitz.) Though Kutuzov knew full well he could not defeat Napoleon, public opinion forced him to fight for Moscow.

On September 5, Napoleon arrived at the Russian village of Borodino to find Kutuzov in a strong defensive position. Though the French army was slightly larger than the Russian — 130,000 soldiers to 120,000 — the latter had more and heavier artillery. Two days later, the French launched their attack. The Russians fought with preternatural obstinacy; their artillerymen, for instance, would continue firing until bayoneted by the French. Both sides suffered enormous casualties, the French 30,000 and the Russians 50,000, and the French lost 40 generals. Only 700 Russians let themselves be taken prisoner. The Russian survivors withdrew — Kutuzov must have an army with which to oppose the French later — and the French continued on.

On September 14, Napoleon entered Moscow. The city was deserted; its governor had ordered that fires be set that night, fires it would take the

French five days to put out. Certain his occupation of Moscow would force Alexander to sue for peace, Napoleon now simply awaited an emissary from the Russian court. Napoleon did not understand that Alexander could not possibly sue for peace and retain his throne: the Russian people hated the French invader, and the loss of Moscow had made Alexander *wildly* unpopular. Napoleon did, however, recognize that all was not as it should be: "If I had sent Talleyrand to Warsaw, I should have had my 6,000 Polish Cossacks, and affairs would have rapidly assumed a different aspect." (While in Moscow Napoleon rescinded his humiliating restrictions on Talleyrand.) In spite of Caulaincourt's repeated warnings about the harshness of the Russian winter, Napoleon continued to await Alexander's representative.

Kutuzov's victory over Murat at Winkovo on October 18 made it clear that Alexander had no intention of negotiating. The following day, Napoleon ordered a retreat. (In retaliation for the defeat at Winkovo and for Alexander's refusing to negotiate, he also ordered one of his officers to blow up the Kremlin, an order the officer would not carry out.) Encumbered by loot, sick and wounded, and 600 pieces of artillery, the French army moved only very slowly. Napoleon at first tried to retreat by a road to the south, but a Russian attack at Malojaroslavetz on October 24 — in which the French suffered 5,000 casualties — induced him to return by the devastated route he had come.

By early November, the French had lost all their horses and were suffering greatly from hunger. Russian soldiers, Cossacks, and peasants would fall upon the French soldiers who went out to forage, as well as upon any stragglers; rather than be killed or die of cold or starvation, many of the soldiers committed suicide. Napoleon reached Smolensk on November 8, but the city had only the scantest of supplies. At Krasnoi the French and Russians fought again; Napoleon was able to extricate his army only by losing almost the whole of his rearguard. He now learned that the Russians had taken Minsk (which was to be his next supply depot) and destroyed the bridge over the Beresina River at Borissov. The French were now very nearly surrounded; Napoleon ordered his papers burnt.

On November 27, Napoleon made as if to cross the Beresina to the south of Borissov, but did so to the north of the town over improvised bridges thrown up by French engineers. The weather now turned markedly colder. On December 6, the French reached Smorgoni. Napoleon now departed for Paris; he traveled by sleigh with a single companion, Caulaincourt. (At one point during their journey, Napoleon said, "That choice [of the abbe de Pradt rather than Talleyrand as my representative in Poland] is what cost me my campaign… Talleyrand would have accomplished more through Madame Tyszkiewicz's salon than Maret and Pradt with all their talking… I have often wished that Talleyrand were here.") Napoleon arrived in Paris on December 14, attributing his defeat to the Russian winter. Of the 160,000 or so French soldiers who entered Russia, fewer than 40,000 would return.

೦ಌ

By 1812, Napoleon recognized that he would not be able to attain his object. (This is not to say he recognized that his object was *unattainable* — he understood the context far too poorly for *that* recognition — only that *he* would not be able to attain it.) Napoleon was coming to see that battle would *not* always answer; neither the great bloodiness of Eylau and Aspern-Essling, nor his victory at Borodino and his taking of Moscow, brought him any closer to his object. Furthermore, at the beginning of 1811 Europe was hit with an economic crisis; though Napoleon had large subsidies paid to French manufacturers, these subsidies were of little help, many of the manufacturers went bankrupt, and unemployment rose. The crisis was chiefly due to the Continental System, as Europe, and perhaps Napoleon, recognized. And by now Napoleon was clearly spent. "One has only a certain time for war," he said in 1805 following Austerlitz. "I will be good for six years more; after that even I must cry halt." Chronic stress is ruinous to health; it leads to obesity, premature aging, the erosion of immune cells, and the degeneration of brain structures (including the hippocampus). Napoleon was by now quite corpulent and drowsy, had aged markedly, and had suffered at least three nervous crises simulating epileptic fits.

Three things suggest that Napoleon now recognized he would not be able to attain his object: he stopped trying, he shut out *military* reality, and he tried to have himself killed.

Napoleon's invasion of Russia was half-hearted. Though Caulaincourt repeatedly warned him about the severity of the Russian winter, while in Paris Napoleon did nothing to prepare his army. (The French horses, for instance, were not shod for ice.) Rather than supervise the movements of the army, Napoleon lingered for two weeks at Vilna. He then halted the army for a whole day so that he might celebrate his birthday. In Smolensk, he retired to his quarters before the battle was over and so achieved little. And rather than exert further pressure on the Tsar while in Moscow, he simply dallied; one of his officers records that he "would pass whole hours half reclined, as if torpid and awaiting, with a novel in his hand..."

Napoleon had long shut out political and economic reality; but he was now shutting out military reality as well. When Caulaincourt warned him that Alexander would lure him into the hinterland so that winter and hunger might do their work, Napoleon retorted, "A battle will dispose of the fine resolutions of your friend Alexander and his fortifications of sand." At Borodino, he refused to encircle the Russians as General Louis-Nicolas Davout urged and instead engaged in a rare and wasteful frontal attack; he then did nothing for a whole day. When told in Moscow that the soldiers would need fleece-lined coats, thick boots, and special capes, and the artillery horses, Napoleon ordered that they be purchased locally — this in spite of his continually being told that none were to be had anywhere near Moscow.

Napoleon studied neither the context nor his opponent with any care. "Without heeding the difficulties with which he was unacquainted," said one of his officers, "he gave orders for enterprises, which, on account of their minutely punctual execution by his generals, entailed great sacrifices of human life." What Napoleon said to Davout in 1811 — when Davout warned him of rising German nationalism — clearly shows his state of mind: "I beg of you not to transmit any such fanciful vaporings to me again. My time is too precious to be spent in the consideration of such nonsense... All this is only calculated to make me lose my time and to sully my imagination with senseless pictures and suppositions."

Napoleon now seemed to care little whether he lived or died. He took a vial of poison, concocted by his physician, with him to Russia; during the horrific retreat, he showed a curious lack of concern for what might befall him. By 1813, he sought to do himself in. During the battle of Arcis-sur-Aube, Napoleon ordered a certain field cleared of soldiers because it was far too hazardous; he then rode out onto the field. When one of his officers began to ride after him, another stopped him with the words: "Let him be! Can't you see that he is doing it deliberately? He wants to put an end to himself!" After one of his officers was killed at Bautzen, Napoleon remained where he was, deep in thought, as bullets and shells flew about him. During the pursuit of an Allied army later in the year, Napoleon rode in the advance guard among the young recruits, the enemy firing continuously upon them. Napoleon could not do — or grow — so he would die.

∾

Soon after Napoleon returned to France, Russia, Austria, and Prussia formed a new coalition. Napoleon could dissolve this coalition simply by returning France to its natural frontiers and by offering concessions to each state individually. "Negotiate," advised Talleyrand. "You now hold pledges in your hands which you can afford to abandon. Tomorrow you may have lost them, and then your ability to negotiate is also lost." All Europe was heartily sick of war, so much so that the monarchs feared a prolongation of the fighting might well lead to popular uprisings. Furthermore, the Emperor Francis and Metternich, wishing neither France nor Russia to be victorious, preferred a general peace and the continuation of a Bonaparte-Habsburg dynasty in France. Napoleon called a Council of State meeting for January 3, but only for show; he could neither renounce his Grand Empire nor relinquish his autocracy in France. It was now quite clear to everyone that Napoleon fought not for France, but for himself.

In response to the formation of this new coalition, in early January Napoleon withdrew French soldiers — but not cavalry — from Spain. He could mobilize 150,000 soldiers by April, but only by calling up the conscripts of 1814 and by drawing on the National Guard. He could do nothing, however, to replace the 80,000 horses lost in Russia. Talleyrand advised Austria to bring its army up to at least 200,000 men so that it would be in a position to impose its mediation. (Metternich would keep Talleyrand informed as it did so.) Talleyrand also induced Savary, the Minister of Police, to collaborate against Napoleon.

In May 1813, Napoleon inflicted defeats on the Allies at Lutzen and Bautzen; neither victory was, however, decisive. On June 4, short of cavalry and facing a sizeable Austrian force, Napoleon agreed to an armistice and a Peace Congress at Prague. Neither Napoleon nor the Allies were in earnest; both sought the armistice simply to give them time to build up their forces. On June 14, Alexander and the King of Prussia signed secret treaties with English representatives pledging not to make a separate peace with Napoleon. Napoleon soon had Caulaincourt request such a peace of the Tsar; he refused.

By the armistice's end on August 10, Napoleon had 470,000 soldiers in Germany, of whom 50,000 were of the Imperial Guard, and 40,000 cavalry. By now, however, the Russians, Prussians, Austrians, and Swedes had half a million men and considerable reserves. The Allies were grouped into three forces: that to the north was under Bernadotte, Napoleon's former marshal and the King of Sweden, that in the center under Gebhard Leberecht von Blucher, a Prussian field marshal, and that to the south under Schwarzenberg, an Austrian field marshal and the former ambassador to France. A French general now in the service of the Russians, Victor Moreau, counseled Alexander, "Expect a defeat whenever the Emperor attacks in person. Attack and fight his lieutenants whenever you can. Once they are beaten, assemble all your forces against Napoleon and give him no respite."

Throughout the autumn of 1813, Napoleon was irresolute and timid. Rather than defeat each of the three forces in turn, he simply *responded* to an Allied attack on Dresden; rather than issue orders, he consulted those about him. One of his officers records: "I saw the Emperor at this time, waiting for news from the Elbe, sitting quite idle on a sofa in his room in front of the large table, on which lay a sheet of white paper which he covered with large Gothic characters... His geographer, d'Ibe, and another assistant sat as idly in the corners of the room, waiting, at their ease, for his orders." Said Marshal Auguste-Frederic-Louis Viesse de Marmont: "One fails to recognize the old Napoleon again during this campaign." In spite of his lethargy, however, Napoleon continued to inflict defeats on the Allies; but they, following Moreau's advice, continually defeated his officers elsewhere, and Blucher wore down his army by continually retreating. In the two months following the end of the armistice, the French lost far more men — through battle, sickness, and desertion — than did the Allies.

On October 16, 160,000 French soldiers faced 300,000 Allies at Leipzig, Napoleon having failed to attack Schwarzenberg before Blucher and Bernadotte could join him. After two days of fighting, the Saxons deserted the French left wing, forcing Napoleon to retreat. Though both the French and the Allies lost 40,000 in casualties, the French lost a further 20,000 as prisoners. And the French retreat induced the Bavarians to go over to the Allies. On November 2, Napoleon crossed the Rhine with only 60,000 men.

The Allies could now cross into France unopposed. Still afraid of Napoleon, and uncertain how the French people would respond to an invasion, the Allies hesitated. On November 15, the Allies offered Napoleon peace on the basis of France's natural frontiers, the Rhine, the Alps, and the Pyrenees. Talleyrand, Caulaincourt, and others leaked word of this offer, hoping French public opinion would force Napoleon to make peace. On the 16th, Napoleon issued a cryptic reply that was received badly both within and without France. "The result of your labors is destroyed," Talleyrand now advised him, "and the desertion of your allies leaves you no other alternative but to treat for peace at once at your expense and at any price. A peace, however bad, must be less disastrous than this war that we cannot win must prove eventually. You have neither sufficient time nor resources to bring about a change of luck, and your foes won't give you a breathing space. They have conflicting interests that you should appeal to, and their various ambitions offer you a chance of bringing about a diversion." By this time the finances of the French government were in ruins, and French army contractors paid with promissory notes.

As the Allies continued to debate whether to cross the Rhine, an emissary sent "by French officials" arrived from Switzerland. He assured the Allied sovereigns and their ministers that, should they invade France, not only would Napoleon not be able to stop them, but they would be "received with open arms" by the French people. The Allies now resolved on invading France. Talleyrand was one of the officials who sent this emissary.

In December, Napoleon restored Ferdinand to the Spanish throne with the words, "I have sacrificed hundreds of thousands of men to make Joseph reign in Spain... It is one of my mistakes to think my brother necessary to assure my dynasty." Napoleon did not understand until too late Spanish loyalty to Ferdinand, or that the Spanish middle class on which he pinned his hopes was far too small to offer him support. Since its beginning, the Spanish war had vitiated French forces throughout Europe. Not only had Napoleon been forced to send contingent after contingent to Spain, but the maladministration of the French forces there, and the resulting corruption, contributed greatly to the moral dissolution of the French army. Furthermore, the continual French defeats in Spain had emboldened the other European states to resist Napoleon elsewhere. Talleyrand may have induced the Spanish royal family — who were still at his country home at Valencay — to delay the negotiations for two months, so that Napoleon would not be able to reinforce his armies elsewhere with the soldiers taken from Spain.

Napoleon now offered Talleyrand the post of Foreign Minister once again. Talleyrand declined, "knowing that we could never agree on the only way out of the maze into which his follies had thrust him." Talleyrand was able to persuade Bourrienne, Napoleon's secretary and a friend of Lavalette's, the post-master general, to share the Emperor's correspondence with him.

In January 1814, the Allies declared that France would be returned to its ancient limits, its frontiers of 1792 — to the frontiers, that is, before Napoleon had fought a single battle. In spite of his being married to Napoleon's sister Caroline, Murat now threw in his lot with the Allies, contributing his 30,000 men to the Austrian army in north Italy. On the 12th, Napoleon ordered Paris fortified and, on the 16th, established a Council of Regency with the Empress as its director. Talleyrand as a Grand Dignitary was made a member, but, as a counterpoise to his influence over the Empress, Napoleon appointed his brother Joseph the Council's Lieutenant-General. On the 24th, the day before he was to leave to join his army, Napoleon called a meeting of his ministers and other dignitaries. Glaring at Talleyrand, he said he knew he would not be facing *all* his enemies while in the field, that some indeed would be in Paris itself. Talleyrand and Joseph calmly continued their conversation in a corner of the room.

On January 29, Napoleon defeated Blucher at Brienne. By February 1, however, Blucher and Schwarzenberg had joined forces, and the French were forced to fall back. Blucher and Schwarzenberg now separated again as they continued their march on Paris. Delighted, Napoleon attacked Blucher on the 10th, 11th, and 14th, inflicting heavy casualties each time; on the 18th, Napoleon caught Schwarzenberg at Montereau and defeated him. Napoleon was trying once more. "As a military *tour de force*," comments Markham, "the campaign of 1814 will stand comparison with that of 1796." Napoleon now ordered Savary to arrest Talleyrand; Savary, however, did nothing:

he was far too occupied putting down an uprising of royalists throughout the French countryside to wish to incite those of Paris as well.

The encouragement of the British Foreign Secretary, Viscount Castlereagh, the rising of Bordeaux in revolt, and their victory over General Nicolas-Jean de Dieu Soult in late February, restored the Allies' pluck. In early March, Napoleon tried to take Blucher in the rear, but was prevented from doing so by the surrender of the French commander at Soissons. Napoleon lost a further 6,000 men at Craonne a few days later; his force was now greatly inferior to that of the Allies. On learning that Joseph was asking the Council of State and National Guard to issue a proclamation in favor of peace, Napoleon wrote Savary: "Let them know that I am still the same man as I was at Austerlitz and Wagram. I want no tribunes of the people: let them not forget that I am the great tribune."

On the 20th, Napoleon repulsed a Bavarian corps at Arcis-sur-Aube. On the following day, he engaged Schwarzenberg, whose army was three times the size of his own; Napoleon was forced to retreat with considerable losses. He now marched eastward, hoping to draw the Allies away from Paris. The Allies were at first inclined to pursue him; should Paris hold out, he would be able to cut their lines of communications and fall upon their rear. From Paris, however, Talleyrand assured the Allies that the city would not hold out against them. Ignoring Napoleon, the Allies continued on. "That's a fine chess move!" cried Napoleon. "Really, I could never have believed that the Allies had a general capable of making it."

Throughout 1812 and 1813, Talleyrand had hoped for a regency under the Empress Marie-Louise, and he would continue to do so — and oppose the return of the Bourbons — until the end of March. He strongly preferred a constitutional monarchy founded on Napoleon's son, a preference Austria shared. But for a regency, Napoleon must be killed rather than simply defeated and forced to abdicate; and England was strongly in favor of restoring the Bourbons. Napoleon had ordered that his wife and son, along with the entire French government, should flee Paris should it be in danger of falling to the Allies. On the 28th of March, the Council of Regency voted on whether the Empress and her son should do so; still hoping Napoleon might be killed, Talleyrand voted against their leaving. So that he himself might remain in the city — and thus become the French government — Talleyrand simply presented himself at the city wall without his passport; in spite of a great show of indignation, he was turned back.

Throughout the day of March 30, the 20,000 soldiers defending Paris valiantly held out against the Allies. That evening, Talleyrand called on Marmont, one of the two commanders of that force. Marmont was with the Russian Colonel Orloff and Napoleon's emissary General Dejean; the first was urging Marmont to surrender, the second — observing that Napoleon would be in Paris the very next day — to hold out. Talleyrand asked if he might speak privately with Marmont; he did so and then, as he took his leave, said to Colonel Orloff, "Please, sir, be so good as to convey to His Majesty the Emperor of Russia the profoundest respects of the Prince de Benevent," to which Orloff replied, "You may be sure, Prince, that I will bring this proof of your political detachment to the knowledge of His Majesty." At 2:00 in the morning, Marmont signed the capitulation; Napoleon was at Athis, only ten miles from Paris. The Allies marched into Paris the following day; both the proclamation Alexander signed and the house in which he stayed were Talleyrand's.

On April 3, Talleyrand, elected by the Senate President of the Provisional Government, induced the Senate to proclaim the deposition of Napoleon. Though Napoleon beseeched his marshals to march on Paris, they refused to do so, and on the 6th he signed an unconditional abdication. (He soon asked Caulaincourt to retrieve the abdication so that he might alter the wording on Italy; he wished to march on that country with his remaining troops and form a kingdom there. Caulaincourt refused.) "We are persuaded," commented the Englishman Lord Rosebery, "that had Napoleon been able to retain and work with Talleyrand, his fall would not have taken place." On receiving his abdication, the Senate voted to recall Louis XVIII, the brother of Louis XVI, the king guillotined in the Revolution.

The Treaty of Fontainebleau of April 11, 1814, signed by the Allies and Napoleon, granted him sovereignty over Elba, an island in the Mediterranean with 112,000 inhabitants, and an income of two million francs. Each member of his family would receive a pension. The Empress Marie-Louise received the Duchy of Parma; though she wished to join Napoleon, her father, the Emperor Francis, and Metternich refused to let her do so. While at Fontainebleau, Napoleon took the poison he had taken with him to Russia, remarking to Caulaincourt as he did so, "I did my best to get killed at Arcis." But the poison had lost its potency, and Napoleon suffered only severe vomiting and convulsions.

After taking leave of his Imperial Guard in the courtyard at Fontainebleau, Napoleon, escorted by four Allied Commissioners and others, traveled to Toulon, whence an English frigate took him to Elba. He took possession of the island on May 4, joined by 700 volunteers from the Guard.

On pledging his oath of allegiance to Louis XVIII, Talleyrand said pointedly, "Sire, it is my thirteenth; I hope it will be the last." Though Louis seems to have wished to govern well — he promised to be a constitutional monarch and to guarantee civil liberties, constitutional rights, and an elected lower house of parliament — he could do little against the ultra-royalists, who were resolved on extirpating all vestiges of the Revolution. (They had, said Talleyrand, "learned nothing and forgotten nothing.") Louis soon declared the French Constitution merely a "Charter" his to grant by divine right, appointed *emigré* aristocrats who knew nothing of war to critical military posts, and entertained a proposal to return all unsold national lands to the Church and *emigres*.

In October, the Allied states of Russia, Austria, Prussia, and England convened the Congress of Vienna to carve up the Napoleonic Empire. Though "lesser states" such as France were merely to be observers at the Congress, nonetheless Talleyrand hoped to attain two objects: the withdrawal of the Allies from France, and a weakening of the Coalition. In spite of the weakness of his own position — France was at first not even permitted to attend the meetings — he attained both. (To Talleyrand's delight, Alexander and Metternich fell out over the Duchess of Sagan, with whom both were passionately in love, and over whom they very nearly fought a duel.) Not only did the Allies withdraw, but they levied no indemnity against France and even permitted the country to retain some of the territories it had acquired. Indeed, so successful was Talleyrand at convincing England and Austria of the danger of Russia and Prussia that they agreed to sign a secret treaty of alliance with France and refused to grant either Russia the whole of Poland or Prussia the whole of Saxony. What Talleyrand did at the Congress — dissolve a coalition against France — Napoleon might easily have done a year-and-a-half earlier, had he been any good at politics.

Heartened by the dissensions at the Congress of Vienna, and unable to support himself and his Guard without the income guaranteed him by the Treaty of Fontainebleau (which the Bourbons refused to pay), on February 26, 1815 Napoleon and his Guard set sail for France. (Neither Talleyrand nor Metternich were in favor of Napoleon's being so close to Europe; but Alexander, viewing Napoleon's propinquity as a nice check on the Bourbons, insisted the Treaty of Fontainebleau be observed.) On the 6th, Talleyrand wrote Louis, "Any invasion by Napoleon of France will be the act of a brigand. He should be treated as such; any action that is permissible against brigands should be taken against him." At his behest, on the 14th the Congress proclaimed that "Napoleon Bonaparte has placed himself outside the bounds of civil and social relations, and as an enemy and disturber of the peace of the world was consigned to public prosecution." Since the whole of Europe would combine once more against him, Napoleon could not possibly hope to win.

On the 20th, Napoleon arrived in Paris, which the Bourbons, most of the French government, and the diplomatic corps had fled. So hated had the Bourbons made themselves in the short time of their rule that Napoleon was received with adulation. He proclaimed that he would be a "constitutional monarch" and institute liberal reforms, and he beseeched Talleyrand to rejoin his government. When Talleyrand refused, Napoleon confiscated his property, reassuring him, however, that it would be returned should he think better of his decision. A French government official recorded that "M. de Talleyrand was the man whose absence [Napoleon] felt most acutely during the Hundred Days, and whose name cropped up most constantly in his conversation and in his references to his past mistakes."

On June 15, Napoleon crossed the Sambre River with 120,000 men, hoping to rout Blucher's force of 120,000 Prussians while Wellington was still some distance away. On the following day, Napoleon fell upon the isolated Prussians, but a mistake by one of his officers enabled them to escape. Though Napoleon might still have saved the situation by destroying either Blucher's or Wellington's force while still isolated, that night he did nothing. On the 17th, Napoleon neither attacked the Prussian army with sufficient force nor pinned Wellington down. "He still possesses his remarkable intelligence," said Marmont. "In this respect he is still the same…but there is no longer any resolution, any will, any character in him. These qualities, formerly so very prominent in him, have vanished. Nothing remains but the mind."

On the morning of the 18th, Napoleon faced Wellington at Waterloo; Napoleon had 74,000 men, Wellington 67,000. Rather than take command of the French forces himself, Napoleon inexplicably had his marshal Michel Ney do so. He also had the preeminent French artillery expert, Antoine Drouot, take command of the Imperial Guard (whose commander was ill), greatly weakening the artillery. Certain the Prussians were *hors de combat*, Napoleon gave his marshal Emmanuel de Grouchy only very imprecise orders on how he should engage them. (Indeed, so careless were his orders that Grouchy would also be nowhere near the field of battle.) A Prussian column soon slipped past Grouchy; a little after noon, it was sighted approaching the French right flank. Though he might still have called off the battle, Napoleon felt certain he could put Wellington to rout before the Prussians could come to his aid.

At 1:30, Ney launched the first attack, four columns of infantry unsupported by cavalry. Using a tactic he had perfected fighting the French in Spain, Wellington had had his soldiers assume a defensive position on a rise. (When the French generals thrashed by Wellington warned Napoleon of the efficacy of such a position, he scoffed, "This will be a picnic.") With volleys of great precision, Wellington's troops decimated the compactly massed French columns. Ney now sent in the French cavalry unsupported by infantry; the cavalry also fell back before Wellington's squares. Wellington was doing to Napoleon what Napoleon had always done to his opponents: pinning him down.

In the early evening, Napoleon was forced to throw his reserves at the oncoming Prussian column. When at 6:30 Ney beseeched him for Guard infantry so that he might make a final assault on Wellington's center, Napoleon replied, "Troops? Where do you suppose I shall find them? Do you expect me to make them?" It was not until 7:30 that Napoleon could free up any of his reserves; Ney at once hurled the five battalions at Wellington's line, but they, too, failed to break through. On seeing the French troops panic at the retreat of the invincible Guard, Wellington launched his cavalry against them, putting the French to rout. Napoleon escaped to Charleroi, so exhausted that he had to be held onto his horse by an aide. The following day, Wellington wrote, "It was the most desperate business I ever was in: I never took so much trouble about any battle, and never was so near being beat." And this against a greatly decayed Napoleon.

Napoleon returned to Paris, where on June 22 he signed his second abdication. He then made his way to Rochefort, where he surrendered to the English. An English ship conveyed him to England, whence another took him to St. Helena, a volcanic island in the South Atlantic 1,200 miles west of Africa.

On July 8 Louis XVIII returned to Paris as the Germans, Prussians, and others ravaged his country. France lost Alsace Lorraine, French Flanders, Franche-Comte, and Burgundy; it would be three years before the Allies once more treated Louis XVIII as an equal. In a rare instance of spite — but one that did not touch his interests — Talleyrand had the Marquis de Montchenu appointed French Commissioner to St. Helena, remarking, "What a punishment for a man of Bonaparte's caliber to be compelled to associate with an ignorant and pedantic gossip. I know him; he won't be able to stand the boredom of it; it will make him ill, and he will die by slow degrees." (Napoleon refused ever to speak with Montchenu.) Napoleon died on St. Helena on May 5, 1821, at the age of 51.

༄

The young king Pentheus of Euripides's *Bacchae*, writes Arrowsmith,

is a deeply unreasonable man, intemperate in anger and utterly unconvinced by reasonable evidence. Around him cluster almost all the harsh words of the Greek moral vocabulary: he is violent, stubborn, self-willed, arbitrary, impatient of tradition and custom, impious, unruly, and immoderate. At times he evinces the traits of a stock tragedy-tyrant, loud with threats and bluster, prone to confuse the meaning of subject with slave. But so, I think, he must be shown in order to be presented for what he is: ignorant of himself and his nature, profoundly *amathes*...

Ranged against Pentheus are Cadmus, Teiresias, the Chorus, and the god Dionysus

who all alike appeal to the massive authority of tradition and folk-belief and constantly invoke against the scoffer the full force of *dike* (custom incarnate as justice) and *sophrosune* (very roughly, humility). Thus in flat ominous opposition to Pentheus's lonely arrogance of the "exceptional" individual, superior and contemptuous, defying the community's *nomos* (custom as law) in the name of his own self-will, is set the Chorus's tyrannous tradition: "Beyond the old beliefs, no thought, no act shall go."

The conflict between them is

a bitter image of Athens and Hellas terribly divided between the forces that, for Euripides, more than anything else destroyed them: on the one side, the conservative tradition in its extreme corruption, disguising avarice for power with the fair professions of the traditional *aretai* (virtues), meeting all opposition with the terrible tyranny of popular piety, and disclosing in its actions the callousness and refined cruelty of civilized barbarism; on the other side the exceptional individual, selfish and egotistical, impatient of tradition and public welfare alike, stubborn, demagogic, and equally brutal in action.

As with Pentheus and those opposed to him, so, too, with Napoleon and the ancient monarchies of Europe...

SURPRISE THE OPPONENT

Alexander rode round the plain on which he would fight the Persian King Darius. He saw how Darius had prepared the field, here leveling the pitch for chariots, there placing snares and stakes into the ground to slow a cavalry charge. Alexander returned to his tent; he sat up into the early hours of the morning, thinking. He then fell asleep.

Alexander continued sleeping late into the morning. Anxious, his officers finally woke him. "How can you sleep," they asked, "as if you had won the battle already?" "Have I not?", replied Alexander with a smile. To see Darius's preparations was to know his plan of battle. Alexander ordered certain changes made to the Macedonian dispositions; in spite of their vast numerical superiority, the Persians were routed, and Darius killed.

"Secrecy," said Richelieu, "is the very soul of all important undertakings." "It is no more possible to preserve secrecy in business without some degree of dissimulation," said Lord Chesterfield, "than it is to succeed in business without secrecy." One of Napoleon's maxims was *toujours confondre*, always confound and perplex. Confounding your opponent will dishearten and disorient him; what is more, *your opponent cannot parry a strike he does not see coming*. Do not favor certain strikes or techniques over others; do not be predictable. Since Napoleon's opponents followed the accepted military principles of the day, he almost always knew beforehand what they would do. And do not signal your strikes as Pompey did at Pharsalus. On seeing Pompey's cavalry massed on his left wing, Caesar knew at once what Pompey would try to do — circumvent his right wing and fall upon his rear — and so created a fourth line of battle to meet it. Talleyrand's success in overthrowing Napoleon was due in large measure to his taking away Napoleon's ability to surprise. Napoleon himself learned only of some of Talleyrand's many strikes against him, learned only very little of how Talleyrand had contributed to his downfall.

Countless instances can be cited of Caesar's attaining his objects through surprise. During the great rebellion of the Gallic War, Caesar was able to elude the Gallic patrols, and so join his legions, by crossing the Cevannes in the dead of winter. In Ravenna on January 10, 49, Caesar spent the day in public, watching gladiators practice. He then took a bath and went to dinner; after a while, he rose from the table and told his guests he would return soon. He entered a hired carriage, took a road that led away from Italy, and then, once out of sight, turned back toward the Rubicon; there he met his companions, each of whom he had sent by a different route. Caesar then stormed down the Adriatic coast road while his opponents were still levying troops. And later, rather than march through Illyria to reach Greece, Caesar crossed the Adriatic — taking the Pompeians wholly by surprise, as they had 110 warships to his 12. In all such instances, Caesar had far fewer men than did his opponents; surprise made him far stronger.

In Napoleon's *corps d'armee* system, each corps was a self-contained unit with its own infantry, cavalry, and artillery; each was of a different size, and the size of each would change during a campaign (or an altogether new corps formed). This would utterly confound his opponent, who might know that a certain corps was in a certain place, but not its size or composition. (With his light cavalry, Napoleon would keep the opponent from conducting reconnaissance.) Furthermore, "it was only very rarely that Napoleon issued any orders dealing with his army as a whole. In most cases, every corps leader received instructions only upon what he himself had to do, while, with respect to the general position of the army, he received additional information only concerning the corps next to his own." (Chandler) And Napoleon was quite as secretive *before* a campaign: he would close France's borders, greatly limit what the French press could report on military affairs, and order the secret police to redouble its vigilance.

STRIKE SWIFTLY AT THE CRITICAL TIME

Just as you must concentrate force at the critical point, so, too, must you concentrate force at the critical time. You must strike the moment a vital point presents itself; not to do so may be to lose all. A vital point may be vital or exposed, or the opponent between a Scylla and Charybdis, only a short while. And you must strike before your opponent has time to organize his resistance (as when Caesar scattered Pompey's levies in northern Italy). "Strategy," said Napoleon, "is the art of making use of time and space. I am less chary of the latter than the former. Space we can recover, lost time never."

Had Pompey attacked Caesar at the height of the Gallic rebellion, when Vercingetorix had united almost all the tribes against him, he might very well have prevailed; but he waited until Caesar had pacified Gaul and could turn his full attention to his Roman opponents. "A capacity which Richelieu possessed to an unusual degree," comments Burckhardt, "was the sense for ripeness; ripeness in men, in times, in circumstances; he never intervened until the moment was ripe." Richelieu was forced to stay his hand for years against many of *les grands* he was bent on striking, until they should make some mistake; once they did, he was upon them. Only by combining his self-contained corps at precisely the right moment could Napoleon hope to win; a bit too early, and the enemy would be frightened away; a bit too late, and he would crush the French. And once battle was joined, Napoleon would carefully observe the action, noting the precise moment to do this or that; only "at the decisive moment, which lies between the winning and losing of a battle," for instance, would he send in the Imperial Guard. All was a question of precise timing.

Once the moment is ripe, you must strike swiftly. Caesar, said Montaigne, "repeated on several occasions that the most sovereign qualities in a commander are knowing how to seize opportunities at the right moment... and acting with speed." Caesar was celebrated for his *Celeritus Caesaris*, for his lightning marches and strikes; Suetonius tells us that Caesar "often arrived at his destination before the messengers whom he had sent ahead to announce his approach," Plutarch that Caesar slept in carriages and litters more often than in beds. Rarely would Caesar wait until all his forces were assembled; he would more often march out with whichever forces he had, hoping the others would soon catch up. Napoleon, too, would strike will great speed. The moment his opponent made a "false movement," the moment he erred in his calculations or dispositions, Napoleon would be upon him. He would frequently ride his horses to death and urge his officers to do so as well.

Striking swiftly will also confound your opponent. Of Napoleon's Italian campaign of 1796, the Italian historian Carlo Botta observes, "His movements and tactics on this critical occasion were...conceived and executed with the rapidity of lightning, nor had the Austrians any notion of what he was doing until Bonaparte had chosen his own ground and entirely changed the state of the campaign." *Within six days*, the French marched over 100 miles and fought two engagements and one battle.

STRIKE IN COMBINATION

Your first strike may not result in a breach, may not break the opponent's equilibrium, may not place him hors de combat. You should, therefore, strike in combination, strike multiple vital points, a single vital point multiple times, or a single vital point and multiple non-vital points. These strikes may be simultaneous or in rapid succession; some will be of greater force than others.

As the opponent reels from your first strike and begins to think how he will respond, strike again, and again, and again. "Toujours attaque," said Napoleon: always attack. In his war against the Habsburgs, Richelieu struck wherever he could, in Europe, America, and Asia. "No discord between Spain and the states within her sphere of influence...and no dissension between Spain and her allies escaped his attention; wherever he saw differences, whether newly emerging or of long standing, he offered his help." (Burckhardt) Such an enfilade not only distracts the opponent from the strike or strikes at his "main body" and scatters his forces, but also demoralizes and disorients him.

To strike in combination is to dictate when, where, and how your opponent will fight. "Make war offensively," said Napoleon; "it is the sole means to become a great captain and to fathom the secrets of the art." "It is contrary to the nature of a true general," said Count Yorck von Wartenburg, "to have his course of action imposed upon him by the enemy, and it was Napoleon's instinctive determination to force his opponent to do as he wished, more than any other consideration, that dictated to him his line of action." Napoleon would "force his opponent to do as he wished" even while on the defensive, as at some points during his first Italian campaign.

To strike in combination well, you must see the whole of your rival, not simply this or that force or position. In early 1800, Napoleon created a reserve army at Dijon; this army would "form the center of the great line of operations, whose right is at Genoa, and whose left is on the Danube." To Napoleon, the whole of this line, the whole of the Austrian forces, were as one. Which vital points you strike, and the order in which you strike them, depends on you, your opponent, and the context. On Richelieu's policy in Germany, Burckhardt comments, "In his view Catholic, Protestant, and class passions were all there to be exploited. The question of which should be exploited in any given instance was purely a tactical one, to be determined by considerations of time and place."

Your strikes should be varied and creative. The historian Robin Lane Fox observes that "the expert use of varied weaponry [was] the main principle of Alexander's military success."

Following a seven months' siege, Alexander took the island city of Tyre by simultaneously having: battering-ships breach various points in the city's walls; infantry storm through the breaches from two other ships; other ships attack the city's two harbors; and, ship-borne archers and catapults strike from all round the island. Against such a combination of strikes, Tyre could not hope to prevail. "Such a mixture of concentrated and diversionary tactics," observes Fox, "is the mark of a great general. . ."

While Microsoft has many sources of income — its Windows operating system and countless applications and other products — most of its rivals have only one or a few. Microsoft is thus able to bundle a new application (such as its video software Media Player) free of charge with every new copy of Windows; its rivals cannot possibly offer their products for free and survive. In a 1988 memo, Bill Gates ordered deep price cuts to cut "Lotus' profit in half;" a Microsoft manager responded with a "Kill Lotus Plan." Microsoft bundled its applications into Microsoft Office and slashed its price; the market share of Lotus 1-2-3 plummeted, and IBM soon bought the company. Following its acquisition of Access in 1992, Microsoft reduced the software's price by 86 percent, greatly hurting its chief rival in such products, Borland International. By pricing its browser at zero, Microsoft forced Netscape to do so as well; its revenues cut off, Netscape could no longer compete with Microsoft in research and development. The quality of Microsoft's browser soon surpassed that of Netscape; by November 1998, Netscape's once highly profitable browser business was valued at zero.

Microsoft's rivals charge that they receive critical information about operating systems such as DOS for Windows long after Microsoft's applications staff. The rivals also charge that the information they receive is incomplete, that Microsoft does not, for instance, disclose some of the Applications Programming Interfaces, or APIs, in its Windows operating system. Since APIs enable an operating system to respond to commands from an application program, the rivals' products do not work quite so well with Windows as do Microsoft's.

On occasion, Microsoft programmers have written secret code into the Windows operating system to hobble, or at least undermine confidence in, rivals' applications and operating systems. In the early 1990s, Microsoft programmers wrote secret code into the beta version of Windows 3.1 telling users whose computers also carried Novell's DR DOS, a rival operating system, "non-fatal error detected." Microsoft also struck at DR DOS through its applications; on detecting DR DOS, the applications would state: "Warning: This Microsoft product has been tested and certified for use only with the MS DOS and PC DOS operating systems. Your use of this product with another operating system may void valuable warranty protection by Microsoft on this product." Microsoft programmers purportedly wrote secret code into Windows 95 hobbling all Internet browsers but Microsoft's own, Explorer 1.0; Netscape Navigator, for instance, would either not work, or not work well, with Windows 95. RealNetworks has charged that Microsoft's operating system disables its software, a competitor to Microsoft's Media Player. In a January 24, 1999 e-mail on Linux, Gates suggests, "Maybe we could define the APIs so that they work well with [Windows] and not the others..."

Just as Microsoft alters its own codes, so, too, does it alter others'. While seemingly embracing an industry-wide standard, Microsoft will make secret changes to the standard so that it works best with the company's own products. In an e-mail, a Microsoft staffer describes this tactic as "Embrace, extend, extinguish." Kerberos, for instance, is an open standard that keeps passwords secure on the web; by adding undisclosed extensions, Microsoft made desktop computers running its software work better with network and internet servers.

Microsoft ties its desktop versions of Windows to its server software; to function fully, Windows must be on both the desktop and the server. Functions that allow group scheduling in Microsoft Office, for instance, operate only on a Windows server running Microsoft's Exchange software. Microsoft Word and Excel let users work on and share online documents; but some of the features of the two require a Web server running Microsoft's Internet Information Server. And such Microsoft applications as its SQL server database and its Web server are designed to run only on Microsoft's operating system.

Microsoft has offered computer makers lower prices for Windows should they drop rival operating systems and applications. Through secret contracts called "Market-Development Agreements," PC makers agreed to hew to Microsoft's terms on marketing, technical specifications, and so on in return for discounts on each copy of Windows (as well as early access to Microsoft technical data). (Microsoft has discontinued such contracts.)

And Microsoft has punished computer makers that offer its rivals' products. When Microsoft learned that one computer maker would offer DR DOS on 10 percent of its computers, the company doubled the maker's price for MS DOS (which was to be loaded on the other 90 percent). Microsoft once insisted that IBM drop competing software lines such as Lotus Smart-Suite and IBM's own operating system OS/2; when IBM refused, Microsoft doubled the price IBM paid for Windows. IBM has said that had it agreed to make Windows the standard IBM operating system, the earnings of its PC units would have been as much as $48 million more over the first year of its licensing agreement with Microsoft.

Microsoft once offered computer makers a considerable discount on MS DOS if they paid a royalty on each computer shipped *whether or not MS DOS was on the machine.* The per-copy cost of MS DOS was $90 or so, the royalty per machine $30 or so. (The royalty depended on the size of the maker; the larger makers paid as little as $7.) The PC makers that opted to pay the royalty —the majority — were not inclined to offer competing operating systems (since they were already paying for MS DOS on each computer shipped). In an August 1997 e-mail to Warren Buffett, CEO of Berkshire Hathaway Inc., a Microsoft group vice president, Jeffrey Raikes, said that others had likened Windows to a "toll-bridge," collecting a toll on every PC sold. (Raikes continued that Microsoft's "real goal" in investing in cable companies and set-top boxes was "to get an 'operating-system' royalty per TV.") The FTC forced Microsoft to cease this practice.

Microsoft has in general sought to increase its leverage over computer makers. By imposing restrictions on the Windows 95 start-up sequence, for instance, Microsoft not only made it more difficult for the makers to differentiate their computers, but also increased their technical-support costs. (On earlier versions of Windows, the makers had been able to install a program welcoming new users and instructing them on how to use the computer.)

CREATE OR EXPOSE A VITAL POINT

It may not be quite so simple. Your opponent may not make a "false movement," may not leave a vital point undefended; if so, you must force him to make a false movement, must create or expose a vital point. You may be able to do so simply by striking him; Napoleon would often sting his opponents "into ill-conceived and ill-timed counterattacks" (Chandler) that would create or expose vital points. Striking the opponent in combination may also create or expose a vital point, as it will stretch him thin.

A vital point may present itself or come into being through deception. "As far as Lorraine is concerned," Richelieu once wrote his sovereign, "for the time being we must dissemble...and, without binding ourselves, so arrange matters as to give them reason to believe that we do not intend to act against them... As soon as the Dutch have taken the field [thus tying down the Spanish forces], we must send in 40,000 men to conquer Lorraine...and we must do so at the precise moment when our action is least expected." If your opponent is ignorant of himself or the context, if he fancies himself quite good at that which he is quite bad, do all you can to fan his delusions. Stoke, too, his conviction that he is superior to you; nothing quite lures an opponent on, or makes him relax his vigilance, as does the conviction that he is far stronger than you. So reliant is life on manner for its judgments, so programmed is it to draw its information from behavior, that manner is one of the better tools with which to deceive.

Perhaps the greatest military genius who has ever lived gained his victories chiefly by creating vital points.

In the months before a campaign, Napoleon would have the French press issue disinformation; at its beginning, he would launch false offensives. As the French army marched toward its destination, Napoleon would have its front continually expand and contract, forcing the opponent to expand and contract his own in turn; his doing so not of his own volition would not only unnerve him, but also perhaps create a vital point in his line, upon which Napoleon would concentrate his forces and strike. Should the expansion and contraction of the French front not create a vital point, Napoleon would try to induce the opponent to attack one or another of the French corps; he would do so by keeping them far apart and thus seemingly isolated. (So flexible was Napoleon's *corps d'armee* system that it mattered little which corps the opponent attacked.) Should the opponent not attack one of the corps, Napoleon would order the nearest corps to engage. Since each corps was a miniature army with its own infantry, cavalry, and artillery, each could pin down an army many times its own size; should the corps begin to give way, Napoleon would send in special reserves to reinforce it.

Once a corps pinned the opponent down, Napoleon would order the other corps to converge on the spot by forced marches. (All the corps were within one or two days' march of one another.) As the other corps arrived, the opposing commander would commit more and more reserves to maintain his numerical superiority — reserves that would be exhausted by the time the main battle began. All the while, a French force of infantry, cavalry, and horse artillery, concealed by cavalry or the terrain, would be marching toward the opponent's flank (that nearest his line of retreat). Once the opposing commander had committed most or all of his reserves, Napoleon would signal this force to attack; lest the commander order a retreat, he would simultaneously order the pinning force to launch a frontal assault. To meet this new French attack on his flank, the commander would be forced to form a new line at a right angle to his main line; having already committed his reserves, he could do so only by drawing troops from the nearest section of his front line. This thinning of the opponent's line at the hinge Napoleon called "the Event."

Napoleon would now signal an elite force of fresh troops to fall upon the vital point where the line bent. This *masse de rupture* was drawn up in the form of a large square, with the Guard Reserve artillery forming the front face, two divisions of infantry forming the sides, and cavalry the rear. The Guard Reserve would gallop to within 500 yards of the opponent's line, dismount, and rip a hole in the line with artillery. The infantry, supported by batteries of horse artillery, would now come up, form into lines, and plunge through the opponent's line. As they did so, the French cavalry would hurl itself upon the opposing infantry, forcing them to form into squares (thus making it more difficult for them to fire upon the French). Napoleon would throw in unit after unit, careless of casualties, till the breach was made; once it was, he would send in fresh cavalry and infantry to widen it. The French cavalry would then reform, storm through the gap, and hew down the enemy. Victory was now Napoleon's; the question was simply how considerable a victory. The French would continue to attack the opponent for days or weeks until he surrendered or was destroyed.

&

On occasion, Napoleon would be faced by, not one, but two or more armies within supporting distance of one another. In such a situation, he would adopt the "strategy of the central position." *Though the French army would be numerically inferior to the opponent as a whole, it would always be numerically superior at the point of attack.* Napoleon would secretly concentrate his forces, attack the middle-most unit of the opponent's army, and destroy it. He now controlled the central position, a vital point: a shorter distance lay between the French and most of the opponent's units than lay between the units themselves. The nearest corps of the French army would attack the nearest enemy unit and pin it down; French reserves would soon join in the attack. Another French corps would first observe and then attack the opponent's next-nearest unit, both to pin it down and to prevent it from coming to the aid of the other. Once the second unit was defeated, Napoleon would have a portion of his army pursue its survivors and a portion turn about and join in the attack on the third unit. After two or three days of battle, little or nothing would remain of the opponent's army.

&

Napoleon's most successful stratagem was *la manoeuvre sur les derrieres*, which he would apply against a single, isolated army. While a French corps pinned the army down frontally, other corps, hidden by cavalry or the terrain, would fall upon the opponent's rear, cutting his communications. As they did so, "corps of observation" would occupy natural barriers such as rivers and mountain ranges to block all crossings and isolate the army further. The opposing commander could now do one of three things: attack the pinning force in strength, attack the French line of communication, or retreat toward the main French army. The commander would find it quite difficult to break through the strong pinning force; and even should he be able to do so, he would only take himself farther from his own bases, with the French in pursuit. To attack the French line of communication, the commander would have to divide his forces into three, one to fight off the pinning force, one to fight off the force to the rear, and one to attack the line; his dividing his forces so would weaken them greatly. (Since the French army lived largely off the countryside, cutting its line of communication would anyhow not be fatal to it.) The third would require the commander to give battle on ground of Napoleon's choosing, his forces disorganized and demoralized. Here again, victory would go to Napoleon.

Austerlitz

Much contributed to dooming the Peace of Luneville of 1801. A rivalry of interests in the West Indies, the Mediterranean, and elsewhere provoked King George III into resuming war against France in May 1803. In March 1804, Napoleon had the Duc d'Enghien seized in the neutral territory of Baden and executed, acts received with horror and indignation throughout Europe. In May of that year, Napoleon declared himself Emperor of the French. The following year, he turned the Italian Republic into a hereditary kingdom, proclaimed himself king, and annexed Genoa to France; all were breaches of the Treaty of Luneville, and all convinced Emperor Francis that Napoleon sought to evict Austria from Italy. Tsar Alexander objected to France's occupation of Hanover and its increasing influence over the German princes, suspected Napoleon would oppose Russian control of Poland, and mistrusted French intentions toward Turkey. In April 1805, England and Russia signed the Anglo-Russian Convention, to which Austria adhered a few months later. (Hoping Napoleon would cede it Hanover, Prussia simply vacillated.) The Third Coalition had come into being, its object the restoration of Europe to the territorial balance of 1789.

The Allies' campaign against France would involve connected offensives by half a million men; Italy would be the main theater of war. The Austrian Archduke Charles, with 100,000 of the finest Austrian troops, was to evict Napoleon's stepson, Viceroy Eugene Beauharnais, from Lombardy and then invade the south of France. A force of English, Russian, and Sicilian-Bourbon troops was to retake Naples and then join the Archduke Charles. The Austrians Quartermaster-General Karl Mack and Archduke Ferdinand with 70,000 Austrian troops, joined by the Russian General Mikhail Kutuzov with 35,000 troops, were to occupy Bavaria, a French ally, to block any French advance through the Black Forest. The Russian Marshal Buxhowden with 40,000 men was to follow Kutuzov into Bavaria, and the Russian Marshal Levin Bennigsen with 20,000 to occupy nearby Franconia. A further 25,000 Austrians, under Charles's brother the Archduke John, were to occupy Tyrol and the nearby Alpine passes; these troops would then go either south into Italy or north toward Bavaria as circumstances dictated. To the far north, a force of English, Swedish, and Russian troops would seize Hanover; the English would also raid the coasts of France and Holland in hopes of inciting rebellions against the Napoleonic regime.

The first riposte would come from General Mack. French troops were in five widely separated regions — Hanover, Swabia, Piedmont, Naples, and (in preparation for an attack on England) northern France — more than 700 miles from Bavaria. Calculating that Napoleon could not reach the Danube in fewer than 80 days, and then with at most 70,000 men, on September 10 Mack invaded Bavaria without awaiting Kutuzov; he occupied the city of Ulm and encamped to the west of it.

As Austrian intelligence reported the French to be still in Boulogne, seven *corps d'armee* of 200,000 men marched separately toward the Danube. To make certain of his lines of communication — which were in danger should Mack cross to the north bank of the Danube, the Russians arrive from the east, or Prussia join the Allies and come down from the north — Napoleon arranged reserve camps and fortified cities along the Rhine and detached a strong force to guard his rear areas. (To meet the threats elsewhere, Napoleon made certain other dispositions: General Andre Massena with 50,000 men was to contain the Archduke Charles in northern Italy, the marquis de Gouvion-St.-Cyr to defend Naples, and Marshal Brune to guard the Channel coast.) As he marched, Napoleon sought to deceive the Allies as to his object. To General Jean-Baptiste-Jules Bernadotte he wrote, "You will announce everywhere that you are returning to France because you are being relieved by Dutch troops." The meeting of Corps I and II at Wurzburg on September 29 was said to be for the purpose of holding joint maneuvers. To distract Mack, Napoleon had his cavalry launch attacks in the Black Forest to the east of the Rhine (whence Mack expected Napoleon's attack to come).

The *corps d'armee* marched southeastward from the Rhine, crossed the Danube — thus placing themselves to Mack's rear — and seized its crossings. It was a perfect *manoeuvre sur les derrieres*, performed on an isolated army. Not until the 30th did Mack learn that he was trapped in the Black Forest; shocked, he withdrew into Ulm. To buy time till Kutuzov might arrive, Mack sought to negotiate with the French; on being shown incontrovertible proof that the Russians were still quite far away, on October 20 "the unfortunate General Mack" surrendered. In a campaign of 26 days, without a single major battle, Napoleon took almost 60,000 prisoners and 200 cannon.

On learning of Mack's surrender, Kutuzov at once ordered his 58,000 Russians and Austrians to retreat over the River Inn. On October 25, Prussia signed the Treaty of Potsdam, by which it promised to join the Allies by early December; once Prussia did so, the Allies would have 400,000 men to France's 60,000. Napoleon must catch Kutuzov before he could cross the Danube and join up with Buxhowden's army of 30,000 men (which was then marching south toward the Danube). The French crossed the Inn on the 28th; in spite of a number of fierce skirmishes with the Russian and Austrian rearguards, the French could not prevent Kutuzov from crossing the Danube.

On November 11, Kutuzov fell upon the isolated French Marshal Mortier at Durrenstein, inflicting heavy casualties. (Rather than support Mortier as Napoleon had ordered, Marshal Joachim Murat took Vienna; his doing so infuriated Napoleon: annihilating Kutuzov was purposeful, taking Vienna not.) On learning that Kutuzov was retiring north towards Znaim, Napoleon ordered Bernadotte over the Danube at Molk and Murat up from Vienna. Murat soon caught Kutusov near Hollabrunn, but the Russian rearguard commander, General Peter Bagration, was somehow able to induce him to accept an armistice. Livid, Napoleon commanded: "Break the armistice instantly and attack the enemy! March! Destroy the Russian army!" Though Murat threw himself at once upon Bagration, the main Russian and Austrian force had by now marched well out of reach. On November 20, Kutuzov joined Buxhowden, forming a joint army of 90,000 men.

His troops exhausted, on November 23 Napoleon called a halt at Brunn. The situation he now faced was as complex as it was daunting. Napoleon had only 53,000 soldiers under his direct command; they were 700 miles from France and dispirited by fatigue, hunger, bitter cold, and word that the English Admiral Nelson had destroyed the French fleet at Trafalgar. The 90,000 Russians and Austrians were well positioned at Olmutz, 30 miles to the northeast of Brunn, with strong lines of communication; both Tsar Alexander and the Emperor Francis were now with the army. At any moment, the Prussians might contribute a further 200,000 men to the Allies. Should the Russians continue their retreat and the French their pursuit, the French lines of communication would become dangerously extended, and both the Prussians (to the north) and Bennigsen (to the south) might well take the French army in the flank. Should the French remain where they were, the Archdukes Charles and John, who were then crossing the Alps, would take the French on one side with 90,000 men, and the Prussians and Russians the French on the other. To retreat to Ulm would be a strategic defeat, and the French would have to recross country they had just denuded.

Napoleon ordered Marshal Auguste-Frederic-Louis Viesse de Marmont south to hold up the Archdukes Charles and John; divisions of General Louis-Nicolas Davout's and Mortier's corps would be within supporting distance of Marmont. His southern flank secure, Napoleon ordered the corps of Marshal Jean Lannes, General Nicolas-Jean de Dieu Soult, and Murat to take possession of the town of Austerlitz and the nearby Pratzen Heights, in Bohemia (now Czechoslovakia); he also ordered a brigade of light cavalry north along the road to Olmutz. Once he had made these dispositions, Napoleon visited the plain of the Pratzen Heights. To the northwest of the plateau, just to the south of the road between Olmutz and Brunn (which ran from east to west), was a low hill called the Zurlan; to the northeast of the Zurlan, and just to the north of the road, lay the smaller hill of the Santon. To the south of the Zurlan, and to the west of the Pratzen Heights, was a valley of marshy fields and ponds through which the Goldbach rivulet ran; to the south of the heights was the Satschan Pond. To the north of the plateau stood the village of Blasowitz, to the east Krzenowitz and Austerlitz, on its western slope Pratzen, to the west Kobelnitz, to the southwest Zokolnitz and Tellnitz, and to the south Aujest Markt. "The Emperor slowly and silently went over this newly discovered ground," wrote his aide the Duc de Segur, "stopping several times on its most elevated points, looking principally towards Pratzen. He carefully examined all its characteristics and during this survey turned towards us, saying, 'Gentlemen, examine this ground carefully, it is going to be a battlefield; you will have a part to play upon it.'"

The weakness and dispersion of the French forces delighted the Allies. To be certain, however, of numerical superiority, on November 27th Francis offered an armistice to give the Archduke Charles time to come up. Napoleon showed himself eager for the armistice, which he sent General Anne-Jean-Marie-Rene Savary to negotiate. While at Allied headquarters, Savary was timorous and indecisive; he learned, however, that while Francis preferred to await the Archduke Charles, he was little listened to since his soldiers composed only one-fifth of the total. Kutusov, too, preferred circumspection, but the Austrian chief of staff Weyrother, the Austrian Generals Kollowrath and Kienmayer, and the Tsar's young aides, all keen to revenge Ulm, were urging the Tsar to attack. Why would Napoleon agree to an armistice, they asked, if not in recognition of his weakness? They also pointed out that they could not remain at Olmutz, since the local food supplies were beginning to run short. Savary returned to Napoleon with a document from the Tsar, addressed to "the Head of the French government," demanding considerable French concessions and cessations of territory. As Napoleon considered this document, Bagration drove Murat's cavalry out of Wischau. Napoleon at once ordered Bernadotte, in Iglau, and Davout, in Vienna, to march for Austerlitz with all speed.

Napoleon ordered Savary to return to Olmutz to request a personal interview with Alexander. Though the Tsar would not himself meet with Napoleon, he would permit his young aide-de-camp, Count Dolgorouki, to do so. Napoleon met the Count at the French outposts, an unprecedented honor, and conducted him to French headquarters. Once there, Dolgorouki lectured Napoleon on European politics and war and then demanded that he renounce Italy and other conquests; Napoleon, diffident and grave, said little. Following this interview, Napoleon ordered his forces to withdraw from Austerlitz and the Pratzen Heights. The Allies now began to move down the road from Olmutz.

On the morning of December 1, Russian columns occupied a hill to the north of the Olmutz road. By the early afternoon, they had mounted the Pratzen Heights; soon the divisions of the Russian General Doctorov and the Austrian General Andrault Langeron had taken up a position on the southeast of the heights, facing the French right. By evening, 85,400 Allied troops and 278 cannon were on the plateau or surrounding plain, with a further 5,000 still on the road from Olmutz. Alexander and Francis established their headquarters in the village of Krzenowitz, to the east of the heights. Napoleon followed these Allied movements with great care; he also inspected the French units and artillery pieces and interviewed local peasants to learn in minutest detail the topography of the plain. As he did so, Bernadotte arrived from Iglau. (Davout would arrive late that night.)

At 1:00 in the morning, the Allied commanders were summoned to receive their orders. Weyrother laid a large map of the plateau and plain on a table and began to read the dispositions he had drawn up. His plan called for turning the French right flank (to the south) by crossing the Goldbach rivulet between the villages of Tellnitz and Zokolnitz; the Allies would then swing north, enveloping the French as they fled for Brunn to the northwest. Five divisions of 59,300 men, under the overall command of Buxhowden, would engage in this attack on the French right. Leading this force would be Kienmayer's Advance Guard of 5,100 men; behind him would come Doctorov's First Column of 13,600, which was to take the village of Tellnitz and then swing north to join Langeron's Second Column of 11,700 troops, which would by this time have taken the village of Zokolnitz, aided by the Russian General Przbyswski's Third Column of 10,000 troops. These three columns would then cross the Goldbach, reunite near Kobelnitz, and attack the French center, which would now form a right angle, the French right flank running east-west, the left flank north-south. As they did so, the Allied Fourth Column of 23,900 men under Kollowrath and the Russian General Miloradovitch would fall upon the "hinge" in the French front. The Austrian cavalry would at first aid in the crossing of the Goldbach and then cut the Brunn-Vienna high road. To the north, Bagration with 13,000 men would press toward Santon Hill, supported on his left by the Austrian Prince Lichtenstein's 4,600 cavalry (which would link the Allied right and center). In reserve, near the village of Krzenowitz, would be the Grand Dukes Ferdinand and Constantine at the head of the Russian Imperial Guard Corps of 8,500 elite horse and foot.

Once Weyrother had finished reading the dispositions, Langeron asked whether the movement of the Allies toward the French right would not invite a French attack on their center. Not in the slightest, replied Langeron; the French could not possibly attack the Allied center: they were far too weak. Why had Napoleon not attacked them as they came down the road from Olmutz, when their forces were weakened by dispersion, and why had he abandoned Austerlitz and the Pratzen Heights, if not out of weakness? Furthermore, the French were in an exceedingly poor strategic position; it would be all they could do to meet the Allied onslaught. Should a French corps or two somehow manage to attack their center, Weyrother continued, the Imperial Guard Corps would cut them to pieces.

Following dinner with his officers, Napoleon retired to bed, a pile of straw on the floor of a peasant's hut. After a short while he rose to inspect the French forces; as he strolled through the encampments, a soldier twisted straw into a brand, others followed, and Napoleon soon found himself returning to his hut by torchlight procession. In the early hours of the morning, Savary roused Napoleon to report that the Allies were slightly stronger than expected to the far south; after making certain changes to his own dispositions, Napoleon fell back asleep.

On the morning of December 2, a thick mist lay on the ground and Pratzen Heights. Napoleon stood atop Zurlan Hill with his chief of staff Louis-Alexandre Berthier, Soult, and other officers and aides-de-camp. By 6:00, the Allied columns had begun to descend the gentle southwest slope of the heights. At 7:00, Kienmayer's Advance Guard fell upon the village of Tellnitz; five times the Austrians and Croats threw themselves at the village, but its defenders, the *Legion Corse* and the *3eme Ligne*, stood fast. At 8:00, Doctorov's First Column appeared out of the mist. Hopelessly outnumbered, the French withdrew to the west, Davout's *chasseurs* and hussars covering their retreat. Fourteen squadrons of Austrian cavalry now stormed past Tellnitz and crossed over to the west bank of the Goldbach, brushing aside the French light cavalry sent to bar their way. Though Doctorov's First Column was now to join Langeron's Second, the latter had been delayed in its descent by Lichtenstein's cavalry, which had had to cross to the north after encamping too far to the south the night before. By now, the mist had cleared sufficiently on the heights — but not on the lowlands — for Napoleon to follow the movements of the Allied columns through his spyglass.

Taking advantage of the delay in the Allied descent, General Friant of Davout's command, joined by the remnants of the *Legion Corse* and the *3eme Ligne*, led a counterattack on Tellnitz, driving the Austrians and Croats from both the village and the Goldbach. As the *26eme Legere* marched south to reinforce the *3eme Ligne*, however, it mistook the *108eme* for the Allies and opened fire. As the *108eme* returned fire, 29 Austrian and Russian units fell upon the village, evicting the French. Langeron's Second Column now arrived to the north of Doctorov's and launched an attack on Zokolnitz; as that village also fell to the Allies, Przbyswski's Third Column attacked Zokolnitz Castle and its walled pheasantry. Allied units soon began to cross the Goldbach rivulet: Weyrother's plan was succeeding.

To the north, Prince Lichtenstein had moved forward against the French left wing with several batteries of horse and reserve artillery; as he did so, a battalion of Russian Guard *Jaeger* and *cuirassier* regiments marched towards the village of Blasowitz. Lichtenstein fired upon the French with artillery and then launched 4,000 of his cavalry against the French V Corps. Lannes's division responded with cannon and infantry and cavalry volleys; as the Austrian cavalry drew back, the French General Kellerman advanced with his cavalry, provoking Lichtenstein into a counter-charge. The French cavalry retreated behind Count Caffarelli's infantry, who opened fire on Lichtenstein's cavalry. Kellerman now charged again, only to be fallen upon by Russian hussars and dragoons; the Russian cavalry continued on through the French lines, forcing Murat and his staff to defend themselves with their sabers.

Napoleon now lowered his spyglass. "How long," he asked Marshal Soult, commander of the French center, "will it take you to move your divisions to the top of the Pratzen Heights?" "Less than twenty minutes, Sire," Soult replied. Napoleon raised his spyglass. A little before 9:00, he judged that Kollowrath and Miloradovitch's Fourth Column had marched sufficiently far down the slope; he ordered the divisions of General St. Hilaire and General Vandamme, 16,000 of the 65,000 soldiers in the French center, all still hidden from the Allies by Zurlan and the mist, to advance. The two columns began to mount the gentle westward slopes of the Pratzen, Vandamme to the left and St. Hilaire to the right, "with great coolness, and at a slow pace." At that moment, Kutuzov and his staff were descending the slope with the Fourth Column. "My God!", cried one of his officers, "those are Frenchmen!" A few hundred yards down the slope, the two French columns could be seen emerging from the mist. Appreciating at once the threat to the Allied center and to the rear of the descending columns, Kutusov hurriedly ordered Kollowrath's Austrians and Miloradovitch's 25 Russian battalions to countermarch and summoned Prince Lichtenstein's cavalry from the north.

To slow the Allied reverse march up the heights, Napoleon ordered Soult's cavalry to fall upon the Allied columns and the French right wing, now reinforced with reserves, to launch an all-out attack. Davout's infantry and six regiments of dragoons drove the Allies back over the Goldbach and into Tellnitz. Friant led the *4eme* and *3eme Ligne* in an attack on Langeron's flank and rear and soon retook Zokolnitz; he then fell upon Przbyswski's column, flinging the Russians back. To prevent the Allies from reinforcing their center with infantry and cavalry drawn from the north, Napoleon ordered Bernadotte's I Corps to take Blasowitz. The French did so; the Allies counterattacked with two battalions of the Russian Imperial Guard and soon retook the village. Murat's cavalry and a column under Lannes moved forward to pin down Bagration's infantry and Lichtenstein's cavalry. The latter fell upon Cafarelli's division, but was driven off by the French light cavalry. Bagration launched a new attack against the Santon, but the French stood fast. Owing to these continual French attacks, only four of Prince Lichtenstein's cavalry regiments could go to the aid of the Allied center.

On the heights, as St. Hilaire stormed through the village of Pratzen, halfway up the slope, Vandamme marched toward the peak of Stare Vinohrady, driving five Russian battalions before him. Elements of the recalled Allied columns now appeared. As 2,500 soldiers of Kollowrath's command and a further nine battalions under Miloradovitch fell upon Vandamme's division, that of St. Hilaire was attacked on the right flank by the rear brigade of Langeron's returning column, by Kollowrath's troops to the fore, and by the Russian General Kamenskoi's reserves on the left. Attacked simultaneously from three sides, St. Hilaire considered retreating until he realized that he could hold only where he stood. More elements of the Second Column now arrived; rather than await the combined attack, St. Hilaire led his men forward in a bayonet charge, throwing the nearest Allied formations into confusion. To aid Vandamme and St. Hilaire, Soult hurried forward with the six cannon of his corps artillery reserve and personally supervised their firing. More and more French troops arrived; by 11:00, they were driving Langeron's column back down into the valley and Kollowrath's Fourth Column toward the village of Krzenowitz. As the Tsar and Kutusov escaped to the east of the heights, Langeron hurried to Buxhowden to report the French attack. Buxhowden was incredulous: "My dear general, you seem to see the foe everywhere." Other Allied officers mistook the French on the heights for Austrians or Russians.

At noon, Napoleon ascended to the highest point of the Pratzen Heights. He was joined by the elite reserve Imperial Guard, a corps of grenadiers, and Bernadotte's I Corps, all crying *Vive l'Empereur!* as they went. So that it might follow the Allied columns down the southwest slope of the heights, Napoleon ordered the whole of the French center to incline to the right. As it did so, the Grand Duke Ferdinand launched an attack on Vandamme's exhausted troops with four fresh battalions of the Russian Imperial Guard infantry and cavalry. The Guard broke through the first French line; the concentrated fire of the second, however, forced it to fall back on Krzenowitz. In inclining to the right, Vandamme had exposed his left flank and rear, which the Grand Duke Constantine now fell upon with 15 squadrons of Guard cavalry, supported by a renewed frontal assault by the Russian grenadiers. As the foremost French battalion formed into a square, the Russians brought up six horse-artillery pieces and ripped a hole into the French line. The French reeled back, the Russian *cuirassiers* and cavalry upon them. Most of Vandamme's soldiers now fled in panic, some almost knocking Napoleon down as they did so. "The unfortunate fellows," records de Segur, "were quite distracted with fear and would listen to no one; in reply to our reproaches for thus deserting the field of battle and their Emperor, they shouted mechanically, '*Vive l'Empereur!*' while fleeing faster than ever." At this Napoleon smiled.

Napoleon now sent forward the French Imperial Guard cavalry. The Russian Imperial Guard repulsed the first two squadrons; three squadrons of horse grenadiers, joined by General Drouet's division and supported by batteries of horse artillery, now hurled themselves at the Guard. As the Russians fell back, Napoleon ordered two squadrons of *chasseurs* of the Guard and one of Mamelukes to deliver the *coup de grace*; within ten minutes, 500 Russian grenadiers lay dead, and 200 members of the Chevalier Guard, the Tsar's personal escort, had been taken prisoner. The survivors of the Russian Imperial Guard now retreated toward Krzenowitz, elements of Bernadotte's command in pursuit. The Allied line was now, at 2:00, without a center. Victory was Napoleon's; but victory would not suffice: as much of the Allied army as possible must be annihilated. The French would follow the very paths the Allies had taken that morning and fall upon the rear of the three remaining columns. Napoleon ordered Bernadotte to hold the Pratzen and Stare Vinohrady with his I Corps; St. Hilaire, Vandamme, and the Imperial Guard were to move south and west to fall upon the Allied left.

Buxhowden was in a perilous position: he was isolated from the rest of the Allied army and could receive orders from neither Kutusov nor the Tsar. As Friant launched a full-scale attack on Zokolnitz (which the Allies had again taken) and others assailed Zokolnitz Castle, St. Hilaire fell upon the nearby pheasantry. As they did so, Vandamme's two brigades and a division of dragoons appeared on the southern edge of the heights. This was too much for the commanders of the Allied left: they now thought only of retreat. Hoping to join the remnants of the Fourth Column, Przbyswsky led his troops to the north toward Kobelnitz. The Fourth Column was, however, in full retreat two miles to the east; the French fell upon Przbyswsky from three sides as he marched, forcing him to surrender with 4,000 of his men. Elements of Doctorov's, Kienmayer's, and Langeron's commands were isolated to the south of Zokolnitz, attacked simultaneously by Vandamme's, St. Hilaire's, and Friant's troops. Other Allied troops were forced away to the northwest.

Napoleon and his staff now reached the southern slope of the heights. Perceiving that the Allies' main line of retreat would take them past Aujest Markt, he at once ordered Vandamme to seize the village. A large battery of Russian artillery, however, slowed Vandamme's descent; Austrian dragoons fell upon other French soldiers as they tried to move 25 cannon toward the village. A battalion of the *28eme Ligne* soon forced its way to the east of Aujest Markt, cutting the road to Austerlitz; as it did so, other French divisions drove the Russian defenders from the village. Napoleon ordered the commander of the 3rd Division of Dragoons to deliver the *coup de grace* to the retreating Allies; inexplicably, the commander did nothing. Livid,

Napoleon at once replaced him with another, but the dragoons could do little against the withering Russian artillery fire.

The main road to Austerlitz now occupied by the French, Buxhowden ordered his men to cross a wooden bridge to the south of Aujest Markt. After he and his staff had crossed, a gun-team broke through the bridge, making it impassable. The troops now began to cross a narrow causeway; as they did so, a French shell struck an ammunition wagon, blocking the causeway as well. Without awaiting orders, the men set out over the ice of Satschan Pond. Kienmayer and Doctorov now arrived with the remnants of the Advance Guard and the First Column; Doctorov ordered *sauve qui peut*, and his men also began to cross the ice. Napoleon ordered the French artillery to fire upon the ice; it soon broke, and an uncertain number of Allies drowned. To the north, Bagration, slowly driven back by the French since midday, recognized that all was lost for the Allies and began his retreat, the French too exhausted for the moment to pursue him. Accompanied only by his surgeon and a single officer, the Tsar was only just able to escape; as soon as he felt himself safe from French pursuit, he dismounted, sat by the side of the road, and wept.

At 5:00, Napoleon ordered the cease fire sounded. The Allies had lost one-third of their force — 15,000 had died or would die of their wounds and 12,000 were taken prisoner — including nine generals, 20 senior officers, and 800 junior officers; they had also lost 180 artillery pieces. The French would continue to pursue the fleeing Allies until the armistice was signed. Only 1,305 French soldiers were killed, 6,940 wounded, and 573 taken prisoner. "Soldats!," began Napoleon's victory bulletin. "Je suis content de vous." To his senior and junior officers he would disburse 2,000,000 francs; to the widows of the fallen he would award large pensions. He would formally adopt all orphaned children; all would be placed in state schools, and the boys later be found posts, the girls provided with dowries.

On December 4, Napoleon met with the Emperor Francis and granted him an armistice, to take effect the following day. As he retreated toward Hungary and Poland, Alexander agreed to Francis's request for a separate peace; the Third Coalition was no more. Disconsolate, the English Prime Minister, William Pitt, died a few weeks later. On the 26th, France and Austria signed the Treaty of Pressburg, by which Austria ceded Venice to

France, the Tyrol, Voralburg, and other Alpine territories to the ruler of Bavaria, and Swabia to the Duke of Wurttemberg. Austria had been evicted from both Italy and Germany.

∾

A few months before the battle of Austerlitz, Napoleon instructed Berthier, his chief of staff, "to entrust someone who is acquainted with German to follow the march of the Austrian regiments, and file the details in the compartments of the box you were told to make for that purpose. The name or number of each regiment is to be entered on a playing card, and the cards are to be changed from one compartment to another according to the movements of the regiments." The Allies followed the movements of the French with far less care; an Englishman with the Allied forces, Sir Arthur Paget, reported, "No one knows *exactly* where the French are, or in what force." The Allies were quite as careless in other matters. Simply because Napoleon's earlier European campaigns had been fought in Italy and he had recently proclaimed himself king of the country, the Allies assumed Italy would be the main theater of war; they thus placed considerable forces far from the true theater of war. Austria followed the Gregorian calendar, Russia the Julian; since the Austrian staff omitted from their calculations the ten days' difference between the two, Kutusov did not arrive at the River Inn on the scheduled *Austrian* date. "This miscalculation," observes Chandler, "was to ruin the balance of the entire Allied scheme." That the Allies' offensives were not simultaneous was greatly to Napoleon's advantage; of their four initial offenses, that of General Mack took place first, in isolation.

Napoleon lured the Allies down from Olmutz through deception. He had only 53,000 troops occupy the Pratzen Heights and Austerlitz, far less than the Allies' 90,000 and a strong inducement to attack. (Once the Allies moved against the French, Napoleon would bring up the corps of Bernadotte and Davout by forced marches, a further 22,000 men whose movements screens of cavalry would conceal.) Napoleon offered other inducements as well. By eagerly agreeing to the Emperor Francis's offer of an armistice, and by having Savary seem apprehensive while at Allied headquarters (with, however, strict instructions to study the Allied commanders), he further suggested French weakness. In his interview with Count

Dolgorouki, Napoleon showed himself diffident, timorous, and indecisive and let the Count lecture him. "The Emperor," Napoleon later wrote, "controlled his indignation with difficulty, and this young man, who wielded a strong influence over the Tsar, returned full of the notion that the French army was on the eve of its doom." (This "coxcomb," as Napoleon was to call him, thought a young man's thoughts.) Following the interview, Napoleon had Soult withdraw from Austerlitz and the heights in a seeming panic. Notwithstanding the objections of the Emperor Francis and Kutuzov, the Allies now resolved to attack.

The Allies were as careless with their plan of battle as with all else. Infinitely pleased with his dispositions (and, it would seem, himself), Weyrother read them "to us in a loud tone and with a self-satisfied air that indicated a thorough persuasion of his own merit and of our incapacity. He was really like a college teacher reading a lesson to young scholars." (Langeron) *Of all those present, only the Russian General Doctorov examined the map carefully.* Some of the Russian generals received the dispositions late — they were delayed by translating them from German to Russian — some did not receive them at all, and most did not understand them once they received them. Furthermore, far too many people — the Emperor Francis, Tsar Alexander, Kutuzov, Weyrother, congeries of staff officers — directed the Allies' affairs. *One bad general is better than two good ones.*

In their being deceived as in their plan of battle, the Allies showed they did not understand their opponent in the slightest. A French officer, Thiebault, said of them, "They seemed to forget that they were dealing with the greatest commander in the world, and they failed to recognize that even his apparently unconsidered actions were the direct reflection of very deep thinking." Like the *optimates*, the Allies wished to fight in the way least inconvenient to themselves; and the inconvenience they most wished to avoid, was that of thinking. Napoleon, to the contrary, understood his opponent well. He knew the Allies would seek to turn the French right flank and place themselves between the French and Vienna, cutting the French line of communication and retreat (turning the opponent's flank was a common 18th-century strategy); knew they would think the Pratzen Heights a superb position from which to turn the French flank; knew they would think Vandamme's and St. Hilaire's troops — that is, the troops they could see — would reinforce the French right (when it was the troops the Allies could *not* see, those of Davout coming up from Vienna, that would reinforce the French right, freeing Vandamme and St. Hilaire to storm the Allied center); knew they would thin their center as they descended the slope, and that they would have far too few reserves to repel a French attack.

The Allies struck the French at a secondary point, a point that simply did not matter. Napoleon applied precisely the right amount of force at precisely the right point; elsewhere he simply pinned the Allies down. (Indeed, so adroitly did Napoleon apply force that the French later had difficulty convincing the Allies that they had not had superior forces all over the field.) The Allies made other mistakes as well. Their columns consisted solely of infantry; without cavalry to conduct reconnaissance, the infantry marched quite without knowing what they would come upon. The Allies lost an hour as Lichtenstein's cavalry crossed in front of the descending Second, Third, and Fourth Columns. "The loss of time," said Napoleon, "is irreparable in war." In the main battle as in the campaign as a whole, the Allies did not attack simultaneously, did not strike strongly. And while the Allies had no secondary line of retreat should the road to Olmutz be cut, had they lost their own to Vienna the French would simply have retreated to the northwest toward Brunn. "Before he fought a battle," said Bourrienne, "Bonaparte never troubled much about what he would do in the event of success, but very much about what he would have to do in the event of failure."

Napoleon later calculated that he could have won the battle of Austerlitz with 25,000 fewer men. He also felt certain he would have won had he simply remained on the Pratzen Heights and fought the Allies from there. "But then," he said, "that would have been just an ordinary battle."

∽

Let us now revisit Bill Gates and Microsoft. Gates has said that Napoleon is his hero; he once went to a costume party dressed as Napoleon. If Napoleon wished to be the Caesar of 19th-century Europe, Gates wishes to be the Napoleon of business. Gates fights no less than did Napoleon; like his hero, he attains his objects chiefly through fighting. Indeed, so similar are Gates's strategies and tactics to Napoleon's that Microsoft's rivals would do well to study the life of the latter.

Like Napoleon, Gates swiftly occupied the center, the operating system, the shared vital point of most of his rivals. Here, in the very heart of the computer industry, Gates creates an infinite number of vital points. Each time a rival applications developer makes a change to its software, it must reveal that change to Microsoft if it is to be certain its software will work well with MS DOS; Microsoft is thus privy to the source code of most of its competitors' products. Like Napoleon, Gates deceives his opponents and others. Where MS-DOS is not a rival's center, Microsoft will express interest in forming an alliance and ask to see the source code of the rival's product. Microsoft will then decline the alliance and later come out with a similar product (as with Go Corporation's operating system for pen-based computers, and Stac Electronics's data-compression software). Or, Microsoft will license technology from another firm (often by buying a considerable share of the firm's stock), create a similar product using that technology, and become a rival to its erstwhile ally (as with RealNetworks). Microsoft: will announce that it will soon release an upgrade that will be superior to a competitor's new product, knowing it will not be able to do so for quite some time (vaporware); always represents itself as wishing only to cooperate; divides its opponents, and delays their acting, by offering them ostensible advantages such as the hope of an alliance. As Microsoft was arguing at its antitrust trial that it should not be forced to disclose its Windows software code to rivals, calling it a "confiscation," Gates was lobbying the FCC to force America Online to disclose the code of its instant-messaging software — a market in which Microsoft was doing less well. Microsoft has tried to dissuade companies from using free open-source software such as Linux, claiming that it "has inherent security risks and can force intellectual property into the public domain." But Microsoft itself has used one such program, FreeBSD, in its own Windows software (such as in the "TCP/IP" section that controls connections to the Internet).

Gates follows other Napoleonic strategies and tactics as well. Microsoft gains its victories chiefly through better strategies and tactics, rather than better products. Once well-positioned, the company: isolates and attacks its rival; surprises its rival, "falls on the rival's rear;" exploits the mistakes of its rival; follows the philosophy of *toujours attaque*. But Gates does not simply *follow* Napoleon's strategies and tactics: he is truly *like* Napoleon. Napoleon could fall asleep at will, as can Gates; Napoleon had a brilliant sense of humor, as does Gates; Napoleon was intemperate, as is Gates, and his manner rankled, as does Gates's; Napoleon was quite a bad horseman, as is Gates a driver. Gates also shows some of Napoleon's solipsism; Philippe Kahn, the CEO of Borland International, one of Microsoft's rivals, once said of him, "He looks at everything as something that should be his. He acts in any way he can to make it his. It can be an idea, market share, or a contract. There is not an ounce of conscientiousness or compassion in him. The notion of fairness means nothing to him. The only thing he understands is leverage." This is Germaine de Stael speaking of Napoleon.

Napoleon and Gates share the same asymmetry: each is or was a far better fighter than his rivals. But why did this asymmetry not enable Napoleon to attain his object, and yet has enabled Gates to attain his? Will doing as Napoleon did doom Gates as it did his hero? It would seem not: the contexts — the political world of Europe in the early 19th century, the business world of the United States in the late 20th and early 21st centuries — differ sufficiently. By the early 19th-century, a state could not create an empire in Europe; in the United States today, a person can create a business empire. Why? While the taking of territory is generally not permitted, the taking of market share most certainly is. Certain geographic territories are recognized internationally as states; no such recognition is accorded market share, or business "territory," which is fluid and ever-changing. (Modern businesses are rather like ancient states.) Law is weak and rather easily gotten round. A state that has been attacked does not engage in legalistic quibbling: it hits back; force, unlike law, is no-nonsense. Furthermore, a single, standard operating system fits the context. Gates's object, then, unlike Napoleon's, would seem to fit its context.

It is highly unlikely that Microsoft's rivals will be able to unite against it. A strong, centralized entity such as Microsoft is far stronger and more stable than a collection of entities divided by a rivalry of interests. That which will most prevent Microsoft's rivals from uniting, is that they themselves are rivals. And Gates is free of some of the traits that doomed Napoleon. Gates is not fixed and immutable; he can grow. He at first dismissed the internet, for instance, as an insignificant technological development; but once he recognized its significance, he redirected the whole of Microsoft. Gates also seems to understand the context far better than did Napoleon. Gates, it would seem, is superior to his hero.

Gates may, however, overreach; like his hero, he perhaps does not see where the limits lie. With Windows XP, the 2001 version of its operating system, Microsoft asked the content providers to its consumer web sites to adopt Microsoft services such as Passport, a "single sign-in" Web-registration service, and Windows Media, the Microsoft format for playing digital music and video. So vociferously did the content providers protest against these requests that Microsoft soon withdrew them. On occasion Gates shows a touch of hubris, that he perhaps fancies himself invulnerable. When one of his competitors said that he would rather negotiate than testify against Microsoft before Congress, Gates responded by e-mail, "I've decided it doesn't make sense for us to meet. While you're in D.C., I suggest visiting the National Gallery and the Smithsonian." Just as Napoleon viewed victory in battle as the solution to every problem, so, too, does Gates seem to view the Windows operating system as the means by which to hold sway in every realm of technology. And, like Napoleon, Gates seems to overgeneralize about humanity, to think that *all* of humanity is simple and gullible, rather than simply the majority. Furthermore, Microsoft's rivals and others are now striking its vital points — such as by creating viruses and worms, a free operating system (Linux), and a free internet browser (Foxfire) — and creating vital points. Perhaps most intriguing, Google is now seeking to make the *internet* rather than the operating system the center, to have the internet be the foundation of applications.

OTHER PRINCIPLES

PARRY THE OPPONENT'S STRIKES

The more your opponent strikes you, the weaker you and your resolve will become, and the less able you will be to strike *him*. You must try to anticipate where your opponent will strike; you must consider your vital points, the opponent, and the context. Caesar's creating a fourth line of battle at Pharsalus to meet Pompey's cavalry, which were far more numerous than his own, is a perfect instance of parrying a strike. Your opponent seeks always to surprise you, you not to be surprised. "One must always assume," said Napoleon, "that the enemy has made movements during the night, in order to attack at daybreak." Richelieu created a superb intelligence service so that he might know what his opponents were plotting against him.

You can parry a strike by striking. When King Juba of Numidia marched against him, Caesar had one of his legates attack Juba's kingdom, forcing Juba to return post-haste. On receiving intimations of a plot against the government, Richelieu said to his King, "One never knows everything about a conspiracy until it has succeeded, and then it is too late... In the course of ordinary affairs, justice requires authentic proof. It is not necessarily so in matters of state. There, occasions arise where one must start with an execution." You can also parry a strike by deceiving. On learning that the Romans would fall upon his army as it marched through a valley the following day, Hannibal had twigs tied to the horns of oxen, the twigs lit, and the oxen sent off by another path. Thinking the lights those of the Carthaginian army, the Romans set out in pursuit. The following morning, the Carthaginians marched through the valley unmolested.

Once you have parried the opponent's strike, try to learn whether the strike or your deflection has created or exposed one or more vital points in your opponent. Hoist your opponent with his own petard. Napoleon favored "a well-reasoned and circumspect defensive followed by a rapid and audacious attack." Richelieu would continually deflect strikes against him, and then use those strikes to bring down his opponents or further his own interests. When, for instance, he caught the Duke of Bouillon allying himself with Spain and plotting to assassinate him, Richelieu forced the Duke to relinquish the territory of Sedan, which he had long coveted.

∾

Far better than parrying the opponent's strikes, is first to lessen your vital points. Caesar's fortifications are an instance of this, as is his changing the order of march when near an enemy: in the usual order, each legion would be followed by its baggage train; when near an enemy, however, Caesar would concentrate his legions, with the baggage well to the rear of the column. Richelieu had a great many bodyguards, Caesar none; one was assassinated, the other not. Whichever vital points you cannot rid yourself of, you must hide. Of the two Gauls who deserted to Pompey at Dyrrhachium, Caesar writes, "These two knew everything; they knew if there was something unfinished on the fortifications, or if something was thought by the military experts to be lacking, and they had observed the times things happened, and the distances between sites, and the varying watchfulness of the guards according to the character and enthusiasm of the man in charge in each case. All this information they presented to Pompey." Shown all the weaknesses in Caesar's line, Pompey was soon able to breach it. And, in striking your opponent, be careful not to create or expose a vital point in yourself. Do not be stung into striking carelessly; one military historian observes that the opponents who did best against Napoleon, were those who remained determinedly on the defensive.

Do not create vital points in yourself. Most vital points are self-created, most misfortunes self-incurred. Had Caesar put his opponents to the sword rather than show them clemency, far more people would have tried to strike him. The vices are so because they create vital points; corruption, for instance, creates vital points that rivals will gleefully strike. You would do well to follow J. Pierpont Morgan's dictum: "Do nothing of which you would be ashamed were it ever to come to light." Do not, in self-seeking, hurt your interests. Of Napoleon's seizing the Duc d'Enghien in the neutral territory of Baden and executing him, it was said in Europe, "It was worse than a crime; it was a mistake." So, too, with much corruption: it is worse than a crime; it creates a vital point in yourself.

Greed creates countless vital points. Caesar felt that greed imperils; he writes in *The Gallic War* that, when pursuing the Eburones, "great care was needed…to keep the individual soldiers safe…for the desire for plunder lured many of them farther afield…" The Roman soldiers who attacked Gergovia in defiance of Caesar's orders did so in hopes of booty; rather than plunder, they died. The aristocratic families of the late Roman republic took so much for themselves and gave so little to others that they were constantly fearful of rebellions, insurrections, and *coups d'etat*. In 88 BC, the people of Asia, incited by Mithridates, King of Pontus, slaughtered 100,000 Roman men, women, and children on a single day, so passionately did they hate the Romans for their exploitation. By paying its soldiery so little, the Roman Senate ensured that the soldiers' loyalty would not be to the state, but to their commander, who provided them with booty and (at the end of their military service) land. (That it was these very soldiers who had created the Empire and thus their fortunes, the senators cared not one whit.) The despoiled hate the despoiler.

The more you exploit others, the more they will benefit from your fall, the more vital points you create in yourself, and the more you provoke them into striking you. When the Goths and Visigoths invaded Thrace in the late fourth century, its Roman inhabitants went into hiding; but soon some workmen "who laboured in the gold mines of Thrace, for the emolument, and under the lash, of an unfeeling master," guided the barbarians to the food stores and places of hiding of the Romans. "With the assistance of such guides," writes Gibbon, "nothing could remain impervious, or inaccessible: resistance was fatal; flight was impracticable…"

TOIL

"Great men are rarely seen to fail," said Napoleon, "even in their most hazardous undertakings. If we study the causes of their successes, we are astounded to see all they did in order to gain them." Only by scrabbling over pathless foothills could Caesar bar the Pompeians' way to the Ebro. Just so with any victory: it goes to the unremitting. In the fall of 1806, on the evening before the battle of Jena-Auerstadt, Napoleon recognized that a French victory depended on their securing a certain hill; the hill had, however, only a single, narrow track, up which the French could not possibly move men and artillery. A staff officer records: "Napoleon sent at once for 4,000 pioneering tools from the wagons of the engineers and artillery, and he ordered that every battalion should work in turn for an hour at widening and leveling the path." The French worked through the night, "lighted at their work by torches," Napoleon himself at first supervising them. By morning, 25,000 men and 42 pieces of artillery stood atop the hill. Success, said Napoleon, is "the infinite capacity for taking pains."

While simultaneously conquering Gaul and directing affairs in Rome, Caesar wrote the *The Gallic War* and *On the Selection of Words* (a work on Latin grammar), while under siege in the palace of Alexandria, *The Civil War*, while traveling to Spain to fight Gnaeus Pompey, *The Journey* (a long poem), following that victory, the *Anticato* (an attack on one of the leading *optimates*), and, all the while, voluminous speeches, letters, and other works. Caesar would dictate correspondence to secretaries or slaves as he went about on horseback or in a carriage or litter. He would accustom his soldiers to toil as well; he would, for instance, make them "turn out when there was no need at all, especially in wet weather or on public holidays. Sometimes he would say, 'Keep a close eye on me!' and then steal away from camp at any hour of the day or night, expecting them to follow. It was certain to be a particularly long march..." (Suetonius) Caesar, comments Meier, "viewed difficulties simply as tasks."

Richelieu would work from 2:00 until 5:00 each morning; sleep until 9:00; work from then until 11:00; walk in his garden with friends; take lunch; work until the evening; take dinner; walk in his garden; and then work until 11:00 — a 14-hour or so day, every day. He fought continuously both within (the *devots, les grands,* and the Huguenots) and without (the Habsburgs) France. Throughout the autumn of 1642, Richelieu: wrote copious letters; held discussions with his secretaries of state and others; directed France's military activities; made arrangements for the return of the Queen-Mother's body to Paris, the settlement of her debts, and disposal of her effects; planned the buildings to be erected at the Sorbonne; and, directed the measures to be taken against those involved in a plot on his life. This was the autumn in which Richelieu lay dying.

"Work is my element," said Napoleon. "I was born and made for work. I have recognized the limits of my eyesight and of my legs, but never the limits of my working power." It was not unusual for him to work eighteen or twenty hours a day, while eating, while in bed, while at the opera. During the fifteen years of his rule, Napoleon dictated 80,000 or so letters and orders — roughly fifteen a day. One historian notes that even his enemies "admitted that his capacity for work was beyond compare; that, at least, of four men in one." "God created Bonaparte," quipped a French prefect, "and then He rested." ("What a pity it is," sighed Talleyrand, "that Napoleon isn't lazy.") "Well, well, Citizens and Ministers, wake up!", Napoleon would cry to his sleepy ministers. "It's only two o'clock in the morning, and you must earn the wages that the French nation is paying you!"

Of Gates one Microsoft programmer said, "Bill did it all. He was the salesman, the technical leader, the lawyer, the businessman... You could go on and on." Gates's "seven-hour turnaround" was renowned: at night, he would return to Microsoft within seven hours of leaving it.

∽

"Health," said Napoleon, "is indispensable in war." Because you must toil so in fighting, because you will feel a passion that is also enervating, *you must husband your strength.* Fatigue is ruinous to both thinking and resolve. You must fight calmly, as being all of a dither is exhausting; you must be loose and relaxed, both physically and psychologically, rather than stiff and tight. You must also focus: trying to think of everything at once is exhausting. And you must sleep well. A natural night's sleep for a human being is 10.3 hours (how long human beings in controlled studies, and the other primates, sleep). Certainly you can function on seven hours of sleep (the average night's sleep in the United States); but you cannot on so little sleep (over a prolonged period) access the deepest regions of your neocortex. An aide to Napoleon, the Duke of Ragusa, said of him, "It has been claimed that he slept very little, but this is quite inaccurate. On the contrary...he required long hours of repose. I have often seen him lie abed for ten or twelve hours together. If it was necessary for him to be wakened, he would put up with it and make amends later on. He often rested before a crisis to husband his strength. He possessed also the valuable faculty of sleeping where and as often as he pleased." You must not only rest, but also exercise and eat well. Your food should be organic and processed as little as possible; our bodies are as little suited to modern food, as our brains are the modern world.

FIGHT AS LITTLE AS POSSIBLE

Following his victory at Waterloo, Wellington, the "Iron Duke," wrote, "I hope to God that I have fought my last battle. It is a bad thing to be always fighting. While I am in the thick of it I am too much occupied to feel anything; but it is wretched just after. It is quite impossible to think of glory... I am wretched even at the moment of victory, and I always say that, next to a battle lost, the greatest misery is a battle gained." You should fight as little as possible in life; fighting continually is far more likely to harm than further your interests. Napoleon is the perfect example of how fighting over-much can make one *less* rather than more secure. *At the height of his power,* following an unbroken string of victories, Napoleon cried, "My enemies make appointments at my tomb!"

Fighting over-much makes others far less willing to cooperate with you. At the end of 1813, a few months before Napoleon's fall, Talleyrand said of him, "His greatest misfortune, his irremediable misfortune is his isolation. He stands alone, quite alone, in Europe, as he wished to do, but the worst of it is that he is alone in France." To be without allies is to be wildly vulnerable. Richelieu worked quite as hard at forming alliances with non-Habsburg states as he did fighting the Habsburgs. Microsoft has come to see that, because of its bellicosity, it is simply not being told of new technologies and lucrative investments and partnerships; information is vital to high-tech organizations, and many others now prefer not to share information with Microsoft. Why does life cooperate? Because it is in its interest to do so. Why did DNA molecules unite to form cells? "DNA molecules make proteins. Proteins work as enzymes, catalysing particular chemical reactions. Often a single chemical reaction is not sufficient to synthesize a useful end-product." (Dawkins) And why did cells unite to form bodies? "The cells [in a body] can specialize, each thereby becoming more efficient at performing its particular task. Specialist cells serve other cells in the [body], and they also benefit from the efficiency of other specialists." (Dawkins)

Fighting over-much makes you predictable. Others will learn how best to fight you. Toward the end of Napoleon's reign, Metternich counseled the Austrian generals, "Use his own tactics. Turn his own methods back upon him... Expect hard knocks and above all be prepared for the unexpected. Oppose him with an adaptability equal to his own... Never regard any battle as a victory until the following day, never admit ourselves vanquished until four days later." Wellington learned how to counter French strategies and tactics by fighting the French in Spain; this knowledge served him well at Waterloo.

Like Napoleon, Microsoft has become predictable. Whenever the company enters a new market, all know precisely what it will try to do: make Windows the standard software of that market, the platform. Microsoft is now trying to make the PC (and thus Windows) the center of home entertainment. Not wishing to pay Microsoft a royalty on each product sold, as computer makers must do, consumer electronic firms such as Sony, Apple Computer, and TiVo either use some other software (such as Linux) or use that software in combination with Windows; by making their products compatible with non-Windows software, these companies ensure that Microsoft will not come to control the home-entertainment market. (Even computer makers such as Gateway now offer their own, Windows-free consumer products; Intel, too, is offering products that can run on *either* Linux or Windows.) Similarly, studios such as Disney, Metro-Goldwyn-Mayer, and Viacom use software from both Microsoft and RealNetworks to sell their films over the internet. So afraid were cable officials at AT&T and TCI that Microsoft would come to control the software in their new cable boxes that they insisted another firm create some of the software and that the software work with Java; thus self-hobbled, the alliance failed, and Microsoft lost much of its $10 billion investment. In television set-top boxes as in consumer electronics, no one will let Microsoft dominate.

Fighting over-much is unhealthy. In the Louvre is a bust of Caesar in his later years: "The brow is furrowed with huge wrinkles, the lean and shapeless face bears marks of intense physical suffering, and the expression is that of a man utterly exhausted." (Meier) In the spring and early summer of 47 BC, as Pompey's successors raised armies and fomented rebellions, Caesar lingered on a Nile journey with Cleopatra; he was exhausted, and he perhaps also wished to escape his cares. By 46 Caesar was so tired that he put scarcely any planning into his final African campaign. By this time he was quite unlike himself; he would draw up poorly thought-through municipal proposals, become enraged if anyone disobeyed his laws, no matter how minor, and savage others and make indiscreet remarks. He was also far less able to ignore slights; during one of the triumphal processions that followed the civil war, the tribune Pontius Aquila refused to rise as Caesar's chariot passed. "Why don't you make me give up the state, Aquila?", Caesar cried, and for days afterwards followed every promise with the words, "*If Pontius Aquila gives me permission.*" In last year or so of his life, Caesar would often say, "I have lived long enough for both nature and fame."

The stakes in fighting are high; much is to be gained and much lost. "The greater the success we seek," said Clausewitz, "the greater will be the damage if we fail." The consciousness of this is wildly stressful, as is continually "reckoning with the mass of possibilities." Caesar, Napoleon, and Richelieu may have suffered from hystero-epilepsy, or "conqueror's syndrome;" all had fits resembling epilepsy. Richelieu would sometimes howl and foam at the lips; on occasion he would crawl under his bed, and only with the greatest difficulty could others persuade him to come out. To his King he once said, "My already depleted forces are daily reduced to such an extent that I am no longer able to endure the unbelievable strain imposed by the actions that have to be taken to ensure the safety of a great State." To God Richelieu once offered to found a Sunday mass in perpetuity if He would deliver him of his headache.

Fighting has unintended consequences. The world is far too complex for us ever to foresee all the consequences of our actions. Meier argues that the dissolution of the Roman republic was largely the result of the unintended side-effects of action; what no one (save perhaps Caesar) sought was the outcome of the action of most. "The context within which a process operates not only involves the subsidiary consequences of actions, but also produces 'consequential actions.'" To better society, and for the sake of the people, in the late 19th century Russian revolutionaries resolved on assassinating Tsar Alexander II. The Tsar's carriage passed; a revolutionary threw his bombs. The explosions killed the Tsar; but they also killed a five-year-old boy, sent by his mother to buy bread.

Fortuna makes Herself felt, as do human selfishness, fallibility, and perversity. Fortuna, said Caesar, "is the sovereign power in all things, but especially in war. By moving small weights in the balance it produces great vicissitudes." Caesar respected *Fortuna* greatly; when during his Gallic triumph the axle of his chariot broke in front of Her temple, Caesar climbed its steps on his knees. One week after La Rochelle capitulated to the French crown, a strong gale destroyed the dike Richelieu had laid across its harbor; one week, and the Rochellois would have been saved. Napoleon's blitzreig on Russia bogged down in the mud of eastern Europe, mud such as no one could remember, mud that caught at men, horses, and wagons. And the winter of 1812 began early and was one of the coldest ever.

In war, said Caesar, "factors that are frequently trifling — mistaken suspicion, or sudden alarm, or religious scruple — have caused great disasters..." On occasion subordinates misunderstand or disobey instructions. Labienus once laid a fine trap for Caesar; but some of the men whom he had hid in an olive grove, fearing they would be cut off, stole away, thus revealing the trap to Caesar. On occasion subordinates are simply careless. Pompey was only four hours' march from the Caesarian legions in Macedonia when his scouts let slip that he was coming; the legions marched with all speed for Caesar. And on occasion the enemy intercepts orders or is informed of them by spies (as when the English learned of the movements of the French fleet through royalist spies, catching it at Trafalgar). The most competent subordinate is still a biological creature; when tired, sleepy, or panicky, he is apt to make mistakes. And no one is omniscient; Napoleon's staff, for instance, overestimated how much grain and fodder the French troops would find in Russia.

Sometimes it is simply better not to fight, simply better to draw in one's horns and vacate the field. "The excellent general," said Sun Tzu, "realizes there are some roads not to be followed, some armies not to be attacked, some cities not to be besieged, some positions not to be contested..." After studying yourself, the opponent, and the context, you may very well come to see that fighting would *not* be in your interests. Rather than try to fight during the worst of the French Revolution (which would have been folly), Talleyrand lived first in England, and then the United States.

There are other ways to attain your object, ways that are generally preferable to fighting. You should in general strive to maintain an *entente cordiale* with others; social life *does* enhance personal survival. Furthermore, some objects simply cannot be attained through fighting. Microsoft, for instance, found that it could induce Japanese game-software writers — among the more creative in the world — to create games for its Xbox only through diplomacy and other means, that fighting would simply alienate them.

Which means is best depends on the context and the individual you hope to influence; usually a combination of these means works best. Just as you must study the person you will fight, so, too, must you study the person you hope to influence. Like Jeeves, you must consider "the psychology of the individual." "Observe their weaknesses, their passions, their humours," counseled Chesterfield, "of all which their understandings are, nine times in ten, the dupes." Always remember the great variation in our species; adapt your methods to the quality of the individual you hope to influence, each after his kind.

You must choose your means with great care. What Chesterfield says of life at court is quite as true of life in society: "The ways are generally crooked and full of turnings, sometimes strewed with flowers, sometimes choaked up with briars; rotten ground and deep pits frequently lie concealed under a smooth and pleasing surface: all the paths are slippery, and every slip is dangerous." Social skills are the tools with which we induce others, insofar as possible, to further our interests. Without *savoir-vivre*, one is always at sixes and sevens with the world. Antonia Fraser remarks of the Stuarts that they were "better in misfortune than in prosperity. Perhaps there was some justice in this; in that their personal qualities so often brought misfortune upon them, it was only fitting that they should be well equipped to endure the slights of adversity." Certain "personal qualities" will deflect misfortune. *You must understand how human beings work*; always remember that others are survival machines for *their* genes, not yours. To be in society is to be the lion tamer in his cage: if you are good with a whip and a chair, you will survive; if not, you will be torn to pieces.

None of these means is perfect; none will bind someone to you forever. Loyalty comes and goes with interests, fluctuations in power, and whims. Labienus was Caesar's faithful adherent before the Gallic war; during the war, he was Caesar's second-in-command — often commanding half the Roman army during the campaign season, and the whole during the winter — and acting governor of Gallia Transalpina; Caesar rewarded him with riches and high position. Many of Caesar's assassins were confidants whom he had richly rewarded; quite a few he had made consul, praetor, or governor of a province. The contingent beneficiary of Caesar's will was his faithful officer Decimus Brutus; Decimus is the conspirator who induced Caesar to come to the curia (and his assassination) in spite of his feeling unwell. Marcus Brutus's mother, Servilia, was Caesar's favorite mistress; Caesar always showed Brutus great favor, sparing his life and those of his friends at Pharsalus, making him praetor and governor of Gallia Cisalpina, and appointing him consul for a future term. It is said that, on seeing Brutus among his assassins, Caesar cried, "You, too, my child?"

"Fear and self-interest," said Napoleon, "are the two levers that move men." We shall take first fear, then self-interest.

Frighten Others

"Generosity is too rarely found to be presumed on," said Thomas Hobbes, "especially in the pursuers of Wealth, Command, or Sensual Pleasure, which are the greatest part of Mankind. The Passion to be reckoned on is Fear." You may be able to frighten your opponent to such a degree that he will submit without fighting; and even if he does not, your rattling him may so weaken his resolve that he will fight less well.

When the tribune Metellus interposed himself between Caesar and the state treasury, Caesar threatened to kill him, adding, "You know well enough that I dislike saying this more than I would dislike doing it." "For the future," said Plutarch, "all Caesar's demands for material for the war were promptly and readily obeyed." When Napoleon, little known, first assumed command of the French army in Italy, one of his generals went about saying, "I don't know what it is about that little bastard that frightens me so." "I, who fear neither God nor Devil," said General Vandamme, "am ready to tremble like a child when I approach him." Following the battle of Austerlitz, Napoleon savaged the 4th Regiment of the Line for having lost one of its standards. "I must own that my flesh crawled," recorded the Count de Saint-Chamans. "I broke into a cold sweat, and at times my eyes were coursing with tears." De Saint-Chamans was not *of* the 4th Regiment; he was simply standing nearby.

A French newspaper reported Napoleon's march on Paris following his escape from Elba. The first headline: "The Corsican monster has landed

in the Gulf of Juan." The second: "The cannibal is marching to Grasse."
The third: "The usurper has entered Grenoble." The fourth: "Bonaparte
has occupied Lyons." The fifth: "Napoleon is approaching Fontainebleau."
The last: "His Imperial Majesty is expected tomorrow in his loyal Paris."
Of Richelieu it was said, "One trembles in his presence." Anne of Austria,
the Queen of France, was one of his bitterest enemies. Richelieu presented
her with correspondence between her and the Habsburgs and intimated that
the children of a treasonous Queen might, "for their own sake," have to be
taken from their mother. Thenceforth the Queen was one of Richelieu's
more loyal supporters.

Apple once provided Microsoft with prototypes of the Macintosh
so that Microsoft could develop application programs for it. When
Apple discovered that Microsoft was using the prototypes to develop a
graphical user interface for IBM, the company threatened to sue Microsoft for copyright violations. Gates retorted that if Apple were to do so,
Microsoft would simply stop developing Excel and Word for the Macintosh, without which Apple might very well fail. Apple did not sue, and
Microsoft went on to develop Windows for IBM. Microsoft compels
its "allies" not to create products — or to assist other firms in creating
products — that compete with its own. As Intel was once considering
whether itself to create software, Gates told the company that Microsoft
would not support Intel's processors if it did so; Intel did not. Microsoft also compelled Intel not to collaborate with Sun Microsystems on
creating Java, a competing operating system. Microsoft induced Compaq
not to feature Netscape on its PCs simply by *threatening* not to supply it
with Windows. Since Microsoft has shown itself quite willing to follow
through on its threats, it is now often able to achieve its aims simply by
threatening.

You must take great care, however, in attempting to frighten others.
Taking fright may simply provoke them into striking first. So alarmed was
Austria by Napoleon's continual hectoring that it secretly rearmed and then
attacked France. Twice Gaston d'Orleans accosted Richelieu with a group
of young men, intent on striking him down; twice Gaston lost heart and
only threatened him. From that point on, all those men — save Gaston, the
King's brother — were doomed; Richelieu would see to that. On occasion
you gain more by reassuring than frightening others. As Caesar showed

his enemies mercy at Corfinium and elsewhere, the Pompeians threatened retribution against all in Italy who did not resist him. Most of Italy now went over to Caesar's side.

Enrich Others

In the ancient world, towns would bestow divine honors on whoever had given them such benefits as a god would bestow; the principal god of the Gauls was the protector of roads and commerce: "When it is a question of money," quipped Voltaire, "everyone is of the same religion." One of the better ways to influence others, is to enrich them. Munificence is as protective to the munificent, as greed is perilous to the greedy.

When consul in 59 BC, Caesar was careful first to obtain what his co-triumvirs Pompey and Crassus desired before seeking their help in obtaining what *he* desired. Then, had Pompey and Crassus not helped Caesar become governor of Gaul, the Senate might very well have declared Caesar's edicts, so beneficial to themselves, invalid. As his successes in Gaul made him more and more powerful, Caesar was careful to augment the power of Pompey with a consulship and governorship of Spain (so that Pompey would not be forced to the side of the *optimates*). Indeed, Caesar was "the one reliable source of help to all who were in legal difficulties, or in debt, or living beyond their means…" (Suetonius)

Suetonius tells us that Caesar "took…pains to win the esteem of kings and provincial authorities by offering them gifts of prisoners…or lending them troops whenever they asked… He also presented the principal cities of Asia and Greece with magnificent public works, and did the same for those of Italy, Gaul, and Spain." Once he conquered Gaul, Caesar did not exploit the country as the *optimates* and financiers had done the East; rather, he imposed only a modest tribute, to be collected by the tribes themselves. "Caesar showed the tribes every possible honor, conferred substantial rewards on their leaders, and imposed no new burdens on the country, so that he might demonstrate to Gaul, exhausted by so many defeats, the benefits of submission and so preserve the peace without difficulty." (Aulius Hirtius) Many of the Spanish communities supported Caesar in his campaign against Afranius and Petreius because they remembered his reducing Roman taxes and tributes while a government official in Spain. When winds blew the Caesarian fleet well beyond Caesar's camp on the Apsus river, the vessels landed in the region of Lissus. Caesar had aided the Roman citizens of this region while governor of Gaul and Illyricum; they now gladly helped the Caesarians with supplies and finding their way. And following his victory at Pharsalus, Caesar reduced taxation on the Roman provinces of the East, which had suffered so from the confiscations of the Pompeians.

One reason Caesar's men were so willing to toil and fight for him is that he rewarded them liberally for doing so. Caesar inspired his soldiers by "making it clear, by the ungrudging way in which he would distribute rewards and honors, that he was not amassing a great fortune from his wars in order to spend it on his personal pleasures or on any life of self-indulgence; instead he was keeping it, as it were, in trust, a fund open to all for the reward of valor…" (Plutarch) Many of Caesar's soldiers were Gauls to whom he had granted Roman citizenship or Latin rights (and from whom the *optimates* would have taken that citizenship or those rights). When at Dyrrhachium Caesar was shown the shield of the centurion Cassius Scaeva, pierced by 120 arrows in defense of his garrison, Caesar rewarded him with a colossal gift and promoted him to *primus pilus*, the senior centurion in his legion; the whole of Scaeva's cohort received double pay and other distinctions. So greatly did the *optimates* love money that they would enrich others only *in extremis* (as when Domitius Ahenobarbus, besieged by Caesar within Corfinium, offered his soldiers some of his land as an inducement to remain loyal).

Whenever France could not itself take the field against its opponents, Richelieu would subsidize those who could. "It is a sign of singular prudence," he counseled his monarch, "to [hold] down the forces opposed to your state…with the forces of your allies, by putting your hand in your pocket and not on your sword…" When there was a risk some of the Protestant states might defect following the death of Gustavus, Richelieu wrote Louis: "One of the things I consider necessary in the initial stages of the new situation created by the death of the King of Sweden is that Monsieur de Charnace should be sent a letter of credit to the value of 30,000 ecus…for distribution to those influential persons…who will not take your money without binding themselves to you." Richelieu also wrote his emissary who was then negotiating with representatives of the Netherlands: "The plenipotentiaries present

when the treaty is concluded must also receive some personal gratification...
It is the King's wish that...92,000 livres should be distributed to the best
possible effect." So regularly did Richelieu pay his informants throughout
Europe that they were referred to as "pensioners."

As with frightening others, you must take care in enriching others.
Since human beings are more apt to be influenced by favors to come than
favors received, you cannot enrich another only once, but must continue to
do so. And, your enriching another may cause him to retire from the lists
rather than continue to collaborate in your interests. On Napoleon's fall
in 1814, General Lefebvre asked, "Did he believe that when we have titles,
honors, and lands, we will kill ourselves for his sake?"

Manipulate Symbols

"The shortest and best way of making your fortune," said Jean de La
Bruyere, "is to let people clearly see that it is their interest to promote
yours." You do so in part through symbols. You must be very careful of
your *existimatio*, of your reputation or prestige. Samuel Johnson once complained to Lord Chesterfield, "Is not a patron, my lord, one who looks
with unconcern on a man struggling for life in the water, and when he has
reached ground encumbers him with help?" The world is a patron, and it
will help you only once you have reached ground (or seem to have done so).
And while you are struggling in the water, the world will indeed look on
with unconcern — or worse. "It lies in men's nature," said Aeschylus, "to
trample on the fighter already down." (In truth, it lies in *life's* nature to do
so, as life evolved to sense and profit from vulnerability.) For our preservation, we seek to influence the world; we sense that we can do so far more
through those with power than those without. Following his abdication in
1814, Napoleon was abandoned by all his ministers save Caulaincourt, and
even by his valet.

In spite of his having no money to speak of, when young Caesar would
always go about with a retinue of servants so that others would think him
important. When a young man, Richelieu wrote a friend asking the cost of
two silver salvers: "I am a poor devil and, as you know, I am unable to create

an impression of wealth. Nonetheless, once I possess a few beautiful silver plates my position will be much improved." (Though he later surrounded himself with luxury, Richelieu himself lived and ate quite simply; the luxury was not for himself, for his sense of self worth, but simply to make others think what he wished them to think.) Talleyrand was once visited by his friend Narbonne, who was at the time quite poor. After a short while, Narbonne said he must leave or else he would not have enough money to pay the waiting coachman. "Why don't you have your own carriage?", asked Talleyrand. "That's a bad joke," Narbonne replied. "You know I haven't got a sou." "You miss the point," rejoined Talleyrand. "You must have a carriage to pay for one."

Through symbols you can not only lift your *existimatio*, but also often induce others to do as you wish. When a member of the Council of State objected that the decorations Napoleon was proposing (such as the Legion of Honor) were "baubles," Napoleon replied, "It is with 'baubles' that mankind is governed." The ultimate disgrace for a Roman legion was to lose its eagle, the symbol of the legion; legionaries would die rather than see their eagle taken by the enemy. Consider: Augustus had far more power than did Caesar, and yet by observing the *forms* of the old republic, by presenting himself as the equal of his fellow aristocrats, he kept Rome quiescent. (As he lay dying, Augustus invited his friends to visit him; he repeated the words actors used on leaving the stage and asked whether they had enjoyed his performance.) Caesar was quite punctilious about ceremonial and religious observances; he would invoke the immortals, sacrifice to the gods, celebrate victories and the Latin games, choose symbolic battle-cries, and so on. Once, when he tripped on landing in Africa, Caesar made a good omen of a bad by crying, "Africa, I have tight hold of you!" At the Congress of Vienna following Napoleon's fall, Talleyrand had extra starch added to his collars so that he might further seem to represent principles and rectitude.

Sacrifice to the Graces

Of all the symbols, perhaps the most influential is manner. And on manner, we can have no better teacher than Lord Chesterfield. "The world judges from the appearances of things and not from the reality, which few are able, and still fewer are inclined, to fathom... Few people have penetration enough to discover, attention enough to observe, or even concern enough to examine, beyond the exterior; they take their notions from the surface, and go no deeper... An air, a tone of voice, a composure of countenance...which are all easily acquired, do the business; and without farther examination, and possibly with the contrary qualities, that man is reckoned the gentlest, the modestest, and the best natured man alive." He continues: "With weak people (and they undoubtedly are three parts in four of mankind), good-breeding, address, and manners are everything; they can go no deeper; but let me assure you, that they are a great deal even with people of the best understanding... I confess I am so made myself. Awkwardness and ill-breeding shock me to that degree, that where I meet with them, I cannot find in my heart to inquire into the intrinsic merit of that person; I hastily decide in myself, that he can have none..."

You are far more likely to attain your objects with a pleasing than a displeasing manner. "Your sole business now is to shine, not to weigh. Weight without lustre is lead. You had better talk trifles elegantly to the most trifling woman, than coarse inelegant sense to the most solid man; you had better return a dropped fan genteelly than give a thousand pounds awkwardly; and you had better refuse a favour gracefully, than grant it clumsily. Manner is all, in every thing; it is by manner only that you can please, and consequently rise. All your Greek will never advance you from secretary to envoy, or from envoy to ambassador; but your address, your manners, your air, if good, very probably may." The degree to which Talleyrand attained his objects through civilities is astounding; the Tsar's advisor at the Congress of Vienna, Pozzo di Borgo, remarked, "Even his civilities are usurious investments which must be paid for by the end of the day." And there is no quality so sterling that uncouthness will not obscure it. "Among men," said Chesterfield, "how often have I seen the most solid merit and knowledge neglected, unwelcome, or even rejected, for want of [the Graces]! while flimsy parts, little knowledge, and less merit, introduced by the Graces, have been received, cherished, and admired... Vulgar low expressions, awkward motions and address, vilify, as they imply either a very low turn of mind, or low education, and low company."

278

Since most others take you at your own valuation, you would do well to show that you hold yourself in high regard. "There is a form of eminence which is quite independent of our fate," said La Rochefoucault; "it is an air that distinguishes us from our fellow men and makes us appear destined for great things; it is the value that we imperceptibly attach to ourselves; it is the quality that wins us the deference of others; more than birth, honors, or even merit, it gives us ascendancy." The world aids those who "appear destined for great things." You would also do well to show that you are self-controlled, are governed by your reason rather than by your emotions; that you have an object; that you are self-reliant; *that you understand how things work*. Your doing so signals the quality of your genes, a signaling that determines whether others will wish to ally themselves or mate with you. Your doing so also declares that you are not to be imposed upon, that your interests are not to be touched, and that, if they are, retribution will follow. *Your manner must bespeak power*, that you have a certain degree of control over the world.

A part of this air is calmness, a cool self-assurance. Calmness bespeaks self-confidence, a certainty that one is equal to all situations, to whatever life may present. "For my part," said Chesterfield, "I see no impudence, but, on the contrary, infinite utility and advantage, in presenting one's self with the same coolness and unconcern, in any, and every company: till one can do that, I am very sure that one can never present one's self well. Whatever is done under concern and embarrassment must be ill-done; and till a man is absolutely easy and unconcerned in every company, he will never be thought to have kept good company, nor be very welcome in it." Neither be nor seem timid; in the gladiatorial contests of ancient Rome, nothing was so apt to bring a vote of death as was timidity. "Assurance and intrepidity," said Chesterfield, "under the white banner of seeming modesty, clear the way for merit, that would otherwise be discouraged by difficulties in its journey…"

We rule over others, Churchill was fond of saying, only by remaining calm. One of Caesar's officers records that, "in an almost hopeless situation, the soldiers found encouragement 'in the expression of their commander's face, in his freshness and wonderful cheerfulness. For he appeared full of assurance and confidence.'" (Meier) "However difficult the situation," writes Gelzer, "he was never embarrassed… Every day there was the possibility of a new development somewhere that could undo everything. Yet notwithstanding this, Caesar could, when he wanted, at any hour of the day display the most fascinating charm, tender consideration, and hilarious good humor." Caulaincourt reported that "not one murmur against the Emperor was heard in the whole course of this disastrous retreat" from Russia, largely because Napoleon remained so calm throughout. And having a calm manner will help you truly to be calm; being calm is calming. Meier observes that "the outward image [Caesar] displayed [of serenity and superiority] may in large measure have determined his inner attitude."

You will not always be able to control your feelings; *but whichever emotion your self-control cannot master, must not breach the wall of your manner.* While we sleep, the brain releases a certain chemical that decouples our brain from our body, thus keeping us from acting out our dreams and thus hurting or attracting attention to ourselves. Just so with your manner: you should detach it from your emotions so that you do not, in acting them out, hurt your interests. Be vigilant over yourself: never speak when you are uncertain what to say, or feel uncertain of yourself; at such moments, simply listen. Above all, avoid *Sturm und Drang*, emotional incontinence; never be all of a dither. Heed Chesterfield:

> The principal of these things is the mastery of one's temper, and that coolness of mind, and serenity of countenance, which hinders us from discovering, by words, actions, or even looks, those passions or sentiments by which we are inwardly moved or agitated; and the discovery of which gives cooler and abler people such infinite advantage over us, not only in great business, but in all the most common occurrences of life. A man who does not possess himself enough to hear disagreeable things without visible marks of anger and change of countenance, or agreeable ones without sudden burst of joy and expansion of countenance, is at the mercy of every artful knave or pert coxcomb... If you find yourself subject to sudden starts of passion...resolve within yourself, at least, never to speak one word while you feel that emotion within you. Determine too, to keep your countenance as unmoved and unembarrassed as possible: which steadiness you may get a habit of by constant attention. I should desire nothing better, in any negotiation, than to

have to do with one of these men of warm, quick passions, which I would take care to set in motion. By artful provocations I would extort rash and unguarded expressions...

Of two rivals for a woman, Chesterfield writes, "If one of [the rivals] has command enough over himself (whatever he may feel inwardly) to be cheerful, gay, and easily and unaffectedly civil to the other, as if there were no manner of competition between them, the lady will certainly like him the best, and his rival will be ten times more humbled and discouraged; for he will look upon such behaviour as a proof of the triumph and security of his rival... It is the same in business: where he who can command his temper and his countenance the best, will always have an infinite advantage over the other." Napoleon remarked on Talleyrand's "absolute facial imperturbability." Talleyrand, said General Lannes, "can be booted in the ass and not show it on his face."

In manner as in thinking, you must go with your interests rather than your feelings. "At courts," said Chesterfield, "there will be always coldnesses, dislikes, jealousies, and hatred; the harvest being but small in proportion to the number of labourers; but then, as they arise often, they die soon, unless they are perpetuated by the manner in which they have been carried on, more than by the matter which occasioned them. The turns and vicissitudes of courts frequently make friends of enemies, and enemies of friends: you must labour, therefore, to acquire that great and uncommon talent, of hating with good-breeding, and loving with prudence; to make no quarrel irreconcilable, by silly and unnecessary indications of anger; and no friendship dangerous in case it breaks..."

What your manner does not reveal, your words must not betray. "A little sincerity is a dangerous thing," said Oscar Wilde, "and a great deal of it is absolutely fatal." Your thoughts are your affair; you should take infinite care in selecting which thoughts you share with others. Meier suggests that Caesar confided only in his daughter, Julia; others "were hardly privy to his concerns and intentions, but were merely given...instructions." When speaking to others about a certain person, say only that which you would be perfectly willing to say to him (and, if at all possible, say it to him first). Do not hope that others will be discreet, that they will keep to themselves that which you should not have said. (And you yourself be discreet; show others that what they share with you will go no further.) To anyone not of your family, say only that which you would be willing to say publicly. *Be reticent.* When a lunatic once cried out to Napoleon, "I am in love with your wife!", he replied, "You should choose someone else to confide in." Do not go about as this lunatic did, confiding in those you should not.

The more you reveal of yourself, the better your would-be opponents understand you, and thus the better can they fight you. "The height of abilities," said Chesterfield, "is to have…a frank, open and ingenuous exterior with a prudent and reserved interior; to be upon your own guard, and yet, by a seeming natural openness, to put people off theirs. Depend upon it, nine in ten of every company you are in, will avail themselves of every indiscreet and unguarded expression of yours, if they can turn it to their own advantage." Remember that you may — and probably will — be hurt every time you commit a solecism, an error of manner or behavior. And the weaker your position, your mode, the more careful you must be, because the more dearly you will pay.

In many contexts, you would do well to hide your virtues; in such contexts, a virtue is taken as a weakness. Most of the virtues of the high quality, are lost on the low; a virtue is for naught, if displayed among those who cannot value it. To his younger brother Pushkin once wrote, "Be on your guard against the kindness of which you are capable; men do not understand it, and they readily take it for servility, always being glad to judge others by themselves." Talleyrand was far more concerned with hiding his virtues than his vices. In 1811, the *Gazette de France* praised the "goodness" of Napoleon, who, joyous at the birth of his son, had granted a petitioner his wish. Enraged, Napoleon had his Minister of Police sack the editor at once. It is not that Napoleon did not *do* kind things; it is rather that he felt a ruler should not be *thought* kind. "A prince who, in the first year of his reign, is considered to be kind," he counseled his brother Louis, King of Holland, "is a prince who is mocked at in his second year." Dostoevsky's novel about a young man who is Christ-like, open, and sweet, in each and every context, is entitled *The Idiot.*

You should be in the field and organization in which your natural self is the ESS. Because genes and childhood are fixed, context is critical. A trait that is adaptive in one context may be quite maladaptive in another; a trait, like a gene, must fit its context: "In a herbivore gene pool, any new gene that conferred on its possessors sharp meat-eating teeth would not be very successful...you cannot efficiently eat meat unless you also have the right sort of intestine..." (Dawkins) Gibbon's "disposition to disregard the customary" contributed to his greatness as a historian, but often offended those with whom he socialized. The singer ejected from the disco, is celebrated in the opera house. Be where your virtues are viewed as such, and your weaknesses are in traits little valued.

To influence others, you must speak well. On a certain debate in the House of Lords, Lord Chesterfield commented: "Lord Macclesfield,...one of the greatest mathematicians and astronomers in Europe, spoke afterwards with infinite knowledge, and all the clearness that so intricate a matter could admit of; but, as his words, his periods, and his utterance, were not near so good as mine, the preference was most unanimously, though most unjustly, given to me. This will ever be the case... Mere reason and good sense is never to be talked to a mob: their passions, their sentiments, their senses, and their seeming interests are alone to be applied to. Understanding they have collectively none; but they have ears and eyes, which must be flattered and seduced; and this can only be done by eloquence, tuneful periods, graceful action, and all the various parts of oratory." Cicero observed that Caesar's style of speaking was "chaste, pellucid, and grand;" indeed, Caesar was as superior in speaking as he was in waging war.

Napoleon once asked Talleyrand how he had come by his reputation as a great conversationalist. "In warfare," Talleyrand responded, "don't you always try to choose the field? Well, I select the field of conversation. I venture only where I have something to say. I ignore all the rest... In a conversation, I let everything go by about which I can offer only insipid comments." Josephine's daughter, Hortense de Beauharnais, said of Talleyrand, "I am certain that his reputation for great cleverness is due not so much to anything unusual that he does, but to the fact that he says so little, but says it so well."

Do not prate; speak of silly things, and the world will think you silly (and unfocused). "Frivolous curiosity about trifles," said Chesterfield, "and a laborious attention to little objects which neither require nor deserve a moment's thought, lower a man, who from thence is thought (and not unjustly) incapable of greater matters. Cardinal de Retz very sagaciously marked out Cardinal Chigi for a little mind, from the moment he told him he had wrote three years with the same pen, and that it was an excellent good one still." Boast, and the world will think you a buffoon. "If you publish your own panegyric upon any occasion," said Chesterfield, "or in any shape whatsoever, and however artfully dressed or disguised, [envy, indignation, and ridicule] will all conspire against you, and you will be disappointed of the very end you aimed at." He quotes Waller, that speaking of himself

> Makes the wretch the most despis'd,
> Where most he wishes to be priz'd.

Caesar felt that boasting and defeat are linked; to show their inferiority, he records the boasting of the Gallic and German commanders. *Do not be eager for applause*; nothing is quite so pleasing as "the white banner of seeming modesty." You should not speak about yourself in part because to do so is to think about yourself; and you should not think about yourself, but about the context.

You should have superb posture; poor posture bespeaks poor self-esteem. (It is well to remember that, in Greek plays, a bent or taut posture showed that the character was of a lesser mode, was subject to great necessity.) Walk and stand as though a string is attached to the top of your head, pulling you up, with your shoulders back; this posture should be perfectly natural and unaffected. Eat well; to eat poorly is to show the world that you are ignorant or do not value yourself or both.

Stoop to Please

Be complaisant; seek to please others. "You must be sensible that you cannot rise in the world," said Chesterfield, "without forming connexions, and engaging different characters to conspire in your point... Those necessary connexions can never be formed, or preserved, but by an uninterrupted series of complaisance, attentions, politeness, and some constraint. You must engage their hearts, if you would have their support... People will not be called out to your service only when you want them; and if you expect to receive strength from them, they must receive either pleasure or advantage from you." He continues: "The heart has such an influence over the understanding, that it is worth while to engage it in our interest... Intrinsic merit alone will not do: it will gain you the general esteem of all; but not the particular affection, that is, the heart, of any. To engage the affection of any particular person, you must, over and above your general merit, have some particular merit to that person, by services done, or offered; by expressions of regard and esteem; by...attentions for him..."

One night in a storm, Caesar and his companions came upon a peasant's hut in which only one could sleep. Declaring that while honors should go to the strongest, necessities should go to the weakest, Caesar had the frailest man sleep inside, while he and the others slept under the projecting roof of the doorway. "When Cicero asked Caesar to take one of his friends on to his staff," writes Meier, "Caesar replied that he would make him king of Gaul and that Cicero should immediately send him another." Not only did Caesar give the friend high position, but he also kept Cicero informed of his progress. Caesar dedicated his work on Latin grammar, *de analogia*, to Cicero; its preface celebrates Cicero as "the creator and master of Latin prose style."

The Wall Street Journal once considered why the Justice Department was not pursuing Cisco Systems for antitrust violations as it was Microsoft. After all, Cisco's core product had a 62% share of the market, the company was acquiring new technologies and "bundling" them with its main products, and three of its rivals had succumbed within the past year. The *Journal's* conclusion: "Where Microsoft seemed to ignore or bully antitrust regulators, Cisco has schmoozed them..." Microsoft was quite late for a corporation its size in creating a government and community affairs division.

Since most members of modern societies feel insignificant, nothing will please them quite so much as your making them feel they are not. "You must carefully watch and attend to their passions, their tastes, their little humours and weaknesses," said Chesterfield. "For instance, suppose you invited any body to dine or sup with you, you ought to recollect if you had observed that they had any favourite dish, and take care to provide it for them; and when it came, you should say, 'You seemed to me, at such and such a place, to give this dish a preference, and therefore, I ordered it; this is the wine that I observed you like, and therefore I procured some.' The more trifling these things are, the more they prove your attention for the person, and are consequently the more engaging. Consult your own breast, and recollect how these little attentions, when shown you by others, flatter that degree of self-love and vanity, from which no man living is free. Reflect how they incline and attract you to that person, and how you are propitiated afterwards to all which that person says or does." (Treat others so when they have neither position nor power, and they will remember forever, particularly as you were quite alone in your solicitude.) But please coolly; if you do so too effusively, the person you hope to please may think you servile or weak.

Just as, when speaking to a child, you adapt your tone and content to those of a child, so, too, should you always tailor what you say to the person with whom you are speaking. *See your audience.* You should, for instance, compliment another, not on his finest trait, but on that which he most values. Richelieu was a great statesman and middling poet; but since he wished to be a great poet, others found they could please him far more by praising his poetry than his statesmanship. In general, however, to make another the center of conversation is to make him feel significant. You should ask about him, his life and views; as he speaks, show your admiration by listening carefully and asking further questions. "The true spirit of conversation," said Jean de La Bruyere, "consists more in bringing out the cleverness of others than in showing a great deal of it yourself; he who goes away pleased with himself and his own wit is also greatly pleased with you." Remember that most human beings would rather be applauded and praised than entertained or instructed. Though almost all men seek *eclat*, few have the gifts to attain it; but a man with middling gifts wishes to be admired no less than does a man with great gifts. And, if you would please others, ignore their solecisms; they will be so very grateful to you for ignoring their lapse in self-control, their imperfection. Not to know how to please others, what to say and what not to say, is to be a child.

How much we are able to please depends in part on our position. In this instance, there is no one ESS; the ESS depends in part on the individual himself. On Napoleon's remarks to his soldiers, Marmont commented, "It was by familiarities of this kind that the Emperor made the soldiers adore him, but it was a means only available to a commander whom frequent victories had made illustrious; any other general would have injured his reputation by it." Richelieu told his sovereign "that a single adverse comment from the monarch could dash men's hopes and undermine their good will, while a cheering word or a sign of appreciation was better able to promote a sense of zeal in the service of the Crown than any gift, however rich." Of Talleyrand Hortense de Beauharnais said, "The vanity of people is what makes Talleyrand so attractive to them. I was a victim of this myself. When he unbends to the extent of speaking to you, he seems utterly charming. And if he goes so far as to inquire about your health, you are prepared to love him forever." As in pleasing, so, too, with all the social forms: your mode affects what you might do and not do, what you might say and not say, what will be permitted you and what not.

Only with those of a certain quality does stooping to please work. Of Pompey Mommsen said, "His was one of those petty and mean natures, towards which it is dangerous to practice magnanimity." With those of *very* low quality, frightening (or fighting) works best.

∾

The corollary to the principle that you should please others, is that you should not *displease* them. "I do not mean by this to recommend to you" said Chesterfield, "...the insipid softness of a gentle fool: no, assert your own opinion, oppose other people's when wrong: but let your manner, your air, your terms, and your tone of voice be soft and gentle, and that easily and naturally, not affectedly. Use palliatives when you contradict...[and] finish any argument or dispute with some little good humoured pleasantry, to show that you are neither hurt yourself, nor mean to hurt your antagonist..." "Nothing is more becoming in a Prince than to speak with constraint," Richelieu counseled his monarch. "He must imitate the queen bee, which has no sting."

Displeasing others may provoke them into striking you. "People will repay and with interest too," said Chesterfield, "inattention with inattention, neglect with neglect, and ill-manners with worse; which may engage you in very disagreeable affairs." No solecism should so upset you as your own. Perhaps because of the great strain he was under, Richelieu would sometimes make cruel remarks, remarks he would usually come to rue. He once asked the unsightly Marquis de Fontrailles to leave the room before a certain ambassador arrived, observing that the latter did not care for "mon-

sters;" with that single remark, Richelieu added a conspirator to a future
plot against himself. If you *should* displease another, strive now to please
him; enmity is only rarely ever implacable.

Never treat another with disdain; never show another you think him insignificant.
Nothing so wounds self-love as does scorn; and thus nothing is so hated.
As Chesterfield observed, a person will forgive you almost anything but
disdain. "Observe carefully," he said, "what displeases or pleases you in
others; and be persuaded, that, in general, the same things will please or
displease them in you... For instance; do you find yourself hurt and morti-
fied when another makes you feel his superiority, and your own inferiority in
knowledge, parts, rank, or fortune? You will certainly take great care not to
make a person, whose good will, good word, interest, esteem, or friendship,
you would gain, feel that superiority in you, in case you have it." (No less
than economic hardship, disdain has been the cause of revolutions; at the
beginning of that of France, soldiers throughout the country rose up and
slaughtered their officers, so greatly did they hate these aristocrats for their
arrogance.) A sense of hierarchy is no less strong in our species than in any
of the other primates. "In Austria," said Talleyrand, "humanity starts with
the rank of baron." To most human beings, humanity starts with the level
the individual has himself attained.

Do not think that by disdaining others (should you do so) that you are
"imperceptibly attaching" value to yourself. "Nothing vilifies and degrades
more than pride," said Chesterfield. "The pretensions of the proud man
are oftener treated with sneers and contempt than with indignation: as
we offer ridiculously too little to a tradesman, who asks ridiculously too
much for his goods..." Indeed, disdaining others is a form of boasting. By
disdaining others, you show the world that you do not feel significant, and
that you are quite willing to sacrifice your interests to feel so (people who
feel significant do not disdain others — consider Einstein); that you are
not self-reliant (you take your sense of self-worth from the status of those
round you; you disdain because you see others do so); that you are governed
by the lower rather than the higher realms of the human brain; that you are a
homunculus, a little man, a "true man of the mean" (indeed, a true primate
of the mean); that you are simple-minded (you think a person his position
only); that you are poor at abstract thinking (that you are limited to the
here and now and do not see that the person you now disdain may one day

be far higher than you); that you are poorly educated and have not been in the wilderness (you have not come to think "human thoughts"); that you simply do not know what you are doing.

(Young men are particularly apt to treat others with disdain, to make themselves "the ultimate perfection." Most burn their bridges *as they come to them,* so instinctive in them is the impulse to compete, to show themselves superior. Young men excel at sniping at one another; sniping is not fighting. A general hostility to all other young men is as callow as it is ruinous to one's interests. A young man uncertain how to behave, would do well to study women.)

Your ideal is that all human beings are equal and should treat one another so. But this ideal is for others, not for yourself. For yourself, you take the more natural and pleasing view: "I am a person of consequence. I signify my being so by speaking only with others of consequence, by disdaining to speak at any length with those of little or no consequence. I save my smiles, charm, and graciousness for those at my order of being or higher. (In truth, I feel uncomfortable speaking with those of lesser mode, feel tainted and debased.) Like Aristotle's youth, I wish to be superior. And if I speak with *everyone,* how are others to know that I *am* a person of consequence? How am *I* to know? What, then, would the marker be? Do people of consequence not congregate? Do they not exclude? How else are we to know we *are* of consequence? For me to be of consequence, others must be of little consequence." (Do state your views so forthrightly; then at least you will not compound the folly of your views with that of muddling reality, of misunderstanding yourself.) This is the reasoning of beasts, the reasoning of the lower realms of the human brain: *he* is strong, so I will treat him well; *he* is not, so I will treat him however I please. Reason so, and you show that you have no need of the last few million years of our evolution.

And of what, precisely, does your specialness consist? Have you contributed to civilization as did Caesar, Montaigne, Gibbon, Mommsen, Talleyrand, Darwin, Austen, Thoreau, or Wharton? Have you pushed the world back from "the lip of the volcano," where one philosopher has so justly observed it now sits? Society tells you that *his* position is not quite so high as *yours;* this is, of course, highly agreeable to you. But society is not considering quality, only power and wealth. Measure yourself, not against the people round you, but against those who contributed most to civilization. Measure yourself, not against gardens, but against jungles.

If you wish to be special, you must be distinctive. However is it distinctive to do what almost all human beings — indeed, almost all primates — do? However is a stone that falls to the ground distinctive? And do you recognize that, by the logic of your thinking, you permit all above you to treat you with disdain? You are, after all, a scullion to as many, as are scullions to you. If someone is uncivil, bumptious, conceited, little, immoral — by all means, without showing that you think him so, speak with him as little as possible. But to disdain another simply because society deems his position the lesser? How monstrous! If you *are* special, you will be so whether you consort with the high or the low; two of the more special people who have ever lived, Caesar and Talleyrand, consorted freely with the riff-raff of their societies. Caesar and Napoleon were far, far superior to their soldiers and yet treated them as comrades. *Their soldiers did not require their disdaining them to recognize their superiority.*

Most of the world is a courtier. Most human beings seek to be with those in high position; biology made them so. "How many friends, how many relatives of a new Minister, spring up in a single night!," observes Jean de La Bruyere. "Some men pride themselves on their former acquaintance, on their having been his fellow-students or neighbors; others ransack their genealogy, go back to their great-grandfather, and recall their father and mother's side, for in some way or other everyone wishes to be related to him… Would those silly men…have said this a week ago? Has the Minister become a more virtuous man, or more worthy of his sovereign's choice, or were they waiting for this appointment to know him better?" Do you not see how little, how callow, how primatial — how *contemptible*, this is? You would do well not to make your ESS quite so obvious.

Neuroscientists at Duke University found that rhesus monkeys would accept less cherry juice if permitted to gaze (via computer) at the higher-ranking members of their troop, and that they would refuse to look at the lower-ranking members unless given additional juice. Be higher than a rhesus monkey; do not simply go with the lower realms of your brain. That which makes us human, that which distinguishes us from the rest of life, is the ability of the higher realms of our brain to predominate over the lower. And do not, as Pompey did, seek the respect of those in high position simply because they *are* in high position. Those in high position may or may not respect what should be respected. Pompey sought to impress the Roman senators with achievement; but the senators did not value achievement in the least.

There is an untrumpeted aristocracy, independent of wealth or position: it is that of quality. The "world of quality" is *not* the privileged classes; it is those of high quality. Wealth and power are not the only modes of consequence; so, too, are learning and *arete*, the traits of the virtuous. (It is low rather than high *sophia* that brings wealth and power. Those who attain them may or may not have high *sophia*; if they do, it is merely by chance.) It is in this that true superiority consists: the ability to distinguish quality rather than class, and the preference to be with the former. All can distinguish class, few quality. (Our species is apt to neglect its higher-quality members — think of Thoreau alone in his hut.) Strip others of their titles and possessions; judge what remains. Caesar judged others, Meier tells us, "not according to their rank, but according to their nature." Remember that Richelieu did not care a fig about Mazarin's title, but only about his qualities. *A human being is not his position.* To suppose him so is to think simplistically, in categories. Of all the queer notions in modern society, this is perhaps the queerest: that a person is solely his profession. In prehistory, when human beings lived in small kin groups, a person was the whole of his traits, characteristics, and skills; he was not a single trait only. To be viewed as such is quite foreign to us. In specializing, as he must do, a human being does not become solely the specialization. And do not take a person at his own valuation, which may be far more or less than that to which he is entitled; self-esteem and quality correlate only poorly.

A high-quality human being treats others well whether they are in a weak position or a strong. "The characteristic of a well-bred man," said Chesterfield "is to converse with his inferiors without insolence, and with his superiors with respect, and with ease." The two are proportionate: the more you do the one, the more you do the other; and the less the self-reliance, the less you do either. If you let yourself feel a *frisson* of pleasure when with those in high position, you will be far more apt to neglect those in low (because you receive no such *frisson* from them). True superiority requires that we treat well all those less intelligent and accomplished. Why disdain those you view as inferior to you? If they are so, it is because they were not so fortunate as you in genes or family or both. Would it not be more fitting to feel compassion for them? (The contempt you feel for the weak comes from the lower realms of your brain; it is the higher that feels compassion.) To treat those below you well is to value yourself: the person with whom you are speaking is significant because *you* are speaking with him. *This* is how a person who truly feels he is significant, thinks.

It is in your interest to treat both those with much power and those with little well. The *optimates* would have done far better to treat Cicero well than with disdain; but they cared far more that he was a *homo novus* — not of the high aristocracy — than that he was a brilliant speaker devoted to the Senatorial cause. It is sensible and prudent to treat well all those who serve your and the group's interests. (If at first you do not see why this is so, simply let the trash pile up in your house; you will soon come to appreciate garbage men.) Others are far less likely to do their work well if you treat them with disdain. Each time you treat another with disdain, you degrade the ESS a bit. (Human quality is apt to correspond with treatment: a human being treated well is generally of far higher quality than a human being treated badly.) And however do you suppose you might lead others while showing them disdain? If you care nothing for your interests, be supercilious.

༄

Observe the social forms; the world cares far less for your views, than that you be agreeable. Your task in life is not to tell others the truth; it is to protect yourself and your family. Do not think it your duty to reform others; it is not. Trying to do so will only displease them, and will anyhow be in vain. You must be very careful not to show others that they present themselves "in two aspects, the actions in one fashion and the speeches in another;" that they are creating their own vital points; that they simply do not know what they are doing. Of the many knaves and fools in the world, Chesterfield said, "Abhor a knave, and pity a fool, in your heart, but let neither of them unnecessarily see that you do so." Tell the truth only where doing so does not hurt your interests. Be careful to keep a strict separation between the social self and real self; the one must not bleed into the other. *If* human quality were higher, *if* human beings were wiser, less selfish, and more benevolent, you could do without a mask; but humanity is what it is. Because social life is simply a contrivance, so, too, should your manner be.

Do Your Work

So: what is a creature that is not fitted to its environment, that evolved in small kin groups and now lives in gargantuan, atomistic societies, to do? However is such a creature to feel a sense of purpose, to feel significant, to attain *dignitas*? Very simply, by doing its work.

That which comes, and will not cease coming, is your work. That which gives you joy and pleasure, is your work. That which calms you, and without which you are agitated and upset, is your work. That about which you truly care, is your work. Your work is where the self is to be found; your work is *you*.

The birds of the field *do* toil; indeed, they do little else. In spite of our complexity, our having distractions and entertainments, what is true of the other creatures is no less true of us: we are our work. "My instinct," said Thoreau, "tells me that my head is an organ for burrowing, as some creatures use their snout and fore-paws..." Each of us has his own instinct, his own distinctive work; our task in life is to discover that work and then devote ourselves to it. Plumb your mind as Thoreau did his pond; find its deepest point, and there you shall find your work (and this is also where happiness is to be found). Your work is where your mind is richest, where it has the most ideas.

Just as you do not dictate what life is, so, too, do you not dictate what your work is; your genes do. Do not say, "I wish to be a writer (or financier or director or philosopher)." Do not fancy yourself this or that; *discover* what you are. Richelieu's wishing to be a great poet did not make him so; his genes made him a great statesman. Submit to your genes.

No one can tell you what your work is. "That which each can do best," said Emerson, "none but his Maker can teach him. No man yet knows what it is, nor can, till that person has exhibited it. Where is the master who could have taught Shakespeare?... Every great man is a unique." It is in the wilderness that we see our work most clearly; in the wilderness, there is no one to follow or impress but ourselves. "Conversation enriches the understanding," said Gibbon, "but solitude is the school of genius." Your work is unique; it has no precedent and imitates nothing. As you do your work, "you shall not discern the footprints of any other; you shall not see the face of man; you shall not hear any name; the way...shall be wholly strange and new. It shall exclude example and experience." (Emerson) Seek suprapersonal legitimacy for your work, and it will not be your work.

A task is *not* your work if you receive no joy from it, and think only of how it will be received. A too-great concern with making a splash among the living belittles our work; water falling into water makes a splash, but leaves no trace of itself. Whatever is *comme il faut* — "as it is done," fashionable — is *not* your work. The great art historian E.H. Gombrich observes that in every society in every age, the mass of artists do what the others do. (This is, after all, how archaeologists date pottery: by its similarity to other pottery of known date.) Be self-reliant even of your work; do not depend on it for enrichment or renown. Your work is also not about the *self*, but rather how the self views something else in the world, an idea, state, or condition. As pleasant as narcissism may be, it is *not* your work.

Doing your work, rather than that which society touts, requires great self-reliance. *You must do what you feel you should do.* "And truly it demands something godlike in him who has cast off the common motives of humanity and has ventured to trust himself for a taskmaster. High be his heart, faithful his will, clear his sight, that he may in good earnest be doctrine, society, law, to himself..." (Emerson) Only *you* will ask that you do your work, but this "simple purpose" must be to you "as strong as iron necessity is to others." (Emerson) The more distinctive your mind, the more distinctive your work, and thus the more self-reliant you must be. Let neither the world nor yourself divert you from your work.

The reason so much of humanity feels it is unsuccessful is that it does not do its work, but the work of others. Only by doing your work will you ever truly feel successful. No amount of fervor or application will make another's work your own; no matter how well you do this work or how many encomiums you receive, you will know that it is not yours. *Do* the work of others to live, if you must, but do not confuse it with your own. The world of affairs consists of those tiny manipulations of our environment that enable us to continue to survive; this world is distinct from that of our work and, if not walled off, toxic to it.

Only rarely is a position within an organization your work; only rarely is an organization's work consonant with your own. No predefined role fits us perfectly; all are at least a little ill-fitting. Each of us yearns for that vehicle through which we can express whatever is great or grand in us; only very rarely is a position in an organization that vehicle. Organizations are assemblies (if not deliberative); as Richelieu recognized, the intelligent only ever form a small minority. Thus whatever you do in an organization will be muddled. In the late Roman republic, said Meier, "infinite effort and ingenuity went into accomplishing very little." Just so with much work within an organization.

Just as Caesar could do his work, express himself, more freely in Gaul than in Rome (because Gaul was wilder and less structured), so, too, can you do your work far better outside an institution. Human beings outside of organizations have created most of our greatest works — consider Socrates, Montaigne, Gibbon, Austen, Pushkin, Darwin, and Wharton. Significance does not come from being a member of a corporate body; the body has magnificent buildings and grounds, complex systems and structures — but where are its great works? Buildings and grounds no more make a corporate body worthy, than manner does a human being.

On Caesar's ignoring affairs in Rome (and the election of Pompey as sole consul) his last two years in Gaul, Fowler comments: "He was intent on finishing his own work, and knew that it was on this that his own future and that of the empire depended, far more than on the caprice or blunders of Pompey and the Senate." So, too, with your work: ignore the "caprice or blunders" of the world; it is your work that will most affect your life. The people and events round you are ephemera; only your work has permanence.

Emerson quotes the Latin proverb, "Do not seek yourself outside yourself." *Do not be governed by baubles.* Titles and honors can be plucked but not eaten; they have no substance, give no sustenance. The accretions of honors, titles, and staff cannot make you feel truly significant; only your work can do that. (To acquire honors is *not* to manipulate symbols as you would wish. The world respects self-reliance, and doing one's own work, far more than it does the acquisition of baubles. How ridiculous Marcus Lepidus seemed to all, when Caesar permitted him a triumph even though he had achieved nothing.) If you do not think your work worthy, all the honors in the world will not make it so; and if you think it worthy, you have no need of honors. The joy of honors is a simulacrum of true joy, the joy of doing your work; once you have tasted that true joy, you will forever disdain honors.

Society makes much ado about nothing, celebrates the swill and dross, the meretricious; it celebrates what should be ignored, and ignores what should be celebrated. In the late Roman republic, only consuls could wear a purple-edged toga, only senators a tunic with a band of purple, only senators and patricians special shoes, and only senators and *equites* a silver ring. Roman aristocrats set great store by these sartorial distinctions. "Even the better men," said Mommsen, "were content when they had gained not power and influence, but the consulship and a triumph and a place of honor in the Senate." (Is there a more paltry object than the flattering of one's self-love?) Following his victories in Spain, Caesar gladly forsook the honor of a triumph so that he might stand for consul. The consulship was substantial and would aid him in attaining his object; the honor was not and would not. It is well to remember that *dignitas* is both rank *and* worth; like the aristocrats of the late Roman republic, however, most of humanity concerns itself far more with rank than with worth.

Of all tasks, only your work gives true, deep satisfaction. "A political victory," said Emerson, "a rise of rents, the recovery of your sick or the return of your absent friend, or some other favorable event raises your spirits, and you think good days are preparing for you. Do not believe it. Nothing can bring you peace but yourself." Caesar, Richelieu, Napoleon, Talleyrand, and Gates all pursued happiness — the free expression of their distinctive gifts.

☙

That which is dashed off is worthless; to be done well, a work requires considerable thought, and considerable thought requires time. "He who improvises," said Titian, "can never make a perfect line of poetry." It is possible to have one superb thought a day and thus 365 a year, but not 365 superb thoughts a day. What you do not see today, you may very well see tomorrow. The more conscious you are of time, the less well you will do your work; the more you hurry, the less your genius will say. Your work, like a small child, requires ever so much time; your work, like a small child, simply does not understand time.

Just as the Qur'an was revealed to Muhammad over 20 years, rather than all at once, so, too, will your work be revealed to you over time. Pushkin took eight years to write the rather short *Eugene Onegin*; the early drafts are poor, the final work incomparable. Gibbon took perhaps fifteen years to write *The History of the Decline and Fall of the Roman Empire* (and the preparation that preceded the writing was far longer). Genius is not the ability to create a great work at the first pass; it is instead the ability to create a great work over time, with much struggle, rejecting much of what it does as it goes.

Take it as given that you cannot do your work well without considerable learning; the *sine qua non* of good work is a good and broad education. It is indeed true, as Newton said, that we see further by standing on the shoulders of giants. Once there, we look where *we* feel we should look; it will not be where the giants looked. But only once there; otherwise we shall see only cuffs.

Inasmuch as possible, free yourself to do your work. Simplify your life; do the work of others as little as possible. Seek to live in obscurity; turn your anonymity and (social) insignificance to advantage. Sir Francis Bacon was one of the more visionary scientists ever to have lived; he neglected his work, however, for the power and attention that came with being Attorney General, Lord Keeper of the Seal, and Lord Chancellor — a choice he greatly regretted at the end of his life. Seek, too, to maintain an *entente cordiale* with others; quibbling takes time and weakens your focus. Caesar's clemency was due in part to his caring so greatly for his work; why waste time in retribution, with so much to be done? When presented with Pompey's correspondence following the battle of Pharsalus, Caesar had it burnt without reading it; reading Pompey's correspondence would not have contributed one whit to Caesar's work, which was of the future. One feels that Caesar constantly said within himself, "More, more, more..."

꩜

Nothing so begets a sense of self as does our work. Not to do your work is to forsake yourself, is never to *be* yourself. Just as you should acquaint yourself with the best the human mind has ever produced, so, too, should you acquaint yourself with the best your own can produce. Do your work, and you will amaze yourself. You will respect yourself most, by doing that which you are best at.

Nothing makes you so self-reliant as does your work, because your work relies wholly on yourself. Indeed, only by doing your work can you become truly self-reliant. As you do your work, only you and it exist; all else — social class, position, disdain — disappears. As you recede from the world, you come to yourself. Your work is your refuge; it insulates you, psychologically, from the world. Your work is your foundation; the more you do your work, the less the world will agitate you.

Do your work, pursue your object, and you will be a far better master of your "jury-rigged brain," of that "infinity of little wheels" within yourself. *Of Human Bondage* is said to be autobiographical, and that Philip's club foot represents Maugham's homosexuality (which was indeed a handicap in his society). Most of us have a club foot, a handicap of one sort or another; nothing helps us to overcome that handicap as does our work. The psychoanalyst Otto Rank counseled Anais Nin that what was black and ugly from her childhood would always be black and ugly, no matter how long or how deeply she might analyze it; all she might do, he suggested, is do her work, counterbalance the ugliness with good. Without our work is dissolution.

Our work keeps us from being frivolous and silly; a mind without its task fills with "cotton, hay, and rags." Without our work, we are all susceptible to being homunculi. Do only little things, and you will yourself be little. Meier observes that the Roman gladiatorial games were "all the more to be relished, the less this people could actually achieve." Without our work, we, too, occupy ourselves with trifles. Our life is an enfilade of short tasks; this, too, contributes to littleness. If we are not to be little, we must work at a single thing over many years. As we do our work, littleness recedes.

Do your work, and you will care little about the attentions of others. Your work will justify yourself, your existence, in your own eyes; you will not need recourse to such silly things as puffing yourself up or disdaining others. (The less the work, the more the puffery.) *This* is the marker you seek, that which will make you special and distinguish you from others. (Another reason human beings disdain those in lesser position is that, by doing so, they reassure themselves that position is all, that they are right to seek titles rather than themselves.) Do your work, and you will celebrate rather than envy others' work, because no one can do *your* work, and so no one is truly your rival. Do your work, and you will have a far more pleasing manner, because you will be far more pleased with yourself. Doing your work will teach you humility, because you will come to see how very difficult it is to do that work well; you can remain puffed up only until your work shows you why you should not be.

&

And what of our work and the world? To the world, it is not *we* that matter, but our work. As with our genes, so, too, with ourselves: "Natural selection favours some genes rather than others," writes Dawkins, "not because of the nature of the genes themselves, but because of their consequences...," that is, because of their work. Why did Louis XIII not rid himself of Richelieu, as so many in his family and court beseeched him to do? Because he recognized that only Richelieu could make his reign great. Why was Napoleon, as Robespierre's "planner," not guillotined with him? Because the Directory appreciated his military skills. Why did Napoleon not simply have Talleyrand shot? It was not only because, with Talleyrand as Foreign Minister, Europe would continue to hope that France would seek peace; it was also because only Talleyrand could extricate Napoleon from his imbroglios. Following his abdication in 1814, Napoleon counseled his successors, "Talleyrand had been betraying me for six months and I knew it, but...my affairs were well managed so long as he was in my service. At the present moment he is indispensable. He is thoroughly familiar with conditions in France and all over Europe, and under present circumstances, moreover, is the only man who can pull people together and get things going... It is a matter of concern to us all that he should remain in the government... *In your own interests he should be retained.*"

The more you do your work, the more the world becomes of your making. Our work is our extended phenotype, a gene's effect, not on the body in which it sits, but on the world (through that body). The more Caesar did his work in Gaul, the more Gaul became his world. And the more you create or influence the world through your work, the more self-confident you will be.

If you would lead others, do your work. Nothing enables us to hold sway over others as does our being far better than they at the work at hand. Napoleon's soldiers fought so valiantly in part because they knew they were being directed by a genius. Massena records that when Napoleon first arrived in Italy, the French officers "imagined from the way he carried about his wife's portrait, and showed it to everyone" — Napoleon had just married Josephine — "and still more from his extreme youth, that he owed his appointment to yet another bit of intrigue... But in a minute or two he put on his General's hat and seemed two feet taller." Competence is the *sine qua non* of leadership; no amount of guile, cunning, or intrigue substitutes for competence. Combine competence and humility, and you shall have the world at your feet (or at least that part of it you would wish to have at your feet).

Only through your work can you achieve *dignitas*, a place of true distinction in society. Only the high-quality will treat you well whatever your position; for all others, you must have *dignitas*. *Dignitas* is a positive asymmetry that keeps others from striking you. To be respected (which is in your interests), you must do your work. "When Alexander's sarcophagus was brought from its shrine," writes Suetonius, "Augustus gazed at the body, then laid a crown of gold on its glass case and scattered some flowers to pay his respects. When they asked if he would like to see Ptolemy too, 'I wished to see a king,' he replied, 'I did not wish to see corpses.'" In modern society, you are insubstantial without your work; it is your work that gives you substance and weight. That ground is most solid, where your work is. And only by doing your work will you be viewed as you are, as the whole of your self, rather than simply your specialization or profession.

Greatness, said de Tocqueville, is what makes life worth living. Plutarch records of Caesar, "As he was reading about Alexander...he wept; when his friends wondered why, he told them, 'Do you not think it a reason for grieving that at my age Alexander was king over so many nations, while I as yet have achieved no glorious deed?'" There is no way round it: only by doing your work can you be great. (Snubbing all the lesser folk of this world, and hobnobbing with all the greater, will not make you great; no one has ever been remembered for whom he snubbed.) "For what we feel to be his greatness," writes Meier of Caesar, "presumably has something to do with the fact that he was his own man." Had Caesar not been "his own man," he simply could not have been great. Nothing gives us "an air that distinguishes us from our fellow men and makes us appear destined for great things" as does our work, because only it *can* destine us for great things. And the greater your work, the more romantic your life will be. "What a romance my life has been," said Napoleon on St. Helena; it was so only because he did his work. Greatness requires a medium; find your medium.

(This is not to say your work will bring you riches or renown; it may very well not. If such things come, all well and good; if not, you shall still have joy, self-sufficiency, self-respect, and an accentuation of the self. Indeed, your work may make you *more* rather than less vulnerable, may provoke others into striking you — as their work did Caesar, Richelieu, Talleyrand, Napoleon, and Gates. So be it.)

We owe a colossal debt to all who have given us great works of art, music, literature, and science. Only through our work can we repay them for their own. *They* contributed to civilization; *they* improved the ESS: let us do so, too. So much that we do, we do only half-heartedly and poorly; in so many realms we are incompetent. It is our work that redeems us. "You were silly like us," wrote W.H. Auden to Yeats. "Your gift survived it all."

SELECTED BIBLIOGRAPHY

Agamemnon, Aeschylus

Alcestis, Euripides, and the introduction by William Arrowsmith

Alexander the Great, Robin Lane Fox

The Ambition to Rule, Steven Forde

Antigone, Sophocles

Austerlitz 1805, Christopher Duffy

Austerlitz 1805, David G. Chandler

The Bacchae, Euripides, and the introduction by William Arrowsmith

Caesar, Matthias Gelzer

Caesar, Christian Meier

The Campaigns of Napoleon, David G. Chandler

Cardinal Richelieu, Anthony Levi

Characters, Jean de La Bruyere

The Civil War, Julius Caesar (Oxford University Press)

Consilience, Edward O. Wilson

The Count of Monte Cristo, Alexandre Dumas

Crime and Punishment, Fyodor Dostoyevsky

Crome Yellow, Aldous Huxley

Cromwell, Antonia Fraser

Cyclops, Euripides, and the introduction by William Arrowsmith

Disraeli, Robert Blake

The Encyclopaedia Britannica

An Enemy of the People, Henrik Ibsen

Essays, Ralph Waldo Emerson

Essays, Michel de Montaigne

Eugene Onegin, Alexander Pushkin

The Extended Phenotype, Richard Dawkins

The Gallic War, Julius Caesar (Oxford University Press)

Gates, Paul Andrews and Stephen Manes

Grey Eminence: A Study in Religion and Politics, Aldous Huxley

Hard Drive, James Wallace and Jim Erickson

Hecuba, Euripides, and the introduction by William Arrowsmith

Heracles, Euripides, and the introduction by William Arrowsmith

The History of the Decline and Fall of the Roman Empire, Edward Gibbon

The History of Rome, Theodor Mommsen

The House of Mirth, Edith Wharton

Julius Caesar, W. Warde Fowler

The Letters of Alexander Pushkin

Letters to His Son, Philip Dormer Stanhope, Earl of Chesterfield

Maxims, Duc de la Rochefoucauld

Meditations, Marcus Aurelius

Metternich, Algernon Cecil

Metternich, Constantin de Grunwald

Metternich, Andrew Milne

Money Talks, Editors of Peter Pauper Press

Napoleon, Felix Markham

Napoleon, F.M. Kircheisen

Napoleon, Eugenii Tarle

Napoleon and Talleyrand, Emile Dard

Napoleon as a General, Count Yorck von Wartenburg

Napoleon's Battles: A History of His Campaigns, Henry Lachouque

The New York Times Science Times

On War, Clausewitz

Orestes, Euripides, and the introduction by William Arrowsmith

Over Drive, James Wallace

Richelieu, Louis Auchincloss

Richelieu, Carl Burkhardt

Roman Lives, Plutarch

Scientific American, "Scars That Won't Heal: The Neurobiology of Child Abuse," Martin H. Teicher

The Selfish Gene, Richard Dawkins

Talleyrand, J.F. Bernard

Talleyrand, Jean Orieux

The Tulane Drama Review, "The Criticism of Greek Tragedy," Volume 3, 1958-59, William Arrowsmith

The Twelve Caesars, Suetonius

Walden, Henry David Thoreau

The Wall Street Journal

Made in the USA
Charleston, SC
08 September 2010